The Economics of the Digital Society

The Economics of the Digital Society

Edited by

Luc Soete

Joint Director, United Nations University-Institute for New Technologies (UNU-INTECH) and Maastricht Economic Research Institute on Innovation and Technology (MERIT), and Professor of International Economics, Maastricht University, the Netherlands

Bas ter Weel

Assistant Professor of Economics and Researcher, Maastricht Economic Research Institute on Innovation and Technology (MERIT), Maastricht University, the Netherlands

Edward Elgar

Cheltenham, UK • Northampton, MA, USA

Published by
Edward Elgar Publishing Limited
Glensanda House
Montpellier Parade
Cheltenham
Glos GL50 1UA
UK

Edward Elgar Publishing, Inc.
136 West Street
Suite 202
Northampton
Massachusetts 01060
USA

A catalogue record for this book
is available from the British Library

Library of Congress Cataloguing in Publication Data
The economics of the digital society / Luc Soete, Bas ter Weel, [editors].
    p. cm.
  Includes bibliographical references.
    1. Information society–Economic aspects. I. Soete, Luc. II. Ter Weel, Bas.

HM851.E26 2006
330.9′051—dc22   2005049821

ISBN 1 84376 774 0

Printed and bound in Great Britain by MPG Books Ltd, Bodmin, Cornwall

Contents

Figures

Tables

Contributors

Eric J. Bartelsman, Department of Economics, University of Amsterdam, Amsterdam, the Netherlands.

Lex Borghans, Research Centre for Education and the Labour Market (ROA), Maastricht University, Maastricht, the Netherlands.

Robin Cowan, Department of Economics and Maastricht Economic Research Institute on Innovation and Technology (MERIT), Maastricht University, Maastricht, the Netherlands.

Paul A. David, Department of Economics, Stanford University, Stanford, CA, USA.

Wilfred Dolfsma, Department of Business, Erasmus University, Rotterdam, the Netherlands.

Chris Freeman, Science and Technology Policy Research, University of Sussex, Brighton, UK.

Rishab A. Ghosh, Maastricht Economic Research Institute on Innovation and Technology (MERIT), Maastricht University, Maastricht, the Netherlands.

Rüdiger Glott, Maastricht Economic Research Institute on Innovation and Technology (MERIT), Maastricht University, Maastricht, the Netherlands.

Harald Gruber, European Investment Bank, Luxembourg.

P. Jean-Jacques Herings, Department of Economics, Maastricht University, Maastricht, the Netherlands.

Jeroen Hinloopen, Department of Economics, University of Amsterdam, Amsterdam, the Netherlands.

Nicolas Jonard, CNRS, CREA, Ecole Polytechnique, Paris, France.

Bernhard Krieger, Department of Economics, University of Cambridge, Cambridge, UK.

Huub Meijers, Department of Economics and Maastricht Economic

Research Institute on Innovation and Technology (MERIT), Maastricht University, Maastricht, the Netherlands.

Joan Muysken, Department of Economics, Maastricht University, Maastricht, the Netherlands.

Gregorio Robles, Experimental Sciences and Technology Department, Universidad Rey Juan Carlos, Madrid, Spain.

Maarten Pieter Schinkel, Department of Economics and the Amsterdam Center for Law & Economics (ACLE), University of Amsterdam, Amsterdam, the Netherlands.

Luc Soete, Department of Economics, United Nations University-Institute for New Technologies (UNU-INTECH) and Maastricht Economic Research Institute on Innovation and Technology (MERIT), Maastricht University, Maastricht, the Netherlands.

Bas Straathof, Maastricht Economic Research Institute on Innovation and Technology (MERIT), Maastricht University, Maastricht, the Netherlands.

Rifka Weehuizen, Maastricht Economic Research Institute on Innovation and Technology (MERIT), Maastricht University, Maastricht, the Netherlands.

Bas ter Weel, Department of Economics and Maastricht Economic Research Institute on Innovation and Technology (MERIT), Maastricht University, Maastricht, the Netherlands.

Thomas Ziesemer, Department of Economics and Maastricht Economic Research Institute on Innovation and Technology (MERIT), Maastricht University, Maastricht, the Netherlands.

Adriaan van Zon, Department of Economics and Maastricht Economic Research Institute on Innovation and Technology (MERIT), Maastricht University, Maastricht, the Netherlands.

Foreword

This volume originated from a set of papers prepared for the annual conference (the so-called 'pre-Adviezen') of the Dutch Royal Economics Society held in December 2000. To these contributions, originally written in Dutch, a number of invited papers written by 'foreign', leading experts in their respective fields were added to provide the present set of contributions on the economics of the digital society. Many if not most of these papers represent research contributions on the economics of technological change, with a direct application to the digital society, carried out at the Maastricht Economic Research Institute on Innovation and Technology (MERIT) at Maastricht University over the last couple of years. All the chapters in the book have been thoroughly revised and refereed before inclusion in the present volume. What appears here are revised versions that take account of those comments. Although the scope of the chapters is fairly broad, it will become apparent that the main theme of the economics of the digital society assures that they are in fact closely interrelated despite the diversity of approach.

The chapters deal with a great many aspects of the digital society and offer a comprehensive picture of the economics behind many of the interesting features of the information society. It has been our aim to bring together and integrate the views of economists and social scientists in closely related fields to provide insight into the influence of the digital society in the core fields of economics. In particular, there are analyses of welfare economics, networks, the diffusion of new businesses and new forms of entrepreneurship, the auctioning of licences, the much-debated role of intellectual property rights and its impact on the diffusion of knowledge, and the upcoming of free software in the open source movement. Furthermore, there are analyses of a number of applications of developments influencing society: the increased work pressure and new diseases affecting the workforce, the economics of digital content, the effects of computer adoption and use on the wage structure and an analysis of the fear of a 'digital divide', the effects of information and communication technologies on the goods and labour market and their interactions, and the macroeconomic consequences of investment in ICT and economic performance and knowledge accumulations. A chapter on the policy challenges concludes this volume.

This study of the digital society is unique in that it addresses most of the economic issues associated with the changes we have been experiencing over the last decades and the ones that will challenge us and our economies in the near future. The chapters of this book therefore provide much useful insight to both social scientists and policy makers interested in the subject. Finally, one may hope they might prove fruitful to further investigation on this important topic.

Luc Soete
Bas ter Weel
Maastricht, March 2005

Acknowledgements

We would like to thank the following persons for refereeing one or more chapters: Irene Bertschek, Lex Borghans, Machiel van Dijk, Arnaud Dupuy, Hugo Hollanders, Anique Hommels, Hans van Kranenburg, Hans Maks, Ferran Mañe, Joan Muysken, Mark Sanders, Bas Straathof, Martin Strobel, Rifka Weehuizen, Henry van der Wiel, Rene Wintjes, Hakan Yetkiner and Lorenzo Zirulia.

In addition, conversations with Lex Borghans and Paul David turned out to be very useful in putting together the present volume. We are most grateful for their input and suggestions.

1.   Introduction and summary

Luc Soete and Bas ter Weel

1.1   MOTIVATION

How important are information and communication technologies (ICT) in explaining fundamental changes in economic outcomes? How should we think about the digital society and what parts of society have changed over the past decades? How have modern economies changed as a result of digital goods and markets, and what are the policy implications and challenges of these changes?

The impact of ICT on economic outcomes and on society in general is founded on a number of technological breakthroughs that seem to be historically unique.[1] The recent consensus is that ICT has affected the design, management and control of production and service systems throughout the economy, based on an interconnected set of radical innovations in computers, software engineering, control systems, integrated circuits and telecommunications, which have drastically reduced the cost of storing, processing, communicating and disseminating information as well as drastically changing the modes of production and the supply of a range of new products and services. The pervasiveness of ICT is not just a matter of new products or industries, but of a radical new technology, which affects every industry and every service, their interrelationships, and indeed the whole way of life of modern societies. In terms of the concept of general-purpose technologies (GPTs) developed by Bresnahan and Trajtenberg (1995):[2]

> Most GPTs play the role of 'enabling technologies', opening up new opportunities rather than offering complete final solutions. For example, the productivity gains associated with the introduction of electric motors in manufacturing were not limited to a reduction in energy costs. The new energy sources fostered the more efficient design of factories, taking advantage of the newfound flexibility of electric power. Similarly, the users of microelectronics benefit from the surging power of silicon by wrapping around the integrated circuits their own technical advances. This phenomenon involves what we call 'innovational complementarities', that is, the productivity of R&D in a downstream sector increases as a consequence of innovation in the GPT technology. These complementarities magnify the effects of innovation in the GPT, and help propagate them throughout the economy.

1

These observations make clear two crucial ingredients of the ICT revolution: its generality and innovational complementarities. The strong effects of both have led to dramatic changes in our economies. To develop these arguments systematically and to answer the questions raised in a comprehensive way, the present volume offers an insight and overview of the changes ICT has brought about in our analysis and understanding of society.

1.2   SUMMARY AND MAIN ARGUMENT

In a certain sense, it is the task of economists to confront technologists with numerous social, economic and societal factors that are related to the diffusion of new technologies, no matter how radical the technology may be perceived to be by the business community and policy makers, scientists and technologists. From the perspective of its social and economic implications and broader societal embedding, the current cluster of ICT represents a potentially radical technological and organisational transformation. The cluster of what is currently described as ICT is based on a broad range of continuous, sometimes radical, converging technological breakthroughs that, when viewed as a group, appear to be historically unique in terms of speed and world-wide impact. Here we briefly review the most important applications and developments.

The first major change ICT brought about was a dramatic technological improvement in the capacity of semiconductors, which led to a giant increase in the capacities and speed of computers to store and process data. Using what is called Moore's Law, these improvements were described in 1965 as a logarithmic increase in the processing capacity of computer chips (e.g. Moore, 1965). This law still seems to apply 40 years after its formulation as clearly indicated on the Intel Website.[3] This trajectory of continuous technological improvement has been described in depth and analysed by a great many economists since the 1980s, so in fact there is not much new to it.[4] The process of technological improvement in semiconductors in particular gained momentum with Intel's invention of the microprocessor in 1971. In other words, the continuous technological improvements over the past 35 years combined with the individualisation of computer use thanks to personal computers has led to the ever-increasing diffusion of ICT applications throughout the various sectors of the economy. Thus ICT – and the increasing power of the (personal) computer in particular – has made its entry in the numerous economic analyses as a general-purpose technology, the diffusion of which is accompanied by a great many organisational changes and tensions leading to different organisational design, productivity changes, and division of labour.[5]

Second, there is the tendency to miniaturise ICT. The impact of ICT miniaturisation has been essential to the physical integration of electronic functions in existing (and new) equipment and has made this equipment itself more handy and efficient in use. Previously it was impossible to apply a lot of the old ICT equipment in both electromechanical capital and consumption goods, simply because it would have taken up too much space. Apart from the development of the miniaturisation of ICT equipment new, user-friendly products as illustrated in the case of the computer by the development of mainframe to mini-computer, PCs, laptops and palms, offer the possibility to include electronic intelligence in practically any existing mechanical apparatus. Thus ICT equipment seems to further increase the efficiency of existing products, whether they are instruments, machines, or household appliances. Miniaturisation also leads to a lower use of energy.[6] Ultimately, the possibilities for ever-increasing miniaturisation open the avenue to nanotechnology, that is, the production of electronic material at sub-micron level that can interact with tiny matter and cells, including live cells. As yet, the latter developments are clearly in their early stages and subject to research in a lot of countries. Nevertheless, these mainly technologically driven developments towards further miniaturisation are important, because they show that the technological trajectory within the ICT sector is far from completed and that the application areas of the technology extend further to other areas and sectors. In other words, ICT is not just limited to the Internet and the computers on our desks.

Third, there are the almost equally radical technological improvements in the area of telecommunication. The developments in the field of optical fibres allow for the transmission of digital signals without noticeable loss of energy. Combined with the trend towards miniaturising IT equipment described above – the routers and networks stations – and the strong expansion of the bandwidth of communication channels, this allows for the development of a communication network infrastructure in which information and communication goods can be supplied at minimal variable cost. Communicating with someone nearby or with someone on the far side of the globe will be virtually the same and the concept of the 'death of distance' is not as farfetched as it may seem, however, keeping in mind that when virtual and face-to-face interactions are complements the demand for real interactions is increasing as well.[7] It is mainly from this perspective that the technological developments in the area of communication technology differ from other, previous breakthroughs in the area of network technology, such as electricity (e.g. David, 1985). Apart from being dependent on the much higher capital costs of the various network stations, an electricity network is also dependent on energy loss over its own network. In other words, in the case of electricity, contrary to ICT, distance continues to be an important cost factor.

Fourth, there are the specific developments in the area of mobile communication. In a certain sense, mobile communication represents the ultimate form of 'reachability'. Physical access to the infrastructure of the network is no longer necessary, but communication can occur from any place. Naturally, the antenna infrastructure continues to be a major cost factor (and the auctions of the UMTS frequencies have proven to be very expensive, e.g., van Damme, 2002), but this is not in proportion to the physical network costs of, for example, the distribution of electricity. As to the rest, the fixed network cost is formed by the property of a piece of space. Hence, mobile communication adds more than just the end of physical distance; it might be described in Marshallian terms as 'any place, any time, anywhere; information and communication is in the air'. It goes without saying that this additional 'reachability' dimension of communication explains the originally unexpected boom in mobile telephone communication in the 1990s. This area, too, is still in its initial stages of further technological development with the third generation telecommunication systems coming on stream only today (e.g. Gruber, 2004).

Fifth, there are the developments in the field of supporting technologies, such as software and other communication standards, in particular the Internet protocols (for example WWW), and mobile communication standards (such as GSM, WAP and UMTS). Software developments have appeared to be essential not only in the development of new information goods such as content, they have also shown to be particularly important in the improvement of the use of the physical communication infrastructure. ASDL, for example, allowed for the better and more efficient use of the old copper telephone lines. On the other hand, the different layers of open Internet protocols are crucial to the development of new information goods and Internet trade in general. Thus the possibilities of communication expand and the tradability of services increases due to new software developments and internationally accepted information and communication standards. Many of these developments face difficulties in terms of the adoption and harmonisation of consistent systems across countries (e.g. Leibbrandt, 2004 for payment systems).

Finally, the digital economy has been struggling with intellectual property rights (IPR) for a while now and the Open Source Movement has been an attempt to make software freely available. Many of the products available in a digital format share the properties of public goods in the sense that these commodities are non-rivalrous. A non-rival good is a commodity for which use of a unit of the good by one agent does not preclude its use by other agents, whereas a rival good is a commodity for which consumption or use is restricted to the buyer of the commodity. In other words, the consumption of a non-rival (or public) good by one individual does not affect or restrain the supply available for other individuals. The recent discussion of copyright protection for recorded music provides a good illustration. The fundamental good produced by the record industry is a long string of sequences of 0s and 1s, which can be reused at no additional cost; so clearly a non-rival good once put on a CD. Napster provided an Internet site that made it possible to freely exchange this string (music) between consumers around the globe. In court Napster attempted to demonstrate that its activities did not reduce the value of the intellectual property protected by the record companies' copyrights by stating that (1) it involved mainly sampling of individual songs (no downloading of full albums) and (2) it engaged primarily in space shifting, using Napster to play a CD already owned. The first argument was used to show that sampling would increase the demand for the artist's CD because it would give the consumer a nice preview of the total album. The second argument was used to make a case analogous to time shifting (e.g., like recording a soccer match to view it later). Both arguments were dismissed in court because Napster substitutes for buying CDs and does not involve 'fair use' of intellectual property rights.[8]

In brief, what is historically unique in terms of technological developments in the area of ICT, is, in a certain sense, the historically long, unremitting technological improvement in various sub-areas, and on the other hand, the exceptional technological spillovers and convergence between the various ICT areas. Central to this issue, however, is the question of to what extent technologically driven developments lead to the emergence of a truly digital society.

1.3   RESEARCH OUTLINE

This book is in 14 chapters. In Chapter 2, Jean-Jacques Herings and Maarten Pieter Schinkel get to the microeconomic core of the digital economy. They introduce the distinction between goods information and information goods. Goods information in particular – the information about goods and services – is readily available in the new economy at lower cost. Information goods, defined as all goods that are also available in digital form, can be used both in production processes and in consumption. Both require an extensive information structure. Herings and Schinkel seem to be moderately optimistic as to the welfare-increasing impact of goods information, because markets become more transparent and transaction costs can be reduced. On the other hand, they fear that dominant suppliers might affect information goods, because the consumer surplus could be skimmed off by consumer lock-in, the build-up of intellectual property rights and further product differentiation. Finally, the information infrastructure leads almost automatically to monopolistic market structures in view of the importance of network effects, both at the individual and the collective levels. Hence there is a need for a diversified public policy that takes account of these various developments, and Herings and Schinkel point to the role of the government in particular as the gatekeeper of the openness of the competition process, if the potential 'world-wide-welfare' gain of Internet is to be realised.

The next three chapters are more concrete applications of some of the microeconomic issues of the digital society sketched by Herings and Schinkel. These chapters deal with innovation in networks, the development of e-businesses and new market structures, respectively. Chapter 3, by Robin Cowan and Nicolas Jonard, presents a microeconomic model for the formation of strategic alliances in a digital world. In the model, innovation results from the recombination of knowledge held by the partners to the collaboration, and public knowledge. As a result of growing IT use, the fund of public knowledge is bigger, and more easily accessible. Hence a positive externality exists, firms drawing from the pool of available knowledge while at the same time contributing to it through the outcome of the R&D alliances they form over time. A tension exists between contributing to and benefiting from the public knowledge, and Cowan and Jonard study this tension as it changes with the relative ease 'cost' of resorting to bilateral agreements versus drawing from publicly available information.

In Chapter 4, Huub Meijers develops a model that uses indivisibilities and adjustment costs to explain the slow diffusion and adoption of e-business practices by firms. Using a model of monopolistic competition, e-business practices are introduced and typically network effects explain the diffusion pattern of this new practice. Since model simulations provide a better understanding of the relation between market structures and the diffusion of new technologies, and of the relation between firm size and the incentive to adopt new technologies, the second part of the chapter shows the diffusion patterns under a number of sets of model parameters. The results show that typically medium-sized firms adopt e-business practices first and that smaller and less productive firms are driven out of the market. On the other hand, some large firms may even rationally decide not to adopt the new practice but are still competitive enough to survive. Increased price competition shows that at first the diffusion process is faster, but that the ultimate diffusion level decreases. From a policy point of view, Meijers' approach shows the need for open standards to foster compatible technologies, thereby increasing the benefits from network externalities. He also suggests that the further diffusion of e-business tech-nologies can be promoted by the introduction of special programmes based on training and the diffusion of knowledge to help smaller firms to over-come problems related to indivisibilities, and by promoting labour market flexibility that reduces adjustment costs which are hampering diffusion among larger firms.

Harald Gruber, in Chapter 5, analyses the European auctions of radio spectrum for the provision of third generation (3G) mobile telecommuni-cations services as a function of the (local) market structure. Unexpectedly high licence fees were observed in some countries, whereas in other coun-tries they were far below expectations. Gruber's aim is to explain the large differences in government revenues between countries using an oligopoly model. The main question is whether market structure is consistent with the licence fee raised, and this question is analysed in terms of overbidding. Overbidding occurs when a firm engages to pay a higher licence fee than the expected oligopoly profit, which encourages a more concentrated industry or collusive behaviour that could lead to a slowdown in the diffusion of new services, with adverse welfare effects. Gruber's line of rea-soning is contrary to the traditional argument that licence fees are sunk costs and thus should not affect post-entry behaviour, but it follows recent experimental research on the sunk-cost fallacy. To illustrate his arguments, he presents a theoretical framework focusing on the interplay between market structure and fixed costs. The features of the model are then con-trasted with the empirical evidence from the European mobile telecommu-nications industry. On the empirical side, this study provides a structured interpretation of the aftermath of 3G licences and an explanation of the newly emerging market structure in the industry.

The contribution of Paul David in Chapter 6 is concerned with the ques-tion of whether the digital society needs the 'old' intellectual property rights institutions. Radical legal innovations in intellectual property pro-tection have been introduced by the little-noticed European Database Directive of March 1996. This initiative poses numerous contentious issues in law and economics. These are likely to create ambiguities for business and non-profit activities in this area for years to come, and the terms on which those issues are resolved will materially affect the costs and organ-isational feasibility of scientific projects that are of global reach and sig-nificance. In general, the conduct of open, collaborative science may be seriously jeopardised by the consequences of the new IPR protections. David's analysis sets out the economic case for the effectiveness of open, collaborative research, and the forces behind the recent, countervailing rush to strengthen and expand the scope of IPR protection. Focusing on innovations in copyright law and the *sui generis* protection of hitherto unprotected content, it documents the genesis and analyses the economic implications of the EC's Database Directive. David concludes his chapter by advancing a number of remedial proposals that are intended to promote greater efforts to arrive at satisfactory policy solutions for this aspect of 'the digital dilemma'.

In Chapter 7, Rishab Ghosh, Rüdiger Glott, Bernhard Krieger and Gregorio Robles give insight into the demographics of the open source movement. Although open source and free software are no new phenomena, they have shown a considerable increase in importance just in recent years. However, many aspects of this domain still appear unknown or even strange. Economic exchange relations, as they occur within the community of FLOSS developers as well as in the traditional parts of capitalist economies, are usually based on the fundamental principles of private property and monetary payments. However, these principles seem not to be applicable to FLOSS, and still this domain functions very well and gains more and more importance in the leading software markets. Based on an online survey of 2,784 open source/free software developers, this chapter provides insights into fundamental features of the FLOSS community and its economic principles. It sheds light on personal features of FLOSS developers, of their work and project organisation, their motivations, expectations, and orientations. Finally, it illustrates the fundamental dividing lines that characterise mainly the FLOSS community and cause its outstanding position, including the distinction between monetary and non-monetary rewards and the distinction between FLOSS and proprietary software.

Bas Straathof and Rifka Weehuizen, in Chapter 8, argue that there is a relationship between new technologies, most notably ICT, and the intensity of work, and between the intensity of work and mental health. They provide a theoretical framework linking technological change to mental health via its effect on the intensity of work, and demonstrate how more rapid technological change can lead to a deterioration of mental health and a greater incidence of burnout. Straathof and Weehuizen start with the observation that technological advances reduce the price of ICT relative to that of human labour, which causes entrepreneurs to automate a larger proportion of routine tasks. As a consequence, workers will carry out fewer routine tasks and spend more time on non-routine activities. It is shown, by means of two different models, that the shift from routine to non-routine tasks affects work intensity such that work pressure goes up. Workers are therefore more vulnerable to developing symptoms of burnout.

In Chapter 9, Wilfred Dolfsma goes into detail about the developments in an outstanding new-economy sector: the content industry, referred to previously as 'the cultural industries'. Dolfsma analyses in sharp detail the big changes that these content or media industries are facing as typical information goods. They are, in Dolfsma's view, representative of what is in store for other sectors. Content goods represent the most important Internet trade, which is illustrated by, among other things, the top three on the list of the most searched for terms on the Internet: games, music and sex. About three million pieces of music are downloaded from the Internet daily. The content industry is thus characterised by continuous and rapid product innovations as a result of digitalisation, special problems related to the preservation of and compliance with existing intellectual property rights such as copyrights, bundled sales via platforms, rapidly changing team working environments with complex non-routine tasks, and so on. This detailed analysis of the media sector leads Dolfsma to argue in favour of more sectoral analyses and studies. Changes in the types of competition can be studied only at a disaggregated level before specific policy can be formulated. The balance between tendencies of monopoly formation and that of market fragmentation can be determined, according to Dolfsma, only at this level. The media sector is also particularly important and instructive from the perspective of the organisation of product innovations. In a certain sense, every new product is an innovation. For decades, media industries have been organised in such a way that they generate an optimal flow of product innovations. Although only a small percentage of the new products become a success, the sector in itself is successful. Teamwork is highly relevant in this process: in the end, truly innovative ideas are created only by the combination of different backgrounds. It looks, so it seems, suspiciously like the academic research community, when the latter is really creative.

In Chapter 10, Lex Borghans and Bas ter Weel discuss the impact of ICT, and of computers in particular, on the labour market. The growing importance of computers has led to a great deal of attention by policy makers on computer skills, which are viewed nowadays as essential qualifications. In the absence of both empirical and theoretical underpinning, however, the real importance of computer skills continues to be unclear. Borghans and Ter Weel use several data sources in their attempt to measure computer skills, the various levels at which computers are used, and the importance of computer use for one's job. They conclude that, in general, the lack of computer skills does not play a limiting role in the workplace. Thus, according to Borghans and Ter Weel, just like the fear back in the 1970s and 1980s concerning large-scale technological unemployment, the fear that without investment in computer skills part of the population will miss the boat, is unjustified. Nevertheless, they believe that, in a lot of professions, labour productivity will increase as a result of the use of computers and more ICT in general. They emphasise, however, the importance of infrastructure and availability of services, not only physical network structure, but also software and information services. In other words, the impact of ICT on the labour market goes beyond the old vision of skill-biased technical change, and brings to the fore a full range of new skills. Rather than with computer skills, this development is concerned with a broader shift from the importance of a variety of skills in today's society.

In Chapter 11, Thomas Ziesemer develops a theoretical model to find the impact of ICT, bargaining power and monopoly power on x-best optimal unemployment benefits and on three market imperfections: search externalities, monopoly prices and variety externalities. The main contribution of Ziesemer's chapter is to consider not only labour-market imperfections (search externalities) but also goods-market imperfections (monopolistic firms and goods-variety externalities). His main result is that ICT and a reduction in a firm's monopoly power increase the optimal level of unemployment benefits, whereas a reduction in a worker's bargaining power reduces the optimal level of unemployment benefits.

Eric Bartelsman and Jeroen Hinloopen, in Chapter 12, also focus mainly on the economic underpinning of cashing in the digital growth promise, by looking at the increase in efficiency in information processing and communication as a result of the use of ICT. This increase in efficiency is translated into a decrease in transaction costs and an increase in the productivity of knowledge workers. According to Bartelsman and Hinloopen, this is translated into a possibly higher growth path of GDP at the macroeconomic level. After all, the lower transaction costs lead to a better match between supply and demand and higher added value per unit of production means. As more firms use ICT in their production process, and as the market share of the ICT-using firms increases and entrants are more productive than firms withdrawing from the market, productivity at the macroeconomic level will therefore also rise. The question is why this process seems to have been set in motion in the United States, but not in Europe. Bartelsman and Hinloopen argue that particularly the investments in ICT capital in Europe lag behind those of the United States. To find an explanation for this, they look at the higher costs of ICT capital in Europe, for example as a result of higher personnel and financing costs and less market pressure. Policy makers should therefore focus on these aspects, if they want to cash in the growth promise of ICT in Europe.

In Chapter 13 Adriaan van Zon and Joan Muysken build a model to analyse the impact of investment in ICT on subsequent knowledge accumulation and eventually economic performance. They formulate an endogenous growth model that incorporates a positive link between the production and the use of ICT on the one hand, and productivity growth at the aggregate level on the other. Van Zon and Muysken do this by introducing ICT capital as a separate factor in the production of final output and in the accumulation of knowledge. This enables them to identify explicitly several transmission mechanisms for the growth effects emanating from the ICT sector, among which is its impact on the process of human capital accumulation that may become much more productive through ICT capital deepening. Thus ICT investment may influence growth performance directly and endogenously. Using the model, they study the structural features (as opposed to the transitional dynamics) underlying the steady-state growth performance of the economy, in which growth is not so much caused by ICT investment, but certainly strengthened by it. They conclude from their analysis that for reasonable parameterisations of the model, a positive link between ICT investment and economic growth does indeed exist. A study of this positive link under three different spillover regimes yields that welfare is positively affected the stronger these spillovers are, but also the more these spillovers are internalised. In addition to this, they find that under a system of decentralised decision-making, the economy will consistently tend to over-accumulate in comparison to the social planner solution. This suggests that there is room for policy intervention aiming to increase the impact on growth of these spillover effects, for instance through education policies that improve computer literacy.

Finally, Christopher Freeman and Luc Soete provide in their chapter, 'A digital society for us all: "old" and "new" policy reflections', a very intriguing view on the policy changes and aspects of the digital society by examining the policy implications made in 1995 in a 2005 context. Their main conclusion is that many of the policy issues debated and discussed ten years ago within the framework of an influential EU advisory expert group in which both Freeman and Soete participated, are today still as valid as ever. As they put it: 'To paraphrase Keynes: policy makers new to the job, who believe themselves to be quite exempt from earlier policy advice, are usually the slaves of some defunct EU policy report'. In short, even when looking at a set of radical general-purpose technologies such as ICT, expert policy conclusions seem to have a stickiness associated with them that makes them relevant for far longer periods than policy makers are likely to be in office and have attempted to implement them.

NOTES

1. See e.g. Freeman and Soete (1990, Chapter 3) for an overview of the development of information and communication technologies into modern ICT.
2. Quoted by Helpman (1998, p. 3).
3. See for example http://www.intel.com/research/silicon/mooreslaw.htm
4. See for example Katz and Phillips (1982), Dosi (1984) and Jorgenson (2001).

5. See for example Freeman and Perez (1988), David (1991), Bresnahan, Brynjolfsson and Hitt (2002), Bertschek and Kaiser (2004) and Borghans and ter Weel (2004).
6. The intensive use and large-scale diffusion of their widespread presence, for example computers, can of course, undo this energy benefit per appliance. According to calculations in the United States, the production and use of computers is responsible for 295 billion kilowatt hours of electricity demand, which equals about 8 per cent of the total American demand for electricity.
7. Cairncross (1997) argues that the revolution we are seeing is the third in a succession of great changes in the technology and cost of transportation over the past three centuries. The nineteenth century was shaped by the falling cost of transporting goods; the twentieth by the falling cost of transporting people; and the twenty-first century will be dominated by the falling cost of transporting ideas and information.
8. The *American Economic Review*, May 2002, published a discussion on the economic perspective of the Napster case. See also David (2001), Borghans (2003) and Soete and ter Weel (2004) for an analysis of access to research data in relation to the developments in the area of ICT.

REFERENCES

Bertschek, I. and U. Kaiser (2004), 'Productivity effects of organizational change: Microeconomic evidence', *Management Science*, **50**, 394–404.

Borghans, L. (2003), 'Nederlandse data zijn te duur', *Economisch Statistische Berichten*, **88**, 132–3.

Borghans, L. and B. ter Weel (2004), 'What happens when agent *T* gets a computer? The labor market impact of efficient computer adoption', *Journal of Economic Behavior & Organization*, **54**, 137–51.

Bresnahan, T.F., E. Brynjolfsson and L.M. Hitt (2002), 'Information technology, workplace organization, and the demand for skilled labor: Firm-level evidence', *Quarterly Journal of Economics*, **117**, 339–76.

Bresnahan, T.F. and M. Trajtenberg (1995), 'General purpose technologies: "Engines of growth"', *Journal of Econometrics*, **65**, 83–108.

Cairncross, F. (1997), *The Death of Distance: How the Communications Revolution Will Change Our Lives*, Cambridge MA: Harvard Business School Press.

van Damme, E. (2002), 'The European UMTS-auctions', *European Economic Review*, **46**, 846–58.

David, P.A. (1985), 'Clio and the economics of QWERTY', *American Economic Review*, **75**, 332–7.

David, P.A. (1991), *The Dynamo and the Computer: An Historical Perspective on the Modern Productivity Paradox*, Paris: OECD.

David, P.A. (2001), 'Tragedy of the public knowledge "commons"? Global science, intellectual property and the digital technology boomerang', MERIT Research Memorandum 2001–003, Maastricht University.

Dosi, G. (1984), *Technical Change and Industrial Transformation*, London: Macmillan.

Freeman, C. and C. Perez (1988), 'Structural crises of adjustment: Business cycles and investment behaviour', in G. Dosi, C. Freeman, R. Nelson, G. Silverberg and L. Soete (eds), *Technical Change and Economic Theory*, London: Pinter, pp. 38–66.

Freeman, C. and L. Soete (1990), *Work for All or Mass Unemployment: Computerised Technical Change into the 21st Century*, London: Pinter.

Gruber, H. (2004), *The Economics of Mobile Telecommunications*, Cambridge: Cambridge University Press.

Helpman, E. (1998), *General Purpose Technologies and Economic Growth*, Cambridge MA: MIT Press.

Jorgenson, D.W. (2001), 'Information technology and the US economy', *American Economic Review*, **90**, 1–32.

Katz, B.G. and A. Phillips (1982), 'Government, economies of scale and comparative advantage: The case of the computer industry', in H. Giersch (ed.), *Proceedings of Conference on Emerging Technology*, Tübingen: Kiel Institute of World Economics.

Leibbrandt, G. (2004), *Payment Instruments and Network Effects*, PhD Thesis, Maastricht University.

Moore, G.E. (1965), 'Cramming more components onto integrated circuits', *Electronics*, **38**, 19 April 1965.

Soete, L. and B. ter Weel (2004), 'ICT and access to research data: An economic review', Working Paper, Maastricht University.

2. World-wide-welfare: A micro-economic analysis of 'the new economy'*

P. Jean-Jacques Herings and Maarten Pieter Schinkel

2.1 INTRODUCTION

Worldwide, there has been – and still is – a lot of interest in what is generally referred to as 'the new economy'. It concerns economics that relates to digital information and the hardware and software that deals with it. The new thing about that form of economics is that, as a result of the digitalization of information, its exchange and multiplication can take place at close to zero marginal costs. With that, comes that an increasingly large number of people have an ever better wall or wireless connection to the new infrastructure that is formed by the world-wide-web. This allows for very fast, inexpensive and extensive transportation of information.

The economic relevance of these developments is large and growing. An ever-expanding economy flourishes on the Internet, in which supply and demand meet in virtual markets. As a result, old physical markets are being substituted at a continuous and rapid rate. On the other hand, many new markets have emerged such as the one for Internet guidance and many new markets will certainly open in the years to come. With that, the Internet is increasingly responsible for added value, which is, despite the burst of an early bubble, reflected in the value of firms engaged in information trade on the stock exchanges around the world.

Two of the many things that are written about the new economy meet the eye. First, the approach taken to understand new economy issues is often a macro-economic one. That is, the effects on macro-economic magnitudes

---

* An earlier edition of this chapter appeared in Dutch as 'World-Wide-Welfare: Een micro-economische analyse van de nieuwe economie' in L. Soete (ed.), *ICT en de Nieuwe Economie, Preadviezen aan de Koninklijke Vereniging voor de Staathuishoudkunde, 2000*, Lemma, Utrecht, 2000. We thank the editors and three anonymous referees for comments that led to the present version.

such as national product, price level or employment are considered. These treatments are typically quite optimistic. National products and employment will rise for long periods of time, and without any inflation to speak of. Sepsis, although heard, often concerns semantic issues – is the new economy new or not new – or earlier eulogies of a macro-economic nature.

Second, it is regularly concluded that understanding the new economy demands a reconsideration of economic theory. Old economic laws allegedly no longer apply, for new ones have replaced them. Demand no longer leads to falls in prices, whereas supply often does. Companies need no longer make profits, but instead should give away their products for nothing. And since traditional economic laws no longer apply, speaking of 'new economics' is justified.

In some sense these two visions are at odds. If one is of the opinion that old theory cannot comprehend new economics, then one cannot support optimism about the effects of the new economy on welfare on the basis of old theories and measurements. And the other way around: optimism on the basis of macro-economic statistics reveals a faith in the applicability of the underlying theory. It is therefore important to find a theoretical structure that can be used to consider the 'new economy's' blessings and plagues.

It is certainly the case that particular traditional insights, such as the existence of a trade-off between unemployment and inflation as represented in the Phillips curve, or measurement methods based on prices, such as inflation indices, are less solid and reliable in an economy in which information increasingly flows at decreasing average costs. The latter corresponds to the paradox on the national product in heaven and in hell. In heaven, there is no scarcity. All commodities are available in abundance. Consequently, all prices, and hence the national product, are equal to zero. In hell, on the other hand, there is a need for energy to keep the temperature sufficiently high. On top of that, everything is scarce and priced highly. As a result, the national product is substantial. Traditional macro-economics has to be careful, therefore, not to measure a preference for hell over heaven.

The questions we are concerned with here are more modest, however: isn't it possible to use the concepts developed in economic theory to consider how to efficiently allocate scarce means over alternative ends in an attempt to shed light on the new economy as well? The discipline in which the allocation issue led to the development of sophisticated models is micro-economics. On the basis of the structure of economies, and the behaviour of consumers and producers in it, micro-economics derives conclusions about social welfare. The latter is a consistently defined concept that is not open to the macro-economic measurement problems pointed at above. Micro-economic theory seems, therefore, particularly suitable for making statements about the new economy. It can serve to give hands and feet to either widespread optimism, or a sceptical attitude.

Since its earliest development, the role of information in understanding societies has been central in micro-economics. Adam Smith's notion of 'the invisible hand' in competitive markets concerns in essence the spread of sufficient information via market prices to ensure that individually optimal decisions are socially optimal as well. Micro-economics seems well equipped to handle information issues, that is.

The applicability of micro-economic theory, however, falls or stands with the presence of scarcity in the new economy. After all, it is the use of scarce means for alternative ends on which the theory concludes, it is scarcity that determines the prices of commodities, and it is the prices of commodities that guide the invisible hand. Yet, digitalized information can be reproduced and transported without loss of quality and at close to zero marginal costs can be multiplied and transported. This seems to challenge the scarcity concept. However, an unbridled production of information leads to a new type of scarcity: the time it takes to select, personalize and consume information. Moreover, there is an artificial way to make information scarce: the granting of intellectual property rights. And a further potential source of scarcity lies in the carriers of information, the information infrastructure.

In this chapter we consider some of the consequences that large-scale traffic of digitalized information can have for the structure of supply and demand, as well as for competitive processes and social welfare. To that end, the following section contains a micro-economic treatment of information and markets that offers a handle for an analysis of the new economy. We introduce the distinction between commodity information and information commodities. Section 3 analyses the consequences of increased commodity information in the new economy. This concerns commodity information on traditional commodities as well as information commodities. Section 4 discusses the specific economic aspects of information commodities. Section 5 considers the carriers of information streams, the information infrastructure, and particularly several important consequences of the private production thereof. Section 6 concludes with concerns about new and specific restrictive tendencies in the new economy.

2.2   INFORMATION AND COMMODITIES

The central aspect of the new economy is its feature that information is reproduced and distributed at extraordinary low marginal costs, with no loss of quality to speak of. The latter is possible because of the form information takes and the rise of new telecommunications networks, with the Internet as a prominent example. We use the term 'information' for everything that can be digitalized; that is, all that can be put in a series of zeros and ones. It is the digitalization of information that facilitates its wide and rapid spread. And even though digitalization is not always fully feasible – after all, a digital signal is only a discrete approximation of an analogue signal – the cut off peaks only really bother the hardened LP record or celluloid film enthusiast. All information – be it newspaper articles, medical records, train schedules or rock songs – can be digitized for practical purposes.

2.2.1 A Classification of Information

In order to unravel the influence of information on the way decisions are made, it is useful to make a categorization. The first and most elementary distinction is that between pure and instrumental information.[1] Pure information – that should be considered distinct from its carrier – is information that is a direct source of utility, or information that is directly used as an input factor in a production process. An example of information as a consumption good is a movie, but then without the cinema. An example of information as a production factor is a word processor, but without the CD-ROM on which it comes. Pure information is a commodity and is therefore characterized just like other commodities, by content, time and place of availability, and state of the world at the time of availability.[2] We refer to pure information as 'information commodity'.

Instrumental information, on the contrary, is information about things that provide direct utility or serve in production. It is commodity information, such as the information that a certain movie plays at a certain time in a certain theatre, or information about the availability of certain types of production factors. Commodity information is in the micro-economic literature generally represented by a probability distribution over the set of possible states of the world. In the case of complete commodity information, there is no uncertainty and the distribution over possible states of the world is degenerated. In the case of incomplete commodity information, however, individuals base their decisions on a non-degenerated distribution. New commodity information generally leads to an update of this distribution.[3]

Where information commodities are a direct source of utility in themselves, commodity information specifies individuals' choice problems over all sorts of commodities that provide utility. It has little value in itself, but derives value from the possibility to make better choices. Commodity information serves to enable one, for example, to better enjoy the information commodity movie by being in time for the show, or to make lemonade more efficiently out of lemons – which in essence is the same. Also, information that producers obtain about the buying behaviour and preferences of their customers features in this categorization under commodity information. Commodity information is information about the elements of the commodity vector, including information commodities. Information is very often available in both forms simultaneously. A film review, for example, is both an information commodity – as it often is amusing reading – and commodity information, since it leads to better choices in the matter of theatre visits. An element of commodity information that attracts a lot of attention in the economic literature is the price of a commodity – whether an information commodity or otherwise.

It is important in this context to note the difference between the interpretation of one piece of commodity information by different individuals. Confronted with a large amount of identical information, different individuals may form similar expectations.[4] Yet, on the basis of the same signals from the outside world, different individuals may also form different expectations. This has to do with both the structure of the view of the world that someone has and the initial probabilities that are assigned to possible developments within that structure. In Section 3 we come back to this.

The indirect value of information may cause commodity information to be traded as if it were a commodity. The information regarding what movie plays when could be offered for sale – generally it is of course offered free. Another, and perhaps better, example of tradable commodity information is the information necessary for the sellers and potential buyers of houses to find each other. The trade in this commodity, which consists of commodity information, earns real-estate brokers their daily bread. Their well-being, however, depends on the latter only.

Although information can therefore be analysed separately from its carrier, to be useful it has to be stored, for example on a DVD, paper, or in human minds. Traditional carriers add characteristics to the combination of information and carrier that make the total product a standard commodity in the economic sense. An example is again the information commodity movie shown in a movie theatre. Since the number of seats in the cinema is limited, a positive price can be charged for this commodity. Also the information printed in the consumers' magazine is tied to a paper carrier that needs to be acquired. Tradable commodity information obtains the characteristics of a traditional commodity, and is characterized by content, time and place of availability, as well as state of the world.

Developments around the information infrastructure, such as wireless Internet, are interesting because they make the tie between information and carrier less rigid. As a result of decreasing scarcity in carriers such as digital memory, the special characteristics of information as a commodity – information commodity and tradable commodity information – play a larger role. The cheaper transportation of information makes the information's location of availability of ever lesser concern. For producers, this implies that a traditionally important element on which to build monopoly power disappears. Apart from that, the technological progress leads to new applications of information, applications that before were simply not feasible or were too expensive.

2.2.2 Specific Characteristics of Information

Both the production and the distribution of information are significantly different from those of physical commodities. This was already recognized by Arrow in the early 1960s, who observed that the production of new information generally requires high fixed costs, which are largely sunk once made. Writing a book, for example, demands a special effort of the writer. Once this production has taken place, however, reproduction is easy and can take place at relatively low marginal costs. This is the case with books since the invention of the art of printing, but more recently it holds for copying computer software as well. The marginal costs necessary for the production of information are nil.

This asymmetry between fixed and marginal costs causes a number of important problems. Because copying is simple, information once produced spreads quickly and easily. As a result, it is questionable whether someone is willing to make the initial investment in the production of new information. After all, there is a real possibility that it will not be possible to earn the investment back. The consequences of this are all the more disastrous when one takes the public good aspect of information into account.[5] Naturally, this is the basis of intellectual property rights, to which we turn in Section 2.4.4.

Information, therefore, can be transmitted from one individual to the next. In that information has the characteristic noted by Arrow that when it is passed on, it remains part of the endowment of the offering party. In most cases this is evident for commodity information, but for information commodities is holds equally true. Trade in information, therefore, typically involves its multiplication. Information is, as a result, not necessarily a commodity for which rivalry exists.

Unintended communication of information can also take place. An example is leakage of information. This happens relatively easily, particularly because information can be exchanged without deterioration and at low costs. In a way, information has as a consequence of these characteristics a natural tendency to spread. In many cases, the leakage of information is actually very desirable. In general it is socially optimal when information, once produced, is made public to as large a group as possible.

Another special aspect of information is that the determination of its value is hard without consuming it. Information, in other words, is an experience good. This causes problems in its transmission. Decisions on the purchase of information, as a consequence, are generally decisions under uncertainty. We return to the specific possibilities that the new economy offers for trade in information commodities.

In many cases, the tendency of information to spread also allows for abuse. People can have an incentive to leak misleading or false information. A traditional example of the spread of such information concerns the announcement of business news in an attempt to manipulate the price of stocks. Some attribute a large part of the gold rush to this effect: land owners spreading the rumour that the mother lode crossed their property, in an attempt to raise the sale or lease price of the lot.

As a result, the reliability of information is an important part of its economic analysis. In order to be able to judge it, it can, for example, be important to know who spread the information, how many others have already used it, and who knows who has what information. That way, it can be determined whether the information was released with specific perverse incentives. Information can, for this purpose, be categorized: first-order information is the actual information and higher-order information is information about the information. To take movies again: a review constitutes first-order commodity information about the information commodity movie, and second-order commodity information about the review, which is the newspaper in which it appeared, or the name and fame of the reviewer.

A special kind of higher-order information is the so-called common knowledge. This is information that everybody knows everybody has. Such information is a strong form of public information, which is information that everybody has, but of which it is not necessarily known that such is the case. It contrasts sharply with private information, which is information that is available only to one individual. The natural tendency of information to spread easily creates a tendency for private information to become public information, and finally common knowledge.

2.3   COMMODITY INFORMATION

Commodity information has been defined in the previous section as knowledge about commodities and services that allows consumers and producers to specify their chosen problems. Commodity information comes in many varieties. When the costs associated with storing and selecting information

are ignored, individual choice making is enhanced with more specific information. After all, more information facilitates comparing different alternatives, while the original option is still available.[6] As a result commodity
information has a derived value for individuals.

2.3.1 The Individual Value of Commodity Information

A somewhat naive approach by which to derive the value of commodity
information is to compare the choices made without and with commodity
information. A conundrum that arises here, however, is that *ex ante* it is not
known what the return of that commodity information will be. Another
problem with simply comparing choices made *ex ante* and *ex post* is that a
choice made after collecting more information can, purely by coincidence,
turn out to be worse than a decision made with less information, even when
the information was actually reliable and valuable.

Collected information can be seen as a series of messages. The joint probability distribution of a message and state of the world depends on the view
of the individual. Assume that someone has the choice between taking
immediate action, or first collecting information with the idea to take
action later. The choice of a particular action, together with the selection
of a state of the world by chance, results in a certain pay-off. Initially, the
individual expects given states to arise with certain prior probabilities. He
or she can choose to collect information on the basis of which to change
this prior distribution. Given the probability with which any particular
message is received, the joint probability of a message and a state, and the
conditional probability of a particular message given the state of the world,
the so-called posterior distribution can be derived using Bayes' law.[7] On the
basis of this model, it is possible to determine whether or not an individual
will collect information. The utility value of a message is then equal to the
utility of the optimal choice made after receiving the message, minus the
utility of the optimal choice made without the message.

The above model also allows for a further sharpening of the distinction between commodity information and information commodities.
Commodity information complies with information defined as follows in
Arrow (1978 p. 7): 'By "information", I mean any observation which
effectively changes probabilities according to the principles of conditional
probability.' This is only part of our definition of information as anything
that can be represented in a stream of zeros and ones. Therefore, music, for
example, is information, while listening to music will scarcely give reason to
reconsider the probabilities with which future developments are foreseen.

As said, the utility value of a message is always non-negative. The
expected value of information is the expected value under the prior utility

values when all possible messages are taken together. It determines how much somebody would maximally want to pay for the use of a certain message service, such as a newspaper, an Internet site or an expert. In this way it is possible to compare the value of information services, and to rank them. Since subjective worldviews determine the value of an information service, individuals rank information services differently. On top of that, the above analysis does not take into account that there are costs associated with the processing and use of information. These capacities differ for different individuals as well. This is one reason why there is such a variety of information services on the Internet.

It is to be expected, for example, that information is different for people with a different attitude towards risk. Intuitively a risk-averse person would want to incur more costs for collecting information before taking a decision than someone with less aversion towards risk. This is not necessarily so, however. If the optimal action without first obtaining information leads with certainty to a particular pay-off, a more risk-averse individual will actually optimally collect less information. The possible variations in income resulting from the new information are not particularly appreciated. The other way around, if collecting information reveals the state of the world with certainty, a risk-averse person collects more information. Extra information, however, always has a non-negative value, for risk-loving and risk-averse people alike.

2.3.2   The Social Value of Commodity Information

A better match between the real probabilities with which events can take place and the subjective expectation of these, therefore, is desirable for the individual decision maker. The significantly improved means of communication in the new economy, therefore, certainly have a private value. Moreover, increased transparency of possibilities and restraints has a positive effect on social welfare as well: it can decrease transaction costs and enhance competition.

General equilibrium models are models in which the social consequences of individual choices in certain economic market structures find expression. Although not inherently, the most important results in general equilibrium models are found in its limit model with rational agents, markets with perfect competition and the absence of transaction costs.

In short, the findings of the general equilibrium research amount to the following. Consider an economy with a complete system of markets, which means that at each point in time there exist markets for commodities that are available at that point in time, but also for all commodities that become available in the future, possibly conditional on the realization of future uncertain events. The information about future commodities that is initially present is in general asymmetrically distributed over the individuals. The equilibrium prices that result in such an economy, however, are such that all existing information is revealed.[8]

It is possible to relax the assumption of the existence of a complete system of markets to the (still strong) condition that a complete system of financial markets exists, or alternatively put, that agents are able to insure themselves against all possible events. This complies with the more general idea that a system with complete financial markets leads to the same result as a system with complete commodity markets.[9] It should be noted however that, although equilibria in both market systems have identical characteristics, the conditions under which coordination on an equilibrium takes place differ.[10]

Outside the context of general equilibrium, auction theory concerns the question of whether perfect competition leads to the complete revelation of all available information. Consider the situation in which an object is auctioned that represents the same value for all, a value that is unknown. Every participant knows this value, however, and the information of all participants together is sufficient to determine the value of the object. For both a decreasing auction and an increasing auction in which the highest bidder pays the second highest bid, the winning bid is equal to the actual value of the object if the number of participants is sufficiently large.[11]

These results are very powerful. They show that in an economy with sufficient competition, information problems play no role: individuals can use market equilibrium prices to obtain all available commodity information. The level of rationality necessary for this, however, is staggering, and by far surpasses the level demanded in a standard general equilibrium model, as it assumes structural knowledge such as insight into the preferences of individuals. The important lesson learned from these models is that commodity prices can reveal quite a lot of commodity information, provided transaction costs are low and information spreads very quickly. It is particularly these assumptions that gain in empirical relevance in the new economy, so that it may enhance the absorption of commodity information in market prices.

2.3.3 A Disequilibrium Approach

In the absence of a complete system of commodity markets, the usual equilibrium concept in general equilibrium theory takes out a loan on rationality. Economic subjects do not only need to know the prices of commodities, they are also required to have insight into 'the model' of the economy. Originally, this is the idea behind the long popular but increasingly questioned 'rational expectations approach'. The idea is that if economists know the model, the economic agents in it should be assumed to be able to know it as well. Therefore, they should not be consistently off the mark in their predictions of equilibrium values. There is, however, an important difference between structural insights into economies and parametric knowledge of them. For both, but especially the latter, an unreasonable amount of information is demanded.

Interestingly enough, the literature on rational expectations as justification of the equilibrium approach has pushed aside the ideas of economists such as Friedrich von Hayek and Kenneth Arrow, which apply, however, much better to the new economy. These scholars argued that competitive economies are not to be praised particularly for the existence of efficient equilibria, but for the fact that the competitive process is an important distributor of information. Rival bids and bargaining will reveal options to others they were previously unaware of, so that prices paid will eventually gravitate towards values that reflect the marginal costs of goods. The competitive process may eventually lead to efficiency, but through an adjustment process in which information plays a crucial role.

It is particularly in this disequilibrium sense that an important influence is to be expected from developments such as the growth of modern information and communication technology. As these technologies accommodate the fast distribution of information, they enhance competition. Consumers are better able to compare prices and qualities of different suppliers, so that margins and intermediaries play ever smaller roles.

Illustrative examples of the latter are brokers in houses, or dealers in second-hand cars. Although these intermediaries do have their own added value in determining the quality of the goods offered, that function apparently does not justify the fees paid for their services in the past. Particularly as a result of the increase in communication that runs via the Internet, these margins have recently decreased significantly. Indeed, for the large part they used to be derived from the difficulties that buyers and sellers in the market have in finding each other. These search costs are the direct consequence of a lack of transparency of markets. In the new economy, a decrease in such costs is to be expected, as is an increase in competitive pressures on both suppliers and demanders. The result is that reality will increasingly become like the competitive general equilibrium models with their nice efficiency properties – be they second-best or first-best. Such is highly socially desirable.

With a flourishing new economy there seem to be both private and social benefits. A better connection between preferences and possibilities on an economy-wide scale can lead to an important increase in social welfare. Nevertheless, it is important to make some qualifications with respect to unbridled enthusiasm based on this type of argument. It follows, for example, that unlimited growth cannot be expected if the benefits of the new economy are particularly found in the resolution of inefficiencies of the old one. Growth is more likely to take the form of a temporary spurt, after which equilibrium is reached at a permanently higher level of welfare. This view may shed light on the burst dot-com bubble, for example.

2.3.4 Information Costs

So far our analysis has assumed that relevant commodity information is readily available at close to zero cost. Collecting, storing and processing information, however, does involve costs. If commodity information can only be obtained and used at a cost, it is still true in general that more information leads to more efficient choices. The efficient amount of information to collect, however, is no longer equal to the total of relevant information. If the marginal contribution to the decision problem is equal to the marginal costs of getting the information, one should stop further inquiries and make a decision.

In many decision problems there is not one single individual who decides, but a group that takes decisions collectively. If the members of the group have different expectations or different objectives, there is a tendency to collect too much information. In the case of different expectations, the reason for this is that these can only coincide when large amounts of identical information are shared. Inefficiently large amounts of information then only serve to justify an otherwise unavoidable decision for all. If there are different objectives, collecting more information helps to put off decisions and keep alternatives open. In both cases abundant information may well have a negative influence on welfare.[12]

There is yet another important social danger that lurks when too much information is available: some options of choice disappear when more information becomes available. Moreover, certain markets exist only by the grace of incomplete information. A well-known example of this is the insurance market. If it is possible to determine with certainty that someone suffers from a certain illness or will be struck by disaster, there is no possibility of insuring against it. In other words, after revelation of the state of the world it is no longer possible to insure oneself. Such can lead to important welfare losses.[13]

The above-mentioned detrimental effects of more information increase the costs of obtaining information. This latter effect is a certain danger that exists in the new economy. As a result of the large supply of information on the Internet, it has become increasingly difficult to separate important from less important, useless, or even false, information. This introduces at least two new problems. First, the overload of information requires storage capacity and time to select valuable and less valuable information.

Second, the reliability of information is not always easily determined and extra costs are incurred in verification.

2.3.5 Virtual Markets

The necessity to select and verify information generates direct costs, but it also has consequences for market structures, especially the structure of virtual markets. These are meeting places of supply and demand that only exist on-line. Whereas the increase in available information reduces the role of certain traditional intermediaries, it also creates room for new ones that select and individualize information. Search engines already do this, albeit quite imperfectly. It is likely that they will be further developed to play into the specific interests of those seeking commodity information. It remains to be seen, however, whether they will ever be able to compete with human consultants. Moreover, if a search engine were to have this potential, it would be likely to exercise a local monopoly power over anyone who used it.

The reputation of suppliers in virtual markets is important in establishing transactions. Concerning commodity information, the Internet creates intervals between the different stages of an exchange. When someone buys a book in a local store, he or she pays while the book is being wrapped up and it can be taken out immediately. A transaction with an Internet bookseller, however, involves an impersonal electronic order, after which it takes some time and risky shipping, before the item, which then has already been paid for by credit, is eventually received. Because there is no cash on the nail, both the method of payment and the delivery require trust of the buyer in the system of the seller, as well as trust of the seller in the credibility of the buyer.

This has several negative effects. Starting entrepreneurs will first have to build confidence among consumers, and this can be very difficult when there are already well-established large incumbents. This is apart from the fact that the incumbent is likely to have other scale economies already, for example in the access to distribution channels. As a result of these problems, market power rises, and can nullify large parts of the efficiency-enlarging possibilities of the increased means for communication. Reputation becomes an important barrier to entry as a result.

Crucial in Internet transactions are the credit card companies. They accommodate the larger part of Internet transactions by means of virtual payments. In order to prevent hesitation and reluctance to trade on the Internet, credit card companies offer a guarantee against potential fraudulent use of credit card numbers. This insurance against fraud is costly, however, which represents a cost typical to virtual transactions that is likely to rise rather than fall.

Another problem is that credit cards are not suitable for all types of transactions on the Internet – particularly not for one-to-one transactions between individuals. Cash payment methods, or bank wires, on the contrary do not fit when transactions are to be completed immediately. For other uses in the new economy it is important to make payments in very small units. An example is downloading information for the price of just a fraction of a cent. Although alternative methods of payment have been developed, confidence problems play an even greater role there.

Confidence issues in payments clearly have the potential to reduce potential efficiency gains. A lack of confidence will put a certain upper bound to virtual transactions. In this context, extensive research has been done into drugs transactions. In the drugs trade there have always existed confidence issues, simply because there is no possibility for falling back on a judicial system for sanctions. Larger transactions are, as a result, split into smaller parts. It has been observed even that dealer and customer exchange little suitcases with drugs and money in several transactions following each other, in order to reduce the risks of unilateral default. The comparable risks of unilateral failure to close a deal in Internet transactions may well put a similar type of upper limit to these transactions. Larger ones will then only take place in a personal meeting – even though parties may still have found each other via telecommunication.[14]

New intermediaries specialize in providing identification methods to reduce confidence problems. Moreover, the increased role of credit card companies as insurance providers leads to a drive for size. After all, the more transactions, the lower the variance in returns caused by non-payment and fraudulent use. Together with the reputation effects that hold for credit card companies as well, this effect kills competition in the payment traffic.[15]

A confidence problem on the side of the buyer is the fact that it is not transparent what consequences placing a virtual order may have for his or her anonymity. In traditional transactions, apart maybe from the local supermarket, some anonymity is guaranteed. Payment can take place with non-traceable money after which the parties split up. Internet transactions, starting from the surfing to obtain information, reveal the preferences and purchases of the customer and offer the possibility to store, and therefore use and exploit, that information for many years to come. Companies have developed protocols to protect private information from being misused. Also, there exist virtual banks where money can be put and from where anonymous payments can be made. It is particularly the lack of transparency concerning the possibilities and impossibilities of undesired use of private information that can be an important cause of reluctance to trade on virtual markets.

Even when the commodity information offered is reliable, it can still be incomplete. It is not easy to compare prices on the Internet: even at a transparent site it demands quite some work to establish the exact total outlay necessary to acquire an item, as this includes transportation and insurance costs, for example. As there does not exist a simple standard by which one can easily compare prices, there remains scope for monopolistic competition and costly intermediaries.

Stronger than this effect, however, is a related drive for intermediaries to keep information dispersed. Suppose that the virtual markets are in perfect competition. Then none of the consumers has an incentive to incur expense in order to search for commodity information, not even when costs are very small. Likewise, websites with comparative price information for homogeneous commodities can only exist by the grace of price dispersion. This type of site therefore has an incentive to leave a certain amount of price dispersion remaining, since that provides the rights to their existence and their profit opportunity.[16]

In a market with sufficient numbers of competing sellers, an efficient and reliable information service gives rise to strong pressures from potential competition. This induces a collective incentive among the sellers to make the Internet into the type of unreliable and uninformative medium that television is with commercials, for example. In that case, the informative role has been pushed away by entertaining and manipulative functions that strengthen the positions of market power. This is a clear and present danger.[17]

2.4   INFORMATION COMMODITIES

In this section we address the second important product of the new economy: pure information in the form of information commodities. The high fixed costs of information commodities make it far from socially optimal to produce all imaginable information commodities, even though the costs of reproduction and distribution are zero. The social benefits of an information commodity need to exceed its fixed costs to make its production desirable. As soon as an information commodity has been produced, and is therefore available, social optimality requires that each and every person who associates a positive value with the information commodity (or would potentially do so after experiencing the commodity), has it at his or her disposal.

Reality differs substantially from this social optimum. Money is made on information commodities by charging non-negligible prices for them and by restricting their distribution. This is not only so for Microsoft's

'Windows' software, but also for publishers of books and music, or for old movies, which are only available on DVD at prices that are excessive when compared to the costs of reproduction and distribution. This is so for a number of reasons, studied in some depth in this section.

2.4.1 Market Structure

The underlying structure of demand and supply for information commodities makes a competitive market structure, with many suppliers behaving like price-takers, very unlikely. The ultimately evolving market structure will display high concentration rates instead. In most cases a natural monopoly will result; or a market structure with one dominant firm and a number of small competitors; or a market structure of monopolistic competition, where a number of firms offer variations of basically the same product.

Even though there are few industries where increasing returns to scale take the extreme form of the production of information commodities, strongly increasing returns to scale are not a new phenomenon. The production of airplanes is a well-known example. Comparably strong increasing returns to scale are also present in the airline industry as long as an airplane is not filled. However, in these traditional industries capacity constraints are much more clearly present than they are in the production of information, which naturally limits the potential benefits from increasing returns to scale.

Although the long-run market structure of information commodities has monopolistic features, the way towards market equilibrium is often characterized by severe competition between producers of the same information commodity. The importance of exploiting increasing returns to scale, namely, creates a first-mover advantage when selling an information commodity in large quantities. There are strong incentives to quickly build up a large market share. This causes large investments in research and development, perhaps excessively large.[18] Moreover, the drive for market share makes substantial outlays on advertising unavoidable.

Another reason for large outlays on advertisements is the fact that information goods are pre-eminent examples of experience goods. An information commodity such as a message service or a television series, with repeated sales and consumption, enables a producer to acquire a reputation for being a high-quality supplier. For an information commodity that is sold only once, it is more difficult to build up a reputation by means of selling high quality. Problems of adverse selection are likely to occur if it is difficult for a consumer to distinguish high-quality from inferior information commodities.[19] Consumers who are not able to assess the value of an information good will infer that the information commodities offered for sale are low quality, and will decide not to buy. This may prevent mutually advantageous trade from taking place.

Sellers may use advertising to escape problems caused by asymmetric information. Suppliers of high-quality information commodities in particular may signal high quality by means of a well thought-out advertisement policy. Suppliers of information commodities with a beneficial price to quality ratio have higher profits per unit sold than suppliers that are less efficient. This increases their incentives to spend money on advertising. In addition to this, advertising outlays may serve to build up a brand name that sustains a strong reputation. This provides producers of information commodities with additional reasons to incur high expenses on advertising.[20]

The road to monopoly is paved with intense price wars that drive prices to nil, should the structure of competition evolve into a Bertrand-type. As a consequence, producers of information commodities have strong incentives to avoid price competition on homogeneous goods. Instead, they seek and protect monopoly positions. The common instruments to achieve these goals are product differentiation, the lock-in of existing customers and the protection of information commodities by means of intellectual property rights.

2.4.2   Product Differentiation

Whenever possible, producers of information commodities will try to differentiate their product from those of their competitors. It is, however, more difficult to differentiate one's product than it may appear to be. Many forms of product differentiation do not stand the test of imitation. This is even more so as the Internet makes imitation quite simple in many cases. On the other hand, the new economy offers possibilities for product differentiation that were traditionally less readily available. The information available on customers, for example, makes it possible to offer a tailor-made information commodity. Information acquisition on customers is possible by studying their past sales records, the terms they used in search engines, as well as their search behaviour on the web. Such information is of crucial importance for formulating advertising strategies, since it allows for well-focused campaigns.

2.4.3   Lock-in

Suppliers of information commodities are certain to use the opportunity of keeping customers once they are acquired by incorporating a sufficient amount of switching costs. In this respect it is helpful to such suppliers that for many information commodities lock-in arises in a natural way. Yet the amount of lock-in is a parameter that can be influenced by the supplier of an information commodity, which will play a prominent role in the strategic plan of many suppliers.

Consider the situation where a number of suppliers each offer a similar information commodity for sale. From the moment a customer has chosen a certain information commodity, it will often be difficult to make use of another supplier because of switching costs. For an information commodity like a word processor, the switching costs do not only involve the investment of the time needed to learn to use a new program. The choice of a new software package often implies the necessity to rework old files, a lack of compatibility with other software, increased difficulty in communicating with others, and so on. Moreover, the possibility to fine-tune information commodities to a specific customer leads to high relation-specific investments, and thereby to lock-in.

After a consumer has chosen a particular information commodity, the producer of that commodity obtains a monopoly position with respect to that consumer when switching costs are high. A consumer who realizes that he or she becomes a sitting duck after lock-in may decide not to buy at all. As a fortunate circumstance, this restricts the possibilities of lock in somewhat. It is also the case that a consumer who will become locked in is in the position to negotiate *ex ante* for attractive discounts. When a sufficient amount of competition is present and consumers are rational, a producer will only achieve a normal rate of return, even in the presence of lock-in, and a form of monopoly power *ex post*. The discount a producer gives initially as a 'teaser' will have to outweigh the consumer surplus appropriated by a producer later as a consequence of consumer lock-in.

Lock-in reinforces the concern of producers to strive for a large market share fast. Waiting too long to land customers has the consequence that many customers are lost forever: they are locked in with rivals. A supplier of information commodities will, on top of that, try hard to further increase switching costs, for instance by selling complementary information commodities, by using long-lasting contracts, and by giving quantity discounts. In particular a monopolist with lock-in customers may cause great harm.

2.4.4 Intellectual Property Rights

Another means producers have available to monopolize information commodities is to build up intellectual property rights (IPRs). The standard economic argument for assigning property rights is that these rights enable producers to retrieve sunk costs by means of a temporary monopoly.

Assigning property rights protects producers of information commodities against reproduction and might thereby create a stimulus to the production of information commodities.[21] This can be achieved by means of patents, copyrights and trademarks. Yet in the case of information commodities, which are so diverse that they have quite different payback periods, easily too much such market power is given. On the other hand the protection of IPRs is not watertight. It is often possible to copy information commodities illegally, even when they are subject to copyright. As long as information commodities are produced, it is perhaps an unfair practice to produce illegal copies, but also a welfare enhancing one. When illegal copying becomes too excessive, then it may cause a restraint on the development of new information commodities, or even bring the development of new information commodities to a standstill.

Nevertheless, it seems quite improbable that the development of new information commodities would come to a stop because of too much unbridled copying. The scale at which illegal copies can be made is subject to limits. Copying sometimes leads to a loss in quality, even when it concerns information commodities. Illegal versions of software for example are often obsolete and, moreover, are not accompanied by technical support. Illegal versions of books, movies and compact disks often do not have everything the original has, such as a nice accompanying booklet and perfect performance. These differences will be reduced quickly by new technological developments. On the other hand, there will be new possibilities for the industry to introduce new differences, thereby enforcing its position. For that matter, there are also indications that illegal copies have positive effects for producers, because it is helpful in getting a larger market share.[22] This implies that producers of information commodities should not be too restrictive in the protection of their intellectual property rights.

In fact, a strategy that is frequently used is to give away information free. This strategy can gain market power in the future. Another reason to achieve a large market share can be found in advertising goals. Suppliers of websites often earn their money through advertisements, or they receive a fee from the provider of the connection on the basis of the traffic they generate. Both for advertising goals and Internet traffic, it holds that more users imply more revenues. This is not without risks for social welfare. Indeed, incentives are no longer determined by the quality of the information, but by the number of people that make use of it. This implies that it pays more to create a website that is somewhat appealing to many people, rather than one that is thrilling for only a small group, whereas the latter is often socially optimal.[23]

Finally, when innovation is both sequential and complementary, there exists both theoretical and empirical evidence that intellectual property rights cause both less innovation and less welfare.[24] Sequential innovation is where each invention elaborates on the one before, and complementary innovation causes some central higher goal to be reached with higher probability. The problem of too strong intellectual property rights protection in this context is that it prevents competitors from making use of existing inventions to generate further innovation. Both sequential and complementary innovations seem to be pervasive in the new economy.

2.4.5 Price Discrimination

Whereas naive contemplation on the new economy quickly leads to the idea that the ideal of the perfectly competitive market is approached more closely, we have already indicated that the new economy offers at the same time ample opportunities to build up and maintain monopoly positions. Subsequently, a producer who has achieved a monopoly position is likely to exploit it to the full, for example using price discrimination. The Internet offers great opportunities to apply price discrimination, precisely because it is in principle open to producers to charge each buyer a different price.

Virtual markets make it possible for producers to capture a larger proportion of consumer surplus than in traditional markets, not only because of the possibility to deal with consumers individually, but also because of the possibility to collect large amounts of information about them. That information can give an indication of reservation prices. The Internet also displays a high degree of interactivity. Search behaviour that reveals certain characteristics of the consumer can immediately be matched by an electronic offer.

There is, therefore, enhanced scope for firms to apply price discrimination of the first degree, making individualized offers. Also, price discrimination of the second degree is applied by offering quantity discounts. Likewise, information commodities are typically offered in a number of forms that are each priced differently – so-called versioning. Versioning is a form of price discrimination of the second degree that is very attractive for the producers of information commodities. For many information commodities it boils down to the firm producing a superior, all-embracing version first, and thereafter it is then fairly cheap to produce a second type of information commodity by elaborating on this and creating simpler variations. Concrete examples are information services that offer for instance financial information, where the price charged for real-time information is a multiple of delayed information, or of enhanced features that are switched off.

We expect that particularly price discrimination of the second degree will be the norm in the new economy. It will occur in its traditional form of quantity discounts, but also take in the somewhat more subtle forms of bundling and versioning. The social implications of these practices are not obvious. Compared to single product monopoly output, versioning – as with second-degree price-discrimination in general – may enhance welfare by making the product available for the low-quality types without infring- ing on the high-quality consumers. In general, however, deliberately dumping-down products at additional costs does not seem to serve welfare well. And indeed it does not when compared to a competitive market. Finally, versioning is likely to be used as a marketing tool. Low costs of reproduction of information commodities, combined with versioning, may make it easier for information commodities to be experienced. Producers may offer free inferior versions of their information commodity as a sample copy to give consumers more insights into its value. As far as this sup- presses the outlays on advertising, it is a positive effect of versioning.

2.5   INFORMATION INFRASTRUCTURE

A third important category for consideration in the new economy is the infrastructure on which information travels. It consists of everything that makes it possible to store, search, copy, filter, manipulate, see, send and receive information. We have already argued that the information infra- structure reinforces the importance of certain less traditional properties of information, and thereby creates part of the specific possibilities and prob- lems of the new economy. The information infrastructure itself, however, also introduces a number of interesting economic aspects.

Where we expect commodity information to cause mainly transparency increasing and transaction costs decreasing effects and thereby ample opportunities for a sunny future, yet foresee scattered showers for informa- tion commodities as a consequence of the dangers of monopolistic market structures, aspects of information infrastructure are likely to give occasion for stormy weather. The reason for this is that specific characteristics of the information infrastructure can easily give rise to a problematic market structure. In this section we look closer into two of these characteristics: network externalities and standardization.

2.5.1   Networks

The information infrastructure of information commodities has positive network externalities.[25] Network externalities are not just a novelty of the new economy, they are also present in traditional sectors of the economy, for instance in railway networks and pipelines for oil or gas. What might be different in the new economy is their abundance, in the form of both physical and virtual networks.

Network externalities exist when the value of a product for one user depends on the number of other users; examples are telephone, e-mail, Internet, fax and modems. The original idea behind network externalities is simple. In a network with n users, there are $n-1$ possible links for each user. The total number of links is then equal to $n^2 - n$. As a result, the value of a network increases quadratically in the number of users. This principle, known as Metcalfe's law, relies on the rather simplistic assumption that each link in a network has equal value as a starting point. A somewhat more economic approach tells us that the first links in a network have the highest marginal revenue, whereas later users show by self-selection they are of lesser value. Nevertheless, it remains true that large connected networks are preferred by everyone over many isolated smaller ones.

In an industry with positive network effects it is often of great importance to have the largest market share. Positive network effects are self-enforcing as the network grows, which makes growing ever more easy. It is only after crossing a certain threshold market share that there is sufficient momentum to generate an explosive growth of the market. This phenomenon is one rationale behind many observations of new economy firms that make losses over prolonged periods. They follow a strategy of building up a large customer base as fast as possible by offering free services, and revenue requirements are postponed to some distant future.

Positive network externalities are accelerated because consumers have an incentive to eventually be part of the largest network. It is therefore of the greatest importance to producers to convince consumers, who have to pay costs and therefore have to make a choice, that their network will be the largest one and that its technology will become the standard. As a result, the announcement of a new product, possibly long before it actually becomes available, may be as important as the introduction itself, since it may make consumers decide not to pass over to the purchase of a competitive product.

The problem of lock-in returns with even greater intensity for information infrastructure aspects. As soon as a consumer has chosen to use a certain technological standard, it will often be very difficult for him or her to pass on to another technology, because of switching costs. Switching from one generation of computers to the next one causes for instance software problems and a need for renewed training of employees. On top of this, there typically are investments in several, complementary and durable capital goods in the case of information infrastructure that are specifically appropriate to a certain kind of information technology, which reinforces the lock-in.

An additional problem for the case of networks is that there is not only individual lock-in, but also collective lock-in. It is not sufficient for a consumer to overcome his or her own switching costs. Consumers have to be convinced that others will do the same. This implies that the disciplining force of potential entrants deteriorates. It is no longer sufficient for entrants to persuade customers on an individual basis. Consumers should be convinced that other consumers will pass on to a new technology as well, which makes entry difficult.

Another consequence of network externalities is that existing technologies, as a consequence of individual and collective lock-ins, are used far past their socially optimal date. The general trade-off for producers is either to develop a completely new technology, or a technology that is compatible with the existing technology. The former is only possible if it concerns a revolutionary improvement over existing technology, which is hardly ever the case. A continuation of extending on old base technology, however, is typically inferior to a quick conversion to a new standard, and often delays technological innovation.

There are common interdependencies between information commodities and information infrastructure. To introduce new technologies, it is often necessary for firms to focus their attention not only on their competitors, but also on firms with whom they may want to collaborate. A prominent example of successful collaboration is the one between Microsoft and Intel. From a competition policy point of view, however, these collaborations may cause the formation of formidable centres of power in the twilight zone between collaboration and abuse of power. The risk of monopolization is, therefore, serious in the presence of positive network externalities. An exception to this might be the case where consumers have such a large desire for variety that several networks may co-exist.

2.5.2 Standards

Information infrastructure uses protocols that rely on standards of communication and inter-compatibility. One can distinguish open and closed standards. The former concern technology that is accessible for all producers, whereas the latter involve technology that is protected by means of intellectual property rights. A closed technology is seemingly more attractive to a producer. An advantage of open technology, however, is that it makes it far easier to build up a large market share fast, and to profit from the advantages that go with that. Moreover, very often producers will have to collaborate, offering complementary products to one another, which is easier in the case of an open technology. The relationship between Microsoft's operating system and application software also shows that an intermediate form may be stable.

An important way to fight the formation of monopolies is by realizing open standards. As soon as a certain technology has the largest network by far, it is possible to promote competition by making this technology an open standard. Standards make switching costs decrease considerably. They enhance the formation of one large network, which is important when there are positive network externalities. An open standard trades competition between networks for competition on a network. Standards can differ immensely with respect to the amount of detail. The more detailed the standard, the less possibilities producers have to differentiate their products.

Governments can play an important role in the creation of standards by establishing independent institutes that set them and keep them pure. Also, governments can set standards 'by example', bearing the initial switching costs by moving to an open standard first.[26] In some cases such an independent institute should have the possibility to impose compensation payments. Conflicts about standards might arise when several companies have an interest in putting forward their own technology as the standard. A role might be played here by auction mechanisms. These could be designed in such a way that the most efficient standard will be realized. A matter of concern, however, is to maintain the independence of such an institute, and to keep social welfare its objective.

We have already observed that as long as it is unclear to consumers whether a certain technology will make it, they will be very reluctant to purchase its compatible products. It is important for producers, therefore, to convince consumers that their technology will break through and dominate. A standard might be helpful to overcome such problems. This provides additional reasons why a standard is not only in the interest of consumers, but often also in the interest of producers. As a result, strong government oversight may not always be necessary to establish a universal standard. It is not inconceivable that the market itself will create institutions that determine standards, for instance in the form of strategic alliances between producers. From a competition policy point of view, such a development is not without danger – an alliance might effectively eliminate competition if it centralizes intellectual property rights and opens standards up only for firms within the alliance.

As soon as a monopoly has emerged, authorities have a number of options. European legislation offers more possibilities here than American legislation does. Government may abstain from intervention, thereby using the argument that it is efficient to have only one supplier in a natural monopoly. This may also be an interesting option when there is a sufficient amount of potential entry. Governments may furthermore improve the conditions under which more entry is possible, for instance by introducing an open standard and pursuing a restrictive policy regarding the protection of intellectual property rights. Current legislation for the protection of intellectual property rights seems far too rigid in this respect. The option of flexibility when it concerns length and scope of intellectual property rights on specific commodities and standards may be most useful to permanently maintain the appropriate balance between sufficient competition and sufficient incentives to innovate.

In the short run, property rights will be less important anyhow, because of the fast pace of technological progress that makes the vast majority of monopoly positions temporary ones only. In the mid-term, under the scenario where rapid technological progress has come into quieter waters, a large number of markets with strong network externalities and huge switching costs may threaten to stabilize into single dominant firms. In such a situation, extensive intellectual property rights protection is undesirable.

Government intervention can break the power of a monopoly in such cases – as in the Microsoft antitrust trials. This is particularly attractive if it is possible to organize competition on a network. In other cases, governments may regulate a dominant firm controlling a network, for instance by installing an independent regulator. An interesting discussion here concerns the scope of the industry to be regulated, because there is simultaneously convergence between industries and globalization of their activities.[27] Sectors that traditionally have been separated from one another, such as the telecommunication, media, and information technology sectors, all produce information commodities and make use of a common information infrastructure.[28] Some of these sectors are not regulated at all. Others, like the telecommunication sector, have to deal with strict supervision. Borders between countries, traditionally greatly influencing trade flows, are hardly important for a medium like the Internet. It is therefore highly debatable whether local regulation of the Internet is meaningful. Instead, global oversight for the information and communication technology sector seems called for. There are, however, also advantages in having several regulators. The case of several regulators makes yardstick competition possible; industry-specific regulators have more specific technological knowledge available and it is often easier to give the right incentives to regulators when they confine themselves to a single industry. These arguments need to be weighed to strike an appropriate balance.

2.6   CONCLUSIONS

There seems to be a sufficient number of similarities between the conditions under which the existing micro-economic theory provides its useful insights, and the fundamental properties of the reality of the new economy. As a consequence, there is no need for a 'new economy' in a theoretical sense.

We distinguish between commodity information and information commodities, where commodity information refers to information about commodities, which is available in the new economy at lower costs and in greater supply than before. This concerns information that facilitates decision-making. Information commodities, on the other hand, are commodities that consist of information. They have an intrinsic value, where commodity information has a derived value. Finally, we consider the flow of both types of information on information infrastructure.

There is reason for moderate optimism with regard to the opportunities offered by the new economy in the area of commodity information. An easy and extensive exchange of commodity information enhances individual decisions, and leads to more transparent and therefore more competitive markets. It is important, however, not to lose sight of the problems for the nature of competitive processes caused by the new economy. Collecting information is costly, which leads to the threat of an inefficient amount of absorption. Information intermediaries will try to find their niches in the selection of information. Firms and credit card companies may profit from problems with trust and deliveries, and even have an incentive to purposely increase these problems. There furthermore is the possibility that firms will attempt to work against greater transparency by applying or strengthening product and price discrimination.

There seem, therefore, ample reasons for being alert regarding developments in the domain of information commodities. Their properties, in particular the presence of large fixed production and distribution costs, and very low marginal costs, may give rise to the emergence of dominant suppliers. Suppliers also have various means to promote such a market structure, for instance far-reaching forms of product differentiation, lock-in of consumers, and the gathering of intellectual property rights. Although increased opportunities to learn about the preferences of consumers may cause great welfare improvements, those same opportunities lead to an appropriation of a substantial share of consumer surplus.

Monopolistic market structures seem inevitable where it concerns information infrastructure. This is mainly because of strong network externalities, both at the individual and the collective level. It is also possible that firms further exploit a dominant position by striving for closed standards that deter new entry effectively, for example by means of the acquired exclusive property rights. The Microsoft case is only the first spectacular instance where the abuse of monopoly power in the information infrastructure has caused the authorities to intervene. There are already several firms in similar positions, and others trying hard to achieve them too. Many more cases are likely to follow.

In general, governments need to watch the new developments closely in order to pre-empt the problems mentioned. The boom of companies that invested in Internet offspring indicates that one may expect niches with a certain amount of protection. One of the courses of action that governments could take is to open up the opportunities for entry of firms and institutions. They can do so by means of direct competition policy, and intervention when companies play too large a role in setting up entry barriers. A good example of an intervention that was too late in this respect concerns the practice of claiming idiosyncratic Internet addresses that were subsequently offered for sale at very high prices. This is a typical form of inefficient speculation. In particular the market for information infrastructure needs to be watched closely by competition authorities. It has a strong inclination to create market structures that are socially particularly undesirable, both from a static point of view, since they restrict the distribution of commodity information and information commodities, and from a dynamic point of view, since they hinder the development of new technological standards.

Even more important perhaps is the role governments need to play as providers of standards and transparency. Though the demand for such services may also provoke privately based responses – such as a virtual consumers' association or specific search engines – the role of the intermediary remains potentially one that has tendencies to disturb competition. Neutrality of government in these matters promotes reliability and transparency. Full exploitation of the potential world-wide-welfare that is offered by the world-wide-web calls for solid, government controlled monitoring of the open network society and its enemies.

NOTES

1. See Hirshleifer and Riley (1995).
2. This coincides with the characterization of commodities by Debreu (1959).
3. See Chapter 7 of Knight (1921) for an interesting discussion of the relationship between risk and uncertainty.
4. See Blackwell and Dubins (1962).
5. For information as a public good see Hirshleifer and Riley (1995), Chapter 6.
6. This is only true if the information does not lead to a reduction in the number of available choices, which can certainly be the case, for example in the purchase of insurance – the so-called Hirshleifer-effect, see Hirshleifer (1971). It is also well-known that when strategic effects are present, less information can lead to more favourable outcomes.
7. Bayesian learning is, as described in the following, widely seen as rational learning. Of importance for its effects is the structural specification of the relations that are to be learned. See on this subject Schinkel et al. (2002).

8. See Radner (1979).
9. See Arrow (1953).
10. An analysis of the conditions under which convergence of a number of price adjustment processes takes place on a perfectly competitive equilibrium can be found in Hens (1997) and Herings (1999).
11. Wilson (1977) and Milgrom (1979) analyse the decreasing auction and Milgrom (1981) the increasing auction.
12. It can also be the case that groups with conflicting objectives collect too little information, and even ignore free information in order to avoid real conflicts, see Hirshleifer and Riley (1995) and Jones and Ostroy (1984).
13. This is the so-called Hirshleifer effect.
14. See Binmore (1994).
15. The developments in virtual banking are of important concern for monetary policy. An increase in this is comparable to the creation of money taking place outside the realm of central banks.
16. See Baye and Morgan (2001) for a formal model of this phenomenon.
17. For further critiques of the idea that the Internet leads to markets with perfect competition, see Dolfsma (1998).
18. For further insights into optimal investment in research and development, refer to Scherer and Ross (1990), in particular Chapter 17.
19. Akerlof (1970) was the first to point out this kind of problem in his ground-breaking work.
20. See Nelson (1974) and Milgrom and Roberts (1986). For an exposition on excess advertisement in Nash equilibrium, see Schmalensee (1986).
21. The United States Congress is obliged by the constitution to promote the progress of science and useful arts by granting exclusive rights to authors and inventors for their writings and inventions during a limited time span.
22. A good example is the commotion around Napster, against which prominent artists like the rock band Metallica protested. We refer to Shapiro and Varian (1999) for a defence of the stance that illegal copies can be beneficial for sales.
23. For a similar example concerning television broadcasts, see DeLong and Froomkin (2000).
24. See Bessen and Maskin (2000).
25. See Katz and Shapiro (1994) for an overview of the area of network externalities.
26. See Varian and Shapiro (2003).
27. See Chapter 7 of Laffont and Tirole (2000).
28. For the specific problems that the convergence of industries poses for regulation, see de Fontenay (1999).

BIBLIOGRAPHY

Akerlof, G. (1970), 'The market for lemons: Quality uncertainty and the market mechanism', *Quarterly Journal of Economics*, **89**, 488–500.

Arrow, K. (1953), 'Le role des valeurs boursières pour la répartition la meilleure des risques econométrie', *Colloques Internationaux du Centre National de la Recherche Scientifique*, **40**, 41–7.

Arrow, K. (1962), 'Economic welfare and the allocation of resources for invention', in R. Nelson (ed.), *The Rate and Direction of Inventive Activity*, New York: National Bureau of Economic Research, pp. 609–26.

Arrow, K. (1978), 'Risk allocation and information: Some recent theoretical developments', *The Geneva Papers on Risk and Insurance*, **8**, 5–19.

Aumann, R.J. (1976), 'Agreeing to disagree', *Annals of Statistics*, **4**, 1236–9.

Baye, M.R. and J. Morgan (2001), 'Information gatekeepers on the Internet and the competitiveness of homogeneous product markets', *American Economic Review*, **91**, 454–74.

Belleflamme, P. (1998), 'Adoption of network technologies in oligopolies', *International Journal of Industrial Organization*, **16**, 415–44.

Bessen, J. and E. Maskin (2000), 'Sequential innovation, patents, and imitation', MIT Working Paper 00–01.

Binmore, K. (1994), *Game Theory and the Social Contract*, Vol. I, Cambridge, MA: MIT Press.

Binmore, K. (1998), *Game Theory and the Social Contract*, Vol. II, Cambridge, MA: MIT Press.

Blackwell, D. (1953), 'Equivalent comparison of experiments', *Annals of Mathematics and Statistics*, **24**, 265–72.

Blackwell, F. and L. Dubins (1962), 'Merging of opinions with increasing information', *Annals of Mathematical Statistics*, **38**, 882–6.

Coase, R. (1972), 'Durability and monopoly', *Journal of Law and Economics*, **15**, 143–9.

Debreu, G. (1959), *Theory of Value*, New Haven, CT: Yale University Press.

DeLong, J.B. and A.M. Froomkin (2000), 'Speculative microeconomics for tomorrow's economy', *First Monday*, **5**, 2.

Dixit, A.K. and J.E. Stiglitz (1977), 'Monopolistic competition and optimum product diversity', *American Economic Review*, **67**, 297–308.

Dolfsma, W. (1998). 'Internet: An economist's utopia?', *Review of International Political Economy*, **5**, 712–20.

Dolfsma, W. (2000), 'How will the music industry weather the globalization storm?', *First Monday*, **5**, 5.

Economides, N. (1996), 'Network externalities, complementarities, and invitations to enter', *European Journal of Political Economy*, **12**, 211–33.

de Fontenay, E. (1999), 'Should the Internet care about regulation: Regulation and convergence', *Netnomics*, **1**, 173–85.

Hens, T. (1997), 'Stability of tâtonnement processes of short period equilibria with rational expectations', *Journal of Mathematical Economics*, **28**, 41–67.

Herings, P.J.J. (1999), 'A note on tâtonnement processes of short period equilibria with rational expectations', *Journal of Mathematical Economics*, **32**, 333–8.

Hirshleifer, J. (1971), 'The private and social value of information and the reward to inventive activity', *American Economic Review*, **61**, 561–74.

Hirshleifer, J. and J.G. Riley (1995), *The Analytics of Uncertainty and Information*, Cambridge: Cambridge University Press.

Jones, R.A. and J.M. Ostroy (1984), 'Flexibility and uncertainty', *Review of Economic Studies*, **51**, 13–32.

Katz, M. and K. Shapiro (1994), 'System competition and network effects', *Journal of Economic Perspectives*, **8**, 93–115.

Klemperer, P.D. (2000), 'Why every economist should learn some auction theory', CEPR Discussion Papers 2572.

Knight, F. (1921), *Risk, Uncertainty, and Profit*, Cambridge: The Riverside Press.

Laffont, J.J. and J. Tirole (2000), *Competition in Telecommunications*, Cambridge, MA: MIT Press.

Menkhoff, R. (1999), 'Java and object standardization in the Internet – a way to more competition in the software industry?', *Netnomics*, **1**, 107–26.

Milgrom, P.R. (1979), 'A convergence theorem for competitive bidding with differential information', *Econometrica*, **47**, 679–88.

Milgrom, P.R. (1981), 'Rational expectations, information acquisition, and competitive bidding with differential information', *Econometrica*, **49**, 921–43.

Milgrom, P. and J. Roberts (1986), 'Price and advertising as signals of product quality', *Journal of Political Economy*, **94**, 796–821.

Muth, J.F. (1961), 'Rational expectations and the theory of price movements', *Econometrica*, **29**, 315–53.

Nelson, P. (1974), 'Advertising as information', *Journal of Political Economy*, **82**, 729–54.

Radner, R. (1968), 'Competitive equilibrium under uncertainty', *Econometrica*, **36**, 31–58.

Radner, R. (1979), 'Rational expectations equilibrium: Generic existence and the information revealed by prices', *Econometrica*, **47**, 655–78.

Scherer, F.M. and D. Ross (1990), *Industrial Market Structure and Economic Performance*, Boston, MA: Houghton Mifflin.

Schinkel, M.P., J. Tuinstra and D. Vermeulen (2002), 'Convergence of Bayesian learning to general equilibrium in mis-specified models', *Journal of Mathematical Economics*, **38**, 483–508.

Schmalensee, R. (1986), 'Advertising and market structure', in J.E. Stiglitz and G.F. Mathewson (eds), *New Developments in the Analysis of Market Structure*, Cambridge, MA: MIT Press, pp. 373–96.

Shapiro, C. and H.R. Varian (1999), *Information Rules: A Strategic Guide to the Network Economy*, Boston, MA: Harvard Business School Press.

Stigler, G.J. and G.S. Becker (1977), 'De gustibus non est disputandum', *American Economic Review*, **67**, 76–90.

Varian, H.R. and C. Shapiro (2003), 'Linux adoption in the public sector: An economic approach', University of California at Berkeley Working Paper.

Vulkan, N. (1999), 'Economic implications of agent technology and e-commerce', *Economic Journal*, **109**, 67–90.

Whinston, A.B., D.O. Stahl and S.Y. Choi (1997), *The Economics of Electronic Commerce*, Indianopolis: Macmillan.

Wilson, R. (1977), A bidding model of perfect competition', *Review of Economic Studies*, **44**, 511–18.

3. Network formation, innovation and IT use*

Robin Cowan and Nicolas Jonard

3.1 INTRODUCTION

This chapter presents a very stylized model of innovation to examine one feature of the information technology revolution. Innovation can be seen as the production of knowledge. It has many different types of inputs, but for our purposes we focus on one of the most important inputs, namely existing knowledge. When a firm innovates, it uses both private knowledge and public knowledge. One of the important features of the IT revolution, particularly as represented by the growth of the worldwide web, is that the fund of public knowledge is bigger, and more easily accessible. It is this feature that we explore here.

Since as early as Schumpeter, economists have acknowledged that innovation consists largely of the recombination of existing knowledge. Recently, however, changes in the knowledge environment of firms have made this recombination more difficult for individual firms: we refer to 'the expanding knowledge base' of firms and industries.[1] The general idea is that in most industries today the technologies both being used and being produced involve technological expertise that covers a much broader range of 'disciplines' than has hitherto been the case (see Weitzman, 1998; Olsson, 2000; Smith, 2000). What this implies is that types of knowledge necessary to innovate and compete successfully can lie outside a firm's main area of expertize. A common way now of coping with this problem is to form an alliance with a firm that has the missing expertize. Inter-firm cooperation can be extremely effective in increasing the circulation of tacit knowledge, and in creating possibilities for a firm to acquire knowledge outside its boundaries, and these cooperative agreements for R&D have grown dramatically in number since 1976.[2]

Firms not only use other firms as sources of knowledge when innovating, they also access the available public knowledge. This is one of the motivat-

* We thank an anonymous referee and the editors of this volume for helpful comments on an earlier draft of this chapter.

ing ideas in new growth theory (Lucas, 1988; Romer, 1986, 1990; for a survey see Jones, 2005), and indeed is one of the sources of external economies discussed by Marshall (1890). The general idea is that a firm's performance is influenced positively by the general knowledge level available to it. In endogenous growth a large pool of public knowledge is sometimes seen representing a source of skilled labour, whereas in Marshall's vision it is actually knowledge 'in the air' that a firm can tap. Practically, this knowledge comes in many forms: the human capital created through formal education; knowledge or information published in scientific or engineering journals or books; public data; presentations at conferences or seminars; patent documents and so on. The more modern statement is that this effect arises from the non-rivalrous nature of knowledge. My using a piece of knowledge does not prevent anyone else from using it, so to the extent that knowledge is public, it can be used by any innovator. For many years, economists modelled knowledge as if all agents had equivalent (free and easy) access to this public knowledge (see Arrow, 1962, or Nelson 1959 for example). This has never been the case for two reasons: first, tacit knowledge is always necessary to access any codified knowledge, and not all agents have the appropriate tacit knowledge at their fingertips. Second, knowledge, even when codified, has a physical location, implying that it is more readily available to some agents than to others. Some have argued that new information technologies have made some inroads into the first issue, perhaps increasing our ability to codify knowledge and thereby reducing the importance of tacit knowledge in some cases, and decreasing the costs of codifying knowledge in others (Cowan and Foray, 1997). But what is even clearer is that the worldwide web mitigates the problems arising from physical distance. The new information technologies have moved the world towards the old idea of knowledge, at least for some parts of the knowledge stock. To the extent that knowledge or information is placed on the web, it really is available to anyone anywhere, at almost zero cost. This is where IT enters in our model. The fall in costs, and increase in performance of information and communication technologies has facilitated codification of knowledge, and has made it easier to store, retrieve and manipulate knowledge once it has been codified. In particular, the ease of accessing codified knowledge means that that knowledge which is made public is of more (net) value to potential users. Thus in a simple model where the two inputs are public and private knowledge, if the body of public knowledge becomes more productive (since it is easier to access and use) it will be more heavily used in producing innovation. Thus in this model the role of IT is to reduce the cost of creating public knowledge and to reduce the costs of using it.

To model strategic technological alliances in their entirety is far beyond the scope of this chapter, and in particular we make no attempt to include any issues of intellectual property rights in our discussion. We are interested, rather, in the nature of the networks of innovators that emerge from a process in which firms engage in bilateral cooperation to produce knowledge. Technological alliances can be very rich and varied, not only in terms of outputs but also in inputs and objectives of the participants, but for our purposes we can focus on a single effect, namely the production of shared knowledge; and consider only two inputs, namely the pre-existing knowledge held by the participants, and publicly available knowledge.

3.2 THE MODEL

The model is in two parts: innovation takes place as a result of the joint effort of pairs of agents, while in parallel a process of network formation and evolution is at work. Regarding innovation, when collaborative R&D is performed by two individuals their knowledge endowments are combined to produce new knowledge, while at the same time they benefit from the 'state of the art' knowledge available within the industry. New knowledge thus created is added to the existing individual endowments. The knowledge production function determines how much new knowledge is generated as a function of the variety of the partners' contributions, that is, how different they are, and the 'innovativeness' of the industry as a whole, which we proxy using the average knowledge level. How pairs form is the second important issue in the model. Agents rank each other on the basis of their expected potential output. As a result rankings change over time because innovation changes individual knowledge profiles. A stable matching always exists (this is shown below) so in each period this stable assignment determines which pairs of agents combine their knowledge. We have assumed here that agents are pursuing knowledge for its own sake, which is unrealistic in general for firms, who pursue knowledge more generally for the sake of profits. To incorporate that explicitly in the model adds significant complication, demanding a fully blown goods market with production and consumption. We avoid that by this simplifying assumption, which, in an industry involved in rapid technical change, will be behaviourally quite adequate. A number of issues are of interest in this model, falling within two broad categories: the process of network formation and evolution; and the properties of knowledge growth. Before examining them, we discuss both matching and knowledge production in detail.

Consider a set $S = \{1,...,n\}$ of individuals engaged in repeated interactions. Each individual $i \in S$ is characterized by a real-valued knowledge endowment in the form of a quantity of knowledge $r_i > 0$ and a composite index s_i representing a type of knowledge between 0 and $\pi/2$. This allows a very simple polar representation of individuals as points in a continuum of knowledge types. At each period, each agent seeks a partner with whom to innovate and increase, as much as possible, his or her current knowledge endowment. The sort of partnerships we have in mind are collaborative agreements such as joint ventures or joint R&D contracts. Hence there is a market for alliances, and the equilibrium behaviour of this market will be studied. An equilibrium on this market will be defined as a situation in which the alliances are all such that there are no two individuals who would rather form a partnership other than with their partner at equilibrium. That is, there are no blocking pairs. Once knowledge has been created and absorbed, which implies in particular that agents' types are modified, a new round of matching begins, yielding a possibly different equilibrium of the market for alliances, based on agents' new knowledge characteristics. It is worth mentioning the resemblance between this market for alliances and the market for marriages in Becker (1962). There as well pairs form in order to jointly produce utility via a household production function that transforms market goods and services into commodities that are not supplied by the market, and from the consumption of which the couple derives utility (love, child care, etc.). In Becker, however, the issue of sharing the benefits from pairing arises naturally, whereas here non-rivalry makes it simpler to find a solution to the problem of constructing a stable assignment.

Innovation as we see it here is a process that combines the knowledge of two partners and produces new knowledge. In this process, diversity of knowledge inputs is central. To focus on one issue we make it so important, in fact, that in terms of agents' contributions, only the degree to which their types differ matters. Indeed two agents whose expertise lies in exactly the same field will in general find only very few synergies, and we make the extreme assumption that they do not find any. Diversity is essential to the innovative process, and positively affects knowledge production. The extent to which diversity matters is the central parameter of the model, and how the system as a whole responds to changes in it is the central question addressed here.

3.2.1 The Roommates Matching Problem

Because we consider a single population of firms rather than two populations (of men and women) our matching is a roommate, rather than a marriage, matching problem. A one-sided, roommate matching problem is defined as follows (see Gale and Shapley, 1962). Each individual $i \in S$ has a strict preference ordering $\angle_i$ over all the individuals in $S - \{i\}$ (a list of the most preferred first). All preferences are complete and transitive, and $\angle$ denotes the profile of the preference orderings of the individuals.

Definition 1: The pair $(S, \angle)$ is called a roommates matching problem.

A matching is a partition of S into $n/2$ disjoint pairs of roommates, that is to say a bijection $\mu{:}S{\rightarrow}S$ such that $\mu(\mu(i)) = i$ for all $i \in S$ and $\mu(i) \in S - \{i\}$ for all $i \in S$.

Definition 2: A matching μ is stable in $(S, \angle)$ if there is no $(i, j) \in S^2$ such that both $\mu(i) \angle_i j$ and $\mu(j) \angle_j i$.

When the condition of definition 2 fails, i and j form a blocking pair: they would both leave their partners to match with each other, and therefore μ cannot be an equilibrium.

In the particular problem examined here, the preference profile $\angle$ is generated by a symmetric function $f: S^2{\rightarrow}R_+$, which associates to any pair of (distinct) individuals (i, j) a value that represents the innovative output of this pair. The profile of preference orderings $\angle$ is then defined by the following rule.

Definition 3: For any $I \in S, j \angle_i k$ if and only if $r(i, k) > r(i, j)$ for all (j, k) in S^2 with $i \neq j \neq k$.

Disregarding cases of indifference (when there are i, j and k such that $r(i, j) = r(i, k)$), it will be shown that a unique stable matching always exists.

3.2.2 Knowledge Production: The Innovation Function

There are many ways to characterize knowledge, none of which is without its pitfalls. For our purposes two aspects of knowledge are important: quantity and type. Recent views of innovation as recombination make it imperative that any formal characterization of knowledge permits that equally knowledgeable agents may know different things. That is, the knowledge of an agent comprises many different types of knowledge. One approach then would be to formalize knowledge as a set of elements, each element representing a different type of knowledge. Agents differ then along many dimensions. This proves cumbersome in implementation however, and is more detailed than necessary for the issues we are exploring here. A simplification of this approach is to represent an agent's knowledge as a pair: one element signifying a quantity of knowledge; the other signifying a type. This representation has the drawback that it takes what is clearly a complex thing, an agent's knowledge characteristics, and reduces it to a pair. But it has the great benefit of simplicity and does capture some important elements of the nature of knowledge, as is discussed below.

A representation of the innovation process should satisfy several minimal requirements. Consider two individuals i and j who conduct innovation jointly. After innovation has taken place, one would expect the following to be true: the knowledge amounts held by i and j have increased; the knowledge types of i and j have changed; the distance between the knowledge types of i and j has fallen.

Operationally, each pair of agents creates an amount of new knowledge determined by the production function, and this amount is simply added to their existing knowledge endowments. The knowledge type of individual i is modified by joint innovation conducted with $\mu(i)$, and changes in the direction of the type held by $\mu(i)$.

Formally, the innovation function is

$$f: S^2 \to R_+ \text{ with } f(i,j) = r^{1-b}|s_i - s_j|^b,$$

with r the arithmetic mean of the knowledge endowments of the firms within the industry, $r = \Sigma r_i/n$.[3] Parameter b measures the importance of diversity in knowledge types in the innovative process. The presence of r reflects the knowledge externality agents benefit from, as a result of inexpensive information technologies making easily accessible an industrywide body of knowledge. It is raised to the power $1 - b$, as b is intended to measure the relative importance of bilateral agreements versus public sources in the knowledge production function. This innovation function is very similar to that in Smulders and van de Klundert (1995) though they use a single firm's knowledge level as the second argument, whereas we use the knowledge complementarity of a pair of firms. In this production function, differences in knowledge types contribute positively to knowledge output. This is contrasted with Peretto and Smulders (2002) for example, in which the ability of a firm to draw on external knowledge (in their case public external knowledge) decreases with the technological distance in knowledge stocks. They explicitly model the economy as a whole, including the introduction of new knowledge types. Our model pertains only to a single industry, which implicitly suggests the assumption that agents are 'relatively' close together in knowledge type. Close enough, at least, that distance between them is a good thing.[4]

Note that f is symmetric in its arguments, a feature which will be essential in proving existence and uniqueness of equilibrium. After innovation, agent i's new knowledge endowment is simply

$$r_i(t+1) = r_i(t) + r(i, \mu(i)),$$

while i's new knowledge type is a linear adjustment to his or her match $\mu(i)$ and the common available knowledge pool. Formally it is written as

$$s_i(t+1) = s_i(t) + b(s_j - s_i) + (1-b)(s-s_i),$$

where the first term in the equation reflects assumption 3, while the second gives the adjustment towards the type of knowledge available from the Internet.[5] As before s is a population mean, here weighted by the relative importance of individuals in the total sum of knowledge, that is, dropping the time argument, $s = \Sigma s_i r_i/(nr)$.

The general intuition is that as an agent uses knowledge or is exposed to it, he or she will assimilate at least part of it, and thereby change the precise area of his or her expertize. The feedback is clear between individuals and the pool: individuals can converge to the pool quickly while the pool, being an average, tends to change only incrementally.

Here we see the two effects of rendering knowledge easily accessible via information technologies: there is a global externality that affects the magnitude of innovative activities and which everyone benefits from; at the same time agents' expertize converge to a common denominator, which could harm long-run growth rates. Depending on the value of b, which can be interpreted as the inverse of the cost of IT, public knowledge is more or less used (and useful) in the innovation process. As it becomes more used, agents' expertize converge towards the mean more rapidly than they converge towards their partners' expertize. This is the effect that drives the results below.

3.3 THE MARKET FOR ALLIANCES: EXISTENCE AND UNIQUENESS

Before turning to the emergence of network structure and the associated knowledge dynamics, we discuss further in detail the market clearing mechanism present in this model. Because any pair of agents assigns the same cardinal value to their match, a unique stable matching always exists, that is, the market for equilibrium always possesses a unique equilibrium. We can prove this by construction, as shown in the following proposition.

Proposition 1: A roommates matching problem $(S, \angle)$ for which the preference ordering of any $i \in S$ is derived from $f:S^2 \rightarrow R_+$, with $f(i,j) = f(j,i)$, admits a unique stable matching.

Proof: The algorithm to construct the stable matching is as follows. Let $S_0 = S$ and $\mu_0 = \{\emptyset\}$. There exists $(a_1,b_1) \in S^2$ such that $f(a_1,b_1) = \max_{(i,j) \in S^2, i \neq j} f(i,j)$. Furthermore as f is an injection, (a_1,b_1) is unique.

Then (a_1,b_1) must belong to any stable assignment, as b_1 is preferred to any other partner by a_1 and reciprocally. No matching that does not involve this pair could be stable. Let then $\mu_1 = \mu_0 + (a_1,b_1)$ and $S_1 = S_0 - \{a_1,b_1\}$. It only involves $n - 2$ individuals with exactly the same preferences as before this operation modulo a_1 and b_1 which have been removed. Again there is a single pair maximizing the innovation function. More generally, define the recursive sequence $\mu_p = \mu_{p-1} + (a_p,b_p)$ and $S_p = S_{p-1} - \{a_p,b_p\}$ where (a_p,b_p) is the unique solution to $\max_{(i,j)\in[S^2_{p-1}]\neq j} f(i,j)$. For $p = n/2$ the unique stable matching $\mu_{n/2}$ of the roommates matching problem is obtained.

Ties do not occur because we work with real numbers. However in case of a tie (that is to say when individual i can achieve the same innovative output with two or more different partners), we resort to an arbitrary rule to guarantee that the score function is still a strict one: we choose the pair involving the individual with the smallest index, and if this is not enough, the second smallest index individual.

3.4   NUMERICAL EXPERIMENT

We study a population of $n = 100$ firms. At the outset individual knowledge types are randomly drawn from a uniform distribution over $[0, \pi/2]$, while all individuals are initially assigned the level $r_i = 1$. Each period, the market for collaborative agreements is activated and firms form pairs in order to innovate. The pairing results in a stable matching, where stability is defined as above (everybody is as satisfied as possible, given everyone else's preferences), and where the value of a pair to a firm is equal to the amount of knowledge produced by that pair. The size of the innovation is determined by the level of public knowledge, and the extent to which the two firms' knowledge types are complementary, as in the above equation. After innovation, the new knowledge is added to the firms' knowledge stocks; the firms' knowledge types change, as described previously; and the public knowledge stock increases by the average innovation size. At the end of the period all pairs disband, and the process begins again in the following period. We iterate this process for 1000 periods, recording data for the whole history of the industry. To measure the effects of the falling cost of IT, we vary the parameter b. That is, for 100 different values of $0 < b < 1$ we do the experiment just described.

A relational network exists in this economy, but in a dynamic rather than a static sense. In any period the static network consists of $n/2$ disconnected pairs. To study the properties of the dynamic network, the list of connections active over time is recorded. This generates a weighted graph, in which the weight of an edge indicates how frequently the two firms have interacted in the history.

Let $G(S,V_t)$ be the graph associated with the stable matching achieved at time $t = 0,1,2, \ldots$, that is $V_t(i,j) = 1$ if $(i,j) \in G_t$ and $V_t(i,j) = 0$ otherwise. The weighted graph recording past interactions is denoted $G(S,W)$, where $W(i,j) = W(j,i)$ is the frequency of activation of the connection between i and j over the history of the industry. For this graph several quantities are of interest. We would like to study the frequency distribution of collaborations and, following Watts and Strogatz (1998), two structural parameters: the average path length and the average cliquishness.[6] However, operating directly on W leads to interpretation problems: weighted graph analogues to cliquishness and path length exist but do not have well-defined bounds, hence are difficult to use and difficult to compare from one graph structure to the next when density varies. To circumvent this problem we translate the weighted graph into an unweighted graph by defining distances between two nodes in the following way.

There are potentially many paths between i and j. Suppose there are Q paths, $p_1 \ldots p_q \ldots p_Q$ between i and j, where $p_q = (i_1, i_2, i_3 \ldots i_l)$, where $i_l = j$. With each path are associated two statistics: path length, $l_{i,j}(p_q)$, which is simply the number of nodes between i and j; and frequency: $F_{i,j}(p_q)$, which can be interpreted as how commonly a path is activated between i and j. It is defined as:

$$F_{i,j}(p_q) = \prod_{m=1}^{l} W(i_{m-1}, i_m)\, cmn$$

If p_q is the path with the maximum frequency, then we define the distance between i and j, $d(i,j)$, as $l_{i,j}(p_q)$.[7]

The average path length is

$$L = \frac{1}{n} \sum_{j \neq i} \frac{d(i,j)}{n-1}$$

and simply measures how distant vertices are on average, which is a global property of the graph. Average cliquishness C is a measure of local connectivity capturing the share of active links between any given vertex's neighbours. It is written

$$C = \frac{1}{n} \sum_{i} \sum_{j,l:d(i,j)=d(i,l)=1} \frac{X(j,l)}{n_i(n_i - 1)/2}$$

where $X(j,l) = 1$ if $d(i,j) = 1$ and 0 otherwise, and where $n_i = \#\{j | d(i,j) = 1\}$ is the size of i's neighbourhood. These two statistics together give a reasonably complete description of the structural properties of the underlying network. We add one simple measure, namely the average degree of the graph

$$D = \frac{1}{n} \sum_i n_i$$

as a measure of the density of the interaction structure.

3.5   RESULTS

We are interested in the effects of the falling cost of IT on network structure and on the growth of knowledge. Because knowledge types converge over time, the long-run growth rate of the economy goes to zero: this is an innovative episode rather than a world with ongoing innovation. Thus we can examine knowledge levels, both in the steady state, and over time. The network, on the other hand, is the result of firms' willingness to combine knowledge of different sorts and evolves as firms' needs and preferences over the population of potential partners change over time.

3.5.1   Knowledge

A common claim is that the information technology revolution will spur economic growth as innovators have better access to the world stock of knowledge and information. What our simple model shows is that this conclusion fails to account for the fact that as a population of agents accesses a pool of information, the knowledge stocks of the agents in that population grows more similar, and thus they can learn less from each other. This is likely to have a negative effect on innovation. The initial amount of diversity in knowledge types sustains innovation and growth as long as it persists, but the more ITs are relied on the faster the convergence to some aggregate composite index of the 'industry knowledge type'. The conduct of joint R&D by partners to an agreement progressively washes away knowledge diversity, and even more so when public knowledge is heavily used.

Figures 3.1a and 3.1b show the relationship between long-run knowledge levels, the dispersion of knowledge levels as measured by the coefficient of variation, and b, the parameter that can be interpreted as the cost of IT. Figure 3.1a shows the nature of the system relatively early in history, namely after only 100 periods. Figure 3.1b shows the system after 1000 periods. By this time the system is effectively frozen – diversity has essentially been eliminated and so innovation has stopped. Both early and late in the history, the relationship between knowledge level and the cost of IT is non-monotonic. Knowledge levels are highest in the extreme situations,

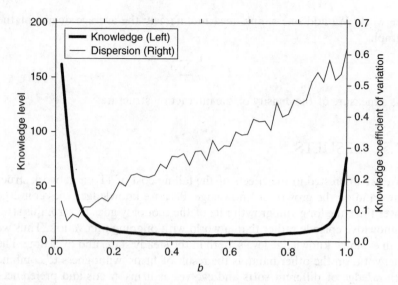

Figure 3.1a   Early knowledge level and dispersion as functions of IT costs

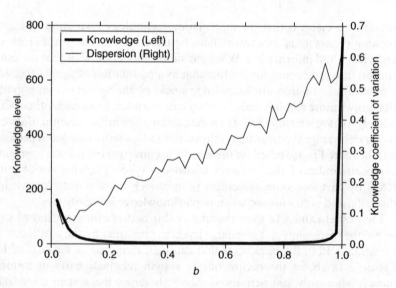

Figure 3.1b   Final knowledge level and dispersion as functions of IT costs

when *b*, the cost of IT, is either very high or very low. Intermediate values of *b* show a deep and wide sink between the extremes.

Figures 3.1a and 3.1b are very similar. The non-monotonic pattern is robust, but when IT is very costly, knowledge levels have grown from roughly 75 at $t = 100$ to 700 at $t = 1000$. Repeated matching continues to produce innovation when public knowledge is expensive (or has low productivity), and thus has less importance in the innovation system. The explanation is that when *b* is small, after a single period of innovation, all agents' areas of expertize make a large shift towards the average expertize. Future innovations are small, since diversity is small among every possible pair. The coefficient of variation in knowledge levels increases with *b*. As IT becomes more expensive, agents innovate largely based on their ability to find suitable partners. Heterogeneity in the population can thus emerge (recall that initially all agents have the same knowledge level), as agents with suitable partners make large innovations whereas those with unsuitable partners make small ones. By contrast, when IT is inexpensive, innovation is driven largely by public knowledge, so all agents' innovations are roughly the same size from the beginning of history, and heterogeneity cannot emerge.

To get a better intuition of the forces at work, and particularly the rapid fall in innovation size entailed by resorting systematically to public knowledge, in Figure 3.2 the re-scaled time series for knowledge growth rates as functions of *b* is shown.

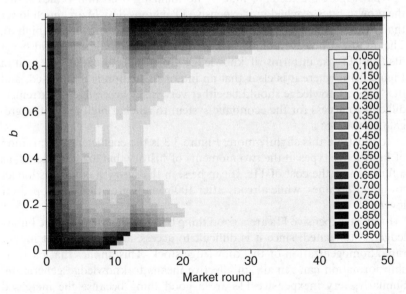

Figure 3.2   Re-scaled knowledge levels over time as a function of IT costs

Figure 3.2 is a two-dimensional view of a 3D histogram in which darker zones correspond to higher values. It has been normalized to facilitate the identification of the parameter configurations generating high growth rates. (For each point in time, the normalized level presented is the actual level over the maximum level observed over all the possible values of b at that point in time; by performing this re-scaling the normalized maximum at any point in time is always 1.) The first conclusion from this figure is that there are two regions of b that have high growth rates of knowledge, namely large and small values of b. But large b and small b generate high growth at different times in history. Hence the industry undergoes a deep change in its early days. First the benefits from cheap ITs are large relative to the costs that come from a rapid decline of knowledge diversity. There is therefore a positive net effect on growth when b changes from an intermediate to a small value. However this quickly reverts and already after the tenth period it is visible that the costs from inexpensive ITs in terms of lost diversity overwhelm the externality benefits from publicly available knowledge. Growth only persists for large b values, that is to say expensive ITs, because only then do the benefits from partnerships remain significant. While a matched pair of agents converge rapidly to each other, they do not necessarily converge to the average expertize, and so are both able to find suitable partners even if they rapidly can learn nothing from each other.

What Figure 3.2 tends to hide by normalizing over all b values is that the growth rates reached in inexpensive IT regions (low b) are much lower than those reached when firms weakly rely on public knowledge (high b). The question, however, of the relative importance of the costs and benefits from IT use in terms of knowledge growth has already been seen in Figure 3.1a, where it is clear that an interior situation is dominated, and that public knowledge should be either very easily accessible or extremely difficult to access for the economic system to reach a high level of aggregate knowledge.

To illustrate this slightly more, Figure 3.3 is the coefficient of variation of knowledge types at the two moments of history that are considered, as a function of the cost of ITs. It can be seen that growth continues longer for larger b values, while already after 100 rounds growth has stopped for low b.

In short, expensive ITs are a good thing because the use of public knowledge is attenuated, since it is difficult to access, and so does not induce rapid homogenization of the knowledge stock. This implies that partnership formation can remain an effective means to knowledge generation. Similarly, very inexpensive ITs are a good thing because the increased similarity effect stemming from drawing more frequently on the public

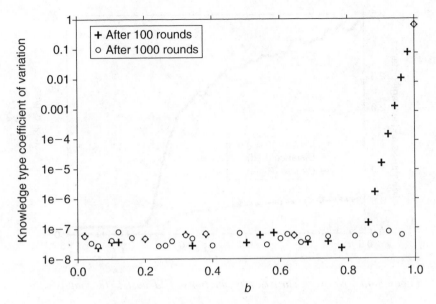

Figure 3.3   Knowledge type dispersion as a function of IT costs

knowledge base is compensated for by the fact that productivity of public knowledge increases, and so initial innovations are much larger. Interestingly, intermediate degrees of accessibility produce the worst, rather than the best, of both worlds.

3.5.2   Network

In this section the properties of the emergent network are discussed. In Figure 3.4a the average number of partnerships is represented, together with the proportion of transitive triples (a transitive triple is a partnership between two of my partners) and the average distance between firms within the industry, after 100 market rounds. Figure 3.4b (see later) represents these same statistics after 1000 market rounds.

The average degree (how many partners the average firm has over the relevant time span) is falling with b, and reaches its lowest possible value of 1 for b close to 0.8. The explanation for this lies in the faster convergence achieved to the average body of knowledge with inexpensive ITs. Very quickly firms carry similar knowledge types and as such start to become indifferent between a large number of potential partners. Pairings become unstable and change often because any is equally bad. For slower

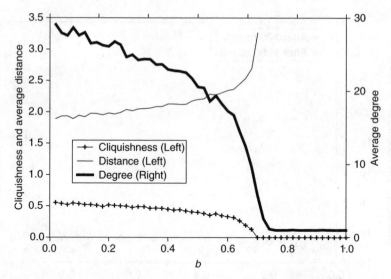

Figure 3.4a   Network statistics as functions of IT costs; 100 rounds

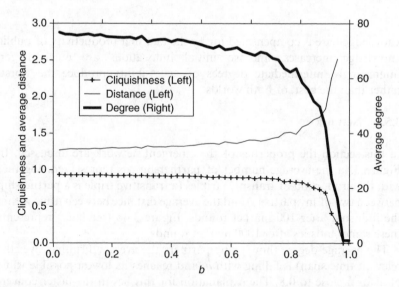

Figure 3.4b   Network statistics as functions of IT costs; 1000 rounds

convergence scenarios (larger *b*) the persistence of inter-individual heterogeneity does not force all the firms to quasi-random choice so quickly and lowers the number of partners to an extent that is increasing with *b*. Finally there is a *b* value such that a single partner for the first 100 periods is still a good thing because convergence has not occurred. There the world consists of isolated pairs. It is easy to see who the market assigns to whom: typically the pair with greatest distance between its members is matched, then *this* is removed and the second pair with largest distance is matched, and so on.

The average distance between pairs corroborates these findings: it tends to increase as density decreases, which is typically what one would expect, until one reaches the point where the graph becomes disconnected into independent pairs, where it ceases to be defined.

The share of transitive triples is also a decreasing function of the cost of ITs, starting around 60 per cent for $b = 0$ and reaching ultimately the value of 0, again at the point where the graph disconnects.

Hence the picture that obtains is one of a densely and randomly connected network, with falling degree as people rely less and less on ITs and focus more and more on the exploitation of (slowly converging) stable partnerships. Rapidly though, as evidenced by Figure 3.4b which provides these results after 1000 periods, things tend to change. In Figure 3.4b it can be seen that types have further converged, so now the critical *b* value for which life-long pairs form is almost 1. Because for any $b < 1$ there is some convergence towards the mean eventually, the population of agents becomes similar enough that quasi-random selection of partners will occur. For low *b* this happens rapidly, for high *b* it happens slowly, which explains the difference between Figures 3.4a and 3.4b.

The patterns for the three statistics are similar to those in Figure 3.4a, with a higher degree for any value of *b* (more indifference cases arise), which yields an almost complete random graph (degree approaching 80 in a graph of order 100) where the share of transitive triples is obviously very high and path lengths are short.

3.6 DISCUSSION

Two aspects of this innovation function deserve note. The first is that knowledge levels of the two partner firms are not included. This is purely to keep the function as simple as possible. Including this feature would not have any effect on the major forces driving the results – it would still be the case that knowledge types converge over time as pairs form and agents access the pool of public knowledge. This will still have the effect of making

variety decrease, and the two sources of the decrease in variety will respond
to the parameters as they do in this simple model.

The second feature of the production function is that a firm not in a pair
(or formally, paired with itself) will have zero innovation, since innovation
as modelled here depends on there being variety in the knowledge of the
two partners. In principle one could add the possibility of individual innovation. If this were present in the model, all else being equal, as knowledge
types converged, eventually firms would stop forming alliances. After this
point, knowledge growth would be driven exclusively by individual innovation. Thus the details of how a firm innovates alone would become central.
If variety is still important, in that a firm benefits from having public
knowledge that is different in type from its own, then the negative effects of
IT would still exist.

In the introduction we discussed the increase in strategic alliance formation in the last two decades. While the model is not meant to explain this
phenomenon (rather it takes it as a starting point) it is suggestive in certain
ways regarding it. One of the accepted explanations for the rise in alliances
is that the knowledge base of industries has broadened, and firms find it
difficult to maintain the variety of human (and physical) capital necessary
to deploy all the types of knowledge they need. An alliance, or set of them,
is a natural way around this problem. What our model suggests is that the
rise in alliances has a limit (other than the combinatorial limit determined
by the number of firms). If knowledge bases converge in the way we have
described, it will become harder and harder for a firm to justify the costs of
an alliance (which in our model were zero, but which are clearly positive
more generally) in terms of its benefits. The sources of continued alliance
formation then will become either a continued broadening of the knowledge base, so that variety in the set of potential partners increases exogenously; or an inherent knowledge capacity constraint at the firm level. That
is, if a firm's knowledge type can only deviate so far from its original type,
or if a firm can only store so much knowledge capital, then the convergence
of firms, both to each other and to the mean, will reach a limit. A positive
amount of variety will still exist in the economy, and so alliance formation
will continue. It is likely to stop growing, however.

3.7 CONCLUSION

In this chapter we have addressed the issue of knowledge growth through
the recombination of existing knowledge when two sources of input exist.
First there is a market for collaborative R&D agreements, assumed to be
at equilibrium; second there is a public knowledge pool (think of the

Internet) to which all firms contribute through spillovers of the knowledge they collaboratively produce, and hence can be seen as a positive externality. The issue is to see how the rise of IT availability (the fall of IT costs) and the related ease of Internet use interfere with the functioning of the market for alliances, both in terms of the growth and distribution of knowledge over the companies, and in terms of the patterns of alliances that emerge. In the chapter innovation results from the recombination of knowledge held by the partners to the collaboration, and public knowledge. A tension exists between contributing to and benefiting from the public knowledge, and we study this tension as it changes with the relative ease 'cost' of resorting to bilateral agreements versus drawing from publicly available information.

We find that, contrary to common opinion, the IT revolution does not necessarily enhance economic growth as a result of innovators having better access to the world stock of knowledge and information. Actually by repeatedly accessing a public pool of information that is a weighted average of what everyone knows, firms' individual characteristics tend to converge, which lowers the innovative potential of the population of innovators. Diversity in knowledge types sustains innovation and growth, but its survival is jeopardized by firms relying heavily on ITs, and the more they do so the faster the convergence is to some aggregate composite index of the 'industry knowledge type'. By comparison, an industry without publicly available knowledge can sustain growth through persistent diversity of endowments much longer. This also suggests that for sustained innovation in an industry over the very long run, recombination will not be enough. There must be some external source of variety in the knowledge base.

NOTES

1. See Cowan and van de Paal (2000).
2. See Hagedoorn (2001) for a review and discussion of this trend.
3. In using the mean knowledge level as the pool of public knowledge we follow Peretto and Smulders (2002), Smulders and van de Klundert (1995), Romer (1990), and others. An alternative (Young, 1998; Aghion and Howitt, 1998; Howitt, 1999) would be to use the knowledge of the most advanced firm as the effective public knowledge.
4. See Swann et al. (1998), for an empirical study of the computing and biotechnology industries that supports the view that diversity in knowledge type is a good thing.
5. The use of the same parameter, *b*, here in both innovation and type-adjustment equations is only to simplify notation. It can be interpreted as the cost of IT, and thus occurs in both places where the cost of IT might have an effect. What is crucial here is that the *relative* importance of the two sources of knowledge in innovation production changes. More complex functions, in which the absolute weights are controlled yields the same qualitative results, but at the cost of an increase in parameters.
6. If one thinks of social networks representing friendship, both have intuitive interpretations. The path length is the number of friendships in the shortest chain connecting two

agents. Cliquishness reflects the extent to which the friends of one agent are also friends of each other.
7. There are other means of translating from a weighted graph to a non-weighted graph, which tend to involve declaring a threshold such that edges with weights above the threshold are assigned a weight of 1, whereas edges with frequencies below the threshold are assigned weights of 0. When reasonable algorithms are used for deciding the threshold (such as assuming that a frequency vector is a multinomial distribution and setting the threshold at 2 standard deviations from the mean), the results are qualitatively similar to those generated by the algorithm we describe here.

REFERENCES

Aghion, P. and P. Howitt, (1998), *Endogenous Growth Theory*, Cambridge, MA: MIT Press.

Arrow, K. (1962), 'Economic welfare and the allocation of resources for invention', in R. Nelson (ed.), *The Rate and Direction of Inventive Activity*, New York: National Bureau of Economic Research, pp. 609–26.

Becker, G.S. (1962), 'A theory of marriage: Part I', *Journal of Political Economy*, **81**, 813–46.

Cowan, R. and D. Foray (1997), 'The economics of codification and the diffusion of knowledge', *Industrial and Corporate Change*, **6**, 595–622.

Cowan R. and Jonard N. (2004), 'Network structure and the diffusion of knowledge', *Journal of Economic Dynamics and Control*, **28**, 1557–75.

Cowan R., N. Jonard and J.B. Zimmermann (2002), 'The joint dynamics of networks and knowledge', in R. Cowan and N. Jonard (eds), *Heterogenous Agents, Interactions and Economic Performance*, Springer, *Lecture Notes in Economics and Mathematical Systems*, **531**, 155–74.

Cowan R. and G. van de Paal (2000), 'Innovation policy in a knowledge-based economy', European Commission, Enterprise Directorate-General.

D'Aspremont C., S. Bhattacharya and L.-A. Gerard-Varet (2000), 'Bargaining and sharing innovative knowledge', *Review of Economic Studies*, **67**, 255–71.

Delapierre M. and L.K. Mytelka (1999), 'Strategic partnerships and the rise of knowledge-based networked oligopolies', in C. Cutler, V. Haufler and T. Porter (eds), *Private Authority and International Affairs*, Binghamton, NY: Suny University Press, pp. 129–49.

Gale D. and L. Shapley (1962), 'College admissions and the stability of marriage', *American Mathematical Monthly*, **69**, 9–15.

Galison, P. (1999), 'Trading zone: Coordinating action and belief', in M. Biagioli (ed.), *The Science Studies Reader*, New York: Routledge, pp. 137–60.

Gibbons M., C. Limoges, H. Nowotny, S. Schartzman, M. Scott and P. Troiw, (1994), *The New Production of Knowledge: The Dynamics of Science and Research in Contemporary Societies*, London: Sage Publications.

Hagedoorn J. (2001), 'Inter-firm R&D partnerships. An overview of major trends and patterns since 1960', in J.E. Jankowski, A.N. Link and N.S. Vonortas (eds), *Strategic Research Partnerships: Proceedings from on NSF Workshop*, Washington, DC: National Science Foundation, pp. 63–92.

Hargadon A. and R. Sutton (1997), 'Technology brokering and innovation in a product development firm', *Administrative Science Quarterly*, **42**, 716–49.

Howitt, P. (1999), 'Steady endogenous growth with population and R&D inputs growing', *Journal of Political Economy*, **107**, 715–30.

Jones, C.I. (2005), 'Growth and ideas', in P. Aghion and S. Durlauf (eds), *Handbook of Economic Growth*, Forthcoming.

Kodama F. (1986), 'Japanese innovation in mechatronics technology', *Science and Public Policy*, **13**, 44–51.

Lucas, R.E. (1988), 'On the mechanics of economic development', *Journal of Monetary Economics*, **22**, 3–42.

Marshall A. (1890), *Principles of Economics*, London: Macmillan.

Nelson, R.R. (1959), 'The simple economic of basic scientific researchs', *Journal of Political Economy*, **67** (3), 297–306.

Noteboom B. (2000), *Learning and Innovation in Organizations and Economics*, Oxford: Oxford University Press.

Olsson, O. (2000), 'Knowledge as a set in idea space: An epistemological view on growth', *Journal of Economic Growth*, **5**, 253–76.

Peretto, P. and S. Smulders (2002), 'Technological distance, growth and scale effects', *Economic Journal*, **112**, 603–24.

Romer, P.M. (1986), 'Increasing returns and long run growth', *Journal of Political Economy*, **94**, 1002–37.

Romer, P.M. (1990), 'Endogenous technological change', *Journal of Political Economy*, **98**, S71–S102.

Smith K. (2000), 'What is the "knowledge economy"? Knowledge-intensive industries and distributed knowledge bases', paper presented to the DRUID Summer Conference on 'The Learning Economy: Firms, Regions and Nation Specific Institutions', 15–7 June.

Smulders, S. and T. van de Klundert (1995), 'Imperfect competition, concentration and growth with firm-specific R & D', *European Economic Review*, **39**, 139–60.

Swann, G.M.P., M. Prevezer and D. Stout (1998), *The Dynamics of Industrial Clustering*, Oxford: Oxford University Press.

Watts, D. and J. Strogatz (1998), 'Collective dyanamics of small-word networks', *Nature*, **393**, 440–42.

Weitzman, M. (1998), 'Recombinant growth', *Quarterly Journal of Economics*, **113**, 331–60.

Young, A (1998), 'Growth without scale effects', *Journal of Political Economy*, **106**, 41–63.

4. Adoption and diffusion of e-business and the role of network effects*

Huub Meijers

4.1 INTRODUCTION

The Internet is an essential part of the infrastructure of the Information Society. It already facilitates a myriad of new possibilities and opportunities to assist and run businesses differently from what we know from the past. Proprietary systems facilitated enterprise resource planning in the 1980s and 1990s, but these systems operated in stand-alone settings. Today these systems are largely replaced by open standard software and what is more, they are connected through networks. It is mainly because of the open standards that many firms have been able to adopt the Internet at low prices and that information can be easily shared. Especially when this information is fed into new communication standards like XML then the communication becomes very smooth and rich (see e.g. Lucking-Reiley and Spulber, 2001). Developing such protocols requires extensive cooperation of buyers and sellers within industries and organizations like RosettaNet support the development of (open) e-business standards.[1]

What we see now is just the beginning of e-business, e-commerce or e-government. However, if we take the long-term view, not only communication about goods, but also the production process itself, will be embraced by this extremely pervasive innovation process. This will happen relatively slowly and its path is difficult to predict because the high degree of complementarity with other developments and applications of information technologies.

It is a well-established view that investment in ICT as such has little impact on productivity and firm performance. Firms need to adjust their internal organization, re-establish competences and responsibilities and re-negotiate and re-discuss contracts and agreements upstream and downstream of the value chain. So gains from investment in ICT will emerge if

* I would like to thank the editors for comments on an earlier version of this chapter.

these investments are accompanied with investments in the internal and external organization. Because of their very nature, this adjustment process is slow and it takes considerable time before efficiency gains are reported.[2] Investigation of productivity effects of ICT investments over time typically shows an inverse U-shaped effect. In the early years after adopting new technologies, the productivity increases, but only marginally. After some years the productivity effects become more sizeable and in the final stage the growth rate of productivity due to ICT investments evaporates (see e.g. Brynjolfsson and Hitt, 2000 and Gretton et al, 2004). The main message however remains the importance of workplace reorganization for success-ful adoption of e-business practices.

Adopting the Internet by firms is positively related to expected market gains (improving the quality and variety of products, improving customer relations and increasing market presence and sales), expected internal cost reduction and expected improved position on the market for inputs. (Hollenstein, 2004). Hollenstein finds, using Swiss-based firm level data, that obstacles for investing in and using ICT for e-business are investment costs and lack of know-how (lack of ICT personnel, information and man-agement problems), and in the case of the adoption of e-sales practices, tech-nological uncertainties also appeared to be obstacles. Concerning firm size and the adoption of ICT, Internet technologies and e-business, Hollenstein (2002) finds that in general larger firms adopted ICT technologies and the Internet earlier than smaller firms – which is to be expected – but also that the intensity of Internet use is larger for medium-sized firms. This indicates that intra-firm diffusion matters and that larger firms adopted ICT and the Internet earlier, but also that it takes more time for them to use these tech-nologies to the full extent. This implies that medium-sized firms face fewer obstacles, or expect to have higher revenues, in intra-firm diffusion of ICT and Internet use. Next to direct investment costs, workplace reorganization and lack of qualified personnel are the main determinants for this difference between large and small firms. Hollenstein (2002), for instance, finds that there is a lack of potential using ICT among smaller firms whereas larger firms face more information and management problems.

In terms of different usage of ICT, using the Internet has shown the fastest rate of adoption. For instance Maliranta and Rouvinen (2004) report that (almost) none of the Finnish firms used the Internet in 1992 whereas it was almost 100 per cent in 2001. Also the use of email has increased remarkably sharply from 20 per cent in 1992 to almost 100 per cent in 2001. The use of communication technologies for electronic data interchange (EDI) also grew in this period but not that spectacularly, from 20 per cent in 1992 to 50 per cent in 2001. One should realize that the concept of EDI was already established in the 1970s and that different communication protocols were used to communicate with upstream and downstream firms. The emergence of the Internet as a more standard communication medium has increased the use of EDI considerably. The usage of Extranet and Intranet technologies (and practices) increased in the period 1992–2001 from 0 to 50 per cent and 0 to 70 per cent, respectively (all data from Maliranta and Rouvinen, 2004). Concerning firm size and the use of ICT, large firms are in general found to adopt Internet and related technologies first whereas smaller firms are the laggards (Clayton et al., 2004). However, e-business practices such as EDI are still mainly done over non-Internet networks by large firms whereas EDI over the Internet is equally developed and diffused among small, medium and large firms (Clayton et al., 2004, p. 244). This suggests that the introduction of the Internet has increased the profitability of medium and small firms to invest in e-business practices and that large firms still stick to the more traditional communication media.

Finally, concerning ICT investments per employee, Becchetti et al. (2003) find that small firms invest per employee twice as much in ICT as larger firms. Disentangling total ICT investment into various components it appears that this finding is driven by hardware and software investments. Investments in telecommunication clearly show the opposite and larger firms invest per employee twice as much as compared to smaller firms. This indicates that there are scale effects at work for hardware and software investments such that large firms have a scale advantage here. For telecommunication the opposite holds true: large firms have a more complex organizational structure, have more often different establishments, and so on, such that there is a higher demand for telecommunication investments.

From the above the question arises of what determines the diffusion process of adopting e-business practices and can we explain the observed diffusion patterns, so this chapter focuses on the adoption and diffusion of e-business. The questions addressed in this chapter are: a) what is the impact of a new (cost saving or efficiency increasing) technology on market structures? b) what is the relation between market structure and the adoption of new technologies? and finally, c) how can we explain differences in the time of adoption of e-business between smaller and larger firms? To answer these questions, the remainder of this chapter is organized as follows: the next section presents a basic model setup where firms with different technologies operate in a market characterized by monopolistic competition. This results in a market equilibrium where firms differ in cost structure and, consequently, have a different size. Given this basic setup, investment in ICT and e-business practices is discussed and I show that both scale advantages and higher adjustment costs for larger firms can explain different size-dependent motivations to adopt or not to adopt this new technology. However, the time dimension is not included and it is shown that more is needed to generate diffusion patterns.

For that reason, network effects are introduced and provide an endogenous time dimension, and complete the theoretical model. Finally simulation results show the basic properties of the model and also show the effects of changing market structures on the adoption and diffusion of e-business practices. It is shown that medium-sized firms are the early adopters; the introduction of e-business practices reduces the number of firms in the market (the least productive, smallest firms are driven out); and that increased price competition reduces the number of producers in the market but also reduces the ultimate relative diffusion level of e-business practices.

4.2 A SIMPLE MONOPOLISTIC COMPETITION MODEL WITH FIRM-SPECIFIC COSTS

This section sets up the basic model, without investments in ICT, along the lines of Montagna (1995). The framework used is a simple monopolistic competition model where each firm produces one variety of final output and each firm also faces specific marginal costs. This market structure is realistic for many markets and it allows for different firm sizes, a property that is used later on. Differences in marginal costs will lead to different prices and thus to firm-specific final demand and output. So by assuming firm-specific marginal costs – because of differences in employed technologies, management quality, or skills of the employees, and so on – it is possible to model different firm sizes in a monopolistic competitive setting. Later on I introduce the adoption of e-business practices and – as discussed above – one of the factors that influences intra-firm diffusion is the size of the firm. So the basic model will provide such a setting.

The demand side is characterized by a representative consumer with a love of variety utility function:

$$U = \left(\sum_{i=1}^{N} x_i^{(\sigma-1)/\sigma} \right)^{\sigma/(\sigma-1)} \tag{4.1}$$

where x_i is the consumption of variety i, N is the number of varieties, and $\sigma > 1$ is the elasticity of substitution between varieties. The representative consumer maximizes its utility subject to the budget constraint

$$P \cdot Y = \sum_{i=1}^{N} p_i \cdot x_i \tag{4.2}$$

where p_i is the price of good i and $P \cdot Y$ is total available income. The aggregate price is defined as:

$$P = \left(\frac{1}{N} \sum_{i=1}^{N} p_i^{1-\sigma} \right)^{1/(1-\sigma)} \tag{4.3}$$

As in Montagna (1995) I assume that nominal income is equal to $Y = A \cdot P^{-\eta}$ where A is a positive constant and η reflects the price elasticity of final demand.[3] Note that I use a partial equilibrium framework where nominal income is not affected by profits and labour income. Maximizing utility subject to the income gives the demand for each variety:

$$x_i = \frac{A}{N} P^{\sigma - \eta} p_i^{-\sigma} \tag{4.4}$$

for all goods i. So the demand for an individual good depends on its own price and on the aggregate price. As long as $\sigma > \eta$ – which I assume to be the case – the demand for an individual good depends positively on the aggregate price and negatively on its own price.

Each firm produces one variety and I assume that firms differ in employed technology, so in marginal costs there is a one-to-one relation between varieties and firms. Since the demand for each variety depends on price p_i firms will face different cost structures leading to different prices and output as we will see below. Firms face a cost structure:

$$c_i = \beta_i \cdot x_i + F \tag{4.5}$$

Where β_i denotes the firm-specific marginal costs and F the fixed per period costs. Although firms face different marginal costs, and will have different market shares, I assume that the fixed costs are firm independent.[4] Note that I also implicitly assume equilibrium in the product market. Maximizing profits subject to the demand function (4.4) yields the familiar pricing function:

$$p_i = \frac{\sigma}{\sigma - 1} \cdot \beta_i \tag{4.6}$$

Such that output for firm i is equal to:

$$x_i = \left(\frac{\sigma}{\sigma - 1} \right)^{-\sigma} \frac{A}{N} P^{\sigma - \eta} \beta_i^{-\sigma} \tag{4.7}$$

So the output per firm is a function of its marginal costs, the aggregate price level and the number of firms in the market. Below I use the basic model to allow for the adoption of new technologies where the size of firms plays a crucial role in the decision to adopt or not to adopt a new technology. From (4.7) it is clear that – within this setup – different firm sizes can only be established by assuming different marginal costs. Following Montagna (1995) I assume that differences between firms are reflected by a spread of marginal costs within an interval between $1 - \delta$ and $1 + \delta$ of the average marginal costs: $\bar{\beta}(1 - \delta) \leq \beta_i \leq \bar{\beta}(1 + \delta)$. All existing firms know their marginal costs, whereas entrants will face marginal costs from a random draw from this distribution, which we assume to be uniform.[5] So an entrant faces fixed costs F and unknown marginal costs which are drawn from a uniform distribution. Existing firms know both the fixed and the marginal costs. Profits can be easily derived from (4.5), (4.6), and (4.7):

$$\pi_i = \frac{\varphi \cdot A}{N} P^{\sigma - \eta} \beta_i^{1 - \sigma} - F \qquad (4.8)$$

with $\varphi = \sigma^{-\sigma} \cdot (\sigma - 1)^{\sigma - 1}$.

Output per firm is determined by (4.7) and total per period profits by (4.8). Finally, entry and exit conditions determine the steady state solution, which depends on the number of firms in the market (N^{**}) and the minimum efficiency β^{**} that is required to obtain non-negative profits. As long as the expected profits are positive, firms will enter the market. This reduces the profits of all firms and leads to bankruptcy of those with the highest marginal costs, hence the marginal firms drop out. But this drop-out increases the average efficiency of production, and it also reduces the aggregate price level and increases aggregate demand, thereby attracting new entrants. In the steady state, the entry and exit dynamics will come to an end and for any number of firms in the market there is a minimum efficiency for which the expected profits are zero. For a given number N^* the entry condition is:

$$V^E = \int_{\bar{\beta}(1 - \delta)}^{\bar{\beta}(1 + \delta)} \Pi(\beta, N^*) f(\beta) d\beta \geq 0 \qquad (4.9)$$

where V^E is the expected profit of the potential entrant, $\Pi(\beta, N^*)$ is the profit function (4.8) and $f(\beta) = 1/(2\delta\bar{\beta})$ is the density function of the random efficiency. So as long as V^E is positive, firms will enter the market and will affect existing firms as described above. Firms will stay in the market as long as their profits do not become negative, that is, as long as $\Pi(\beta^{**}, N^{**}) \geq 0$. This continues until this term equals zero. Solving for $V^E(N^{**}) = 0$ and $\Pi(\beta^{**}, N^{**}) = 0$ gives the number of firms in steady state:

$$N^{**} = \frac{1}{2\delta} \frac{\varphi A}{F} P^{\sigma - \eta} \frac{1}{2 - \sigma} \bar{\beta}^{1 - \sigma} ((1 + \delta)^{2 - \sigma} - (1 - \delta)^{2 - \sigma}) \qquad (4.10)$$

and the efficiency cut-off point:

$$\beta^{**} = \bar{\beta}\left(\frac{1}{2\delta}\frac{1}{2-\sigma}((1+\delta)^{2-\sigma} - (1-\delta)^{2-\sigma})\right)^{\frac{1}{1-\sigma}} \qquad (4.11)$$

which is the same as in Montagna (1995) except for the average efficiency term $\bar{\beta}$.[6] The characteristics of the steady state with fixed average marginal costs are extensively described in Montagna (1995). The next section introduces a new technology that reduces the marginal costs of those who adopt that technology. Here we concentrate on the effect of an overall decrease of marginal costs. From (4.11) it is clear that a decrease of the average marginal costs (a reduction in $\bar{\beta}$) will proportionally decrease the minimum entry point β^{**}. The effect of an overall increase in efficiency on the number of firms (and thus varieties) includes a direct effect, but also an indirect effect through changes in the aggregate price level and thus changes in aggregate demand. In the steady state the aggregate price level is given by:

$$P = \left[\frac{1}{N^{**}}\int_{\bar{\beta}(1-\delta)}^{\beta^{**}}\frac{N^{**}}{\beta^{**} - \bar{\beta}(1-\delta)}p(\beta)^{1-\sigma}d\beta\right]^{\frac{1}{1-\sigma}}$$

$$= \frac{\sigma}{\sigma-1}\left[\frac{\beta^{**2-\sigma} - [\bar{\beta}(1-\delta)]^{2-\sigma}}{(2-\sigma)(\beta^{**} - \bar{\beta}(1-\delta))}\right]^{\frac{1}{1-\sigma}} \qquad (4.12)$$

The effect of an overall change in the marginal costs $\bar{\beta}$ on the number of active firms in the steady state depends on the elasticity of substitution between products as well as on the aggregate price elasticity. From (4.10) it follows that the number of firms depends negatively on the average marginal costs. This is the direct effect at firm level only, however. Since an overall change in the marginal costs also affects the aggregate price level – through changes in β^{**} and of course through $\bar{\beta}$ itself in (4.12) – total final demand also changes and the final effect on the number of firms that remain in the market depends on σ and η.

Figure 4.1 displays $dN^{**}/d\bar{\beta}$ for various values of both elasticities. For $\eta > 1$ (an elastic output market) a decrease in the marginal costs will decrease the price of each individual good (see equation (4.6)), thereby decreasing the aggregate price level, which in turn has a more than proportional demand effect (due to $\eta > 1$), which attracts new firms, so $dN^{**}/d\bar{\beta}$ is negative if $\eta > 1$. The opposite is true for $\eta < 1$ and for $\eta = 1$ there is no effect of a change in the average marginal costs on the number of firms. The latter can be easily detected from (4.10) since the change in the aggregate

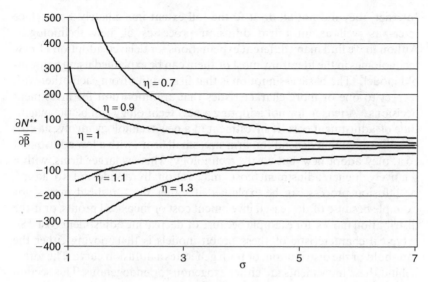

Figure 4.1   Effect of a change in average marginal costs on the number of firms

price level is equal to the change in the marginal costs and with $\eta = 1$ the effects cancel out each other in the number of active firms in steady state.

The analysis so far is restricted to the case in which all firms adopt a new technology, and does not allow for diffusion of new technologies. Firms differ from each other with respect to the marginal costs, but the technology is drawn from a uniform distribution and firms do not choose the employed technology. The effect of an overall increase in efficiency, that is by decreasing the average marginal costs, and the effect on the number of firms crucially depends on the aggregate price elasticity as well as on the elasticity of substitution between varieties. Based on this basic setup, the next section allows for the adoption of e-business practices and firms will choose to adopt or not to adopt these practices, mainly depending on the investment costs as well as on the adjustment costs needed to reap the benefits of ICT investments. Medium-sized firms are likely to be the early adopters. The time dimension is introduced afterwards, however.

4.3   ADOPTING E-BUSINESS

It is obvious that not all firms use the Internet for their transactions, communication, and marketing from the outset and even if firms moved to the

Internet, they did not all do it to the full extent immediately. So we face inter- as well as intra-firm diffusion processes of new technologies. Although we find many different explanations for delayed adoption of new technologies in the literature, most of them can be explained using a threshold model.[7] The basic assumption is that firms differ from each other with respect to one or more characteristics that are important for investment decisions.[8] A reason for not adopting a new technology can be the magnitude of adjustment cost. If investment in a new technology involves a cost of adjustment that depends on firm size, small firms, with a low adjustment cost, may adopt new, but costly, technology, whereas larger firms, with a relatively higher adjustment cost, may rationally decide not to adopt. A diffusion process can be explained if either the threshold moves, for example because of decreased investment cost or increased profits, or if the distribution moves, for example because of decreasing adjustment costs. So a typical characteristic of these probit models is that moving either the threshold or the distribution, or both generates a diffusion curve. The forces behind these movements are either exogenous or endogenous. This section focuses on the gains and costs of adopting a new technology – e-business practices – whereas the next section introduces the time dimension that generates diffusion patterns.

For the model developed in this section we start from the basic setup as described above, where firms differ in size (because of different initial technologies) and adoption costs of Internet technologies (or ICT in general) are related to firm size. Investing in the Internet involves an adjustment cost because the entire internal (administrative) structure of firms has to be adjusted for a successful transformation towards Internet-based commerce. This implies that for instance larger firms may experience a relatively larger adjustment cost than smaller firms do, just because of their more complex internal structure, which is consistent with the findings of Hollenstein (2002). On the other hand, larger firms may benefit from economies of scale of training and implementing new systems, whereas small firms may face indivisibilities of for instance hiring specialized ICT personnel.

So as well as the direct investment costs of IT hardware and software, firms face other costs and obstacles that have to be taken into account. Moreover, such additional adjustment costs are larger than the capital investments in many cases, as reported by for example, Brynjolfsson and Hitt (1996), and Bresnahan et al. (2002). There is also evidence that reorganization of the workplace is necessary in order to reap the gains from ICT investments; see for example, Arvanitis (2004), Bertschek and Kaiser (2004) and Borghans and ter Weel (2004). In a survey-based study, Hollenstein (2004) also finds such a relation but in addition he finds evidence that the lack of know-how is an obstacle for the successful adoption of the Internet and Internet-based commerce. Moreover, firm size is shown to be a significant determinant in such adoption processes. Because of their complexity, large firms face higher reorganization costs and need more high-qualified personnel to successfully implement new technologies. On the other hand, small firms – and especially micro firms with fewer than 10 employees – face the problem of finding financial resources to invest in ICT and also face indivisibilities with respect to (qualified) ICT personnel. The latter implies that small firms face higher costs or larger obstacles to invest in ICT. So firms face two different costs: the reorganization costs on one hand and investment costs on the other. The latter include learning/training, setting up new systems, converting databases, and so on, and are very likely to increase with firm size, but less than proportionally because of positive scale effects. As noted above, reorganization costs are likely to increase more than proportionally with firm size as complexity increases. It should be noted that successful implementation of ICT in business is not limited to setting up and maintaining a corporate website or using email for all employees. Successful use of ICT implies connection of internal information systems with similar systems of suppliers and customers such that logistic processes are automated and optimized. Moreover, in many cases purchasing intermediate goods can be done via electronic auction marketplaces such that prices will drop, inventories can be decreased and overall efficiency increases.

The above implies that the investment costs can be written as a function of firm size. More specifically, both the reorganization costs and the additional investment costs are a function of output. Concerning investment costs we assume:

$$ic(x) = \varepsilon_0 + \varepsilon_1 \cdot x^\varepsilon \quad \text{where } \varepsilon_0, \varepsilon_1 > 0 \text{ and } 0 < \varepsilon < 1 \qquad (4.13)$$

So the investment costs are equal to ε_0 for firm size equal to zero and are increasing, but at a diminishing rate with respect to firm size. Reorganization costs are represented by a similar function:

$$r(x) = \lambda_0 \cdot x^\lambda \quad \text{where } \lambda_0 > 0 \text{ and } \lambda > 1 \qquad (4.14)$$

which is also increasing but at a faster rate because of the greater complexity of larger firms. So total investment costs are equal to the direct investment costs plus the two additional cost components:

$$i(x) = ic(x) + r(x) \qquad (4.15)$$

The benefits from investing in e-business technologies are modelled by a reduction in marginal costs. Here I assume that marginal costs decrease by a percentage Δ for those who invest in e-business, so $\beta_i^n = \beta_i^o \cdot (1 - \Delta)$ where superscripts o and n denote old (pre-investment) and new (post-investment) situations, respectively. Note that we do not include intra-firm diffusion in the model; it is simply assumed that firms either invest in e-business or not, but if they invest, they do it to the same (full) extent. From (4.8) this implies that the gross (expected) profits increase by:

$$\Delta\pi_i = \left(\frac{\varphi \cdot A}{N} P^{\sigma-\eta}\right) \cdot \beta_i^{o1-\sigma}((1 - \Delta)^{1-\sigma} - 1) \tag{4.16}$$

where I assume that firms disregard the influence of their own investment decision on the aggregate price level and on the number of firms in the industry, as is done above in the basic setup. Investigating the relation between increased profits resulting from investing in the new technology and firm size, that is, rewriting equation (4.16) in terms of the output of each firm, we arrive at:

$$\Delta\pi(x) = \varphi\left(\frac{\sigma - 1}{\sigma}\right)^{1-\sigma}\left(\frac{A}{N} P^{\sigma-\eta}\right)^{\frac{1}{\sigma}}((1 - \Delta)^{1-\sigma} - 1)x^{\frac{\sigma-1}{\sigma}} \tag{4.17}$$

which is positive for any output x. Inspection of the first and second derivatives with respect to output shows that the first derivative is positive and the second derivative is negative. So the gains from investing in a new technology are positive (as expected), and are larger the larger the firm is but at a less than proportional rate, so additional profits per unit of output decrease with firm size. The concavity of this relation depends on the elasticity of substitution between different varieties, and for large values of this elasticity the relation becomes nearly linear. Estimates of this elasticity show values of 6–12 (Broda and Weinstein, 2004), depending on the level of detail in the classification employed. (Broda and Weinstein, 2004 found an elasticity of 12 in the case of an 8-digit classification and 6 for a 3-digit classification). Similar results were found earlier by Gasiorek et al. (1991).[9] An elasticity of substitution of 6 corresponds to a profit margin of 20 per cent and a value of 12 reduces the margin to 9 per cent, which seem reasonable values.[10] The relation between firm size and increased profits because of investment in new technology is rather concave for small values of the elasticity of substitution but becomes nearly linear for larger, and more reasonable, values of this elasticity.

Considering the costs of investing in e-business it is obvious that the above-mentioned gains imply increased profit flows in the future, so these future net gains have to be discounted. However, assuming that firms do not expect other firms to invest in e-business too and that their own

decision does not affect the aggregate price level and aggregate demand –
an assumption that is consistent with the monopolistic competitive market
setting – firms will invest in e-business if the investment costs are smaller
than the gains, so if:

$$i(x_i) \leq \int_0^{t_1} \Delta\pi_i \cdot e^{-rt} dt = \frac{1}{r} \cdot (1 - e^{-rt_1}) \cdot \Delta\pi_i \quad \text{so if} \quad r' \cdot i(x_i) \leq \Delta\pi_i \quad (4.18)$$

where r' is implicitly defined in (4.18). Note that firms do not differ from
each other with respect to the planning horizon, so this term is equal for
all firms.

Confronting these costs with the gains from investing in e-business technologies and using reasonable values of the elasticity of substitution
between different varieties of final goods determines which firms will invest
in that technology and which firms will rationally decide not to adopt the
technology. A typical example is given in Figure 4.2 where I assume that the
gains from investing in e-business increase over time, for the moment due
to an exogenous process. The costs are depicted by the convex curve ($ic(x)$)
and the discounted gains by the concave curves, for the moment at three
different points in time, at t_0, t_1 and t_2. At t_0, no firm will adopt the new
technology because the costs exceed the discounted gains. At t_1, the gains
have increased and firms with size within the interval $x_{1,0}$ to $x_{1,1}$ will invest,
whereas smaller and larger firms do not. If the gains from the new technology increase further, more and more firms will invest in it. Ultimately,

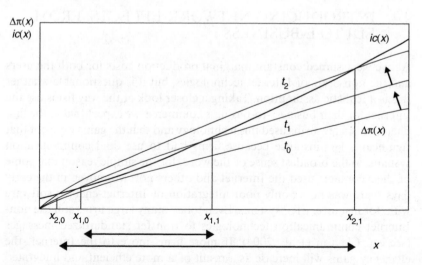

Figure 4.2 Profits and costs of investing in e-business practices

all firms will have invested in e-business, except for the very small ones for which the scale is too small so the gains do not exceed the (fixed) investment costs (ε_0). It is obvious that this process depends on the parameters of the model, and in particular on the cost structure. If workplace reorganization does not matter, the cost curve becomes concave as a result of the scale benefits of investing in and using Internet technologies, and in such a situation large firms will start to invest first in the new technology and smaller firms are the laggards. For very high reorganization costs, the cost curve becomes highly convex and typically the medium-sized firms will invest in the new technology first. Both the larger and smaller firms are now the laggards. Confronting this with the empirical findings as discussed above, where indeed the medium-sized firms are the early adopters, this implies that reorganization costs matter so the cost curve becomes convex. Moreover, if the gains and costs functions as depicted in Figure 4.2 reflect reality, there is a faster diffusion of the new technology among larger firms relative to small firms. Moreover, the very small (micro) firms will not invest in e-business because of the initial fixed costs, which are not covered by the increased profits.

To finalize the model, the diffusion process should be endogenized and either the costs structure or the discounted gains from investing in e-business processes should change over time. The next section shows that network externalities can be the driving force for such a process. After that some simulation experiments show the properties of the model.

4.4 INTRODUCING NETWORK EFFECTS: FROM EDI TO E-BUSINESS

Above we assumed constant marginal production costs for both the users and the non-users of Internet technologies, but it is questionable whether this is a realistic assumption. Taking a closer look at the way firms use the Internet for their business-to-business commerce, we expect that in the first phase, only a few firms used this technology and that the gains were not that significant. For instance because firms had to use dual communication systems, in the broadest sense of the word, for the simple reason that some of their contacts used the Internet and others not. Moreover, in the early days there was no or only poor integration of Internet-enabled software with, for instance, ERP systems. Even today many large firms still use non-Internet communication technologies to transfer standardized messages (see e.g. Clayton et al., 2004). If more firms move to the Internet, the efficiency gains will increase as a result of a more efficient and integrated approach, because of increased competition on the market for intermediate goods and cheaper and better (integrated) software packages. This means that the efficiency gains of using the Internet will increase if more firms move to it. That is, the efficiency gains of using the Internet for business-to-business commerce can be characterized by network externalities, which means it becomes more efficient for every user if more firms move to Internet-based e-business practices. Although I do not specify the exact underlying process very precisely, I assume that the efficiency gains are an increasing function of the number of e-business users.

In this respect, a comparison with Internet technologies and the longer existing concepts of Electronic Data Interchange (EDI) is useful. EDI is based on standards concerning the exchange of data in the sense that the format of the business documents to be exchanged is standardized. Although the idea of standardization of these messages is useful, the EDI concept has some drawbacks, one of which is the enormous amount of different standards. Almost every industry has its own standards, so to do business with many different industries, for instance for the purchase of intermediate goods, a firm has to implement all these different standards.[11] The second drawback is that the EDI concept is limited to the format of the documents to be exchanged, that is, it is limited to the format of the messages. The way firms exchange information, that is, the formats firms use to exchange the messages, is not standardized in the EDI concept. This is exactly the point where the Internet comes into the picture. On the Internet, the messages as such are not standardized but the way information is transferred is laid down in open protocols. Currently both protocols are to be integrated through a new Internet standard XML that allows for standardized messaging via the Internet. This process of standardization increases the number of applications and, even more important, increases the compatibility between various systems.

This implies that the efficiency gains of using the Internet for business-to-business commerce can be characterized by network effects, hence it becomes more efficient for every user if more firms move to the Internet. This means that the marginal cost of the users decrease with the number of users. Next to this, it is only natural to expect that there is some upper limit of these efficiency gains so the second derivative of the marginal cost with respect to the number of users is positive and becomes zero, so the marginal costs reach some lower limit asymptotically. Hence, the decrease of marginal cost is rather large at the beginning of the diffusion process but becomes smaller and smaller as the number of users increases. To be more precise, I assume that:

$$\beta_i^n = \beta_i^o \cdot (1 - \Delta(m)) = \beta_i^o \frac{1 - \Delta_0}{\gamma + (1 - \gamma) \cdot \alpha^m}$$

$$0 \leq \alpha \leq 1, \gamma > 1, \Delta_0 > 0, \Delta(m)' > 0, \Delta(m)'' < 0 \qquad (4.19)$$

where β_i^n denotes the marginal costs of firm i that introduced e-business, based on its original cost structure β_i^o and the reduction $1 - \Delta(m)$ in marginal production costs for a firm using ICT, given that m other firms also adopted the new technology; α controls the speed at which the marginal cost declines and γ determines the level of the asymptote. If the number of users is zero, the marginal costs are equal to $1 - \Delta_0$ times the original marginal costs, whereas for a large (infinite) number of users the reduction in marginal cost becomes $(1 - \Delta_0)/\gamma$.

A crucial aspect at this point is the treatment of expectations of firms regarding the network effects. As will become clear below, the model becomes very complicated if firms take the adoption decisions of other firms and the future gains resulting from network effects into account when making their own investment decision.[12] Moreover, these effects depend on the firms' characteristics concerning the gains and costs of investments in e-business and in order to be able to take these effects into account, all firms should have knowledge about these characteristics of all other firms. This is a very strong assumption indeed. Therefore the expected marginal cost reduction of a user in period t is equal to $[1 - \Delta(m_{t-1})]$. The (expected) marginal cost of the non-users remains the same as before at β_i^o. So the model now includes an endogenous force that increases the gains of adopting e-business practices if more and more other firms adopt it too. However, adoption of a more efficient technology also implies changes in the market structure and changes in the incentives to adopt the technology. The result of these different forces cannot be traced analytically and the model characteristics are presented through simulation results.

4.4.1 An Example

This section illustrates the working of the model by presenting simulation results. I start from a steady state situation where 250 firms (N^{**}) are active in the market.[13] At a certain point in time a new technology becomes available and some firms will invest in the new technology in this period. In their decision process, firms do not take network effects into account – they are treated as externalities – but they will appear after this initial investment. This increases the gains from adopting e-business practices and also increases the potential gains for non-users, which attracts some other firms to invest in e-business too, thereby increasing the network effects for all users. Moreover, because the marginal costs of the users of e-business will drop, their output price will also decrease and their market share will increase at the expense of the non-adopters. Some non-adopting firms will then face negative profit and will disappear from the market. Above I showed that the number of firms remains the same if the marginal costs of *all* firms decrease

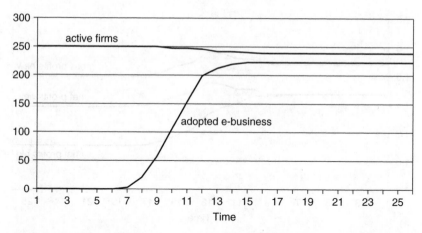

Figure 4.3   The number of active firms and number of users of e-business

if $\eta = 1$. Moreover, the efficiency cut-off point β^{**} was reduced by the same amount as the reduction of marginal costs of all firms. This result was obtained by moving from the initial to the new steady state, whereas the intertemporal dynamics include the bankruptcy of marginal firms on one hand but also the entry of new firms on the other because of the decreased marginal costs. Figure 4.3 shows that the number of active firms decreases if we do not allow for new entrants, and the introduction of new technology will drive out the marginal firms and create opportunities for new firms. This is in line with Schumpeter's theory of creative destruction. The crucial question in this dynamic process is how the entry costs of entrants relate to the reorganization costs of existing firms. In the basic setup firms do not face entry barriers, so starting a new firm does not differ from continuing an existing one, except for the marginal cost structure, which is uncertain for an entrant and known by an existing firm. Continuing along this line of reasoning, organization costs are zero whereas reorganization costs clearly are not. If that were the case, new entrants would not only fill up the gap that occurs due to bankruptcy of the marginal firms, they would also threaten the position of others due to their relative cost advantage so driving even more existing firms out of the market. The other extreme is that entrants face a similar cost structure as compared to existing firms, so they bear the same investment and adjustment costs if they invest in e-business, even when setting up a new firm, and in that case the number of new firms is equal to the number of firms that went bankrupt.

Here entry is ruled out (except in obtaining the initial steady state) and the aggregate price level falls as more firms adopt the new business

The economics of the digital society

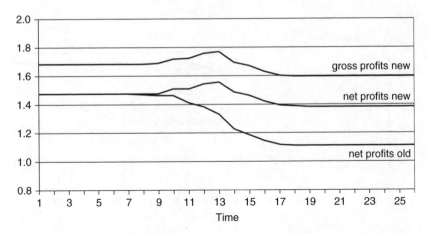

*Figure 4.4   Profits of an early adopter (net profits of the new technology
            exceed the net profits from the old technology, so adopt)*

practices and as marginal costs fall. Consequently, total aggregate demand
will increase. As more firms use the new technology, network effects
increase the profits for all users as well as the expected profits for non-users,
and some will also invest in the new technology. In the first stage, the
number of users increases exponentially whereas due to the combination
of decreased market power and ceasing network effects, the number of
adopters decreases at the end of this process. The entire process creates a
diffusion curve as depicted in Figure 4.3 and in this particular simulation,
some firms – those that survive – will face too high investment costs and
will rationally decide not to invest in the new technology. Note that indeed
the total number of firms in the market falls over time.

The profits are given in Figure 4.4 for an early adopter and in Figure 4.5
for a non-adopter that stays in the market.[14] Indeed, the profits of non-
users decrease as more firms invest in e-business practices and produce at
lower marginal cost and thus sell more products. The profits of the users
even increase at the beginning of the diffusion process: the gains due to the
network effects exceed the decreasing market power. However, as the
network effects become smaller and smaller, the decreasing market power
becomes more important as a result of which the profits of the users will
decline. However, even in that phase of the diffusion process, the decrease
in the profits in the non-users exceeds the decrease of the users such that
the difference in profit between users and non-users still increases. This
implies that still more and more firms will invest in e-business practices.
Finally, the difference becomes too small and the diffusion process stops.

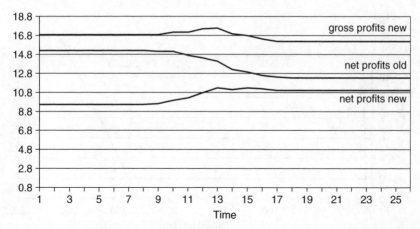

Figure 4.5 *Profits of a non-adopter that remains in the market (net profits of the new technology remain below the net profits of the old technology, so do not adopt. The firm still makes positive profits)*

The difference in the alternative net profits for a non-adopter decreases but the gap is not closed, so this particular (large) firm does not invest in e-business practices, as depicted in Figure 4.5. In this particular example, all small firms that do not adopt e-business will disappear from the market but some large non-adopting firms still manage to make profits and survive.

Finally, investigating the relation between firm size and time of adoption, Figure 4.6 shows that relatively small firms adopt first (in period 6) and the group of adopters spreads in both directions. Output size in Figure 4.6 refers to the final output, after adoption, and it is clearly shown that the largest firms that adopt e-business practices become larger and leapfrog non-adopting firms in terms of output size.

4.5 MARKET STRUCTURE AND ADOPTION OF NEW TECHNOLOGIES

This last section presents the behaviour of the model in a different market structure. What happens if the elasticity of substitution is higher? On the demand side, an increase of σ (viewed in a comparative static way) implies that differences in prices between varieties become more important than differences in qualities. So consumers are more sensitive to price

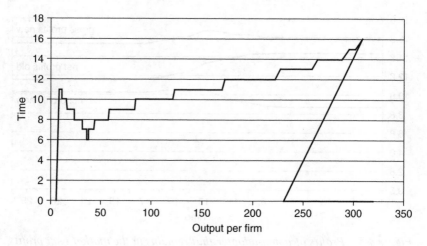

*Figure 4.6   Firm size (after adoption) and time of adopting the new
              technology*

differences and firms experience increased price competition, which
decreases both the cut-off point β** and the number of active firms in the
market N**. The least productive firms are driven out and consequently
the average productivity increases. An increase of σ also decreases the
markup margin, so prices of all varieties decrease. The aggregate price
level falls because of the increased average productivity and because of the
decreased price margins. Aggregate demand consequently increases. For
individual varieties, two different effects are at work. First of all we
observe a rotation of the demand function where the demand for more
expensive varieties fall compared with less expensive varieties. Second,
since all prices decrease, aggregate demand increases and there is an
outward shift of the demand curve. The result is that demand increases for
the cheaper varieties (i.e. those produced by the more productive firm),
whereas demand decreases for more expensive products, conditional on
a unit aggregate price elasticity ($\eta = 1$) as is the case in the present model
simulations. Profits develop in a similar way: highly productive firms
increase their profits because the lower profit margins are offset by
higher volumes, whereas less productive firms experience a decrease in
profits, both compared to the initial value of σ. The decision to introduce
e-business practices is also affected by these changes. For the most productive firms, the introduction of e-business yields higher gross profit
gains as compared to the original market structure. For the least productive firms the opposite holds true. However, most productive firms also
become bigger, so adjustment costs are higher. Given the values of the

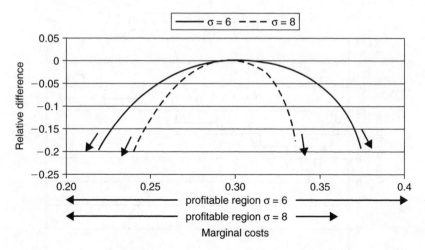

Figure 4.7   Relative net difference in profits

parameters, and in particular the value of λ (= 1.8) in equation (4.14), the increase in adjustment costs outweighs the increase in net profit gains for the largest firms, so they will adopt e-business practices at a later stage or even not adopt at all. This effect is displayed in Figure 4.7, which shows the net difference in profits firms expect to achieve by the introduction of e-business practices at the beginning of the diffusion process. The profitable region in terms of marginal costs is initially between 0.2 (which is equal to $\bar{\beta}(1 - \delta)$) and about 0.4, the value of β^{**}. Firms with marginal costs of 0.3 experience a positive net difference in profits when they adopt e-business practices, and they will adopt these practices first while both more and less productive firms will delay adoption.[15] An upward shift of the elasticity of substitution reduces the upper boundary of the profitable region (β^{**} is reduced to about 0.35) but also reduces the net differences in profits for both the most productive and less productive firms, that is, the larger and smaller firms. For medium productive, medium sized firms the net difference in profits increases to the extent that more firms will adopt the technology at the beginning of the diffusion process. Hence an increase in the elasticity of substitution between varieties increases competition and the market becomes more concentrated. Fewer firms survive in the steady state. The largest and smallest firms will delay or even suspend adoption whereas medium sized firms will adopt earlier. This is depicted in Figure 4.8: e-business technologies are introduced in period 6 and more firms than before invest in it immediately. This continues to be the case for some years and after that the speed of diffusion slows down.

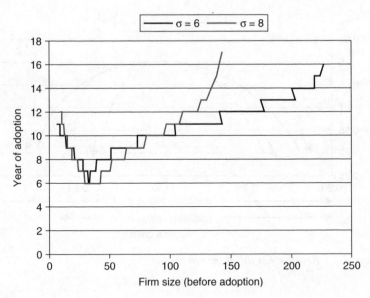

Figure 4.8   Increased competition and time of adoption

So even though network effects are stronger in the first instance (since more firms invest in the new technology), the direct gains and costs as described above remain important.

Taken together, this implies that an increase in the elasticity of substitution first of all decreases the number of active firms in the market, while larger firms, given their marginal costs structure, become bigger and smaller firms become smaller. The adoption decision is affected in two ways and includes a shift in both costs and gains. Large firms experience higher profit gains from adopting e-business practices but also face higher adjustment costs. Small firms experience decreasing adjustment costs but even more decreasing profit gains. In both cases these firms will postpone, or even cancel, adoption. For medium-sized firms the shift in gains outweighs the shift in costs, so they will adopt earlier. Comparing the diffusion processes in both cases, the number of adopters increases in the first stage but also slows down faster. In the end fewer firms will adopt the new technology, both in absolute terms and in relative terms. At first sight this may be a counter-intuitive effect since increased price competition would increase the need for new, more efficient, technologies. However, the size of firms is also affected (large firms become larger and small firms become smaller) and adjustment costs and scale effects have an impact on the decision to invest in new technologies.

4.6   CONCLUDING REMARKS

To summarize, this chapter presents the diffusion of e-business practices as an endogenous process where network externalities, firm size and changing market structures are the main determinants. The dynamics of this system imply that in the initial phase of the diffusion process, the profits of adopters increase and non-adopters face a declining market share and declining profits. This is caused by monopolistic price setting behaviour. Because of network effects the gains from adopting e-business practices increase and more firms invest in these practices, competitive pressure increases even more among both the users and the non-users and implies decreasing profits for all, except for those who adopt the new technology. Some firms do not survive this process and, depending on the elasticity of final demand, new entry will occur.

The continued diffusion of e-business practices decreases marginal costs and also decreases the aggregate price level, thereby increasing aggregate demand. In simulation examples the final rate of diffusion is below 100 per cent and in the new steady state the market returns to a situation with reshuffled profits. Reorganization costs reduce the probability that large firms will adopt new work practices, and typically medium-sized firms are the most successful in incorporating these practices, one of the observed notions. Whether large firms will eventually adopt is not determined by the theoretical model and is a matter of parameter values.

Finally, increased price competition through an increased elasticity of substitution decreases the total number of firms in the initial (pre e-business) era. Compared to a market with a lower elasticity of substitution, profits of the largest firms increase and profits of smaller firms decrease. This also reshuffles incentives to invest in e-business practices. The speed of diffusion increases in the first instance but, because of adjustment costs and changing market structures, fewer firms, both in absolute and in relative terms, eventually adopt the new technology. Increased (price) competition leads to fewer firms in the market and larger aggregate output. The spread of e-business practices is hampered, however.

From a policy point of view the model shows that further promotion of open standards is beneficial to achieve high adoption rates of e-business practices, that is, increased ICT investment and increased benefits from this investment. It also shows that small firms drop out of the market due to indivisibilities, lack of knowledge, and so on. Special programmes focused on these firms, where skills and knowledge can be shared more easily, could overcome this problem. Finally, adjustment costs of large firms are the last main driver of the diffusion process and increased flexibility of the labour market could reduce such costs and thereby foster e-business practices among firms.

NOTES

1. See www.rosettanet.org.
2. See Milgrom and Roberts (1990) for an early view, Brynjolfsson and Hitt (2000) for an overview, and Arvanitis (2004) for a more recent brief overview of the empirical literature.
3. See e.g. Helpman and Krugman (1989), Chapter 7, for a similar approach.
4. Although introducing firm-specific fixed costs (larger firms experience larger fixed costs) will lead to a different outcome in quantitative sense, it will (in general) not lead to different qualitative results. Introducing firm-specific fixed costs complicates the model results considerably, however.
5. Note that Montagna (1995) assumes that the average efficiency is equal to unity. Since we allow for new technologies, this assumption is not appropriate in our case, but it does not alter the model in a qualitative sense.
6. Note that the solution is given for $0 < \delta < 1$, $\sigma > 1$ and $\sigma \neq 2$.
7. The literature on adoption and diffusion can be divided into epidemic diffusion models, rational adoption models and strategic adoption models, see e.g. Thirtle and Ruttan (1987) and Reinganum (1989).
8. An exception is the game theoretic explanations where changing market structures take care of a changing environment such that identical firms in the absence of risk and uncertainty make different choices; see e.g. Reinganum (1989).
9. In their industry-based classification they report variety demand elasticities varying between 6 and 8 for paper & printing, chemical products, and office machinery & precision instruments and 20 and above for metalliferous products, transport, food products, and textiles, clothing & leather (Gasiorek et al., 1991, p. 15).
10. Note that values of σ between 1 and 2, as used by Montagna (1995), result in profit margins of above 100%, which seems unreasonable.
11. Some efforts have been made, especially by the UN, to come to an international standard across all sectors of industry called EDIFACT (EDI for Administration, Commerce & Transport) but not all companies have embraced this.
12. For a two-period adoption model with perfect foresight, see for instance Katz and Shapiro (1985). Two periods would be far too small to make our point in this chapter and are ruled out.
13. In this simulation, δ (the distribution parameter of marginal costs) is set to 0.8, the variety elasticity (σ) is 6, and the price elasticity of aggregate demand (η) is set to 1. The average marginal costs ($\bar{\beta}$) are equal to 1, fixed investment costs (f) are 0.5, whereas the number of potential firms (N) is 2000. The scale parameter (A) is adjusted to 5579.5 so that the number of firms in the 'profitable' interval ranging from $(1-\delta)\beta$ to β^{**} corresponds to the theoretical value, thereby allowing the density of firms within this interval to be fixed, which is needed within the simulation module. The initial gains from investing in e-business (Δ_0 in equation (4.19) are set to 0.02, α is set to 0.9999 and γ to 1.2. Finally, in the cost structure of investing in e-business, ε is set to 0.5, ε_1 to 0.05, λ to 1.8 and λ_0 to 0.05. Given these parameters, the theoretical value of N^{**} according to equation (4.10) is 250.015 in the initial steady state, which is equal to the simulation results.
14. The difference between gross and net profits is determined by the total investment costs of adopting e-business.
15. As explained, because of network effects the curve will shift upwards, so more firms experience positive gains from adopting the technology at a later stage of the diffusion process.

REFERENCES

Arvanitis, S. (2004), 'Information technology, workplace organisation, human capital and firm productivity: Evidence for the Swiss economy', in *The Economic Impact of ICT: Measurement, Evidence and Implications*, Paris: OECD, pp. 183–211.

Becchetti, L., D.A. Londono Bedoya and L. Paganetto (2003), 'ICT investment, productivity and efficiency: Evidence at firm level using a stochastic frontier approach', *Journal of Productivity Analysis*, **20**, 143–67.

Bertschek, I. and U. Kaiser (2004), 'Productivity effects of organizational change: Microeconometric evidence', *Management Science*, **50**, 394–404.

Bresnahan, T.F., E. Brynjolfsson and L.M. Hitt (2002), 'Information technology, workplace organization, and the demand for skilled labor: Firm-level evidence', *Quarterly Journal of Economics*, **117** (1), 339–76.

Borghans, L. and B. ter Weel (2004), 'The division of labour, worker organisation, and technological change', Working Paper MERIT.

Broda, C. and D.E. Weinstein (2004), 'Globalization and the gains from variety', National Bureau of Economic Research Working Papers: 10314.

Brynjolfsson, E. and L.M. Hitt (1996), 'Paradox lost? Firm-level evidence on the returns to information systems spending', *Management Science*, **17**, 541–58.

Brynjolfsson, E. and L.M. Hitt (2000), 'Beyond computation: Information technology, organizational transformation and business performance', *Journal of Economic Perspectives*, **14**, 23–48.

Clayton, T., C. Criscuolo, O. Goodridge and K. Waldron (2004), 'Enterprise e-commerce: measurement and impact', in *The Economic Impact of ICT: Measurement, Evidence and Implications*, Paris: OECD, pp. 241–60.

Gasiorek, M., A. Smith and A.J. Venables (eds) (1991), *European Integration: Trade and Industry*, London: CEPR.

Gretton, P., J. Gali and D. Parham (2004), 'The effects of ICTs and complementary innovations on Australian productivity growth', in *The Economic Impact of ICT: Measurement, Evidence and Implications*, Paris: OECD, pp. 105–30.

Helpman, E. and P.R. Krugman (1989), *Trade Policy and Market Structure*, Cambridge, MA: MIT Press.

Hollenstein, H. (2002), 'Determinants of the adoption of information and communication technologies: An empirical analysis based on firm-level data for the Swiss business sector', Working Paper, Zurich.

Hollenstein, H. (2004), 'The decision to adopt information and communication technologies: Firm-level evidence for Switzerland', in *The Economic Impact of ICT: Measurement, Evidence and Implications*, Paris: OECD, pp. 37–60.

Katz, M.L. and C. Shapiro (1985), 'Network externalities, competition, and compatibility', *American Economic Review*, **75**, 424–40.

Lucking-Reiley, D. and D.F. Spulber (2001), 'Business-to-business electronic commerce', *Journal of Economic Perspectives*, **15**, 55–68.

Maliranta, M. and P. Rouvinen (2004), 'ICT and business productivity: Finnish micro-level evidence', in *The Economic Impact of ICT: Measurement, Evidence and Implications*, Paris: OECD, pp. 213–60.

Milgrom, P. and J. Roberts (1990), 'The economics of modern manufacturing: Technology, strategy, and organization', *American Economic Review*, **80**, 511–28.

Montagna, C. (1995), 'Monopolistic competition with firm-specific costs', *Oxford Economic Papers*, **47**, 318–28.

Reinganum, J.F. (1989), 'The timing of innovation: Research, development and diffusion', in R. Schmalensee and R.D. Willig (eds), *Handbook of Industrial Organization*, Amsterdam: North-Holland, pp. 850–908.

Thirtle, C.G. and V.W. Ruttan (1987), *The Role of Demand and Supply in the Generation and Diffusion of Technical Change*, Chur: Harwood Academic Publishers.

5. Radio spectrum fees as determinants of market structure: The consequences of European 3G licensing*

Harald Gruber

5.1 INTRODUCTION

Market entry in mobile telecommunications is based on a licensing process for scarce spectrum resources. Whereas initially the assignment of licences was based on administrative procedures (e.g. 'beauty contests'), there is a trend towards market-based mechanisms such as auctions.[1] All European countries assigned radio spectrum for the provision of third generation (3G) mobile telecommunications services[2] around the years 2000–2001. The licence assignment procedures varied across countries, but the majority made recourse to auctions. Auctions were an innovative method and produced several surprising results – unexpectedly high licence fees were observed in some countries, whereas in others they were far below expectations. Some of these outcomes, especially the disappointing ones, were explained to some degree by differences and inconsistencies in auction design (Klemperer, 2002). But several points still beg an explanation, especially the high licence fees. However, the administrative procedures for licence assignments, such as a beauty contests, also produced disappointing results on several occasions. The economists' typical argument in favour of an auction revolves around the assertion that it is a market-based mechanism, and hence best to select the agent with the highest willingness to pay. That implicitly would make sure that the most efficient use is made of a scarce public resource. However, the track record emerging from 3G licensing in Europe throws some doubt on whether performance in attracting efficient firms has improved through auctions. For this purpose a close look is taken at the actions of governments and firms in the aftermath of the 3G

* The author would like to thank Bas ter Weel and an anonymous referee for helpful comments. The entire responsibility for the views expressed remains with the author and they need not necessarily reflect those of the EIB.

auctions in Europe. The first 3G auctions in Europe, in particular in the UK and Germany, led to licence fees that were far above expectation. This induced several observers and governments to benchmark the success of a licence assignment by the size of the fee.[3] The fee appeared to be determined rather by the financial resources available than by the intrinsic value of the object at stake. This means also that little concern was expressed in Europe regarding the compatibility of the fees with the envisaged market structures. This study abstracts from public finance considerations and looks at the implications of the size of licence fees for the evolution of market structure.

Mobile telecommunications technologies come in generations and with each new generation governments have the opportunity to design market structure anew by assigning new radio spectrum licences (Gruber, 2005). The observed trend suggests that governments increased competition in the market by assigning an increasing number of licences as new generations of technologies were introduced.[4] As Dana and Spier (1994) have shown in a model of auctions and endogenous market structure, the government's incentives to increase or decrease the number of firms depend on the amount of information available. Incomplete information induces a bias toward less competition relative to complete information. Given the fast technological change and the high uncertainties regarding the market prospects for mobile telecommunications, market valuations by firms and governments may diverge strongly.[5] With 3G governments wanted to continue the trend of increasing the number of firms in the mobile telecommunications industry, but at the same time they allowed for a mechanism for escalating licence fees. The main question addressed is whether the chosen market structure, as given by the number of licences to be assigned, is consistent with the licence fee raised. Suppose that industry profits fall with the number of firms in the market, there appears to be a trade-off between the number of firms and the licence fees that can be paid out from expected oligopoly rents. 'Overbidding' would then occur if a firm engages to pay a higher licence fee than the expected oligopoly profit. It is argued that overbidding may lead to a much more concentrated industry or encourage collusive market behaviour. If auctions encourage overbidding, problems of time consistency or regulatory policy may emerge, especially with respect to the regulatory commitment to enforce competition and rapid diffusion. If high licence fees should lead to higher levels of concentration and prices, a slowdown in the diffusion of new services could be the consequence, with adverse welfare effects. This line of reasoning is contrary to the traditional argument that licence fees are sunk costs and thus should not affect post-entry behaviour, but it follows recent experimental research on the sunk cost fallacy (Offerman and Potters, 2000). To illustrate the arguments, a theoretical framework is presented, focusing on the interplay between market structure and endogenously determined fixed costs.[6] The features of the model are then contrasted with the empirical evidence from the European mobile telecommunications industry. On the theoretical side, this approach complements the line of research on the design of market structure (e.g. Dana and Spier, 1994; Grimm et al., 2003). On the empirical side, this study provides a structured interpretation of the aftermath of 3G licences and an explanation of the newly emerging market structure in the industry. It thus puts a new perspective on the stylised facts indicated by the growing number of detailed empirical studies of the European 3G market.[7]

The study is arranged as follows. Section 5.2 presents the theoretical model to analyse the market structure as a function of licence fees. Section 5.3 presents background information on the mobile telecommunications industry in Europe. Section 5.4 describes the design of market structure for the 3G markets across European countries and the results of the licensing procedures. Section 5.5 makes a critical assessment of the outcomes and comments on the developments successive to the auction. Section 5.6 concludes.

5.2   THEORETICAL FRAMEWORK

5.2.1   The Model

Consider a homogeneous goods industry with Cournot competition[8] and with the following inverse demand function $p(Q) = s/Q$, where s is a parameter for market size and Q is total quantities sold at price p. Assume constant marginal costs c. It can be shown that in a Cournot equilibrium with n (where $n > 1$) identical firms (where quantity supplied by each firm is $q = Q/n$) the equilibrium price is $p = nc/(n-1)$. As typical for a Cournot model, price is above marginal cost and declining with the number of firms. The fixed entry cost F sets an upper bound on entry. At a Cournot equilibrium the profits for each firm are

$$\Pi(n, s, F) = (p - c)q - F = s/n^2 - F \qquad (5.1)$$

The Cournot equilibrium number of firms n^* is determined by the following zero entry condition:

$$\Pi(n^*, s, F) > 0 > \Pi(n^* + 1, s, F) \qquad (5.2)$$

Neglecting the integer problem, from equation (5.1) one can derive the following expression:

$$n^* = \sqrt{\frac{s}{F}} \qquad (5.3)$$

Thus one can derive relationships between the equilibrium number of firm, market size and entry costs: $dn^*/ds>0$ and $dn^*/dF<0$. The equilibrium number of firms thus increases with market size and decreases with fixed costs.

5.2.2 Regulatory Failures

Let us now relate this model to an industry such as mobile telecommunications. Using the above comparative static features, considerations can be made regarding the impact of changes in exogenous variables, such as technology or policy changes, on the equilibrium number of firms. To start with, suppose there were no spectrum constraint. As seen above, with free entry, the Cournot outcome would be n^* firms and zero profits.[9] If however entry is regulated and the number of firms set at $\tilde{n}$, then three cases are possible:

$\tilde{n}>n^*$ this case implies excessive entry and negative profits.

$\tilde{n}=n^*$ this case corresponds to the free entry outcome with zero profits.

$\tilde{n}<n^*$ in this case regulated entry is less than the free entry outcome with positive profits. These 'oligopoly rents' decrease as the number of firms increases.

To make the issue of licence fees explicit, it may be useful to redefine the fixed cost F as follows: $F=I+L$. This means that the fixed cost is split into network investment[10] costs I and licence fee L. Equation (5.3) can therefore be rewritten as

$$\hat{n}^* = \sqrt{\frac{s}{I+L}} \qquad (5.4)$$

that is, $\hat{n}^*$ defines the equilibrium number of firms when a licence fee $\hat{L}^*$ is involved. Likewise n^* defines the equilibrium number of firms when a licence fee is zero. Abstracting again from the integer problem, we have $\hat{n}^*<n^*$ for $\hat{L}^*>0$, that is, with licence fees we should have a smaller equilibrium number of firms than with zero licence fees, as licence fees are equivalent to increasing fixed entry costs; $\tilde{n}$ is fixed by the regulator and L could be decided either by the regulator or by the firm. It is important that the licence fee L is consistent with the total number of firms that are supposed to coexist in the market. According to the 'policy' variables L and $\tilde{n}$, a series of relationships between variables n^*, $\hat{n}^*$ and $\tilde{n}$

are possible. The most interesting cases of regulatory failure are as follows:

> *Case 1. Excessive entry:* $\tilde{n} > n^* > \hat{n}^*$. Here the regulator provides more licences than the equilibrium number of firms at zero licence fee. This is a case of excessive entry and thus not a stable market structure even with a zero licence fee.
> *Case 2. Excessive licence fee:* $n^* > \tilde{n} > \hat{n}^*$. In this case the licence fee has been set at such a high level that an otherwise (i.e. with zero licence fee) viable market structure becomes unstable. In this case, the competitive equilibrium would lead to $n = \hat{n}^* > \tilde{n}$.
> *Case 3. Excessive profits:* $n^* > \hat{n}^* > \tilde{n}$. In this case the licence fee is low enough that all firms can coexist with non-negative profits. In this case a licence fee has extracted only some of the oligopoly profits.

5.2.3 Endogenous Licence Fees

Assume now that firms decide on the licence fee to pay. Firms therefore play a two stage game. In the first stage they decide on the licence fee and in the second stage they compete *à la* Cournot. Licence fees thus can be considered as an endogenous sunk cost. The Nash equilibrium outcome is as above and equation (5.4) may be rewritten as

$$\hat{L}^* = s/n^2 - I \cdot \qquad (5.5)$$

where $\hat{L}^*$ is the level of licence fee that drives industry profits to zero. The iso-profit relationship between the number of firms (market structure) and licence fee is illustrated in Figure 5.1. The curve is the graph of the zero profit combinations.[11] Right from the curve industry profits are negative (due to excessive entry or excessive licence fee, i.e. cases 1 and 2) and left from the curve industry profits are positive (excessive profits, i.e. case 3). Thus for any $\tilde{n} = \hat{n}^*$ chosen by the regulator, we need $L = \hat{L}^*$ to have an equilibrium. Otherwise licence fees have post-entry effects: if $L > \hat{L}^* \geq 0$ we have excessive entry. With $L < \hat{L}^*$ we may have a stable market structure, but excessive profits may create allocational problems. Thus both cases may impair the efficient working of the market.

There are many ways of determining the size of the fee. If there is competition among firms for the licence, the size of the fee offered by an individual firm becomes a determinant for spectrum allocation. Competition for spectrum licences increases the licence fee and thus may endogenously affect market structure. In principle, a higher licence fee tends to reduce

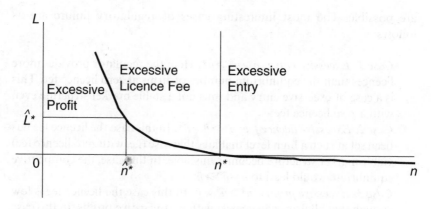

Note: The curve is the graph of the zero profit combinations of the number of firms (market structure) and licence fee. Right from the curve industry profits are negative and left from the curve industry profits are positive.

Figure 5.1   The iso-profit relationship (with zero profit)

the equilibrium number of firms in the industry. The government typically determines how many licences will be granted and thus sets exogenously the number of firms in the industry. If firms set the licence fee, the endogenously determined licence fee might become incompatible with the exogenously set market structure. If, for instance, firms are paying too high licence fees, exit of some firms may be necessary to re-establish non-negative profits. As will be seen later, among the several allocation mechanisms, auctions are most likely to produce 'excessive entry' and thus the highest probability that actually some firms may exit after having been allocated a licence. By fixing the number of licences at the outset the government sets the market structure exogenously. The traditional argument in favour of an auction is that it allocates the spectrum to the most efficient firm that should value it most. The validity of this proposition is however based on two premises. First, the government does not licence too many firm (i.e. avoids case 1). Second, firms do not collude once they have entered the market. This second point is developed in more detail in the following.

5.2.4   Post-entry Effects

Suppose that the number of licences is set at ñ, and that the zero profit condition is fulfilled with a licence fee of at most $\tilde{L}$, given the technology. If firms bid $L > \tilde{L}$, then there are negative profits in the industry, unless some exit occurs. If industry profits rise as the number of firms declines, it is easy to show that a monopoly would pay the highest licence fee, as a monopoly has the highest rents to dissipate.[12] A tension therefore emerges between the objective of extracting high licence fees from spectrum assignment and having as many as possible firms in the industry.

Any specific licensing policy for the underlying services needs to be justified. The policy maker typically wants to assign the licences to the firms that are best at diffusing the associated services in question. There are two major decisions to be taken: the number of licences to be allocated and the determination of the licence fee. If prices are driving market growth, then the effect of the number of licences essentially depends on the type of competition. If Bertrand competition were prevailing, then two firms would be enough to establish competitive prices. If Cournot competition were prevailing instead, then the price would be a decreasing function of the number of firms. If price were a determinant for market growth, this would increase with the number of firms. From this it follows that in order to have the largest number of firms in the market the licence fee should be zero.[13]

The second question relates to the post-entry effects of licence fees. Economic theory would suggest that up-front sunk cost should not interfere with post-entry competition as pricing decisions are based on marginal costs. But what if excessive licence fees were paid? Suppose, for example, that in a duopoly framework the duopoly profit is less than the licence fee paid. In that case there are two options for the firm: exit or collusion. With the exit of one firm, the remaining firm could reap monopoly profits and thus break even. If on the other hand the government can credibly precommit a duopoly structure, then firms need to collude to reap monopoly profits to repay the licence fee. High licence fees therefore could lead to higher prices than there would be without a licence fee. As such, licence fees could be seen as an inducement for collusive behaviour. Moreover, market growth would be lower.

As a result of the previous discussion, the question arises as to whether competitive auctions for licences provide incentives to establish escalating licence fees. Put in another way, can auctions for licences induce credible signalling for collusion at the post-entry stage? Consider the case of an auction for two licences. If post-entry collusion is ruled out, auctioning with firms with identical cost structures would lead to licence fees that drive profits to zero. Licence fee L would be equal to the duopoly firm's profit $\Pi(2) = L$. In other words, licence fees extract perfectly all oligopoly rents. (But we know also from the previous discussion that a Cournot duopoly firm's profit is less than half of the monopoly profit) $\Pi(1): \Pi(2) < \Pi(1)/2$. From this one can derive an excessive licence fee that would be profitable with collusion as long as it was in the range $\Pi(2) < L < \Pi(1)/2$. In other words, spectrum allocation through auctions could lead to extraction of monopoly profits with collusion, and not necessarily to the allocation of the scarce resource to the socially best use.

5.2.5 INTERNATIONAL ASPECTS

This model allows also for analysing the consequences of licence fees for international shifting of oligopoly profits. Consider two countries with different policies for assigning licences. A country that establishes a small licence fee benefits from the fact that firms have less incentive to collude. With Cournot competition, the largest possible number of licences should be granted to have low prices and highest levels of diffusion. Oligopoly rents would not go to the government, but rather be shared among consumers and producers. Prices should be low and market penetration high. In the country that chooses high licence fees, possibly determined through competitive auctions, there may be an inherent incentive for firms to collude. In that case monopoly prices would be charged. Most of the rents would go to the state via the licence fee. However, there would be high prices and therefore lower market penetration.

Differences in the licensing regimes across countries can have implications for firm performance. To illustrate this point, consider the following simple framework. Suppose there are two identical countries denominated 1 and 2. Each country has one firm, called firm 1 and firm 2 respectively, but each firm can reciprocally operate in both countries. Finally suppose that each firm has a cost advantage when operating on the domestic market compared to when operating in the other country (e.g. lower marginal costs due to information advantages). With Cournot competition, this leads to higher market shares for the domestic firm on the domestic market.

Assume now that country 2 establishes a licence fee and thus extracts some oligopoly profit. This puts firm 2 at a disadvantage because it has a larger market share in a low profit market (country 2) and a small market share in a high profit market (country 1). For firm 1 the reverse holds: it has low market share in a low profit market and a high market share in a high profit market. Hence firm 1 has higher total profits than firm 2. Not asking for licence fees could also be seen as a subsidy to firm 1, especially from country 2's perspective. Legitimate questions then arise us to whether the two firms are now forced to compete on unequal terms, whether the absence, or in any case inequality, of licence fees is distorting subsidies and whether coordination of the regulatory frameworks within countries participating in a common market is desirable.

Finally, there are also issues concerning lump sum transfers of rents. Firms active in country 2 pay a higher licence fee than in country 1 for two reasons: first, because there is an auction which drives up the licence fee;

second, because there is no licence fee in country 1, firms have more funds available to spend on a licence in country 2. Thus firms active in country 1 could employ some of the forthcoming rents from country 1 in country 2 the bid for the licence.

5.3 THE MOBILE TELECOMMUNICATIONS INDUSTRY IN EUROPE

The cellular mobile telecommunications industry became the first major laboratory of competitive supply of telecommunications services in a sector where the natural monopoly paradigm was prevailing. However in many countries this opportunity of competition was picked up only after some delay. Initially most countries viewed mobile telecommunications as just an additional new business of the state-owned telecommunications monopoly. The development of the cellular network was a means of honing the innovative capabilities of national equipment suppliers. Analogue cellular mobile telecommunications (first generation mobile technology or 1G) started during the first half of the 1980s in most European countries. In the early days of mobile telecommunications, licences were typically granted on a first-come-first-served basis, if not automatically, to the incumbent fixed line telecommunications operator. A few countries granted a second licence, which was assigned through an administrative tender procedure (or 'beauty contest').

On the occasion of the introduction of the digital technology (second generation mobile technology or 2G), based on the GSM standard, the European Commission started to actively promote a coordinated approach with more competition. Member countries were instructed to grant at least three licences for digital services. Entry in GSM was typically of the sequential type, with the 1G incumbent typically entering first. As Gruber and Verboven (2001) have shown, the heterogeneity in the timing of the licences has important implications for the diffusion path of technologies. There are generally three or four firms in each European national market[14] with a relatively stable market structure.

It is in any case fair to say that during the first generation and also at least during a large part of the second generation technology the mobile telecommunications market was in an 'excessive profits' situation. These technologies were far more successful in the market than originally expected and produced huge oligopoly rents. Table 5.1 lists the profitability of selected European mobile telecommunications firms in 1997, a period of high growth in the mobile telecommunications market, and in 2001, the year when most 3G licences were auctioned. It shows that in 1997 for some

Table 5.1   Profitability of selected European mobile telecommunications firms

Firm	Country	ROCE* (per cent)	
		1997	2001
TIM	Italy	137.1	15.8
Telecel	Portugal	65.5	28.0
Mannesmann	Germany	41.9	n.a.
Sonera	Finland	18.4	7.8
Comviq	Sweden	17.9	n.a.
Netcom	Norway	14.2	10.0

Notes:
* ROCE = return on capital employed; n.a. = not available

Source: Warburg Dillon Reed (1998) and firm accounts.

firms, such as TIM, profitability in terms of returns on capital employed (ROCE) could be even above 100 per cent. Other firms such as Telecel, Mannesmann and Sonera have a ROCE that is still several multiples of typical industry average of around 15 per cent. This profitability however declined rapidly in the following years, mainly as a result of enhanced competition in the market and also expenses for acquisitions and licences. For instance, for TIM the ROCE has fallen to 15.8 per cent by 2001. Likewise Telecel and Sonera saw a sharp drop in profitability. For some firms in Table 5.1, such as Mannesmann and Comviq it was difficult to find comparable data because they became involved in mergers and acquisitions, and hence only consolidated data are available. International comparisons of profitability are however always difficult because of differing accounting standards across countries. But the general pattern of decline in profitability over these years is also confirmed by the very detailed industry data from the UK regulatory authority. Table 5.2 shows some profitability indicators for the four firms in the UK mobile telecommunications market as calculated by the regulator Oftel (2002). The ROCE suggests a large difference in the level of profitability. Moreover, all firms with the exception of Orange display a decline in profitability over time. Oftel has calculated an average cost of capital of 15 per cent for mobile firms. All firms other than Vodafone had profits falling below this level from 1999 onwards, which means that only Vodafone had remained profitable. The lack of profitability of One2One (later called O_2) and Orange is also to a large part explained by their later entry compared to Vodafone and Cellnet

Table 5.2   Profitability indicators of mobile telecommunications firms in the UK

	1997	1998	1999	2000	2001
ROCE					
Vodafone	92	76	53	50	45
BT Cellnet	20	12	8	c.	n.a.
One2One	−18	−5	−23	c.	n.a.
Orange	5	5	10	n.a.	n.a.
EBITDA margins					
Vodafone	43	37	27	28	21
BT Cellnet	20	11	5	8	7
One2One	−23	−7	−20	−13	n.a.
Orange	−8	5	4	7	10
Revenue per calling minute (in pence)					
Vodafone	55.0	44.0	31.9	24.2	19.5
BT Cellnet	58.8	45.4	36.3	23.8	16.4
One2One	7.8	10.5	11.2	11.7	12.7
Orange	36.2	32.6	25.7	18.0	14.0

Notes:
ROCE = return on capital employed, in per cent
EBITDA margin= Earnings before interest, taxes, depreciation and amortisation, as percentage of total revenues
c. = confidential
n.a. = not available

Source: Oftel (2002).

BT (later called T-Mobile). Orange is nevertheless moving against this trend, displaying an increase in profitability. This differentiated picture observed for ROCE is also reflected by the EBITDA margin (i.e. earnings before interest, taxes, depreciation and amortisation, as percentage of total revenues), which may also be seen as a proxy for operating efficiency. Vodafone has by far the highest margin. Of the late entrants, Orange can be seen as improving its margin, exceeding that even of BT Cellnet. Finally Table 5.2 lists also the revenue per calling minute as an indicator of profitability. Again here we have a large difference across firms, with Vodafone the highest prices and One2One the lowest, and a general pattern of decline.

Regulatory activity in the mobile telecommunications industry is less than in the fixed line telecommunications industry, as the sector is considered as being liberalised and competitive. Thus regulatory action in most cases is limited to market segments where there is scope for abuse of market power, such as interconnection. Firms with 'significant market power', that is, with market shares typically in excess of 25 per cent, are subject to separate accounting in order to establish cost-based pricing in interconnection.[15] There is the presumption that regulatory action or entry would drive profitability towards the average level of the economy. As already shown for the UK, there is evidence that later entrants in the market have much lower rates of return.[16] There was even a case of exit in Italy, where in 2002 the smallest and latest (fourth) entrant, Blu, left the market.[17] It has also to be said that in most of the European countries licence fee were either zero or relatively modest, especially when compared to what would be paid for 3G licences.[18] The struggle for survival of fourth entrants in some countries would suggest that a three or four firm market structure has come close to the zero profit entry condition in the industry. Thus more than four firms is likely to constitute 'excessive entry' in the 2G market.

A widely followed business growth strategy for external growth was internationalisation through acquisition of existing firms and bidding for new licences.[19] The best example for this is the astonishing growth of Vodafone, which developed from a UK firm to the largest internationalised mobile telecommunications firm worldwide. But there are also other examples of this kind, such as Orange and T-Mobile. Most of the firms adopting this expansion strategy have experienced rapid deterioration of their profitability and credit rating. Investor sentiment about those firms shifted from optimism to deep pessimism, creating substantial financial difficulties for many firms, which compounded the burden deriving from financing the acquisition of 3G licences subsequently to the bust of the financial bubble in 2000.

Also technical difficulties hampered the introduction of 3G technology, as it concerns after all the establishment of a new technology on a very large scale. Whereas the first and second generation of mobile telecommunications systems were mainly designed for voice transmission, the next technological step is the development of systems for data transmission. 3G systems substantially increase data transmission rates and also allow moving images to be sent. These services will be provided with one of the five competing internationally defined technology standards. The member states of the European Union committed themselves to introducing 3G under the heading of Universal Mobile Telecommunications System (UMTS), a concept developed by the European Telecommunications Standard Institute (ETSI). The European interest was in making UMTS backward compatible with the existing GSM installed base.[20] The first adoptions of third generation systems were expected to occur in 2002 in Europe and Japan. In Japan it happened earlier, though with slower than expected adoption of 3G services by the users. In Europe launch dates, officially set for January 2002, were delayed by more than a year. The first commercial launch was undertaken by subsidiaries of the multinational firm Hutchinson, under the label 3, in Italy and UK during the second quarter of 2003 (ITU, 2003). Equipment problems, especially the limited availability of 3G handsets, were one of the main reasons for delays in introducing 3G services. Moreover, the incumbent firms in the market were not particularly keen on promoting 3G services, as they had invested in upgrading their 2G networks to deliver several services, such as multi-media messaging, that 3G is supposed to provide. Thus only the new entrant '3' had a genuine interest in advancing quickly on the diffusion of 3G services.

Other countries, such as the USA are delaying the development of third generation systems, also because of the slow development of the second generation systems which have been introduced late and are using a range of different, non-compatible technologies (ITU, 1999). On one hand, competition among different 2G systems slowed down diffusion compared to a market with an established technology standard (Gruber and Verboven, 2001). On the other hand, competition among 2G systems provided the opportunity for establishing CDMA[21] as one of the mobile telecommunications systems in the US market already during the 2G era. Because 3G technologies are based on the working principle of CDMA, firms having a CDMA system for 2G services do not need to acquire additional radio spectrum as 3G services can be provided by simply upgrading the current system. A standard may therefore be helpful in quickly diffusing a given technology, but it may delay the emergence of a new, superior technology.[22]

5.4   THE DESIGN OF MARKET STRUCTURE FOR 3G MARKETS IN EUROPE

The entry pattern for the 3G market had a completely different design from previous technology generations. With 1G and 2G markets the evolution of the market structure emerged from a sequential licensing of new entrants, typically starting either with a monopoly (for most 1G services) or with a duopoly (for 2G services). For the 3G service industry the design of the market structure entailed simultaneous entry of a relatively large (4–6 firms) number of firms. Apparently little attention was devoted to the zero profit entry condition in the design of market structure. The $n+1$ rule of thumb (with n being the number of incumbent 2G firms) was typically applied for determining the number of 3G licences. This rule of thumb had a twofold purpose: to create more competition at the pre-entry as well as at the post-entry stage. At the pre-entry stage, new entry would be encouraged to join the competition for the market; at the post-entry stage, new entry should increase competition in the market. In this game the incumbents were presumed to have a strategic advantage. Without increasing the number of licences, pre-entry competition for a licence would have been weak. Thus the additional licence would have given the new entrants incentives to bid for a licence. This would also help to improve the terms on which governments assign a licence, in particular it would increase licence receipts when combined with an auction process. For the post-entry stage it was expected that additional entry would increase competition, leading to lower prices and better service. However, there was little testing on whether the market would accommodate $n + 1$ firms in a competitive setting.

Concerning the allocation method, one half of the EU countries opted for a market-based mechanism such as auctions and the other half has opted for a beauty contest. Italy adopted a hybrid approach, using a beauty contest first, followed by an auction (see Table 5.3). In general the multiple round ascending auction was chosen, with the exception of Denmark, which opted for a sealed bid auction.[23] There was substantial variety in the outcomes across countries, only in part explained by the different assignment method used. The most striking differences can be observed within the group of countries that organised auctions. Figure 5.2 shows the evolution over time of the auction receipts across the different countries. It shows a pattern of decline over time. There is a growing literature trying to rationalise these results, with explanations relying on arguments of bad auction design, collusion and political interference (see Klemperer 2000, 2002, and Cramton, 2002). There is however the indisputable fact that auctions have, on a per capita basis, yielded much more than beauty contests, as can be seen from Table 5.3. This lists the countries in the order of per capita licence fees. The UK and Germany, with a licence fee per head in excess of €600, are far above other countries. But auctions are not a guarantee of high fees. In the cases of Greece and Belgium, the results were considered as disappointing. The licence fee was low in those countries because there were fewer bidders than licences, even lower than in the beauty contest in Ireland. As expected, beauty contests were much more prone to political interference. For instance in countries like Spain and France the licence fee was repeatedly modified following the successes and failures of auctions in other countries. The French government raised the licence fee proposed by the regulator by a factor of three, only then to cut it to one ninth of this after the poor success in attracting bidders.

In the cases where firms were allowed to shape market structure themselves the results were particularly surprising. Germany and Austria auctioned frequency blocks instead of single licences, which to a certain degree

Table 5.3   The 3G licence assignment in the European Union

Country	Incumbent firms	3G licences planned	3G licences granted	3G licences not assigned	Assignment method**	Licence fee/ population (euro)
UK	4	5	5	0	A	634
Germany	4	4–6	6	0	A	615
Italy	4	5	5	0	BC+A	212
Netherlands	5	5	5	0	A	186
Austria	4	4–6	6	0	A	101
Denmark	4	4	4	0	A	96
Ireland	3	4	3	1	BC	92
Greece	3	4	3	1	A	45
Belgium	3	4	3	1	A	44
Portugal	3	4	4	0	BC	40
France	3	4	3	1	BC	21
Spain	3	4	4	0	BC	13
Finland	3	4	4	0	BC	0
Sweden	3	4	4	0	BC	0
Luxembourg	2	4	3	1	BC	0

Notes:
* Initially only two licences were assigned, a third was awarded to the third incumbent during a second tendering in 2002.
** A = Auction; BC = Beauty contest

Source: European Commission (2002a).

allowed market structure to be determined endogenously during the auction. By using frequency blocks any market structure up to the maximum of six firms becomes possible, allowing market structure to become an outcome of the licence process itself. In both cases the least concentrated market structure emerged.

Views on the 3G market structure vary widely. Looking at all countries, the number of 3G firms ranges from three to six (see column 5 in Table 5.2). In four countries (i.e. the Netherlands, Denmark, Greece and Sweden) the regulator did not contemplate an increase in the number of licences, which means that in those countries an increase in the number of mobile telecommunications firms would only occur if at least one of the incumbents do not receive a 3G licence. It turned out that in all cases, except Greece, one incumbent did not receive a licence. What is also striking is that in three cases of administrative procedures (France, Ireland and Luxembourg), the number of licences eventually granted was smaller than the planned

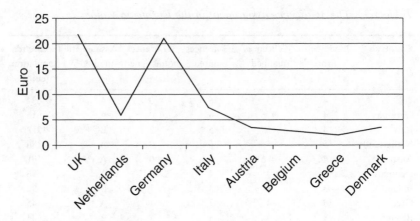

Source: European Commission (2002a).

*Figure 5.2   Licence fees in 3G auctions in chronological order
                (€/head/5 MHz)*

number.[24] With auctions instead, the maximum number of licences granted
was always achieved, both when the number was fixed or when endogenously determined (Germany, Austria).

A substantial part of the critique of European 3G licensing concerned
the sequential assignment process across European countries. Sequential
licensing may have strong implications for bidding behaviour in auctions
and is not yet fully understood from a theoretical point of view. However,
theory predicts that winning bids in sequential auctions should have a
declining price profile because of reduction of risk and learning effects.
This would be in line with the empirical observation as shown in Figure 5.2.
An example of decreasing prices in multiple objects in sequential auctioning is the 'afternoon effect' (McAfee and Vincent, 1993), which can be
explained by the willingness of risk adverse bidders to pay a risk premium
at an early stage. In that case simultaneous auctioning would be more
efficient than sequential auctioning. The high licence fees derived from the
(early) auctions in the UK and Germany had apparently left countries with
later assignment dates in an unfavourable position. Several bidders, typically the local subsidiaries of multinational firms, were facing increasingly
difficult access to finance and thus had to revise their bidding strategies, in
particular towards demand reduction. Late coming countries found it
increasingly difficult to attract bidders for 3G licences as the licence process
unfolded. Thus it appears that firms' bidding strategies were a function of
the financial resources available rather than the intrinsic value of the licence

at stake. The drying up of financial resources also had implications for countries that did not organise auctions, but set minimum fees for beauty contests. For instance the beauty contest in France had to be deferred because only two firms were interested in the beauty contest for the four licences, which however came with a relatively high minimum licence fee. This high fee reduced the demand for licences to below the number of licences on offer. To attract further firms in a second round of bidding, the government had to lower the minimum fee. This price reduction was retroactively granted also to the two firms that had already received the licence with the higher fee.

5.5   THE AFTERMATH OF 3G LICENSING

The 3G auctions delivered mixed results. Taking licence fees as a parameter of success, some auctions were very successful but others were complete failures (Cramton, 2002; Klemperer, 2002). Even for apparently well-designed auctions, there is evidence that bidders' actions were not always consistent with rational decision making (Börgers and Dustmann, 2002). Moreover, the view has spread that 'successful' auctions were delivering licence fees that were far too high for the revenues expected to be generated by 3G services.[25] The observed renegotiations of licence conditions from licence assignments achieved by beauty contests suggest weaknesses in this assignment method (as well as of governments) too.[26] But what became more worrying was the perception by some firms that they may have been subject to the 'winner's curse', that is, to have paid too much for the licences.[27] Financial concerns did not only arise from the burst of the speculative bubble in the financial markets, but also from the sobering thought that the whole market potential for 3G services could be much lower than expected, whereas both investment and operating costs could be much higher. Gruber and Hoenicke (2000) elaborate on the question of whether the speed of adoption proposed and the size of required investments are warranted by a sufficiently high level of demand. In a simulation exercise they showed that revenues from new data services have to increase by a very large proportion to make 3G services profitable. It is unclear which type of 3G applications requiring large data transmission should generate those revenues; moreover, firms are exposed to a high risk of introducing the new technology too early. Detailed technical surveys suggest that the investment required for a 3G network infrastructure is much higher than it was in comparison to a 2G infrastructure, and operating costs are likely to be higher as well (European Commission, 2002a). If this were so, then a less concentrated market structure than with 2G services may not be supported in the

3G market and exit would be necessary.[28] Thus the $n + 1$ rule, the prerequisite for multiple round ascending auctions to work, may have turned out not to be appropriate.

This suggests that several European countries are in a situation of 'excessive entry', and the competitive market equilibrium should therefore be restored through exit. In principle, there are alternatives to exit, such as, for instance, collusion, or cost reduction through measures such as softening the terms of licensing conditions (e.g. softer conditions for licence fee payments and network investment), or sharing costs. However these ex post changes in the licence terms could only be accommodated to a very limited extent as otherwise the licences granted by the regulators could be legally challenged by firms that did not win licences or did not apply in the first place. The reputation and credibility of governments is thus at stake. Ultimately high licence fees may undermine the time consistency of regulatory policies.

A number of events happening after 3G licensing[29] showed how difficult it may become for governments to enforce the terms on which the licences were assigned. One can observe a general trend towards delaying the build-out of networks and the supply of 3G services, with the main purported reasons being technical difficulties and non-availability of equipment, in particular handsets. Moreover, increasing scepticism has arisen about the market potential of 3G services. Several firms that received a licence have decided to postpone the building of the network infrastructure, thereby not respecting the regulatory commitments. This means that they risk losing the licence when the regulator checks on the implementation of the licence conditions.[30] Other firms decided even to hand back their licence to the regulator, forgoing the licence fee paid (such as in Norway).[31] With the justification of reducing costs, several firms have also started to build networks on a shared basis with their competitors; for instance, the German Chancellor called on operators to cooperate in building out the networks.[32] National regulators are observing such schemes with close interest and also with apprehension. The European Commission (2001) has expressed concerns about network sharing, as this may be a potential means for collusion. However most national regulators encouraged network sharing, in particular when it was deemed to accelerate the pace of introduction of 3G services. In several countries the terms of the licence obligations were eased.[33] Moreover, regulators signalled flexibility in interpreting the licence obligations, in particular on the timing of start of service and the extent of 3G network coverage.

These adverse market developments also precipitated situations that were initially not considered; for instance, the scenario of what would happen if a firm did not want to exercise the rights entailed by the licence.

Can such a licence be entirely sold to another new entrant or can only the spectrum be sold. In the first case market structure would be maintained, but in the second case we would have a higher level of concentration with an increase in the inequality of the spectrum distribution. In some countries firms have already made official statements that they would forgo the licence. In Germany for instance the firms Mobilkom and Quam decided to abandon the building of a 3G infrastructure. Mobilkom sold the 3G network infrastructure it had already in place to existing 3G firms, but it was unable to sell the licence because of lack of interest. There was no firm interested in acquiring the licence because of its attached network build-out obligations. At the same time existing 3G licence holders were not entitled to buy the spectrum. In 2003 the firm thus decided to return the licence to the regulator, forgoing the upfront licence fee of €8.4 billion with little hope of receiving any compensation. Thus in Germany two firms have already exited the 3G market. Also in many other countries, such as Italy, Austria, Sweden and Portugal there have been announcements by firms, typically the new entrants, that they would not build the 3G network infrastructure. In Spain, the spectrum can be traded, and in principle the whole licence can be sold to another firm. The new entrant, Xfera, decided to sell part of the spectrum that it had been assigned to one of the other 3G firms. Thus adjustments to the market structure as designed by governments are widespread.

A further not yet fully resolved issue emerges from the reuse of licences that have been returned. The first case of this kind was presented in Norway, where two firms out of four handed back the licence. When the government auctioned the two licences again in September 2003, only one bidder expressed interest. A licence was eventually awarded to the firm '3' at a significantly lower price than at the previous auction. However, the existing licence holders were compensated by a softening in network build-out obligations.

Reported anecdotal evidence provides support for the excessive entry hypothesis in several countries. High licence fees exacerbated this situation, as for instance in Germany and Austria. By auctioning frequency blocks, these countries chose a mechanism of determining market structure endogenously. The outcome was that six firms were awarded a licence, the maximum number of firms. Moreover, for Germany the least concentrated market structure was combined with exceptionally high licence fees.

There is a broad consensus among economists about the advantage of auctions as a means of allocating scarce public resources. However auctions may lead to surprising outcomes, also because some underlying behavioural assumptions may be violated in practice. For instance, in-depth studies on the consistency of the bidding behaviour in Germany and the UK[34] cast doubt on the assumption of rationality of firm behaviour. Hence the postulate of the auction process as a more efficient allocation mechanism of a scarce resource may require qualification.

5.6 CONCLUSIONS

This study has analysed the relationship between radio spectrum licence fees' consequences and market structure in the mobile telecommunications industry. A theoretical framework illustrated the regulatory trade-off in designing market structure for 'natural oligopolies' and the scope for extracting oligopoly rents through licence fees. The number of firms a competitive market is able to support decreases as the licence fee increases. The market structure as designed by the regulator may be overridden by firm behaviour, in particular when entry costs can be determined endogenously. It has been shown how firms might have an incentive to 'overbid' for licences because they could induce more relaxed competition in the post-entry stage.

The empirical relevance of this result was illustrated with reference to the assignment of third generation mobile telecommunications licences in the European Union and by contrasting the outcomes derived from beauty contests and auctions. The auction receipts varied hugely across countries. In some countries they were far above expectations. They are also likely to be incompatible with economically viable operations in the industry. The already observed exit of new entrants from the 3G market supports the hypothesis of excessive entry. Likewise, there are increasing calls for leniency in antitrust enforcement, softening of regulatory obligations and outright calls for subsidies. All this suggests that in several cases the design of the market structure prior to the assignment of the licences was inadequate. The widely adopted $n + 1$ rule for 3G licences, while effective in creating competition for entry, seems not to lead to a viable competitive market structure in the 3G market. This problem of excessive entry is exacerbated when market structure is determined endogenously. The cases of Austria and Germany show that the auctions led to the least concentrated market structures.

Auctions have traditionally been justified as an efficient means of putting an economic value on a scarce resource and of allocating it to the firm that uses it most efficiently. While auctions introduced more efficient allocation of the spectrum in the USA, also because they relieved the Federal Communications Commission from what was considered the overly high administrative burden of assigning the very large number of licences, in light of the European experience a more qualified judgement may be necessary. Many governments stated that the policy objective for assigning a licence is to introduce new mobile telecommunications services at low prices. According to the model presented, this would be achieved by allowing the highest number of firms to enter the market. Asking for licence fees however would reduce the number of firms the market could support in a competitive equilibrium, thus increasing prices and hence reducing the speed of diffusion. Therefore gauging the success of the licence assignment procedure by the revenues raised may be misleading. It has been shown that auctions may induce excessive entry compared to the fee paid. This could then impair the government's ability to enforce the terms of the licences. Licence fees therefore could prove counterproductive in promoting quick diffusion of a new technology, either because of a more concentrated industry or because of the incentives for collusion.

The lesson to be drawn for the design of market structure is that the choice of the licence allocation mechanism has crucial importance for the post-entry performance. The issue can be put boldly as the regulator having to determine whether there should be competition *for* the market or competition *in* the market. This may also require a rethink of the recourse to 'market-based' allocation mechanisms for public goods. Finally, in light of the observed exit of firms one may also conclude that spectrum is not any more a scarce economic resource for the provision of mobile telecommunications services. This point provides scope for stimulating further research on these issues.

NOTES

1. An extensive economic literature has developed on these issues. For surveys see McMillan (1994) and Cramton (2002). In the USA auctions were initially introduced to simplify the huge administrative task of the Federal Communications Commission in assigning several hundred licences. Over time however the revenue-raising aspects with auctions became predominant in the discussion.
2. 3G mobile telecommunications services refer to enhanced mobile telecommunication services such as video telephony or internet access that become feasible thanks to the higher transmission speed of the network. For more details see Gruber and Hoenicke (1999).
3. See for instance Binmore and Klemperer (2002). The total spectrum fees for 3G frequencies as collected by governments over the years 2000–2001 exceeded 100 billion euros (European Commission, 2002a). In comparison, the spectrum auctions organised in the United States over the years 1994–2001 yielded some 40 billion dollars (Cramton, 2002).
4. Previous empirical studies (Gruber and Verboven, 2000, 2001) have looked at the determinants of the diffusion of mobile telecommunications services, finding that increasing the number of firms is typically conducive to a faster diffusion of mobile telecommunications services.
5. As will be seen later, for GSM services both firms and governments initially made cautious market growth assumptions, but actual growth vastly exceeded initial expectations.

For UMTS instead, the high licence fees could discount the expectation of very rapid market growth, with firms being far more optimistic than governments.

6. This approach has similarities with the endogenous sunk cost literature. For instance, in Sutton (1991, 1998) sunk costs refer to, respectively, advertising expenditure and research and development (R&D) costs.

7. See, for instance, European Commission (2002a) and Curwen (2002).

8. As will be seen later, the Cournot competition assumption is supported by empirical evidence for the mobile telecommunications industry.

9. Let us abstract here from the integer problem.

10. The network investment costs cover a wide range of costs, including also those related to uncertainties in technological development, such as delays in the availability of suitable equipment. A further analysis of this is not within the scope of this study, but the qualitative effects on changes of the costs on equilibrium outcomes are comparable to changes in licence fees. Hence greater uncertainty about technological development compounds the effects deriving from an increase in the licence fee.

11. This curve would of course shift with changes in the key variables. For instance, an increase in I, which could be due to higher infrastructure costs following increased technological uncertainty, would shift the curve to the left. Likewise a reduction in infrastructure cost, which could be due to infrastructure sharing among firms, would shift the curve to the right.

12. As argued by Grimm et al. (2003), if a bidder could get all the spectrum, the winner of the auction would monopolise the market.

13. Empirical studies show that Cournot competition is a better description of what is actually happening in the mobile telecommunications industry (Parker and Röller, 1997). Moreover, Gruber and Verboven (2000, 2001) found evidence that the speed of diffusion of mobile telecommunications increases with the number of firms.

14. The exceptions are the Netherlands with five firms and Luxembourg with two firms (see also Table 5.3).

15. This was the case with the regulation in place in the European Union until 2003. With the new regulatory framework these requirements have been further relaxed, with the aim of bringing telecommunications regulation closer to competition law.

16. For instance, Oftel (2002) shows for the UK industry that the early entrants BT-Cellnet and Vodafone have a big competitive advantage because they can operate a less expensive GSM network at the 900 MHz frequency range compared to the later entrants One2One and Orange, which have to operate a more expensive GSM network at the 1800 Mhz frequency range.

17. The spectrum was sold on equal terms to the three remaining firms.

18. Total licence fees collected in the EU for 2G licences amounted to €10 billion, whereas for 3G licences it was, as already mentioned, in excess of €100 billion (European Commission, 2002a). On the licence fees paid for 2G spectrum see Gruber (1999).

19. For an extensive account of diversification strategies see Whalley and Curwen (2003).

20. European policy makers were very keen on introducing early third generation systems, also for reasons of industrial policy (European Commission, 2001). Early adoption of UMTS is seen as key for preserving the worldwide lead in mobile telecommunications technologies established with GSM (see European Commission, 1997). Thus member states of the EU were instructed to provide 3G licences in order for the first 3G technology-based services to become available by 2002. For the expected evolution of 3G mobile telecommunications see Gruber and Hoenicke (1999, 2000).

21. This stands for Code Division Multiple Access.

22. On this trade-off between standard setting and competition among systems see also Shapiro and Varian (1999).

23. A sealed bid auction is a more efficient design when the number of licences to auction is equal to the number of incumbents. The Netherlands did not stick to this, using a multiple round ascending auction for five licences with five incumbents. The result was a short auction with fees falling far below the government's expectations.

24. Notice that in Luxembourg this happened with a zero licence fee.

25. The European Commission (2002a) indicates some countries where this could be the case. The study also mentioned that some network build-out proposals presented even in beauty contests with zero licence fees may also be too ambitious to be supported by the market.
26. The European Commission (2002b) has criticised the non-coordinated licence allocation mechanisms adopted across the EU. However, the Commission could not do very much about this as licensing is the prerogative of member states and the only aspects it could enforce were transparency of the process and non-discrimination.
27. Some firms, such as Telefonica and KPN have in fact fully written off the 3G licence fee, setting the accounting value of the licence equal to zero.
28. The study for the European Commission (2002a) reports also findings from a simulation exercise that the market structures in Germany, the Netherlands, Sweden and the UK are unlikely to be able to support all firms.
29. Such events are regularly reported in the trade press and on specialised websites such as www.totaltele.com
30. The 3G subsidiaries of the Spanish firm Telefonica did so in Germany, Austria and Italy, where they were all new entrants.
31. In September 2003 Norway awarded this licence, after a second beauty contest, to Hutchinson, at zero licence fee. For the second licence that became available no firms expressed interest.
32. See the German newspaper *Frankfurter Allgemeine Zeitung* of 14 March 2002.
33. For instance, in Italy and Sweden the lengths of the licences were renegotiated, extending the licence period from 15 to 20 years.
34. See Grimm et al. (2001) and Börgers and Dustmann (2002).

REFERENCES

Binmore, K. and P. Klemperer (2002), 'The biggest auction ever: The sale of the British 3G licences', *Economic Journal*, **112**, 74–96.
Börgers, T. and C. Dustmann (2002), 'Rationalising the UMTS spectrum bids: The case of the UK auction', mimeo, University College London, January 2002.
Cramton, P. (2002), 'Spectrum auctions', in M. Cave, S.K. Majumdar and I. Vogelsang (eds), *Handbook of Telecommunications Economics*,. Vol. 1, Amsterdam: North Holland.
Curwen, P. (2002), *The Future of Mobile Communications: Awaiting the Third Generation*, Basingstoke: Palgrave.
Dana, J.D. and K.E. Spier (1994), 'Designing a private industry. Government auctions with endogenous market structure', *Journal of Public Economics*, **53**, 127–47.
European Commission (1997), 'On the further development of mobile and wireless communications', *COM(97) 217 final*, Brussels.
European Commission (2001), 'The introduction of 3G mobile communications in the EU – State of play and the way forward', *COM(2001) 141 final*, Brussels.
European Commission (2002a), *Comparative Assessment of the Licensing Regimes for 3G Mobile Communications in the European Union and their Impact on the Mobile Communications Sector*, Final Report, 25 June 2002, Brussels.
European Commission (2002b), 'Towards the full roll-out of third generation mobile communications', *COM (2002) 301 final*, Brussels.
Grimm, V., F. Riedel and E. Wolfstetter (2001), 'The third generation (UMTS) spectrum auction in Germany', CESifo Working Paper No. 584.

Grimm, V., F. Riedel and E. Wolfstetter (2003), 'Implementing efficient market structure. Optimal licensing in natural oligopoly when tax revenue matters', *Review of Economic Design*, **7**, 443–63.

Gruber, H. (1999), 'An investment view of mobile telecommunications in the European Union', *Telecommunications Policy*, **23**, 521–38.

Gruber, H. (2005), *The Economics of Mobile Telecommunications*, Cambridge: Cambridge University Press..

Gruber, H. and M. Hoenicke (1999), 'The road ahead towards third generation mobile telecommunications', *Info*, **1**, 253–63.

Gruber, H. and M. Hoenicke (2000), 'Third generations mobile: What are the challenges ahead?', *Communications and Strategies*, **38**, 159–73.

Gruber, H. and F. Verboven (2000), 'The diffusion of mobile telecommunications services in the European Union', *European Economic Review*, **45**, 577–88.

Gruber, H. and F. Verboven (2001), 'The evolution of markets under entry and standards regulation– the case of global mobile telecommunications', *International Journal of Industrial Organisation*, **19**, 1189–212.

ITU (1999), *World Telecommunication Development Report 1999*, Mobile Cellular International Telecommunications Union, Geneva.

ITU (2003), 'The evolution to 3G mobile. Status report', *ITU News Magazine*, International Telecommunications Union, Geneva.

Klemperer, P. (2000) 'What really matters in auction design', *Journal of Economic Perspectives*, **16**, 169–90.

Klemperer, P. (2002), 'How (not) to run auctions: the European 3G telecom auctions', *European Economic Review*, **46**, 829–45.

McAfee, P. and D. Vincent (1993), 'The declining price anomaly', *Journal of Economic Theory*, **60**, 191–212.

McMillan, J. (1994), 'Selling spectrum rights', *Journal of Economic Perspectives*, **8**, 145–62.

Offerman, T. and J. Potters (2000), 'Does auctioning of entry licences affect consumers prices? An experimental study', Center Working Paper no. 53, Tilburg University.

Oftel (2002), 'Vodafone, O₂, Orange and T-Mobile', *Office of Telecommunications*, December 2002, London.

Parker, P.M. and L.-H. Röller (1997) 'Collusive conduct in duopolies: Multimarket contact and cross-ownership in the mobile telephone industry', *RAND Journal of Economics*, **28**, 304–22.

Shapiro, C. and H.R. Varian (1999), *Information Rules. A Strategic Guide to the Network Economy*, Boston, MA: Harvard Business School Press.

Sutton J. (1991), *Sunk Cost and Market Structure*, Cambridge, MA: MIT Press.

Sutton, J. (1998), '*Technology and Market Structure. Theory and History*, Cambridge, MA: MIT Press.

Warburg Dillon Reed (1998), *The European Cellular Growth Analyser*, July 1998, London.

Whalley, J. and P. Curwen (2003), 'Licence acquisition strategy in the European mobile communications industry', *Info*, **5**, 45–59.

6. Does the new economy need all the old IPR institutions and still more?*

Paul A. David

6.1 INTRODUCTION

My question in this chapter's title signals the deliberately provocative line of argument developed in the following pages. To many writers in the business press, academic economists, lawyers and policy makers, the centrality of information technologies and information goods in the phenomena that are associated with the New Economy has suggested that the world has now entered the epoch of 'Intellectual Capitalism'. Accordingly, it is claimed that the inherited regime of intellectual property rights (IPR) institutions must be protected from the disruptive effects of the rapid advance of digital information technologies and computer-mediated telecommunications, further strengthened, and harmonized globally.

Yet, much of the justification for that view, and hence for the sanguine and in some quarters enthusiastic view of recent trends in the elaboration and extension of IPR protections, rests on little evidence and inadequately careful economic analysis. There are respects in which the new technological setting is increasing the seriousness of the drawbacks of using legal monopolies to solve the problems that the 'public goods' features of information pose for competitive markets. But the latter problems, although long familiar to economists, are beginning to look increasingly tractable without recourse to IPR protection.

A case therefore can be made that the developed and developing economies have a common interest in halting, and, indeed, reversing the encroachments on the public knowledge commons that have resulted from the excessively enthusiastic application of copyright and copyright-like protections. That interest lies not only in reducing the impediment that the

* An early version of this chapter was presented at the Conference on 'The New Economy in Development', held at the UN University – WIDER, in Helsinki, Finland on 10–11 May 2001. I am grateful to the conference organizers, and hope that the exposition of my views in the subsequent drafts has been improved by my effort to respond to the questions and comments that were forthcoming from the conference participants on that occasion.

enforcement of recent IPR provisions poses to global scientific collaborations, but also in protecting opportunities for future commercial exploitation of emerging peer-to-peer networking technologies.

6.2   ICT AND 'WEIGHTLESS' GOODS AND SERVICES IN THE NEW ECONOMY

The twentieth century witnessed a transition to 'knowledge-driven' productivity gains and economic growth in the industrially advanced economies, a process that spread within a widening circle among the latecomers to industrialization. All economic activity is, and always has been, knowledge-based, in the sense that the state of the art in production, the conventions of commerce, and the norms of consumption all entail possession of information and cognitive skills. In the knowledge-driven economy, by contrast, the continuous search for new, reliable knowledge and the generation and absorbing of new information are centrally responsible for structural change and material progress. Consequently, the focus of attention in the search for improved efficiency has moved from perfecting the management of routine to sustaining the capacity for problem identification and solution. Accordingly, an increasing share of society's domestic resources has come to be devoted to activities of the latter sort, in the course of which heterogeneous intangible knowledge assets are formed and recombined to generate further knowledge assets. Recent decades have seen a significant acceleration in the pace of this historical transition. This developmental surge has been quite evidently associated with the dramatic advances in ICT, especially with the progress of digital computing and its convergence with telecommunications. The cluster of innovations – very large integrated circuits on silicon wafter, digital switches, electro-optical networks, and computer operating systems and applications – that has made possible the phenomenon of the Internet, can be conceptualized as having provided a new and potent general-purpose technology (GPT). This is a tool set that may be utilized in many ways; combining with, transforming, and thereby enhancing the productivity and profitability of other, pre-existing technologies and organizational modes, the digital GPT cluster is not displacing 'the old economy' but instead manifesting its potential for 'renewal'.

   A central feature common to the multiplicity of diverse processes of economic renewal that presently are underway is their intensified dependence on the generation, capture, processing, transmission, storage and retrieval of information. The spectacularly declining costs of performing those activities promote this intensification, and induce the search for still newer uses toward which the accumulating bodies of information can be put in order to form the capabilities that we refer to as 'knowledge' – which includes the capacity to find – or impose – order (information) on the myriad streams of data that now can be captured and subjected to systematic analysis. The collection of data and the preservation of information extracted from them are hardly new human activities. But the great reduction in the technologically mandated costs, and the enhanced accuracy and scale on which this can now be done challenge the capacities of individual human beings to attend to, and focus on the signals that are likely to prove significant.

6.3 DIGITAL DATABASES' GROWING ROLE IN COMMERCE AND SCIENCE

It is for this reason, as well as the greatly increased technical ease of data capture and manipulation, that distributed databases and the tools to work with them have grown increasingly prominent on the landscape of the digitally 'renewed economy'. The knowledge-driven society is coming to rely more heavily on, and find new and more productive uses for, the rather mundane entities that we call 'databases'. These objects are in a sense paradigmatic of the enhanced role and social value that 'information assets' of all sorts are coming to acquire in the modern, digital economy.

Scientific and scholarly inquiry has long created collections of objects and observations as a means of preserving materials that could form the basis of later study and forming the necessary support for the collective memory that allows the cumulative advancement of knowledge. In former times scientific databases were comparatively small (10 kilobytes), and feasible for individuals and small groups of researchers to compile, annotate and maintain by labour intensive methods; they often were published as typeset tables or simple, on-line documents.

Recently, however, the size and complexity of scientific databases has grown enormously, and with that the potentialities of exploiting that data have also mounted. The necessary activities are absorbing increasing resources from publicly funded research programmes in science and engineering, and there has been a commensurate expansion in the pressure on researchers to find ways of extracting revenues from these 'assets', so as to defray the costs of creating and maintaining them. In some degree, that pressure reflects the perception that the commercial database business can be a lucrative one.

Thus it is pertinent to notice that the development and 'on-line' databases have been proliferating in the world of business as well, and for many of the same reasons. Yet, the rapid growth of the commercial database industry in the USA during the 1990s, summarized by the statistics in Table 6.1, might be seen as presenting something of a puzzle to those who regard the necessity of stronger protection for intellectual property rights in the 'new economy environment' to be a self-evident proposition. That is because the 1991 decision of the US Supreme Court (in the case of *Feist Publications v. Rural Telephone Service Co.*) removed the remaining shreds of legitimacy draped around the argument that the producer of a database was entitled to the protections of copyright law on the basis of the sheer 'sweat of the brow' effort invested in the activity of compilation, regardless of whether or not such investment had involved a significantly original, creative achievement.[1]

Both before and following the 1991 *Feist* ruling, copyright applied to the original selection, coordination, and arrangement of data within a database; many defendants in the USA therefore have been found liable for copyright infringement since 1991. Industry proponents of *sui generis* legislative protection voiced alarm that comprehensive electronically stored databases, being works of especially 'low authorship' and containing material that was in the public domain, would not meet the standard set by copyright law; that there was a compelling need in this case – as elsewhere – to modify existing IPR institutions to protect incentives for productive investments in this form of information asset from being undermined by 'electronic piracy' in the new technological environment that the convergence of digital computing and advanced telecommunications had created.

Just how limited the lost 'sweat of the brow' protection was for database producers could not be so readily perceived by observers who were not steeped in the intricacies of the US courts' treatment of copyright infringement claims. Nor was it evident to inexpert participants in the debates over the significance of the *Feist* ruling that most of the databases of substantial commercial valuable (i.e. those really worth 'pirating') contain many linked fields, and the selection and arrangement of data in these is a

Table 6.1   Performance of US database industry post Feist v. Rural Telephone (1991)

Performance indicators	1991	1997	% change
Number of databases	7637	10338	35
Number of files within databases (billions)	4.0	11.2	180
Number of online searches (millions)	44.4	88.1	98
Private sector's share in number of databases	*	0.70	78

Note: *The private sector's share in 1977 was 0.22.

sufficiently complex task to constitute some minimal level of creativity on the part of the author. US copyright law clearly prevents the wholesale copying of such (non-trivial) database structures, and thus affords their publishers significant protection even in the post-*Feist* era. These points were still less discernable to spectators in Europe, among them the members of the European Commission's High-Level Expert Group who, at just that point in time, were considering policies to promote the development of 'the Information Society' (see also David, 2001).

Yet, had they looked more closely at the prevailing business practices, the High-Level Group would have discovered that a wide variety of other appropriation devices was available and was being successfully deployed by US database businesses (Maurer, 1999). In the case of the so-called 'full text' databases, which often consist entirely of copyrighted documents, the contents do not lose their protected status by virtue of having been incorporated into a database. Another appropriation device available under existing law is the use of copyrighted enhancements: databases frequently are sold in a package along with advanced software. Because software is copyrightable (and in some instances patentable), would-be database copiers must either try to market a version of the material that is likely to be less useful, or make their own investment in developing search tools to package with the copied contents. Furthermore, technical database firms in the USA were availing themselves of a variety of 'self-help' protections against free-riding. Custom and semi-custom databases prepared for a small number of users provide virtually automatic protection against third parties and, more generally, contracts between the owners of such databases and their customers that limit the latter's right to use and/or disclose the contents to third parties are enforceable as trade secrets, even where the underlying information and data cannot qualify for statutory protection.

Where information was distributed to larger numbers of customers, the industry availed itself of the use of 'shrinkwrap' and 'clickwrap' licences, search-only and password protected websites, and the frequent updating of contents, editing and enhancements of search facilities – all of which are especially valuable to researchers in rapidly changing branches of science. Besides these means, Maurer's (1999) survey of industry practice found that a significant number of products are sold without any protection at all, sometimes for comparatively high prices. The explanation offered is that large vendors can afford to circulate catalogues that enable them to reach a small number of customers who are prepared to pay high prices for comparatively obscure titles, whereas the smaller would-be copiers cannot afford the expense of trying to bring their wares to the attention of those same purchasers.

Thus there was little if any substance to the rationale that was produced by the EC's High-Level Expert Group in their 1992 draft Directive, which called on the member states of the EU to implement statutory protections for intellectual property in the form of databases: their argument was that such protection was needed to 'level the playing field' so that European database creators could compete on less disadvantageous terms with their American counterparts. Nevertheless, later sections of this chapter are devoted to examining the practical consequences that were to flow from this policy initiative, which eventually took shape as the EC Directive for the Legal Protection of Databases, of 11 March 1996, and the implications that the repercussions of its implementation may carry for the future.

But, to understand both its symbolic and practical significance, one has first to appreciate the background of economic thinking that saw the US removal of copyright protection from databases to be problematic, and thus could regard Europe as having been presented with a significant opportunity for an industrial policy coup by creating a *sui generis* property right in databases. Databases, although works of 'low authorship' and therefore lacking most of the rhetorical supports available to those seeking protection of 'creative' works, were very much about knowledge and information, the stuff at the core of the ICT revolution and the knowledge-driven economy.

Yet, by the same token, they were recognized as being problematic commodities for market economies. The conceptual foundations for such a view had been thoroughly prepared by the development and popularization – at least in economic policy circles – of a sophisticated general rationale for the protection of IPR. That now-traditional rationale rests on the microeconomic analysis of the production and distribution of knowledge and information.

6.4   KNOWLEDGE, INFORMATION ECONOMICS AND THE 'THREE Ps'

Knowledge may be viewed as a commodity, but it is not a commonplace commodity. Nor is information, which we may distinguish from the cognitive human capabilities subsumed under the label of 'knowledge'. Through the process of codification, some, but not all forms of knowledge, can be reduced to information, which renders it more readily transmitted, classified and stored. Even so, information, like knowledge remains highly differentiated, and not being homogeneous it has no obvious natural units of measurement. It can have utility as a pure consumption good or as a capital good, and often as both. It is unusual in that, as a pure capital good yielding a stream of material benefits when combined with other kinds of assets, information and knowledge possess intrinsic values. Such is the case, for example, with regard to information about the operation of a cost-saving manufacturing process, or the design of a product with better quality attributes.

A property still more remarkable than those already noticed is information's extreme *indivisibility*, coupled with its durability: once a bit of knowledge has been obtained, there is no value to acquiring it a second time, or a third. There is no societal need to repeat the same discovery or invention, because a piece of information can be used again and again without exhausting it. Related to this, and of even greater import, knowledge differs from ordinary 'private' commodities in being what economists refer to as a *non-rival* good: it can be possessed and enjoyed jointly by as many as care to make use of it. While this observation forms the point of departure of the classic analysis of the economics of R&D due to Arrow (1962), it hardly can be claimed as a modern insight.

Consider the following passage in a letter written in 1813 to Isaac McPherson, a Baltimore inventor, by Thomas Jefferson:

> If nature has made any one thing less susceptible than all others of exclusive property, it is the action of the thinking power called an idea, which an individual may exclusively possess as long as he keeps it to himself; but the moment it is divulged, it forces itself into the possession of every one, and the receiver cannot dispossess himself of it. Its peculiar character, too, is that no one possesses the less, because every other possesses the whole of it. He who receives an idea from me, receives instruction himself without lessening mine; as he who lights his taper at mine, receives light without darkening me. That ideas should freely spread from one to another over the globe, for the moral and mutual instruction of man, and improvement of his condition, seems to have been peculiarly and benevolently designed by nature, when she made them, like fire, expansible over all space, without lessening their density in any point, and like the air in which we breathe, move, and have our physical being, incapable of confinement or exclusive appropriation. (Koch and Peden, 1972, pp. 629–30)

It seems clear that Jefferson grasped the essential point that the cost of transmitting useful knowledge in codified form is negligible in comparison to the costs of creating it; and saw that were it not for society's need to encourage the pursuit of ideas by rendering such pursuits economically viable, such information should be distributed freely.[2]

Non-rival possession, low marginal cost of reproduction and distribution, which makes it difficult to exclude others from access, and substantial fixed costs of original production, are the three properties familiarly associated with the definition of a 'public good'. As is well known, when these characteristics are present, competitive markets – in which price tends to be driven down to the costs of supplying the marginal unit of the commodity – in general perform quite badly; competitive producers' revenues will not even cover their full costs of production, much less appropriate anything approaching the use value of the goods to the public. Indeed, the attempt to make the beneficiaries pay for value received would so reduce demand as to result in an inefficiently low level of its consumption.

In the literature of public finance economics, three principal alternative allocative mechanisms are proposed as solutions to 'the public goods problem'. One is that society should provide independent producers with subsidies financed by general taxation, and require that the goods be made available to the public freely or at a nominal charge. A second mechanism would have the state levying general taxes to finance its direct participation in the process of production and distribution, furnishing and managing the requisite facilities, and contracting where necessary with private agents to carry out this work. Here, again, the objective is to supply the good without having to charge for it. The third solution is to create a publicly regulated private monopoly, which would be able to charge consumers prices that will secure a 'normal' rate of profit. This does not guarantee that consumers will be lined up to purchase the goods and services in question. In other words, the legal right to exclude other producers from the market for a product does not, in and of itself, create a profitable monopoly of that line of business.

While the elements of non-excludability and 'non-rivalry' that are present in information qualify this commodity to be regarded as a 'public good' for purposes of economic policy analysis, ideas and information remain distinguished in two respects from the mass of conventional public goods, such as traffic lights, flood control systems, airport beacons and radar landing beams, and the like. The first difference is that the attributes of the commodity – that is, typically, the complete contents of the information itself – will not be known beforehand. Indeed, it is not known automatically to all the interested parties even when the new knowledge becomes available in codified form. This *asymmetry in the distribution of information* greatly complicates the process of arranging contracts for the production and use of new knowledge.

The second differentiating feature is *the cumulative and interactive nature of knowledge*. It is particularly evident that the stock of scientific and technological knowledge grows by incremental additions, each advance building on and sometimes altering the significance of previous findings in complicated, and often unpredictable ways.[3]

The importance of the foregoing differentiating features notwithstanding, it is useful to notice a striking correspondence between the three solutions for the standard public goods problem – subsidies, direct production, and regulated monopoly – and the three main institutional arrangements that may be deployed to address the so-called 'appropriability problem' to which the public goods characteristics of information give rise. In order to encourage the provision of public goods in the shape of scientific and technological knowledge, modern states typically are found to be deploying several of these concurrently. For the sake of brevity, I have referred on previous occasions to the three principal institutional devices as 'the three Ps': public *P*atronage, the legal exclusive ownership of (intellectual) *P*roperty, and *P*rocurement by state agencies through contracting arrangements. Each of these mechanisms, however, exhibits some special deficiencies as well as some specific virtues in its effects on resource allocation; none among them offers a perfect solution to the problem. I will focus here on intellectual property rights, and examine the virtues and deficiencies of the less often discussed case of the protections afforded by the copyright system. But the advantages and deficiencies of the alternative mechanisms also deserve at least brief notice.

The term 'patronage' stands for the system of awarding publicly financed prizes, research grants based on the submission of competitive proposals, and other subsidies to private individuals and organizations engaged in intellectual discovery and invention, in exchange for full public disclosure of their creative achievements. It may be said to characterize the pursuit of 'open' scientific inquiry, and the dominant institutional and social mode of organization associated in western democratic societies with the conduct of academic science.

'Procurement' is associated with governmental contracting for intellectual work, the products of which it will control and devote to public purposes. Whether or not the information thereby produced will be laid open for public use is a secondary issue, albeit an important matter for public policy. 'Sensitive' defence-related research usually is conducted under government auspices in secure, closed laboratories; whereas much public contract R&D and the scientific work of governmentally managed laboratories and (agricultural) experiment stations is undertaken with the intention of wide dissemination of the findings.

The third arrangement is for society to grant private producers of new knowledge exclusive property rights to the use of their creations, thereby forming conditions for the existence of markets in these forms of intellectual property, and enabling the originators to collect (differential) fees for the use of their work by others. Here, under the Property rubric, are found the specific legal contrivances of the patent and copyright, and, somewhat more problematically, the trade secret.

6.5 PATENT AND COPYRIGHT SYSTEMS IN ECONOMIC THEORY AND HISTORY

The creation and assignment of intellectual property rights convey a monopoly right to the beneficial economic exploitation of an idea (in the case of patent rights) or of a particular expression of an idea (in the case of copyright) in return for the disclosure of the idea or its expression. This device allows the organization of market exchanges of 'exploitation rights', which, by assigning pecuniary value to commercially exploitable ideas, creates economic incentives for people to go on creating new ones, as well as finding new applications for old ones. By allocating these rights to those who are prepared to pay the most for them, the workings of intellectual property markets also tend to prevent ideas from remaining in the exclusive (secret) possession of discoverers and inventors who might be quite uninterested in seeing their creations used to satisfy the wants and needs of other members of society. Thus a potential economic problem that is addressed by instituting a system of intellectual property rights is the threat that unfair competition, particularly the misappropriation of the benefits of someone else's expenditure of effort, may destroy the provision of information goods as a commercially viable activity. The nub of the problem here is that the costs of making a particular information good available to a second, third, or thousandth user are not significantly greater than those of making it available to the first one. Ever since the Gutenberg revolution, the technical advances that have lowered the costs of reproducing 'encoded' material (text, images, sounds) have also permitted 'pirates' to appropriate the content of the first copy without bearing the expense of its development. Unchecked, this form of unfair competition could render unprofitable the investment entailed in obtaining that critical first copy.

Producers of ideas, texts, and other creative works (including graphic images and music) are subject to economic constraints, even when they do not invariably respond to variation in the incentives offered by the market. If they had no rights enabling them to derive income from the publication of their works, they might create less, and quite possibly be compelled to spend their time doing something entirely different but more lucrative. So there is an important economic rationale for establishing intellectual property rights.

To summarize, the 'property' solution, which creates rights for the fruits of intellectual creations, possesses a number of definite virtues. These may be quickly adumbrated for the case of patents. The patent provides an obvious and recognized solution to the economic problem of the intellectual creator. By increasing the expected private returns from innovation, it acts as an incentive mechanism to private investment in knowledge production: (1) patents facilitate the market test of a new invention because they allow disclosure of the related information while (in principle) protecting against imitation; (2) patents create transferable rights (by granting a licence, the owner of the knowledge allows it to be exploited by other agents) and, therefore, it can help to structure a complex transaction that also concerns unpatented knowledge; and (3) patents are a means to signal and evaluate the future value of the technological effort of the companies that own them (which is particularly useful in the cases of new or young companies for which other classes of 'intangibles' cannot be used for proper evaluation).

This way of providing market incentives for certain kinds of creative effort leaves the valuation of the intellectual production to be determined *ex post*, by the willingness of users to pay; it thereby avoids having society try to place a value on the creative work *ex ante* – as would be required under alternative incentive schemes, such as offering prospective authors and inventors prizes, or awarding individual procurement contracts for specified works.

But establishing a monopoly right to exploit that 'first copy' (the idea protected by the patent or the expressive material protected by copyright) turns out not to be a perfect solution. The monopolist will raise the price of every copy above the negligible costs of its reproduction and, as a result, there will be some potential users of the information good who will be excluded from enjoying it. The latter represents a waste of resources, referred to by economists as the 'deadweight burden of monopoly': some people's desires will remain unsatisfied even though they could have been fulfilled at virtually no additional cost. This is but one of the things that are likely to go awry in the case of patent protection. As is quite well known, the first to invent and first to file basis for awarding patents creates incentives for duplicative 'races' that result in socially excessive R&D expenditures. Similarly, patents may be sought and used strategically as tools to raise rivals' costs by confronting them with the threat, if not the actuality of infringement suits.

Not surprisingly, then, the subject of intellectual property policies has proved troublesome for the economics profession, as it presents numerous situations in which the effort to limit unfair competition and provide adequate 'market incentives' for innovation demonstrably may result in a socially inefficient resource allocation. Human institutions, however, rarely are perfect. From the viewpoint of both legal theory and economic analysis there is therefore much to be said for regarding patent and copyright institutions as remarkably ingenious social contrivances, whereby protection of the discoverer's or inventor's exclusive right to exploit new knowledge commercially is exchanged for the disclosure of information that creates a public good; and, moreover, a public good that may be drawn on to produce additional discoveries and inventions.[4] This is managed by leaving the economic value of the right to be determined by the workings of the market and thereby removing it from the realm of political discretion.

Yet it ought not to be supposed that the actual provisions of the laws affecting intellectual property rights fully honour this social bargain. True, no patent is valid that does not describe the invention in 'clear, precise, and exact terms', thereby disclosing sufficient information to enable second-comers to produce the invention without 'undue experimentation'. American patent law is unusual in going farther than this, in requiring the patent applicants to disclose the best mode in which they contemplate implementing their invention. But in practice these provisions often prove insufficient to overcome the effects of the economic incentives that patentees usually have to withhold some pertinent information, either for their private use or as a basis to extract additional rents for the transfer of know-how that is complementary to that disclosed by the patent.

Delays in the release of information add to the academic research community's concerns over the way that the workings of the patent system restrict access to new scientific and technological findings. US patent law follows the principle that priority in invention, rather than being first to file a patent application, is what matters; it therefore allows applicants a one-year grace period after publication. But most foreign systems award patents on a 'first to file' basis, which means that even American researchers are induced – by their own or their supporting organization's commercial goals – to delay publication of their findings and inventions until they have prepared patent applications to secure rights in other countries. During the two decades following the passage of the 1980 Bayh-Dole Act, which authorized universities in the US to seek patents on innovations arising from federally funded research projects, there has been more-or-less continuous modification of institutional rules in the direction of lengthening the permissible duration of delays placed on the publication of research findings for purposes of allowing the filing of patent applications.

From the standpoint of academic researchers the greatest deficiency of the statutory disclosure requirements imposed by patent laws is simply that little scientific or technical data may be divulged in meeting this stipulation, so that the patent itself is of only limited interest and serves mainly as a notice that the patentees may be willing to supply more useful information for some fee. Moreover, researchers' ability to make use of such information as the patent does divulge is by no means assured until the end of its life; the patent not only excludes others from selling the invention, but also prohibits them from making and using it. That the use of an invention for purposes of research, and hence in generating further discoveries and innovations, ought not be proscribed has long been recognized by patent case law in the US: researchers have been allowed to defend themselves from infringement suits on grounds of 'experimental use' – so long as the infringer is able to show that no commercial benefit was derived thereby.[5]

The same situation does not arise with conventional copyright protection, since what is being protected is the published form in which ideas have been expressed; only that which is fully disclosed can qualify the author for legal protection against infringers. Inasmuch as it is difficult, if not impossible to establish that unauthorized copies were made of a text that had not been made public in some way, authors seeking legal protection for their work have every incentive to hasten its disclosure. Moreover, in recognition of the cultural and scientific benefits of exegetical and critical writings, and further research based on published information and data – not to mention the interests of authors in having such usage made on the basis of accurate representations of their work – statutory exceptions traditionally are provided to permit 'fair use' infringements of copyrighted material. Largely for these reasons, this form of intellectual property protection historically has not raised serious objections on the grounds of impeding rapid access to new scientific or technological data and information. But the situation has changed in recent years.

6.6 THE RELENTLESS 'POLICY PUSH' FOR A STRONGER GLOBAL IPR REGIME

The economic prominence of intellectual property and efforts to strengthen the legal protections afforded patents copyrights and trademarks, have been growing continuously since the 1970s. The value of intellectual property is increasing as a share of average total firm value; the number of patent applications is rising at double-digit rates in the major patent offices; and licensing and cross-licensing are being employed with greater frequency than ever, particularly so in high-technology industries.

The greater intensity of innovation, characteristic of the knowledge-based economy, and the increase in the propensity to patent (that is, the elevation of the ratios of patents to number of innovations, and of patents per real dollar expended on R&D, indicate the emergence on new strategies and managerial approaches to research and business innovation. According to Kortum and Lerner (1988) these have been the main drivers of the recent quantitative trends. Some 147 000 US utility patents were granted in 1998, corresponding to an increase of 32 per cent compared with 1997. Over the past 10 years both patent applications and patent grants have increased at a rate of about 6 per cent per annum, compared with about 1 per cent per annum in the preceding 40 years.

There is a qualitative aspect to the growth of patenting as well. Patents are being registered on new types of objects such as software (17000 US patents during 1999, compared with less than one-tenth that number in 1992) and genetic creations; and they are being issued increasingly to new actors, namely universities and other public sector research organizations. This general trend is also reflected in the increase in exclusivity rights over instruments, research materials and databases. While all of this may be seen as contributing to a dramatic expansion of 'the knowledge market', the proliferation of exclusive rights on whole areas of intellectual creation, equally, represents an unprecedentedly large incursion into what formerly was the public domain of scientific and technical data and information.

Many factors explain this broader trend. The first factor is simply that a patent is becoming an intangible asset of increasing importance: for new and/or small companies because this is sometimes the only reliable way to signal their value to the market and, more generally, for many established firms engaging in innovation-based competition. A second factor is the increasing value of strategic use of patents as entry-deterring threats, or bargaining chips for future negotiations over cross-licensing of patents. With the current (or expected) strengthening of national and regional legal systems of intellectual property, the expected benefits of amassing portfolios of legal rights to exclude began to outweigh their costs.[6]

The third factor has been reflected in changes of patenting policy in the US and Europe. Patenting policy decided by the patent offices and courts deals obviously with the interpretation of the three basic patentability criteria, which always have played a role of regulation, blocking or slowing down of private appropriation in certain fields. Today, pro-patenting policies of patent offices mean that patentability criteria have gradually been eased and extended to new subject matter areas. Many research results become patentable, as a result of both legal (court) and patent office decisions. The increasing ability to patent fundamental knowledge, research tools and databases is part and parcel of a broader movement towards strengthening IPRs.

Other important factors relate to changes at the institutional level. Powerful commitments to basic research by private firms in certain sectors (for instance, the case in the genomics area where we can observe the emergence of a new generation of firms that are highly specialized in fundamental research and are, therefore, in direct competition with the public research institutions). Changes in the behaviour of universities and public institutes have contributed significantly to increased patenting in the US, particularly in the biotechnology and medical devices fields; more generally universities have become more and more oriented towards exploiting the intellectual property system as a means of capturing revenue, and demonstrating a commitment to the promotion of economic development in their regions.

These trends do not necessarily lead to an excess of privatization of knowledge. In many cases the establishment of intellectual property rights strengthens private incentives, allows the commitment of substantial private resources, and thereby improves the conditions of commercialization of inventions. Moreover, the establishment of private rights does not totally prevent the diffusion of knowledge, even if it does limit it. Finally, a large proportion of private knowledge is disseminated outside the market system, either within consortia or by means of networks of trading and sharing of knowledge, see von Hippel (1988).

Nevertheless, there clearly is ground for concern when all these developments show a general shift from one view to another of the role of IPRs: traditionally, IPRs are considered as one of the incentive structures society employs to elicit innovative effort. They co-exist with other incentive structures, each of which has costs and benefits as well as a degree of complementarity. The new view is that IPRs are the only means to commodify the intangible capital represented by knowledge and should therefore be a common currency or 'ruler' for measuring the output of activities devoted to knowledge generation and the basis for markets in knowledge exchange.

The restructuring of the legal regimes relating to patents and copyrights, and the adjustments of behaviour to the new incentives created by those institutional innovations are likely to impact the organization and conduct of scientific research and publishing. Indeed, they seem bound to figure among the more prominent unexpected consequences of the very same digital infrastructure technologies that were created by publicly sponsored scientists and engineers. Unfortunately, at least some of these repercussions now appear to be detrimental to the long-term vitality of the practice of 'open' science in the world's academic research communities. Such an untoward effect will not follow from the technology itself. It comes, instead, from the lack of appropriate concern for maintaining a healthy balance between the domain of publicly supported knowledge production and exchanges, and the sphere in which private, proprietary R&D and profitable businesses flourish based on information goods.

One source of difficulty in preserving such a balance is quite immediately apparent. An attractive short-run strategy of business development entails utilizing enhanced information processing and telecommunications in conjunction with the assertion of private property rights over the mass of publicly provided data and information products. Rather than having to produce wholly new content for distribution via the new and more effective technical facilities, an obvious first line of enterprise is to make use of what comes freely and most readily to hand. Ever since the introduction of printing with moveable type, the history of new publication and broadcast media has shown how automatic it is for entrepreneurs to seek first to draw on content that was already available in the public domain.

Hence, one can expect that this approach will continue to be tried, exploiting larger and larger portions of the body of codified scientific knowledge and observational data that has been built up under public patronage and maintained as a common, readily accessible research resource. Sometimes the commercialization of public databases makes good economic sense, because private firms may have technical or marketing capabilities that would add value for a variety of end users of publicly generated data, whereas existing government agencies or NGOs lack that competence. Such was shown to be the case in regard to the distribution and packaging by commercial weather information services of data gathered by the US National Oceanic and Atmospheric Administration (NOAA).

But the possibility of seriously adverse consequences elsewhere in the national research system, from ill-designed policies and programmes to promote proprietary exploitation of public knowledge resources, also needs to be recognized. Consider what ensued in those circumstances from the Reagan administration's sponsorship of the Land-Remote Sensing Commercialization Act (1984), under which the responsibility for the operations of the Landsat system of remote sensing satellites was transferred from NOAA management, and a monopoly on Landsat images was awarded in 1985 to the Earth Observation Satellite (EOSAT) Company, a joint venture of Hughes and RCA. The price of Landsat images immediately rose tenfold, from $400 per image to $4000. This permitted EOSAT to attract profitable business from commercial customers and the federal government, although virtually none from academic and independent researchers. Indeed, the impact of the privatization of Landsat operations on basic research being conducted by university groups around the world was quite devastating, as, they suddenly went from being 'data rich' into a condition not of actual 'data poverty' so much as one of data 'non-entitlement'.[7]

The EOSAT Co. secured its monopoly position in the market for satellite images by virtue of being given physical control over the source of (Landsat) images, which, having been accumulated over many years as a by-product of the Cold War, formed a data resource that for all intents and purposes could not be regenerated. Yet it is equally possible to imagine that a similarly damaging outcome for academic researchers would follow from the exercise of the market power that a commercial provider of a scientific database might gain under intellectual property protection; especially under a legal regime that granted indefinitely renewable copyright protection to the database contents, whether or not the data were otherwise copyrightable.[8]

The recent extension of copyright to software has itself permitted a breach of the disclosure principle that parallels the one already noted in regard to patents. Under American copyright law (in order to qualify to pursue infringers for damages) it is sufficient to register only some sample extracts of a computer program's 'text', rather than the entire body of code. Moreover, there is no requirement whatsoever to disclose the underlying 'source code'; copyright protection can be obtained on the basis of a disclosure of just the machine language instructions, which, even were they to be divulged in their entirety would be difficult and costly to interpret and re-utilize without access to the source code. While this practice surely can be seen to violate the principle that no burden of 'undue experimentation' should be placed on second comers, the latter requirement is one that holds only in the case of patent law. It never was contemplated that one might be able to register a text for full copyright protection without practically disclosing its contents to interested readers.

A further, more generally disconcerting set of developments may prove quite destructive to the effectiveness of traditional safeguards against 'fair use' exemptions for research (and educational) purposes – even where such provisions continue to be made. This threat has emerged only recently in the form of digital technologies that limit 'on-line' copying of electronic information. Advanced encryption systems now underpin many computing and communications security services, and permit a wide variety of security objectives to be achieved by establishing discretionary control over access to encrypted data, along with assurance for both users and service provider of message authentication and data integrity, as well as privacy and confidentiality goals. There are other techniques for marking and monitoring the use of distributed digital information, such as 'water marking', which attaches a signal to digital data that can be detected or extracted later to make documentable assertions about its provenance, authenticity, or ownership; also, 'fingerprinting', which embeds a mark in each copy that uniquely identifies the authorized recipient.

'Self-help' or 'copyright management' systems that make use of encryption or prevent unauthorized copying of 'cleartext' allow copyright holders to enforce their legal claim to capture economic value from users of the protected material and, moreover, enable selective access to elements of content that makes it more feasible for the vendor to engage in price discrimination. Marking and monitoring techniques, in contrast, do not allow direct enforcement of copyrights, but can be used to deter unauthorized copying and distribution of information by facilitating tracking of errant data to the original recipients who were responsible for its unauthorised use.

These advances in digital technology have a direct economic effect that is efficiency enhancing, insofar as they reduce the costs of enforcing a statutory property right and thereby securing whatever societal benefits copyright legislation is designed to promote. In the currently prevailing enthusiasm for stronger intellectual property protection, however, the American drafters of the 1998 Digital Millennium Copyright Act included a provision that prohibits the circumvention of 'any technological measure that effectively controls access' to a copyrighted work, and outlawed the manufacture, importation or public distribution of any technology primarily produced for the purpose of such circumvention.[9] The problem posed by this statutory reinforcement for applications of novel self-help technologies is simply that it may render impossible the exercise of 'fair use' of copyrighted material by researchers and educators, leaving the provision of information access for such purposes as a matter for the discretion of copyright holders.

This is not the only serious assault on the traditional means of permitting publicly supported open science communities to pursue their work untrammeled by the protections afforded to copyright owners. As attractive as the prospect of more powerful 'self-help' technologies may appear to be in curtailing 'digital piracy', such remedies would create a threat to the achievement of a reasonable regime for the allocation of scientific and technological information goods while providing protection for private investments in information goods. One way in which it is feasible to approximate the efficient workings of a system of discriminatory pricing for data and information is to allow educators, scholars and researchers to invoke 'fair use' exemptions from the requirements for licensing material that is copyrighted or otherwise legally protected by statute. In effect, this approach would set differentially lower prices for the use of information goods in producing and distributing knowledge – indeed, prices that approximate the negligibly small marginal costs of digital reproduction and transmission.

Thus far we have considered only the most straightforward and obvious of the potentially adverse consequences of turning over parts of the public knowledge domain to information monopolists. The staking out of property rights to scientific knowledge has potentially serious and subtler implications for the circulation of information and its use in research. These may be grouped, for the sake of convenience, under the general heading of 'transaction costs increases'. First, it is possible that IPR-related transaction costs may increase so much that the result can be the blockage of knowledge exploitation and accumulation. Policy makers and academics alike have focused especially on the tragedy of the anticommons in biotechnology and microprocessors, the potentially deleterious effect of strong IP protection for databases on academic science, and the extension of patentability to new subject such as patents, and more recently business methods (e.g., Cockburn and Griliches, 1988 and Hall and Ziedonis, 2001).

Second, efforts and costs devoted to sorting out conflicting and overlapping claims to IPR will increase as will uncertainty about the nature and extent of legal liability in using knowledge inputs. Again policy makers and academics are concerned with the increase of litigation costs, including indirect costs, which may distort the innovative behaviour of small companies. As put well by John Barton there is a problem when 'the number of intellectual property lawyers is growing faster than the amount of research'.[10] That has been happening in the US, but the emergence of similar trends in the EU show that the scope of the problem is global.

6.7 IMPLICATIONS OF THE EU's *SUI GENERIS* PROPERTY RIGHT IN DATABASES

A new and quite unexpected direct threat to the academic research enterprise in science and engineering has emerged since the mid-1990s as a result of the extension of *sui generis* copyright protection to databases, even to databases containing non-copyrightable material. This institutional innovation emerged first in the European Union Directive on the Legal Protection of Databases (issued 11 March 1996), which directed member states to create a new broadly comprehensive type of intellectual property that was free from a number of the important and long-standing limitations and exceptions traditionally provided by copyright law, in order to safeguard access to information used in socially beneficial, knowledge-creating activities such as research and teaching. The EU Database Directive applies equally to non-electronic and electronic databases, even though, as will be seen, it originated as a strategic 'industrial policy' response to the commercial development of on-line (electronic) databases in America.

Further, as a device to secure international acceptance of the new approach initiated by this directive (which remains binding on the member states of the European Union, in the sense of requiring implementation in each of their national statutes) reciprocity provisions were included. The latter in effect threatened the commercial creators of databases who were nationals of foreign states outside the EU with retaliatory infringement of copyright material in their products, unless their respective governments became signatories to a World Intellectual Property Organization (WIPO) draft convention on databases which had been framed to embody the essential provisions of the *sui generis* copyright protection established under the 1996 EU Directive.[11]

The European Commission's strategy succeeded in setting in motion an administration-initiated legislative response in the US Congress, which has spanned a succession of draft statutes that have to date generated intense but inconclusive lobbying activity in Washington. The response began in May 1996 with the introduction at the behest of the US Patent and Trademark Office of House of Representatives of a bill, H.R. 3531, short-titled the 'Database Investment and Intellectual Property Antipiracy Act of 1996'. This first and ill-considered rush to legislate soon encountered opposition from the US academic research community and non-commercial publishers of scientific information. But although that attempt proved unavailing, the legislative genie has been let out of the bottle, with the result that the 104th Congress has two further pieces of legislation. The first of these is 'The Collections of Information Antipiracy Act', H.R. 345, introduced in January 1999, essentially recapitulating the quite pernicious approach taken in the original administration-inspired legislative proposal in 1996. A second bill, 'The Consumer and Investors Access to Information Act', H.R. 1858, was introduced in May 1999, and contains provisions protecting access to database information that are rather more responsive to the objections raised during 1997 against H.R. 3531. This too failed to gain sufficient support from the Senate Judiciary Committee, but in the following session of Congress its proponents were able to muster the strength needed to move the bill forward to the floor of the House of Representatives, and a parallel version is making headway in the Senate. A rapid review of the main features of the EU's Database Directive of 1996 highlights aspects of the national statutes that have been implemented in the UK, Germany, Italy and many other member states, as well as by a growing number of the accession countries.[12] Even if the US database legislation that emerged form Congress turned out to be less extreme in some respects, as presently is thought likely, significant pressure could subsequently emerge for international harmonization – and the experience of such efforts is that they invariably harmonize at the higher standard of protection, because no nation's negotiators are sanguine about yielding the existing rights of their compatriots.

To begin with, the EU Directive's *sui generis* approach departs from the long-established principles of intellectual property law by removing the distinction between protection of expression and protection of ideas, a distinction that is central in US copyright law and was embodied in the TRIPS agreement adopted by the WTO. Compilers of databases in the EU will now be able to assert ownership and demand payment for licensing the use of content that is already in the public domain, including material that otherwise could not be copyright-protected. In complying with the Directive, member states will not be providing any specific incentives for the generation of new database content (such as scientific data and information, for example), as distinguished from new compilations. Nor can it be thought that copyrights in databases are being granted as part of a social bargain, in exchange for the public disclosure of material that hitherto was not revealed.

A second distinction fundamental in copyright law, that between original expressive matter and pre-existing expressive matter, has been discarded by the wording of the Directive, because the latter fails to attach any legal significance to the difference between expressive matter that already exists in the public domain, and matter that is original and newly disclosed. Domestic laws and national courts that reaffirm this omission in effect will allow a database maker to qualify for renewal of the 15-year term of exclusive rights over the database as a whole – by virtue of having made a 'significant investment' in updates, additions, revisions.[13]

Strict limitations on re-use of database contents are imposed by the Directive, requiring third-party regeneration or payment for licences to extract such material. This would inhibit the integration and recombination of existing scientific database contents with new material to provide more useful, specialized research resources.

But regardless of whether or not it is possible in theory to regenerate the raw contents of a database from publicly available sources, under the terms of the Directive, investors in database production can always deny third parties the right to use pre-existing data in value-added applications, even when the third parties are willing to pay royalties on licences for such use. It would therefore be possible for an initial database producer simply to block subsequent creation of new, special-purpose databases which reproduced parts of existing compilations, wherever the regeneration of such data *de novo* was infeasible or terribly costly (as in the case of years of remote-sensing satellite observations, or data-tracks from high energy particle collision detectors, or multi-year bibliographic compilations of scientific publications and citations thereto).

Where a database maker also held the exclusive rights to license previously copyright-protected publications, it would be entirely proper under the terms of the Directive to refuse third parties licences in that material, while incorporating it within a database protected under the terms of the EC Directive. There are no compulsory licensing provisions under the Berne Convention on copyrights, and these are likewise excluded under the TRIPS agreement. By following suit and excluding conditions for compulsory licensing, as well as omitting to provide remedies for abuse of the legal protections newly accorded to database investors, the Directive opens the door for the construction of indefinitely renewable monopolies in both regeneratable and non-regeneratable scientific data.

The Directive abandons the principle of 'fair use' for research, as distinct from extraction and use of data for purposes of 'illustration in teaching or research'. How 'illustrative use' is to be interpreted remains ill defined, pending some infringement litigation that would provide opportunity for a court ruling in the matter. But the current consensus among IPR scholars is that 'illustration' falls far short of the normal scope of research use of copyrighted material. Such an interpretation is consistent with the fact that the absence of fair use exclusions for research (and research training) creates the prospect of a two-way squeeze on public sector funded research programmes, as the costs of obtaining commercially supplied data are likely to rise. The tenfold rise in the unit prices of remote-sensing satellite images that immediately followed the privatization of LANSAT satellite operations in 1985, and its withering effects on university-based research projects, might well be recalled in this connection. Continuing pressures for cuts in government budgets, taken in combination with the priority that tends to be accorded to near-term applications-oriented research vis-à-vis exploratory science, is likely to encourage derogation to commercial database generators of the function of compiling, updating and publishing databases that were created by, and remain of continuing relevance for, basic public sector research. There is a two-fold risk in this situation: one is the threat to data quality in the separating of the database creation and maintenance from the scientific expertize of the research community that creates and uses the data; the other is the resulting squeeze on public research resources, as already restrictive appropriations would have to be spent on purchasing data and database licences.

When considering the benefits to society of enabling the appropriation of the value of this facility (and ones like it in other research fields) for users who seek to exploit it in conducting commercially oriented research – say, in developing new genetic diagnostic kits, or new drug therapies – the question to be asked is what effect doing so will have on the probability of valuable discoveries both in the near term and over the longer run. Seeking to apply the rights granted by the EC's Directive for the Legal Protection of Databases (11 March 1996), and to partition and restructure the 'information space' so as to readily extract licensing fees from users, would have the predictable effect of curtailing searches that were not thought to have a high expectation of quickly finding something with high 'applications value'. In other words, the probabilities of unexpected discoveries would be further reduced by the economically restricted utilization of the facility. Targeted searches may be quite affordable, but wholesale extraction of the data-spaces' content to permit exploratory search activities is especially likely to be curtailed.

The adverse influences of the consequent 'lost discoveries' also are likely to ripple outwards. This is so because the development of new and more powerful search devices, and techniques of pattern recognition, statistical analysis, and so forth, are more likely to figure among the discoveries that would be made collectively through the exploratory use of a facility by a larger number of searchers. Therefore, some cost of extracting economic rents from this construct today will most likely come in the form of smaller benefits (and the sacrifice of reduced applications-oriented research costs) in the future. In addition, one should consider the possibly serious inhibiting effect of setting up a 'model' of IPR exploitation of such structures on the construction of some new, presently unimagined information tools that would require the assembly (and licensing) of myriad information components from many diverse sources.

A concrete illustration of the creative power of collaborations built to exploit enhanced digital technologies is provided by the vast, multi-dimensional 'information space' that has been built up over the course of many years by the research community whose activities are coordinated today by the European Bioinformatics Institute (EBI). This 'virtual library' is a dynamic collective research tool rather than a simple repository of information. The ordinary conceptualization of 'a database' is too static and, in a sense, too pre-structured, to comprehend the potential for discoveries that have been created by this collective construct. Yet, as the EBI's Director has testified, this information space began to be formed long before the research communities involved gave any consideration to intellectual property right restrictions on the use of the information contents that were being linked for subsequent retrieval and analysis. The implication was clear that it would be far more difficult in today's environment to create this particular research tool.[14]

6.8 RECONSIDERING THE TRADITIONAL ECONOMIC RATIONALE FOR COPYRIGHT PROTECTION

The advent of technologies that have greatly reduced both the fixed and the variable costs of reproduction and transmission of information elicited strong defensive reactions from business publishing interests that previously enjoyed a measure of protection from their possession of superior, decreasing-cost production facilities. It was said that unrestricted use of plain paper photocopiers in the hands of readers threatened the profitability of conventional publishers. But more careful economic analysis has shown that such is not necessarily the case; indeed, just the opposite might be true.

Under the traditional analysis of the social efficiency of copyright, it was held that stringent protection against unauthorized copying could cause social as well as private losses from underutilization of the intellectual asset, where the cost to consumers of obtaining an unauthorized copy was greater than the amount would be charged by a copyright holder who had a strict enforceable monopoly. This is tantamount to the conclusion that strengthening copyright protection could enhance social welfare even without stimulating the production of new works of authorship, so long as lax restraints on copying resulted in the demand for authorized copies ('originals') being reduced greatly in relation to total consumption of the work in question (e.g. Johnson, 1985 and Novos and Waldman, 1984).

But this line of argument rests crucially on the supposition that the private cost to the consumer of obtaining a close substitute by copying an authorized 'original' was greater than the copyright monopolist's marginal costs. However, Liebowitz (1985) pointed out that this latter assumption has been invalidated by advancements in copying technologies. The complementarity in production between authorized 'originals' and low-cost copies could mean (under conditions in which the demand for copies of such works was sufficiently price elastic) that a more permissive law regarding copying – by allowing utilization of highly efficient copying technology – actually could increase the effective demand for 'originals' as well.

Furthermore, it turns out that the best way for business to exploit the potential monopoly power conveyed by legal protections for 'intellectual property' is not always that of trying to extract the maximum consumer surplus from each individual user. Even traditional 'content owners' of information goods such as books, video recordings, CDs, software programs, and the like may be able to reap greater profits by allowing 'sharing' (the *free* copying for use) of information goods among certain groups of consumers. The candidate groups would be those whose members were closely integrated socially, and whose collective willingness to pay exceeded the sum of their individual revealed demands for the commodity in question (see further David, 2001).

This represents an important qualification of the widely asserted claim that digitally assisted, low marginal cost reproduction encourages 'piracy' (unlicensed copying and redistribution) which must be injurious to copyright holders, and therefore warrants introduction of stronger protections against all unauthorized copying. In the context of the present discussion, therefore, it is especially appropriate to point out that spatially distributed scientific and engineering research *networks* are in a sense paradigmatic of the self-selected producer groupings whose information goods requirements might be more profitably met by publisher/vendors who permitted, or actually facilitated free (intra-group) sharing.[15]

The key condition for arguments of this sort is that allowing customers to 'bundle themselves' into such consumer units permits increased aggregate sales, so long as the groups are 'natural clubs' – such as families and scientific research teams – that organized themselves for some other purpose than spreading the fixed costs of acquiring access to the copyable information product. But, in actuality, the restrictions on group membership could be dispensed with in technological circumstances that restricted the ease of producing copies; where the latter were embedded in a physical medium, such as a printed book, publishers could benefit from the formation of club-like organizations that aggregated individual consumer demands–effectively 'bundles'. The English book trade thus came eventually to take a tolerant, and even appreciative view of the local commercial circulating libraries that arose during the eighteenth century to cater to the growth in demand for popular literature (e.g., Roehl and Varian, 2001).

It is said that economists are the sorts of scientists who like to show that things that are observed to work in practice also can work in theory. So it is reassuring that the experience of commercial circulating libraries conforms with the result of microeconomic models that demonstrated that lax restraints on copying (or free sharing) could be compatible with profitable publishing. But more recent and more intricate theoretical arguments have raised rather more profound challenges to the traditional rationale for copyright protection in the digital information age. In a pioneering and mathematically elegant dynamic general equilibrium analysis, Boldrin and Levine (2002a and 2002b) show that even in the absence of any restrictions on the re-copying of a new information good – restrictions that legal owners of copyright are permitted to impose on their customers and licensees – competitive markets can support a socially efficient equilibrium in the production of information assets, and in the intertemporal flows of consumption utilities these yield.

The underlying idea here is that although unrestricted copying eventually will drive the price of the marginal copy to zero, this doesn't happen very quickly; even if new technology has made copying rapid and essentially costless at the margin, Boldrin and Levine (2002a and 2002b) point out that consumption use may degrade the reproduction rate, and the supply of copies cannot instantly undergo infinite expansion. Hence, the possessor of a 'first copy', that is, the original instance of the intellectual or cultural work, has an asset that can command a positive price under competitive conditions. Its price reflects the present value of the future flow of marginal utilities that subsequent copies will yield to impatient consumers. Thus the notion that the infinite expansibility of information, by permitting 'free-riding' on the part of consumers, would leave the producer of the first copy with nothing for his or her efforts, is unjustified because the process takes time, and there is a value to reading the best seller, or the latest DNA sequence sooner, rather than later.

Still more recently, this line of analysis has been taken a very significant step farther by Quah (2002): it turns out that the ability of competitive equilibrium prices to support the socially efficient dynamic allocation – maximizing the present value of the future stream of consumers' utilities – survives the complete removal of all the restrictions that copyright law (and analogous *sui generis* legal protections for works of 'low authorship') allows possessors of 'the first copy' to impose on licensed users. Whereas in the analysis of Boldrin and Levine the terms of the weaker licence permit purchasers to make copies only for future consumption purposes, Quah's analysis shows that the first copy can command a positive value even when those copies can be sold in competition with the copies being supplied by the holder of the original instantiation of the information good – so long as the rate at which copies can be generated remains bounded from above.[16]

Commercial database firms in the US appear to have understood at least one facet of the economic reality that is reflected in these theoretical propositions. Copyright, or other legal protections of the content of their databases was not necessary for them to run profitable businesses, in part because they could charge a premium to customers who wanted access to early updates of the contents, and did not restrict them putting the information they extracted into other, equally unprotected databases.[17] To be sure, these results do not go so far as to say that the competitive market valuation of the 'first copy' always would be sufficiently large to cause every possible information asset to be created. The cost of the creative effort may be too large, but then we do not ask competitive markets for conventional commodities to provide them even when the cost of doing so exceeds what the utility maximizing consumers would be willing to pay.

Viewed from the vantage point of these deepening doubts about the old rationale for legal monopolies in readily copyable and ubiquitously shareable information goods, the current rush to tighten the copyright regime and encourage strict enforcement of 'anti-piracy' provisions of all kinds, may at some date in the not-so-distant future come to be perceived as having been a serious mistake. This is so not only because it will turn out to have been unnecessary for the socially efficient production and distribution of an increasingly important class of commodities in the New Economy, or because it will have consequences that were injurious to the conduct of open science. Those will be bad enough, but policy makers are likely to suffer more obloquy if it begins to be evident that their enthusiasm for entrenching all the old IPR institutions was antithetical to the development and exploitation of new and more profitable business opportunities. This prospect is not merely a fantasy.

Among at least some leading innovators concerned with the future trajectory of e-commerce, there is growing recognition that the conventional regime of proprietary controls over the use of information by industry may hinder the exploitation of new profit opportunities being created by digital, networked technology. Within the domain of Internet-based media industries, a new landscape of what are referred to as 'peer to peer' (P2P) services has emerged, featuring shared storage, shared information and shared processing. The new P2P applications devolve significant autonomy and control to independent nodes in the network; they capitalize on under-utilized network-connected computing resources at the edge of the network; they operate as transparent end-to-end services across an Internet of uneven and temporary connections. One vision of the future sees the greater effectiveness of this comparatively unstructured and self-organized mode of producing and delivering new information to individual users as the basis for new and competitive commercial services; that these will challenge the incumbency of traditional business forms in information-intensive production and distribution activities.

Not surprisingly, therefore, spokespersons for P2P business applications have been worried by the threat that proprietary standards strategies on the part of platform vendors would create barriers to collaborative computing, in just the same way that scientists engaged in distributed Internet projects worry about IPR-created barriers to the flow of information, and the diminishing future prospects for easy voyages of exploration in 'information space'. Here is Esther Dyson's (2000, p. 8) formulation of the threat to P2P, and a possible means of avoiding it:

> The growth of P2P services will be retarded if this world fragments into warring proprietary platforms, forcing users to make unpalatable choices and killing synergistic network effects. Some existing proposed standards fit naturally into P2P models, including simple object access protocol (SOAP) and universal discovery description and integration (UDDI). . . . At some point it will make sense to have at least *de facto* standards for common P2P elements. Standards bodies [which under ANSI rules preclude adoption of proprietary specifications that are not freely licensed] provide a place for industry participants to gather, compare notes, identify shared challenges and find common ground.

At the 2001 Economic World Forum meeting in Davos, Switzerland, Richard Li, executive Chairman of Pacific Century CyberWorks, is reported to have voiced essentially the same worries: 'his biggest concern about the development of broadband technology was the conservatism of many content providers who were determined to retain copyright protection and unwilling to consider creative new business models. That element is probably the missing slice – for the time being' (*International Herald Tribune*, 30 January 2001, pp. 1, 16).

Significantly enough, the emerging P2P approach to network-based computing and computer-mediated telecommunications services, and the demonstrated capacity of that non-hierarchical form of machine organization to mobilize distributed intelligence for the rapid solution of new problems, has strong elements of homomorphism with the historical functioning of 'invisible colleges' in the open science domain (see David, 1997 and David et al., 1999). What has changed, of course, is the qualitative effects of the technological capacity to link 'distributed intelligent resources' in a host of differentiated sub-communities at negligible cost; and to thus provide spectacularly rapid capabilities of searching the 'information spaces' thereby created.

What hitherto was the peculiar organizational facility for discovery and invention that the commercially unpressured pace of open scholarly inquiry afforded practitioners of 'open science' may become a much more widely relevant mode of generating innovative information goods that customers are willing to pay for.

The transformation that appears to be bringing the world of P2P network-based commerce and the world of 'invisible colleges' of academic inquiry into closer alignment with regard to their working modalities is certainly an intriguing development, and one that is potentially promising for the future synergetic interactions between those two spheres of human endeavour. It stands in much greater need of concerted public policy support than the present impetus being given to the negotiation of university–industry collaborative research agreements whose IPR provisions accede to the monopoly-protecting strategies familiar to conventional R&D-intensive businesses in the chemical, pharmaceutical and electromechanical engineering industries.

My point in drawing attention to the parallels between the organization of open-science communities, and the information-intensive strategies emerging in the domain of cyber-commerce is simply this: policy makers in the industrially advanced countries, and those in other regions who are echoing their views, may be making a serious error in pressing university- and public institute-based research groups to involve themselves in conventionally securing and 'managing' proprietary rights to the use of new knowledge. However fashionable this current policy trend may be at present, those subscribing to it may be found to have been trying to ride the wave of the past – at the expense of building the wave of the future. In actuality, if such efforts to create 'wealth from knowledge through IPR' succeeded, the result might be to have rendered more difficult their economies' eventual development of novel kinds of computer network-intensive service organizations, and the other new lines of e-business to which those would lead.

Rather than seeing 'open science' communities as asserting claims that stand in the way of the exploration and exploitation of profitable business opportunities built on exclusive ownership and control of digital content, their characteristic mode of disclosure and data sharing might well be regarded as a precursor and paradigm of future 'New Economy' activities that will fully exploit the potentialities opened by the Internet. To put this thought into proper historical perspective, the ethos and mode of organization that have been associated historically with publicly supported scientific work groups (at least since the seventeenth century), now could be coming into its own as the basis for new forms of *commercial* activity feasible in the Digital Age. This certainly is what some observers of the open source software movement now suggest.[18] What policy-making for economic development in the twenty-first century ought to consider carefully, therefore, is how to avoid promoting an entrenchment of durable IPR protection regimes that could fatally obstruct that evolution.

6.9 MODEST PROPOSALS: IPR POLICIES TO PRESERVE THE PUBLIC KNOWLEDGE COMMONS

What sort of intellectual property arrangements will be best suited to the socially efficient exploitation of the production and consumption possibility emerging in the 'weightless economy,' and to the construction of the 'digital information spaces' in which globally collaborative programmes of discovery and invention are likely to flourish?

The policy position on copyright and copyright-like protections of intellectual property that I have advanced on previous occasions and continue to advocate here is of the meliorist, rather than the radical variety (e.g. David, 2001). This is not because I am not attracted by the elegance of the idea of creating a positive right to 'fair use' of legally protected information, and research tools, for educational and research purposes. One might be tempted to think along such lines by the recent indications that WIPO is aware of the existence of a connection between intellectual property and human rights. The joint panel discussion organized by WIPO and the Office of United Nations High Commission for Human Rights, to commemorate the 50th anniversary of the Universal Declaration of Human Rights, addressed issues such as biodiversity, the production of traditional (ethnic) knowledge and innovation, the right to culture, health, non-discrimination, and scientific freedom.

Another possible straw in the wind is to be seen in Article 10 of the European Convention on Human Rights, which prescribes the right to freedom of speech as protecting not only the positive right to expression, but the right to receive information. Yet the involvement of human rights counts in intellectual property law is likely to be a distant and incremental evolution, if it happens at all. It therefore seems expedient to attend to less far-reaching means of improving the present state of affairs.

Developed and developing economies alike have a shared interest in halting and, if possible, reversing the trend toward the further strengthening and extension of property rights regimes to every conceivable form of 'information'. My convictions in this regard have crystallized as a response to the prospective implications of the European Union's database legislation, the proposals for similar *sui generis* protections that surfaced in the US Congress, and the alarcity with which the European Commission's Information Society Directive (2001) followed the US Digital Millennium Copyright Act (1988) in introducing new criminal law sanctions to reinforce the effectiveness of digital 'self-help' technologies such as watermarking and encryption. These institutional changes appear to me as last-ditch efforts to entrench an approach to intellectual property rights that is being rendered increasingly obsolete by the technological developments that are driving the 'New Economy'. Yet, worse than exemplifying ingenious adaptations to preserve the workability of an old legal regime, the continuation of this trend may seriously curtail the benefits developed and developing societies alike are able to derive from vastly expanded access to scientific, technological and cultural knowledge.

When considering the available courses of action to counter threats to the pursuit of knowledge arising from recent innovations intended to strengthen intellectual property protections, distinctions of two kinds help to simplify the discussion, although not the problems that need to be addressed. First, there is an obvious difference between the altered terms and the scope of statutory intellectual property protections, on the one hand, and on the other hand, legislative steps designed to reinforce the use of technologies of 'self-help' that enable copyright owners to more perfectly control the dissemination of digital content (whether that is legally protected or not). A second distinction has to be drawn between the situation of countries where legislative innovations affecting intellectual property may be under consideration, and those cases in which such statutes already are *faits acomplis* – so that the questions of practical interest concern implementation and enforcement.

For most of the nations of the world, the appropriate recommendations in regard to both the technological and the legal measures that would restrict access to digital data used for research and training would seem to follow Nancy Reagan's admonition to youths who are offered the opportunity to experiment with addictive drugs: 'Just say "No"!' It is relevant that this option remains one that is open to all the countries, developed and developing alike, that are signatories to the TRIPS agreement and, of course, to those who have not yet joined the WTO. To date, at least, there is no international convention in force for the legal protection of databases and the articles of the TRIPS agreement do not pertain to database protection per se. Thus, unless a case were successfully to be made for interpreting the *sui generis* protections for databases created by the EC Directive of 11 March 1996 as somehow being covered under copyright, nothing in the TRIPS agreements would oblige other nations to follow the (misdirected) leaders in this particular regard. Such an interpretation, moreover, would be utterly tendentious in view of the numerous respects in which the terms of the EC Database Directive has been seen to deviate from the principles embraced by national and international copyright law.

Much the same general position may be advanced in regard to the possible products of the legislative drive to provide legal reinforcement for technological measures of 'self-help' on the part of copyright owners. As has been noted (in section 6.4, above), the US Digital Millennium Copyright Act (1998) includes provisions making it illegal to furnish – whether by importation or manufacture, and whether by sale or free distribution – all means of circumventing 'any technological measure that effectively controls access' to a copyrighted work. As dubious and in some respects as counter-productive as these sections of the DMCA have been found to be, by both legal and technical experts,[19] it remains quite conceivable that an effort will be made to press other countries into following suit. In an immediate sense, however, the issue in this case is not one of legal principle, but instead belongs to the wider and unresolved debate about the feasibility and desirability of uniform international standards of *enforcement* of intellectual property rights.

Nothing presently compels countries that are signatory to the TRIPS agreement to arrive at uniformity in the degree of enforcement of their intellectual property laws. It is true that the international conventions and laws governing patents, trademarks, copyrights, trade secrets, industrial designs, semiconductor mask works, and still protections, all must be 'effectively implemented and enforced' by each of the nations belonging to the WTO. Nevertheless, the term 'effectively' remains subject to considerable variations in interpretation. In addition, the agreement explicitly recognizes several bases for exemptions from the provisions made for protection of the rights of owners of intellectual property, including appeal to 'fair use' or 'public interest' (Articles 13, 17, 24, 27:2, 30 and 37). It may be argued, therefore, that inasmuch as national governments under the agreement retain the right to create a haven for 'fair use' of protected intellectual property in the public interest, their ability to effectively exercise that right would be impeded by requiring that they prevent their own nationals from circumventing unilaterally imposed access-blocking technologies in order to avail themselves of those 'fair use' exemptions for those very same scientific research and training purposes.

The foregoing remarks obviously apply to the situation in which the developing economies find themselves with respect to intellectual property protections that would have seriously inhibited worthy 'public interest' activities, had not the latter gained statutory exemptions under the laws' provisos for 'fair use'. It remains an interesting question as to whether its sphere of applicability extends still farther: could it also encompass retroactive remedial legislative actions on the part of the economically advanced member states of the EU that have not yet implemented the EC Directive on the Legal Protection of Databases in their national laws? Whereas some countries, such as the United Kingdom, were quick to implement the Directive without entering any exceptions or liberalizing interpretations, others European states, such as the Netherlands as well as Greece, Ireland, Italy, Portugal and Spain, have not rushed to comply with its terms. This has opened a window for attempts to modify the Directive's force by suitable interpretations in the way it is implemented. But rather than leaving it to individual members to undertake to ameliorate the harm that a literal acceptance and enforcement of the text of the Directive might do to the scientific research community in Europe, it would be far more satisfactory for the EC to now propose a 'harmonized' set of fair use exemptions, as a minimal remedial step.

That solution, however, is most unlikely to emerge spontaneously, not even in the wake of the departure of EC Commissioner Bangemann, and the scandal-prompted reforms undertaken by the new leadership of EC President Roman Prodi; some very considerable amount of political pressure would have to be brought to bear on the Commission, and a coalition formed among the smaller member states who have yet to implement the Directive would seem to be among the few plausible ways in which such pressure could materialize. Yet, in view of the politically fragmented condition of Europe's basic science research communities, the prospects of an effective coalition emerging would remain rather remote unless it were to be energized by business corporations similar to those in the US who have lobbied actively against counterpart database legislation. The political economy of the question, therefore is likely to turn not on the longer-run implications for science and technology in Europe, as the logic of economic analysis might dictate, but instead on whether or not there exists a significant section of European industry that comes to perceive a direct and immediate source of harm to their economic fortunes in the extraordinary nature of the protections allowed by the EC's Database Directive.

The important broad principle to be established is a simple one: whatever legal rights societies construct regarding 'intellectual property,' whether under international patent and copyright regimes or by *sui generis* protections (inadvisable as these may be, on other grounds), the licensing terms available to 'owners' should never be allowed to create inefficient artificial impediments to the intensive utilization of the contents of virtual archives and information tools. As I have argued, this principle may be just as important for the future of new commercial ventures based on computer-mediated telecommunications as it is for the health of fundamental, exploratory inquiries organized under the auspices of non-profit institutions. How should such a principle be applied in practice? In the view of most economists, the 'first best' allocation system in situations where goods are produced with high fixed costs but far lower marginal costs, is to apply what is known as the 'Ramsey pricing' rule. This fits the case of information products such as scientific publication and data, where the first-copy costs are very great in relationship to the negligible unit costs of copies. Ramsey pricing in essence amounts to price discrimination between users whose demands are inelastic and those users for whom the quantity purchased is extremely price-sensitive. The former class of buyers therefore will bear high prices without curtailing the quantity purchased of the goods in question, and hence not suffer great reductions in consumption utility on that account, whereas the low prices offered to those in the second category will spare them the burden of economic welfare-reducing cutbacks in their use of the good.

The case might then be made for treating scholars and public sector, university-based researchers as having highly elastic information and data demands. Such a characterization would follow from considering that this category of knowledge-workers is employed on projects that have fixed budget allocations from public (or non-profit) entities, organizations that are expected to promote the interests of society at large. As there is strong complementarity between their data and information requirements, on the one hand, and on the other resources they use in their research, the effects of raising the real price of this input are tantamount to sharply reducing the quantity of useful work that such projects can accomplish so long as their budgets remain fixed. Obviously, there is no workable economic or political mechanism that would serve to 'index' the nominal value of public research budgets on the prices of commercially provided data. Even were such mechanisms to be found, commitment to implement them on the part of the rich societies would most likely result in pricing the use of scientific information and data beyond the reach of many poorer societies.

The general thrust of the policy advocated here is thus quite simple: statutes that would establish legal ownership rights for compilers of scientific and technological databases should also include provisions mandating compulsory licensing of scientific database contents at marginal costs (of data extraction and distribution) to accredited individuals and research institutions. The implication is that the fixed costs should be covered by lump sum subscription charges, which would be waived in the case of researchers engaged in constructing and maintaining these databases under the auspices of publicly supported projects.

A fully consistent, albeit still bolder, recommendation would be to have the same provisions applied more broadly. They could be extended to all users of such data and information resources who agreed to distribute the data they generated on the same basis as that on which they had been able to access the data used in creating it. That universal application of the so-called 'copyleft' principle in the GNU General Public License leaves open the possibility to commercial ventures of licensing and direct marketing of ancillary and complementary goods and services. By such means the firms might recoup the fixed costs of the contribution to the 'information infrastructures' that they would participate with publicly sponsored researchers in helping to create.

Further and still more far-reaching reforms affecting patents on research tools follow from this approach. The first would institute a public policy of 'patent buy-outs', under which public tax revenues would be used to purchase the rights to this class of inventions, and place them in the public domain. A possible device to prevent confiscation of valuable patents at arbitrary low compensation, or the award of an inappropriately high 'prize' to the patentee, would take the form of the following provision: such inventions would be made legally subject to compulsory licensing at a 'reasonable' royalty rate and the (regulated) rights to the revenue stream would then be publicly auctioned, with the government standing ready to acquire the rights for the public domain by default if a pre-announced 'reservation' price was attained by a private purchaser.

It is true that there are some well-known circumstances in which significant patent protection might be warranted by the high fixed costs that public regulatory policies impose on the private developers of innovative commodities that are readily 'reverse engineered' and cheaply copied – for example, by the extensive field testing requirements for pharmaceutical products and medical devices. But these represent the exception rather than the rule, and the end products themselves typically do not have the essential 'public goods' properties associated with information good's and information tools. Rather, it is the product safety-testing information regarding new pharmaceuticals and other complex and potentially dangerous products that actually constitute the 'public goods'. Yet even here it should be pointed out that a convincing economic case has still to be made for using legally constructed monopolies to solve the resulting appropriability problem, rather than, say, public procurement contracts for safety-testing.[20]

6.10 CONCLUSION

The American poet Robert Frost's ode to individualism celebrates the stone fences that distinguish the rural landscape of upland New England: 'good fences make good neighbours'. Perhaps this is so where the resource involved is land onto which the livestock from neighbouring farms otherwise may wander to graze and thereby destroy the provender of the animals already pastured there. But is it so, too, when one scientist pores over the data gathered by another? Simple consideration of the 'public goods' nature of information tells us that such is not the case.

Information is not like forage, depleted by use for consumption. Datasets are not subject to being 'over-grazed' but, instead, are likely to be enriched and rendered more accurate, and more fully documented the more that researchers are allowed to comb through them. It is by means of wide and complete disclosure, and the sceptical efforts to replicate novel research findings, that scientific communities collectively build bodies of 'reliable knowledge'. Thus there is good reason for hesitating to embrace 'private property rights' as a universal panacea, for that is a system of resource allocation that has been found to work well in the domain of conventional commodities that are exhausted in the process of use and cannot be simultaneously enjoyed by many.

By contrast, in the realm of knowledge, information and scientific data, an overly literal application of the metaphor of 'property', one that emphasizes the desirability of socially enforced rights to exclude trespassers and to alienate 'commodities' by means of exchange, may lead towards perverse economic policies in the field of scientific and technological research. By its very nature, the alternative to proprietary research – the pursuit of 'open science' – requires patronage from external sources of grant and contract funding, or from those who are personally engaged, and often from both.

The central problems facing researchers in the developing countries are rooted in a lack of adequate material resources to pursue their work in the effective, open mode of cooperation with scientists throughout the world. Thus it is tempting for them to think of embracing proprietary research as the solution to the income constraints under which they presently labour. The same thought occurs quite naturally to those who wish to help these less advantaged colleagues. After all, this course of 'self-help' in meeting the rising costs of modern scientific research demonstrably has proved attractive to the administrators of many far better endowed universities and public institutes in the industrially advanced regions – and also to individual researchers who see in it a means of further advancing both their work and their material standard of living.

In the developed countries this course has provided, at best only a small margin of incremental research support, averaging 8–10 per cent among research universities in the US. Yet, in some fields, and particularly in the life sciences, where the share of funding from industrial sources approaches 25 per cent at the leading institutions, the commercialization movement is perceptibly encroaching on the culture of academic research and challenging the ethos of collaborative, open science. Consequently, we must worry that applying the same 'remedy' to mend the economic disabilities of open science in the developing countries would have more profound transforming effects, and might in the end result in further isolating researchers there from the remaining sources of cooperative exchange with publicly supported colleagues and institutions elsewhere. Yes, in the private property rights system we have a readily prescribed and potentially potent 'cure' for the condition of impoverished open science. Unfortunately, it is one in which the patients die. We really do need to think of something better.

NOTES

1. The practical importance of the 'sweat of the brow' argument for the legal protection of database investors in the US has tended to be exaggerated. Legal opinion is divided on the question, but, as Maurer and Scotchmer (1999, n. 3) have noted, courts in New York and California – the two main jurisdictions where intellectual property litigation traditionally occurred – did not accept this argument for extending copyright to databases. Both before and following the 1991 *Feist* ruling, copyright applied to the original selection, coordination, and arrangement of data within a database; many defendants in the US therefore have been found liable for copyright infringement since 1991. See also Maurer et al. (2001).
2. This does not mean that knowledge of all kinds can be transferred at low marginal costs. Uncodified knowledge, which in many instances resists codification and remains 'tacit', is more difficult to transmit between agents, except through personal communications that take the form of demonstrations. On the implications of tacitness in regard to science and technology policies, and the economics of codification of knowledge, see Cowan et al. (2000).
3. Thomas Jefferson remarked on this, too: 'The fact is, that one new idea leads to another, that to a third, and so on through a course of time until someone, with whom no one of these ideas was original, combines all together, and produces what is justly called a new invention.' (Koch and Peden, 1972; p. 686).
4. For the legal and economic interpretations see Dasgupta and David (1987 and 1994) and David (1994).

5. Dam (1999, pp. 7–8) points out that because the case law has tended to reject the 'experimental use' defence against infringement suits whenever the researcher might profit, this exception to patent protection is less likely to prove beneficial for academic researchers in fields like biomedical sciences, where even publicly funded 'basic' research may yield short-term economic payoffs. Given the case law precedents in the US, the drive on the part of university administrators to exploit patent rights under the provisions of the 1980 Bayh-Dole Act may thus be seen as contributing indirectly as well as directly to creating more formidable barriers to the ability of academic researchers to rapidly access new research tools and results.

6. See Hall and Ziedonis (2001) for the defensive use of patent portfolios in an industry that prior to the 1980s had been characterized by low propensity to patent.

7. The introduction here of the term 'non-entitlement' is a deliberate allusion to Amartya Sen's observation that people starved in the Indian famine of 1918 not because the harvest was inadequate to feed them, but because the rise in grain prices had deprived them of 'entitlement' to the food that actually was available.

8. It will be seen (from the discussion below) that such also may be the import of the European Commission's Directive on the Legal Protection of Databases, issued on 11 March 1996.

9. See Digital Millennium Copyright Act (1998), United States Code, 17, Section 1201.

10. This pithy comment was made by Stanford Professor of Law, John Barton, in the concluding remarks of his seminar on international trends in intellectual property protection, presented at the Stanford Institute for Economic Policy Research Workshop on Science, Technology and Economic Policy in Winter Quarter, 2000.

11. The 1996 draft was entitled: 'Basic Proposal for the Substantive Provisions of the Treaty on Intellectual Property in Respect of Databases . . .', WIPO Doc. CRNR/DC, Geneva, 30 August. It has been pointed out that in this regard, as well as in others, the EU Directive called for a departure from the principle of administering commercial laws on a 'national treatment' basis, under which a country's domestic laws (whether for intellectual property production, or unfair business practices) should treat foreign nationals like one of the country's citizens. The principle of national treatment is embodied in Article 3 of the TRIPs agreement, as well as more generally in the Paris Convention (on patents and trademark protection) and the Berne Convention (on copyright protection). Objections to this departure were recorded in the testimony of the General Counsel of the US Department of Commerce (Andrew J. Pincus), in the 106th Congress House Hearings on H.R. 1858 (1999): section F.

12. See National Research Council (1997), pp. 148–53, for material underlying this and the following discussion.

13. The EC Directive on Databases, note 52, article 7(1), provides an initial 15-year term from the date of completion; 7(2) extends protection for an additional 15 years if the database 'is made available to the public in whatever manner' before the initial term expires; 7(3) allows 15-year renewals for '[a]ny substantial change, evaluated qualitatively or quantitatively, to the contents of a database . . . from the accumulation of successive additions, deletions or alterations, which . . . result in . . . a substantial new investment.' Under US copyright only the additions and revisions themselves – which would be considered as 'derivative work' from the prior original expressive matter – would be entitled to fresh legal protection.

14. See Statement by Graham Cameron, in *IPR Aspects of Internet Collaborations*, European Commission – DG Research, Strata Programme Working Group Report, EUR 19456, Brussels (April) 2001.

15. Moreover, in 'the knowledge society' – where collaborative generation of new ideas and practices is expected to characterize a larger and larger segment of business activity, the scientific research network, conceived of as a form of 'competence-based club', may become a paradigm for an economically much larger part of the market for information goods that are research inputs.

16. The increasingly rapid rate of copying that Quah's (2002) analysis contemplates is

alluded to by the reference to '24/7-time' – the continuous, 'round the clock every day of the week' pace at which the Internet permits economic activity to run. In the limit, where copying becomes infinitely rapid, Quah finds that the intuition of the traditional economic argument that competitive markets will fail is regained. The first copy (asset price) and the price of the marginal consumption flow both go to zero.

17. As has been pointed out, US database firms also provide a variety of complementary services, including efficient and rapid search algorithms, which also contribute to the profitability of their operations in the absence of intellectual properly protection for the database contents.

18. See, for example, 'The Organization and Viability of Open Source Software: A Proposal to the National Science Foundation', P.A. David (Principal Investigator), Stanford Institute for Economic Policy Research, 22 January 2001.

19. On the question of 'counter-productive' effects, Dam (1999) notes the testimony by cryptography experts to the effect that the wording of the 1998 DMCA (US Code, 17, section 1201) would make it illegal even to devise and distribute algorithms used in testing encryption systems by trying to defeat them, and, more generally would greatly impede research aimed at making such devices cheap and faster to apply. This point nicely recapitulates the larger theme that what the would-be protectors of technological innovation most frequency fail to grasp is that information is an input in the process of generating new knowledge.

20. Purely fiscal arguments would have to show the existence of socially more productive alternative uses of the claims on resources used (or withheld by their owners) as a consequence of the state's reliance on general tax revenues to provide product and process safety information on which to base its regulatory decisions. It might be noticed that there already is a specific (and hidden) form of state subsidization of private investment in field trials of drugs and medical devices: in the UK, for example, the hospital and clinical facilities of the National Health Service are placed at the disposal of the researchers who conduct those trials on behalf of the commercial developers of the innovations.

REFERENCES

Arrow, K. (1962), 'Economic welfare and the allocation of resources for invention', in R. Nelson (ed.), *The Rate and Direction of Inventive Activity*, New York: National Bureau of Economic Research, pp. 609–26.

Boldrin, M. and D.K. Levine (2002a), 'The case against intellectual property', *American Economic Review*, **92**, 209–12.

Boldrin, M. and D.K. Levine (2002b), 'Perfectly competitive innovation', Staff Report 303, Federal Reserve Bank of Minneapolis.

Cockburn, I. and Z. Griliches (1988), 'Industry effects and appropriability measures in the stock market's valuation of R&D and patents', *American Economic Review*, **78**, 419–23.

Cowan, R., P.A. David and D. Foray (2000), 'The explicit economics of codification and tacit knowledge', *Industrial and Corporate Change*, 9, 211–53.

Dam, K.W. (1999), 'Intellectual property and the academic enterprise', Working Paper Chicago Law School.

Dasgupta, P. and P.A. David (1987), 'Information disclosure and the economics of science and technology', in G.R. Feiwel (ed.), *Arrow and the Ascent of Modern Economic Theory*, New York: New York University Press.

Dasgupta, P. and P.A. David (1994), 'Toward a new economics of science', *Research Policy*, **23**, 487–525.

David, P.A. (1994), 'Positive feedbacks and research productivity in science: reopening another black box', in O. Granstrand (ed.), *The Economics of Technology*, Amsterdam: Elsevier Science.

David, P.A. (1997), 'Communication norms and the collective cognitive performance of "invisible colleges" ', in G.B. Navaretti et al. (eds), *Creation and Transfer of Knowledge: Institutions and Incentives*, Berlin: Springer Verlag.

David, P.A. (2001) 'A tragedy of the public knowledge "commons"? Global science, intellectual property and the digital technology boomerang', MERIT Working Paper 2001–2003.

David, P.A., D. Foray and W.E. Steinmueller (1999), 'The research network and the "new economics" of science', in A. Garmbardella and F. Malerba (eds), *The Organization of Innovative Activities in Europe*, Cambridge: Cambridge University Press.

Dyson, E. (2000), Esther Dyson's monthly report, **10**, 8.

Hall, B.H. and R.H. Ziedonis (2001), 'The patent paradox revisited: An empirical study of patenting in the U.S. semiconductor industry, 1979–1995', *RAND Journal of Economics*, **32**, 101–28.

von Hippel, E. (1988), *The Sources of Innovation*, New York: Oxford University Press.

Johnson, W.R. (1985), 'The economics of copying', *Journal of Political Economy*, **93**, 158–74.

Koch, A. and W. Peden (eds) (1972), *The Life and Selected Writings of Thomas Jefferson*, New York: Modern Library Editions.

Kortum, S. and J. Lerner (1998), 'Stronger protection or technological revolution: What is behind the recent surge in patenting?', *Carnegie-Rochester Conference Series on Public Policy*, **48**, 247–304.

Liebowitz, S. (1985), 'Copying and indirect appropriability: Photocopying of journals', *Journal of Political Economy*, **93**, 945–57.

Maurer, S.M. (1999), 'Raw knowledge: Protecting technical databases for science and industry', Report Prepared for the NRC Workshop on Promoting Access to Scientific and Technical Data for the Public Interest.

Maurer, S., P.B. Hugenholtz and H. Onsrud (2001), 'Europe's database experiment', *Science*, **294**, 789–90.

Maurer, S.M. and S. Scotchmer (1999), 'Database protection: Is it broken and should we fix it?', *Science*, **284**, 1129–30.

National Research Council (1997), *Bits of Power: Issues in Global Access to Scientific Data*, Washington, DC: National Academy Press.

Novos, I.E. and M. Waldman (1984), 'The effects of increased copyright protection: An analytical approach', *Journal of Political Economy*, **92**, 236–46.

Quah, D. (2002), '24/7 Competitive Innovation', LSE Working Paper.

Roehl, R. and H.R. Varian (2001), 'Circulating libraries and video rental stores', *First Monday*, **6**, 8.

7. Free software developers: Who, how and why*

Rishab A. Ghosh, Rüdiger Glott, Bernhard Krieger and Gregorio Robles

7.1 INTRODUCTION

A large part of the worldwide market for software is dominated by so-called proprietary software, which means that the buyer and user of a software product is not allowed and not able to read and change the source code of the program.[1] Microsoft Office is surely the best-known example of proprietary software. Representatives of proprietary software companies argue that this limitation of the users' opportunity to customize software according to individual needs and preferences is necessary because otherwise the property rights and liabilities of the software companies as well as growth prospects and job opportunities in the software industry as a whole would be jeopardized.[2]

In contrast to this viewpoint, developers of Free/Libre/Open Source Software[3] (FLOSS) argue that the user should generally be entitled to read and change the source code. Well-known examples of this kind of software are the Linux operating system or the Apache web server. FLOSS developers distribute their products on the basis of licence agreements that require anyone who improves a certain software program to distribute the revised version further only by disclosing the source code again.[4] The reasons for this standpoint have a practical and a political dimension. The practical one is that standardized software hardly meets the interests and needs of any individual user and that therefore each user should be allowed to adapt a software product to his or her personal needs. The political one is that software is considered as pure information that should be freely (or at very

* The authors wish to thank Paul David, Bas ter Weel and the referee for their comments, which helped a lot to strengthen our argument. We would also like to thank Steffen Kühnel for his methodological advice. This chapter is based on the results of the FLOSS Developer Survey, carried out as part of the FLOSS Project, supported by European Union funds under the 5th Framework Programme (IST), June 2001–October 2002. The final report is available at www.flossproject.org/report.

low costs) accessible to everyone in order to make the information society work.[5] This attitude is by no means anti-commercial, since 'free' in 'free software' is meant as in 'free speech', not as in 'free beer'. (Stallman 2002) Many successful business models have developed around FLOSS products and provide distribution and consultation services, like the Red Hat or SuSE distribution platform for Linux.

The political dimension illustrates that many FLOSS developers define themselves not only by technical but also by socio-economic terms. They claim that FLOSS is more than just a matter of software products, projects or licences, and perceive developing FLOSS as a distinctive 'way of life'. The community dynamics of developers as well as the existence of a freedom-based 'hacker' culture are emphasized, both claimed to be essential for understanding the FLOSS phenomenon (O'Reilly 1999, pp. 34, 36).

Although the sharing of non-proprietary software occurred in academic and some commercial labs as early as the early 1960s (Lerner and Tirole 2000, pp. 4–5), the dynamics of FLOSS as a mass phenomenon started to unfold with the founding of the Free Software Foundation in 1985 and was reinforced by the growth of the Internet in the 1990s. In 1997, the founding of the Open Source Initiative again accelerated the dynamics of the FLOSS movement. During these years, FLOSS products experienced a triumphal march and captured a considerable share of important parts of the software market, namely the market for operating systems and for web servers. Success factors for FLOSS products are the short period of time in which they can be developed and their high quality, compared to many proprietary software products (Wheeler 2002). Both advantages derive from the specific way in which FLOSS is developed, that is by using network externalities of highly volatile groups of independent software developers who communicate and interact via the Internet (Raymond 1998a, 1998b; Stallman 1999; Ghosh 1999; Bonnaccorsi and Rossi 2002; Garzarelli 2002). The large numbers of developers that are involved simultaneously in the various software developing projects provide fast progress and continuous debugging on a large scale that cannot be reached at the level of development teams in proprietary software companies. FLOSS has therefore been expected to provide a means to overcome the so-called 'software crisis', that is that software is considered to take too long to develop, to exceed its budget, and not to work very well (Feller and Fitzgerald 2000, p. 58). Some authors like therefore to consider the process of FLOSS development as continuous creation and reconfiguration of communities of practice (Moon and Sproull 2000; Franke and Shah 2001; Scacchi 2002).

However, despite the fact that FLOSS is widely used today and is the subject of much discussion in the academic literature as well as the trade and popular press, many aspects of the FLOSS phenomenon remained puzzling. A still too common question is frequently asked – how is it sustainable? There is an unwillingness to take the sustainability of this model as proven by time – the free software movement is two decades old and has been growing at an exponential rate since its inception; it has proven exceedingly attractive to commercial businesses with almost every major player in the ICT industry backing it in some way or another. This unwillingness stems from an underlying question – in its simplest form, 'if they aren't paid, why do they do it?' Who typically becomes a FLOSS developer, how these developers work together, and how they are integrated and involved in the community are further questions that are directly related to this subject. Answers to these questions do not only provide more general knowledge about the phenomenon and its community, they are also important in the context of discussions about efficiency, productivity, and future developments of FLOSS.

Research in the topic of FLOSS development and the related community has unfortunately not yielded a comprehensive and unequivocal picture, but rather one of very different facets and even contradictions. Conceptions of FLOSS developers have long been dependent on either generalizations of characteristics that were found in particular software projects or on assumptions about the 'nature' of FLOSS developers gained from conversations, publications and speeches of the spokespeople of the community. Besides these conceptions, others appear to be determined by prejudiced stereotypes generated outside the field of software.[6] Conclusively these conceptions show a wide and contradictory variety, ranging from high-skilled specialists, to young amateurs to political activists. A key issue of the discussion about FLOSS developers is the degree of professionalism and expertise there is within the community, as this can clearly be expected to affect strongly the efficiency of work within the community and the quality and competitiveness of FLOSS products. Besides demographic facts this discussion covers the educational and professional background of FLOSS developers as well as socialization patterns in and through the FLOSS community and the organization of work.[7]

The same puzzlement applies to the motivations that are assumed to drive the FLOSS community. Suggestions to form a clear-cut label for the FLOSS community range from fun and reputation concerns, which assume a certain sense of 'hackerism' (Raymond 1998a, 1998b; Torvalds 1999, 2001; Himanen 2001; Shah 2003), to monetary and career concerns (Lerner and Tirole 2000; Lee et al. 2003), thus stressing pure materialism. Since the FLOSS phenomenon has clearly changed from a rather small community of software professionals to a mass phenomenon, we think that any attempt to label this community in a narrow sense must fail. Instead, we suggest understanding the FLOSS community as a wide and multifaceted institution, thus assuming a large and sometimes contradictory variety of different types of members and motivations. This would not only acknowledge and integrate the different aspects of the discussion on that topic, but it would also help to gain a broader understanding of the different ways and directions in which the community as a whole is advancing.

7.2 THE DATA

It is not the purpose of this chapter to dwell on the gross oversimplification of human motivation inherent in the fundamental 'why' question, which is asked, unfortunately, most often by economists, but simply to provide some answers based on empirical evidence that was gained from the FLOSS developer survey. This survey was started in February 2002 and ended at the beginning of April 2002. It was intended to obtain insights into the motives of software developers to develop, distribute and exchange Open Source/Free Software and into the ways in which the FLOSS community is organized, as well as to gain information on demographics (including income levels – in response to the 'if they're not paid' question). Key issues of the examination in this context were:

1. the relationship between non-monetary motives of software developers to provide Open Source/Free Software, such as the wish for a good reputation, and monetary motives, such as the wish for better paid jobs;
2. software developers' perception and valuation of the Open Source/ Free Software domain compared to that of commercial software;
3. personal backgrounds of software developers.

The developer survey was conducted in the form of an online (web-based) survey. The questionnaire consisted of closed questions, that is, every question was associated with a variety of possible answers the developer had to choose from. The questionnaire covered the following topics: work situation and experience, personal features (age, sex, status, etc.), involvement and activity in the Open Source/Free Software community, activity in the commercial software area, motives for involvement in the Open Source/Free Software community (especially the role of monetary and non-monetary remuneration), comparisons of experiences in the Open Source/Free Software community and in the field of commercial software, remuneration of contributions to the FLOSS scene.

The scope of the survey was not limited, neither by the number of interviewees nor by countries or similar criteria. The FLOSS team utilized the well-known phenomenon that questionnaires of this type tend to be distributed within the FLOSS community by the developers themselves, thus enabling the project team to reach a large and diverse part of the whole group under consideration.

Since the questionnaire, once developed, was posted to a few FLOSS communities and then distributed further within the whole community by FLOSS developers themselves, the survey covered a broad scope of their community as a whole. Within the two months during which the survey was conducted, 2784 FLOSS developers filled in the online questionnaire, a number that provides a good basis for a deep-grounded description and analysis of the realm of FLOSS development.[8] The size of the sample is, thus, smaller than the size of the sample of the WIDI survey,[9] but considerably larger than the sample size of the 'hacker survey' of the Boston Consulting Group and OSDN (Lakhani et al. 2002).[10]

7.3   WHO IS DOING IT? PERSONAL FEATURES OF FLOSS DEVELOPERS

7.3.1   Gender

The survey on FLOSS developers confirms the findings of the WIDI project that women do not appear to play a prominent role in the development of Open Source and Free Software; only 1.1 per cent of the FLOSS sample is female. Although women are clearly underrepresented in programmers in industrialized countries, too, this extremely low share of women in the FLOSS community cannot be compared to gender structures in IT professions: according to Suriya (2003), the proportion of women programmers at in the end of the 1990s and the beginning of the new millennium varied between 22 per cent (North and Latin America, UK, Germany) and 33 per cent (Finland). We expect two reasons to explain the low incidence of female FLOSS community members: first, it may be that women within the community show less willingness to reply to surveys in general. Second, we assume that the young age of the community together with the very young average age of the community (see below) and the fact that the community is centred around a technical issue promotes the interests and habits of men rather than of women, especially when they are in adolescence. Indeed, we found that the average age of women is slightly higher than that of men (28.8 years compared to 27.2 years) and that women form a large proportion of programmers and other professions, but a lower proportion of software engineers, consultants, executives and students than men. In addition, while only 16 per cent of the male community members have a professional background outside the IT sector, the respective share of female community members is 25 per cent. Finally, the proportion of those who had joined the FLOSS community in the last four years before the FLOSS developer survey was conducted is slightly higher in female than in male developers, and there was only one woman in the FLOSS sample who had belonged to the FLOSS community for more than nine years. These findings suggest that the channels into the FLOSS community differ considerably between men and women in the sense that women enter the community later in their life-course and after they have already attained some experience in programming or in professions outside the IT sector, whereas men join the community quite early in the life-course and mainly from professions or studies in the IT sector.

7.3.2 Age

The age of the respondents ranges from 14 to 73 years, while there is a clear predominance of people between 16 and 36 years. Only 25 per cent of the respondents are older than 30 years, and only 10 per cent are older than 35. The average age (mean) of the respondents is 27.1 years. The standard deviation is 7.2 years, which indicates quite a large spread within such a young group. However measures of skewness (1.33) and kurtosis (2.84) indicate that the age distribution of the FLOSS developers does not follow the normal distribution pattern, but is significantly shifted towards the younger ages.[11] Despite the astonishingly high maximum age we can thus conclude that members of the FLOSS community are extraordinarily young, usually around the mid-twenties.

The question on the year in which the respondents started to develop FLOSS revealed that the main dynamics of FLOSS development took place in the second half of the 1990s. Still, some of the respondents claim to have started with FLOSS in the 1950s, and others ticked a year in the 1970s or 1980s. However, until 1990 only 8.2 per cent of the sample were already active in the FLOSS scene, and just in the following years the development accelerated considerably. Although the dynamics have accelerated again from 1998 onwards, the average starting year (mean) was 1996.7. The standard deviation of 4.46 years underlines again the strong dynamics of the FLOSS phenomenon in the 1990s. The distribution of this variable within the sample again does not correspond to normal distribution and is shifted towards the later years of the 1990s. Skewness is −2.6 and kurtosis is 13.32, indicating quite a broad peak of the distribution curve.

The starting age of the FLOSS developers ranges between 10 and 55 years. Only 7 per cent started below an age of 16 years, one third was between 16 and 20 years old, another third between 21 and 25, and a quarter was older than 26 years when they started developing FLOSS. The average starting age is 22.9 (standard deviation: 6.32). The measures for skewness (1.44) and kurtosis (3.52) show again that the distribution of the starting age does not follow the normal distribution pattern and is shifted towards the younger ages.

Altogether, the results suggest that developing FLOSS is more populated by the younger generation than by experienced software developers. However, taking into account that Open Source/Free Software is by no means a phenomenon of only the recent years, the young age of FLOSS developers cannot be explained only by generational effects. Changes in the frame settings for the production of software – like increasing capital investments and the new organization structure in FLOSS projects (see Lerner and Tirole 2000, p. 1), together with the growth of the Internet seem to be the key factors for the increasing attractiveness of FLOSS for young people.

7.3.3 Familial Background

Roughly 60 per cent of the developers live in a kind of partnership, only two fifths are single. Further examination of the data revealed that 17 per cent of the FLOSS developers have children, of which almost half have one child, 31 per cent have two children, 14 per cent have three, and 6 per cent have more than three children. Thus participation of developers in the FLOSS community is not necessarily driven by socialization motives or by the willingness 'to be a member' of that community. FLOSS is not a substitute for non-virtual relationship, but fulfils other personal needs, which will be considered below in the section on motivations of FLOSS community members. The FLOSS community can be considered as a large community of practice, as membership is not defined by official status but by participation, as it develops informally around things that matter to people (in this case software), and as it produces a shared repertoire of communal resources (routines, sensibilities, artefacts, vocabulary, styles, etc.) (Wenger 2000).

7.3.4 Educational Level of FLOSS Developers

FLOSS developers have a rather high educational level. University degrees are held by 70 per cent of developers, while another 17 per cent have a high school dipolma. However, a PhD is clearly not a necessary prerequisite to become an FLOSS developer, as only 9 per cent of the respondents show such a high degree. This result corresponds widely to what is known from other surveys in the field of FLOSS (e.g. WIDI Survey; Dempsey et al. 2002). Thus FLOSS obviously attracts young or skilful people, but not

Table 7.1 Educational level of FLOSS developers by age and marital status

All respondents	Age (years) (%)			
	14–23	24–30	>30	Total
A-level / apprenticeship	51.4	21.4	14.8	30.0
University–Bachelor	31.7	32.5	33.3	32.4
Universty–Masters or PhD	17.0	46.0	51.9	37.6
Pearson Chi-Square:		291.179		
Somers'd		0.316		
Respondents 24 years old and older	Marital status (%)			
	Single	Partner	Married	Total
A-level / apprenticeship	25.4	19.8	11.5	19.0
University–Bachelor	31.4	32.7	34.8	32.9
University–Masters or PhD	43.2	47.4	53.7	48.1
Pearson Chi-Square:		27.232		
Lambda		0.00		

Source: © 2004 International Institute of Infonomics / Merit.

blue-collar workers or housewives who learn the art of programming in their free time. This result can be explained by the fact that programming requires capacities in abstract and formal reasoning, which are usually developed in the course of higher educational attainment.[12] Since the FLOSS community has developed as a community of practice around the matter of software, we think that this explanation holds true for the community as a whole, although programming is not at all an activity that is performed by or required from all FLOSS community members – some members translate code or texts for web-sites, others provide or maintain technical infrastructures, and so on.

The educational level of FLOSS developers increases with age, which is explained by the fact that higher educational degrees require more time than lower degrees. In order to eliminate this youth bias, we removed the respondents below 24 years of age from the following analysis. Table 7.1 shows that singles have lower educational levels than those who live in a partnership, whereas married developers have the highest educational level. Despite removing the youngest group of FLOSS community members, this finding is still explained by the age structure of the FLOSS developers: while the average (mean) age of singles and those who live in a partnership

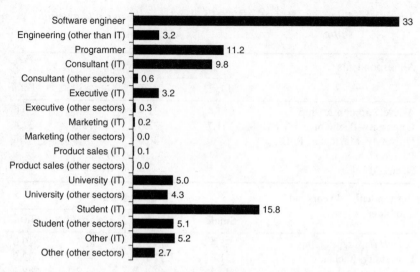

Figure 7.1   Professional structure of FLOSS developers

is about 29 years, the average age of the married is almost 34 years, which is clearly above the overall average age of 30.7 years.

7.3.5   Professional Background

Software engineers provide one third of the sample and thus the largest single group. With a share of 16 per cent, students are the second largest group, followed by programmers and IT consultants. Executives, marketing and product sales experts do not have a significant impact on the professional structure of the FLOSS community. Not surprising, professions and university courses related to the IT sector play a vital role for FLOSS development. Eighty-three per cent of all developers in the sample are employed in the IT sector or deal with similar tasks at universities (Figure 7.1).

7.3.6   Employment Status

Almost two thirds of the FLOSS developers within the sample are employees, but a relatively high proportion, of 14 per cent, is self-employed. Students and people who claim that they are not working currently make up a fifth of the sample. A more sophisticated view that combines employment status and professional background of the FLOSS community members allows us to distinguish between those who show no professional or occupational background at all (unemployed or not

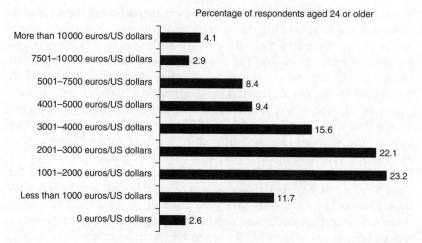

Percentage of respondents aged 24 or older

More than 10 000 euros/US dollars	4.1
7501–10 000 euros/US dollars	2.9
5001–7500 euros/US dollars	8.4
4001–5000 euros/US dollars	9.4
3001–4000 euros/US dollars	15.6
2001–3000 euros/US dollars	22.1
1001–2000 euros/US dollars	23.2
Less than 1000 euros/US dollars	11.7
0 euros/US dollars	2.6

Figure 7.2   Monthly gross income of FLOSS community members

working for other reasons: 4.8 per cent), pure students (14.5 per cent), semi-professionals (students who have an IT-related job: 8.4 per cent), and the large majority of professionals (73.3 per cent).

7.3.7   Income

Overall FLOSS developers are not really high earners, which is still con-firmed when those community members below an age of 24 are excluded from the consideration of monthly gross incomes (Figure 7.2). Three per cent do not earn anything, and another 35 per cent reach no higher gross income than 2000 euros/US dollars per month. A further 22 per cent earn between 2000 and 3000 euros/US dollars, and 16 per cent reach an income level of 3000 to 4000 euros/US dollars. Eighteen per cent earn between 4000 and 7500 euros/US dollars, and only 7 per cent reach an income above 7500 euros/US dollars (the survey was conducted at a time of relative euro–dollar parity).

7.3.8   Nationality, Residence and Mobility Patterns

Although the FLOSS survey was not designed to provide any representa-tive data on developer nationality or residence, like many surveys including WIDI and FLOSS-US[13] it shows that a majority of developers are based in EU countries. Regarding the residence of the community members, we found the highest shares in France (15 per cent), the United States of

America (13 per cent), and Germany (13 per cent), whereas Italy, UK, the Netherlands and Spain form the second important group, providing shares between 6 and 8 percent. Thus the global distribution of FLOSS developers obviously does not follow the pattern that is determined by the overall impact of the Internet in different countries. According to the SIBIS (Statistical Indicators Benchmarking Information Society) 2003 report, countries like the USA, Denmark, Finland, the Netherlands, Sweden, Switzerland and the UK provide the cluster with the highest impact of Internet use, whereas Germany belongs to a cluster with medium impact and France, Italy and Spain belong to a cluster with a low impact of the Internet (Technopolis 2003, p. 47). We assume that public awareness of the Open Source Software phenomenon and of trouble with proprietary software, such as lack of quality or a perception of an overly strong market power of proprietary software companies, play a role for the observed nationality pattern of the FLOSS community, as many countries in the EU and the EU as a whole developed policies towards open source software.[14] The strong incidence of US FLOSS community members is surely a result of the fact that the FLOSS community has its origins in the USA.

Figure 7.3 provides a summary of the mobility patterns of developers, that is nationality subtracted from country of residence. Unsurprisingly, this reflects mobility patterns in the ICT industry, with the US showing the largest net positive inflow of developers.

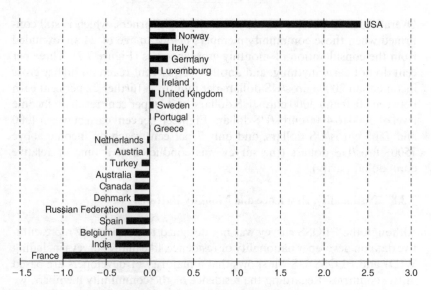

Figure 7.3   Country-based mobility balances

7.4 HOW IS IT DONE? PATTERNS OF PROJECT AND WORK ORGANIZATION IN THE FLOSS COMMUNITY

7.4.1 Time Spent on Developing Software

Although developing FLOSS could be considered as the core activity of the FLOSS community and despite their evident strong professional background, most community members (nearly 70 per cent) spend no more than 10 hours per week developing FLOSS.[15] Another 14 per cent spend an amount of time on FLOSS that could be compared to professional part-time work (11–20 hours per week), and 9 per cent spend 20 up to 40 hours per week on the development of FLOSS. Finally, for 7 per cent of the sample the time used for developing FLOSS exceeds 40 hours per week.

This surprising result can partly be explained by the fact that developing FLOSS is not at all a matter of 'leisure work' at home, as 95 per cent use FLOSS at work, school or university. Another part of the explanation for the low amount of time that most community members spend on developing FLOSS is that half (52 per cent) of them do not only develop FLOSS, but also proprietary software. Figure 7.4 shows the amounts of time the developers spend for developing proprietary software in comparison to the pattern of time spent for developing FLOSS.

The patterns of time spent on the development of FLOSS and of proprietary software are clearly converse, which appears to be explained easily by the simple fact that those who spend a lot of time on FLOSS have less time for proprietary software and vice versa. However, a deeper insight into

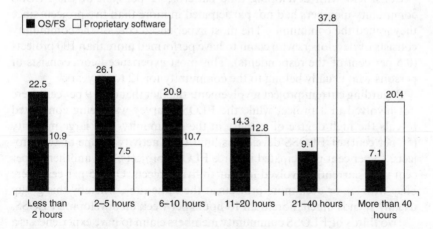

Figure 7.4　Time spent on development: FLOSS vs proprietary software

the data shows that this assumption does not reveal fully the reality of FLOSS community members, at least not the reality of the most active ones, as 38 per cent of those who spend more than 40 hours per week on developing FLOSS spend also more than 40 hours per week on developing proprietary software.[16]

Although age and duration of membership in the FLOSS community showed a highly significant impact in the model, a regression analysis revealed that socio-demographic factors, as they are discussed above, do not suffice at all for explaining the differences in the pattern of time spent on developing FLOSS.[17] Apparently other factors that could not be controlled properly in the FLOSS survey, such as workload in the professional life, present involvement in software projects, familial restrictions, or similar factors, played a much more decisive role for these differences.

7.4.2 Degrees of Activity within the FLOSS Community

Regardless of whether the FLOSS community is considered as a community of 'hackers' or a community of career-concerned materialists, FLOSS developers are usually assumed to be very focused and active in pursuing their purposes. However, we have already seen that the amounts of activity of community members concerning the development of FLOSS are diverse. But there are other vital aspects of activity within the FLOSS community than developing time patterns, such as project experience in terms of participation in and leadership of projects, and involvement in developer networks, which is measured by the number of regular contacts with other developers within the community.

Consistent with developing time patterns, 72 per cent of the FLOSS community members had not participated in more than five projects since they joined the community. The most experienced core of the community consists of developers who claim to have performed more than 100 projects (0.5 per cent of the respondents). This most experienced core consists of persons who usually belong to the community for 12 to 20 years.

Regarding current project involvement, the fact that only 9 per cent were not involved in a project while the FLOSS survey was being conducted reveals the high degree of activity in the community. The large majority (56 per cent) of FLOSS developers limit their activity to one or two projects, 15 per cent participated in three FLOSS projects, and another 15 per cent were currently involved in four to five projects. Only 5 per cent were busy with six or even more projects at the same time, whereby this group usually spends much more than 10 hours per week on developing FLOSS.

Two thirds of FLOSS community members claim to have experience as a leader, administrator or coordinator of FLOSS projects, but only 2 per cent of the developers have led more than five projects. FLOSS project leadership is not significantly correlated with socio-demographic and national variants. We assume that project participation and leadership, like the time that can be used for developing FLOSS, is highly dependent on factors that were not asked explicitly in the FLOSS developer survey, like the overall amount of time that is spent on work, family-life, friends, hobbies and other leisure activities. These time patterns obviously rely only indirectly on professional and civil status, since a person in a certain social situation might prefer to set aside a lot of time for family-life, friends or hobbies, while another person in the same social situation might prefer spending a lot of time on FLOSS activities. This lack of knowledge on the respondents' lifestyles and time-consumption patterns explains why the socio-demographic factors of the FLOSS data show such a weak impact on community life. Conclusively, the socio-demographic environment of the FLOSS community members provides an important field for further research.

As a specific feature of the development of FLOSS, everybody in this community is free to take up existing software code, to refine it, and then to distribute it again. FLOSS projects are thus usually aligned with a high degree of collaboration and communication between numerous people. Therefore members of the FLOSS community often stress the socializing effects of collaboration according to the principles of this community (Butler et al. 2002; von Hippel and von Krogh 2002; Lakhani and von Hippel 2000). However, how such collaboration is structured has usually been investigated on the level of single projects, like the Linux kernel project (Ciborra and Andreu 2001; Dempsey et al. 2002), and from the viewpoint of all contributions to this project. The crucial question is how the individual developer perceives collaboration and how he communicates with others in the community. Due to different life-styles, different degrees of engagement in the community and different social capacities, it is assumed that there are strong differences in the socializing behaviour of FLOSS developers and in their perception of their FLOSS-related environment. For instance, a developer who takes up software codes of other developers may consider himself as part of the FLOSS community as a whole, not caring who these other developers are; or he may consider himself as part of a team, regardless of its size and whether he knows the other team members personally or not; or he may consider himself as a performer in a one-man project, leaving thoroughly aside the contributions of others. Of course, this problem cannot be clarified by means of an online survey.[18] However, the FLOSS survey allows a first approach to this problem by assessing the number of contacts with other FLOSS developers within the community.

The results of the survey show an unexpectedly low degree of network activities within the FLOSS community, as two thirds of the sample show no contact at all with other community members or have contact with a very limited number of other FLOSS developers: 17 per cent of the FLOSS developers do not maintain any regular contact at all with other members of the community, another 26 per cent report regular contact with one to two other FLOSS developers, and 24 per cent have regular contact with three to five other developers. Some 15 per cent have contact with six to ten developers, 13 per cent have regular contact with 11 to 50 other developers, and 5 per cent report regular contact with more than 50 other developers. Like the other activity-related items, the networking activity of FLOSS community members can hardly be explained by socio-demographic factors. A regression analysis revealed that, although age and period of time belonging to the FLOSS community show a significant impact, altogether these factors explain only 4.3 per cent of the variance.

7.5   REASONS TO PARTICIPATE IN THE FLOSS COMMUNITY

There is a large variety of assumptions why people join the FLOSS community and 'work for free'. Reputation, mainly in the form of peer recognition, is often mentioned as a key motivator for people to participate in the FLOSS community, sometimes associated with a strong refusal of the role of monetary rewards (see for instance Raymond 1998a, 1998b; Kohn 1987).[19] Other developers emphasize that the most intriguing thing about developing FLOSS is that other people use their products and are fascinated by them (Torvalds 1999). This can of course be interpreted as a certain desire for reputation. However, instead of 'doing it for the glory' (Raymond 1998a, 1998b), the hope that one's products are employed by others depends less on one's personality and more on the outcome of one's work.

The personal need for a specific software program or functionality is considered as another important factor motivating people to join and contribute to the FLOSS community (Searls 1998). Lakhani and von Hippel (2000) distinguish three kinds of motivators – the personal need for FLOSS, the wish for reputation among developers, and intrinsic joy in programming. Similarly Shah (2003) emphasizes a specific need for software as the main reason for people's initial involvement, while in the long run fun becomes a more important motivation for people to continue.

Some authors point out that direct or indirect rewards are as essential for the functioning of the FLOSS community as for any other organization that develops and distributes software. Ghosh (1999) explains that developers always get more out than they possibly can put in, but only if people keep contributing together. Implicitly he thereby assumes reciprocity on a large scale. Ousterhout (1999, p. 44) stresses that free software needs profit and states 'sooner or later, every successful open-source software package will have one or more profitable businesses associated with it', which he considers to be not only a historical artefact, but also a necessity. Consequently, Lerner and Tirole (2000; see also Lee et al. 2003) argue that the whole open source phenomenon can be explained by 'simple economics'. They refer mainly to monetary and career concerns.

Hars and Ou (2001) however illustrate that the motivations for participation in open source projects are more complex than expected. They observe a mixture of internal motivators, such as self-determination, altruism and community identification, and external motivators, such as selling products, human capital improvements, self-marketing and peer recognition. In general, the external factors are comparable to Lerner and Tirole's (2001) category of 'signalling effects'. Hars and Ou found that external factors play a more significant role than internal ones. Another interesting result of their study is that students and hobby-developers show the strongest internal motivation, while salaried and contract programmers show a strong interest in being paid indirectly for their efforts.

Empirical analyses of FLOSS community members' motivations have clearly revealed that signalling functions play only a very unimportant role compared to other motivators.[20] Bonnaccorsi and Rossi (2003), who have compared several of these empirical studies, showed that in all of them studies social motivations played a much more important role for FLOSS developers than signalling effects or peer recognition (see also Ghosh 2003, pp. 12–15).

The FLOSS survey allowed examination of the role of direct and indirect monetary rewards in the community as well as the importance of community-oriented, political, software-related, career-oriented and monetary aspects in the individual motivations of FLOSS community members.

7.5.1 Direct and Indirect Monetary Rewards from Software and FLOSS

Because a large number of FLOSS developers deal with software on a professional basis, it is clear that many of them earn their main income from administrating, supporting or developing software. Three quarters of the sample earn their main income from (any) software development.

However, this finding does not tell anything about the role of FLOSS as a source of income, because there is no distinction between FLOSS and proprietary software in this question. Figure 7.5 provides an overview of the extent to which the developers in our sample receive direct and indirect payments and non-monetary rewards from developing Open Source/Free Software. As one can achieve different kinds of rewards for contributions to FLOSS, we allowed the respondents to tick more than one answer. Therefore, the percentages add up to a value that is higher than 100.

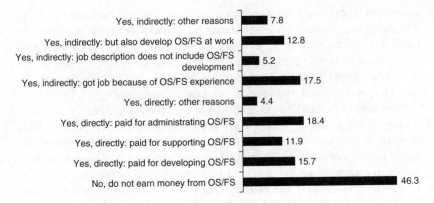

Figure 7.5   Direct and indirect rewards from FLOSS: 'Do you earn money from FLOSS, either directly or indirectly?'

Almost half the sample (46 per cent) does not earn money from FLOSS, neither directly nor indirectly. In turn, this means that the majority of the FLOSS developers receive some kind of reward for contributions to FLOSS. Comparing the amount of monetary and non-monetary reward with regard to the respective proportions of developers in the different items, both kinds of rewards seem to have the same importance for the community. Within the scope of directly earned money from FLOSS, administrating plays a more important role than developing FLOSS. Within indirect earnings, to get a job because of expertise in FLOSS issues is observably the most important factor, followed by the development of FLOSS at work.[21]

7.5.2   Motivations for Developing Open Source/Free Software

We were interested in the motives of people to participate in the FLOSS community from two different perspectives. First, we wanted to know which motives had been causal for them to join the community, and second, we were interested in the motives that keep the developers staying in this community. Figure 7.6 illustrates the answers to these two questions, whereby the respondents have been asked to limit themselves to a maximum of four answers.[22]

Most of the respondents ticked reasons that were connected with the individual skills level, but there is also evidence of a social aspect. Almost eight out of ten software developers started with FLOSS because they wanted to learn and develop new skills, and half the sample claimed that they wanted to share their knowledge and skills with other software developers. Not surprisingly, with regard to the reasons to stay in the community we observe that the first reason has lost some of its importance, while the second reason has increased.

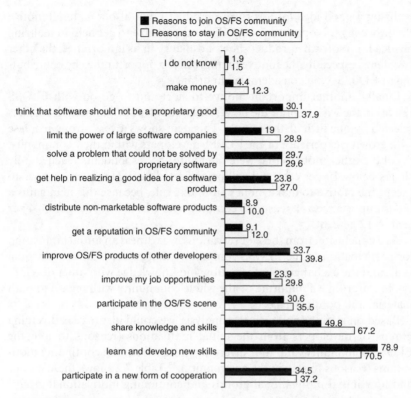

■ Reasons to join OS/FS community
□ Reasons to stay in OS/FS community

I do not know	1.9 / 1.5	
make money	4.4 / 12.3	
think that software should not be a proprietary good	30.1 / 37.9	
limit the power of large software companies	19 / 28.9	
solve a problem that could not be solved by proprietary software	29.7 / 29.6	
get help in realizing a good idea for a software product	23.8 / 27.0	
distribute non-marketable software products	8.9 / 10.0	
get a reputation in OS/FS community	9.1 / 12.0	
improve OS/FS products of other developers	33.7 / 39.8	
improve my job opportunities	23.9 / 29.8	
participate in the OS/FS scene	30.6 / 35.5	
share knowledge and skills	49.8 / 67.2	
learn and develop new skills	78.9 / 70.5	
participate in a new form of cooperation	34.5 / 37.2	

Figure 7.6   Reasons to join and reasons to stay in the FLOSS community

The second important group of reasons is provided by motives that reach proportions of between 30 per cent and 35 per cent and ranges from socializing aspects of the community (participation, collaboration), to software-related to political aspects: 35 per cent of the sample emphasized their wish to participate in new forms of cooperation that are associated with FLOSS development, and another 34 per cent emphasized aspects of the goods produced in FLOSS by stating that they wished to improve software products of other developers. Almost 31 per cent stated that they wanted to participate in the FLOSS scene, and 30 per cent were convinced that software should not be a proprietary product. It is noteworthy that all these reasons increase in importance after the developer has joined the community and gained some experience, which particularly applies to the product-related and the political item.

The third important group of motives, featuring shares between 20 per cent and 30 per cent, again comprises product-related issues ('solve a problem that could not be solved by proprietary software' and 'get help in realizing a good idea for a software product'), but also a material motive ('improve my job opportunities'). While the motive to get help in realizing an idea for a software product shows no change in its importance, the other two items, especially the motive to improve job opportunities by contributing to FLOSS, gain considerable importance.

Finally, another important motive to start and to go on with FLOSS resides in the wish to limit the power of large software companies, which is selected by one fifth of the sample. This item shows a very strong increase with growing experience of the FLOSS developers within their community.

All the other motives that were offered to the respondents reached only shares below 10 per cent and will be neglected here. However, we have to except the motive to make money from this rule, because this item gains a lot of importance as a reason to continue with FLOSS, growing from 4 per cent to 12 percent.

As a conclusion from these observations, we witness an initial motivation for participation in the FLOSS community that rather aims at individual skills and the exchange of information and knowledge with other developers, but over time a maturing of the whole community with regard to both material and political aspects.

Based on a factor and a cluster analysis, we could identify six diverging groups of developers from the initial motivations (reasons to join the FLOSS community) and four diverging groups from the continuing motivations (reasons to stay in the community).[23] Table 7.2 shows these groups and how initial motivational groups and continuing motivational groups are related to each other.

The first initial motivational group is enthusiastic about FLOSS in many respects, with the exception of monetary and career concerns. Its members show an extremely strong impact of a desire for software and skills improvements, but also of ideological aspects and reputation. The second initial motivational group, 'software improvers', shows only a strong impact of software-related motivations, while skills-related motivations and monetary and career concerns do not motivate this group. FLOSS community members strongly driven by a wish for gaining a reputation in the community provide the third initial motivational group. While monetary and career concerns still play a role as motivators in this group, ideological motivations play no role at all, and the role of software-related motivations is also limited within these 'recognition seekers'. The fourth initial motivational group clearly consists of 'materialists', as they show very strong and exclusive motivation by money and career concerns. The fifth initial motivational group within the FLOSS community consists of 'ideologists' who are clearly driven by the wish to abolish proprietary software in favour of free software and who want to limit the power of

Table 7.2 *Flows from initial to continuing motivational groups within the FLOSS community*

	Initial motivational groups					
	Enthusiasts 4% of respondents	Software improvers 10% of respondents	Recognition seekers 11% of respondents	Materialists 12% of respondents	Ideologists 17% of respondents	Utilitarians 46% of respondents
	Per cent within continuing motivational groups					
Continuing motivational groups						
Recognition seekers (12% of respondents)	33.7	6.0	41.6	14.1	7.2	5.8
Skills improvers (33% of respondents)	32.7	22.8	37.0	26.3	43.6	31.1
Software improvers (24% of respondents)	30.8	37.5	13.0	39.4	14.4	23.2
Ideologists (31% of respondents)	2.9	33.7	8.4	20.2	34.7	39.9

large software companies. Finally, the sixth initial motivational group appears opposed to the 'enthusiasts'. While enthusiasts are driven by almost all facets of FLOSS that could be covered by the items we offered as motivators, members of this group show quite disparate answering patterns with regard to the 13 items offered as motivating factors in the FLOSS questionnaire. Obviously, they follow no unique motivation, but consider the FLOSS community as a means that allows them to realize a great variety of interests and needs. Therefore, we would like to call this group 'utilitarians'.

As indicated in the header of Table 7.2, utilitarians play the most prominent role when motivations to join the community are considered. This result suggests that apparently most people who join the community have no clear concept of what they expect from this step and what its outcome will be. 'Ideologists' provide the second largest initial motivational group, which highlights the importance of the political dimension of the FLOSS community for attracting new members. While software itself, reputation and material concerns provide shares of respondents between 10 and 12 per cent, enthusiasts provide clearly the smallest initial motivational group.

Regarding the continuing motivational groups we observe dissolution of the initial enthusiasts, materialists and utilitarians to the benefit of a new group that is strongly driven by the wish for skills improvement, while the fact that recognition seekers and software improvers have remained reflects the above-mentioned trend towards professionalism and objectification. Ideologists did not disappear either. Moreover, as shown in Table 7.2, people who continue their participation for ideological reasons make up a considerable proportion of the FLOSS community, equally as large as the proportion of the skills improvers. While software improvers still provide roughly one quarter of the FLOSS community, recognition seekers play the least important role in quantitative terms.

As shown in Table 7.3, enthusiasts represent a larger than average proportion of those who are married and older than 30 years. They have typically lower educational levels. Regarding employment status, they are usually employed, but provide also the highest share of unemployed compared to the other initial motivational groups. They make up comparably high proportions of software engineers and programmers. With regard to the period of time enthusiasts belong to the FLOSS community it turned out that this group typically consists of 'old hands'.

Regarding marital status, age, employment status and duration of membership in the community the socio-demographic structure of software improvers resembles very much the structure of enthusiasts. However software improvers clearly have higher educational levels and their main professions are as in consultants, managers and university staff.

Table 7.3   Socio-demographic structure of initial motivational groups

	Initial motivational groups						
	Enthusiasts	Software improvers	Recognition seekers	Materialists	Ideologists	Utilitarians	Total
Civil status							
Single	35.4	35.6	44.3	34.2	41.7	45.1	41.4
Partner	38.5	39.6	35.7	40.4	38.9	35.3	37.3
Married	26.0	24.8	20.0	25.3	19.3	19.6	21.2
Contingency coefficient:				0.093**			
Current age							
14–23 years	36.9	28.8	45.7	29.0	37.9	33.7	35.0
24–30 years	35.0	36.5	39.7	42.1	37.9	42.4	40.2
Older than 30 years	28.2	34.7	14.6	29.0	24.1	23.9	24.9
Contingency coefficient:				0.140**			
Highest educational level							
A-level / apprenticeship	34.7	27.6	40.8	26.0	26.9	28.7	29.7
University–Bachelor	35.8	23.8	34.2	36.5	35.7	31.3	32.6
University–Masters or PhD	29.5	48.5	25.0	37.5	37.4	40.0	37.7
Contingency coefficient:				0.146***			
Employment status							
Self-employed	9.4	14.5	15.4	18.4	12.1	14.2	14.3
Employed	67.7	67.6	59.7	70.4	63.7	63.3	64.5
Student	17.7	13.3	23.1	7.2	20.1	18.7	17.4

Table 7.3 (continued)

	Initial motivational groups						
	Enthusiasts	Software improvers	Recognition seekers	Materialists	Ideologists	Utilitarians	Total
Unemployed / not working	5.2	4.6	1.8	4.0	4.1	3.8	3.8
Contingency coefficient:				0.136***			
Profession							
(Software) engineers	43.3	30.9	38.2	42.7	32.8	36.6	36.5
Programmers	14.4	11.1	13.1	11.8	10.6	10.3	11.2
Consultants	8.2	14.4	5.1	15.8	9.4	9.9	10.4
Executives, marketing and sales managers	2.1	4.5	2.9	4.3	3.4	4.2	3.8
University staff	8.2	14.4	6.2	6.1	7.7	10.8	9.3
Students	18.6	16.0	27.3	11.5	26.0	21.1	20.9
Other professions	5.2	8.6	7.3	7.9	10.1	7.1	7.9
Contingency coefficient:				0.189***			
Duration of membership in FLOSS community							
Up to 1 year	20.4	20.4	30.8	29.9	35.1	23.2	26.9
2–5 years	46.6	44.2	47.0	39.9	44.3	44.9	44.4
More than 5 years	33.0	35.4	22.2	30.2	20.6	31.9	28.8
Contingency coefficient:				0.144***			

Significance level: $**p < 005$; $***p < 001$.

Recognition seekers provide one of two initial motivational groups that are strongly represented by students, although they feature also above average shares of software engineers and programmers. Accordingly they are typically single and quite young. They usually belong to the community for a medium or short period of time.

Materialists are most typically living in partnerships and the share of married materialists is also above average. Like enthusiasts and software improvers they are typically older than 30, but in complete contrast to these two groups materialists are clearly new to the FLOSS community, as the above average share of those who have belonged to the community for one year or less shows. They usually have a bachelor degree and are employed or self-employed. Their professional structure appears as a mixture of the structures of the enthusiasts and the software improvers, as they show high proportions of software engineers, but also of consultants and managers.

Ideologists provide the second initial motivational group that is represented by students, but in contrast to recognition seekers they show a comparably high number of people over 30 years and a higher educational level. The proportion in employment is also higher within this group than within the recognition seekers. Like recognition seekers, they belong to the community for a short period of time.

As utilitarians provide the lion's share of the initial motivational groups, they do not differ notably from the average.

Regarding the continuing motivational groups (Table 7.4), we found that recognition seekers and skills improvers are very similar in their socio-demographic structures. Members of these groups are typically single, very young, and have comparatively low educational levels. A comparatively high share of students makes up both groups. Differences are only that recognition seekers make up a relatively high proportion of unemployed and they typically have belonged to the community for a medium period of time, whereas skills improvers are relative newcomers in the community.

Software improvers differ in some respects from their counterparts among the initial motivational groups. As a continuing motivational group they are typically married, in the middle-age group (that is, younger than the initial software improvers) and self-employed (rather the employed or unemployed). Their professional structure and their membership in the community do not differ with regard to initial software improvers.

Typical features of ideologists are that they are comparatively older, have high educational levels, and have a relatively high proportion who do not belong to the community for more than one year.

Table 7.4 Socio-demographic structure of continuing motivational groups

	Continuing motivational groups				
	Recognition seekers	Skills improvers	Software improvers	Ideologists	Total
Civil status					
Single	44.5	46.4	35.8	38.3	41.4
Partner	35.8	37.0	38.2	37.8	37.3
Married	19.7	16.7	26.0	23.9	21.2
Contingency coefficient:			0.112***		
Current age					
14–23 years	44.7	39.9	26.8	30.9	35.0
24–30 years	36.6	40.6	46.3	34.3	40.2
Older than 30 years	18.7	19.5	26.9	34.8	24.9
Contingency coefficient			0.179***		
Highest educational level					
A-level / apprenticeship	34.6	33.2	26.6	24.8	29.7
University–Bachelor	35.6	30.4	34.6	31.6	32.6
University–Masters or PhD	29.8	36.4	38.8	43.6	37.7
Contingency coefficient:			0.105***		
Employment status					
Self-employed	13.4	11.2	18.5	14.8	14.3
Employed	60.0	63.8	66.1	66.6	64.5
Student	21.4	20.8	12.6	15.2	17.4
Unemployed / not working	5.2	4.1	2.9	3.5	3.8
Contingency coefficient:			0.127***		

Profession					
(Software) engineers	34.5	37.1	37.7	35.1	36.5
Programmers	13.1	10.3	11.4	11.3	11.2
Consultants	11.0	8.0	13.4	10.2	10.4
Executives, marketing and sales managers	3.4	1.9	5.2	5.6	3.8
University staff	7.2	10.6	9.7	7.8	9.3
Students	23.1	24.1	15.9	20.6	20.9
Other professions	7.6	7.9	6.8	9.5	7.9
Contingency coefficient:			0.143***		
Duration of Membership in FLOSS community					
Up to 1 year	25.4	30.0	21.5	29.2	26.9
2–5 years	50.8	44.4	44.4	40.3	44.4
More than 5 years	23.9	25.6	34.1	30.5	28.8
Contingency coefficient:			0.111***		

Significance level: ***$p < .005$; ***$p < .001$

7.6 CONCLUSIONS

Although the FLOSS community appears to be very homogeneous with regard to the age and gender structure of its members, the FLOSS survey clearly revealed that it is a very diverse community in many other respects. It comprises students as well as professionals, software experts as well as managers. Moreover, the community members differ considerably with regard to the ways in which they contribute to the community, as we found very dissimilar patterns of time consumption for developing FLOSS and for project and network activities. One of the most surprising results in this respect was surely the rather low average amount of such activities, as FLOSS developers are often considered to be always busy and working day and night. Due to the homogeneous aspects of the community structure, socio-demographic factors are rather limited in explaining the observed differences in the behaviour of the community members, and other factors in their everyday life apparently play a more important role in these differences.

The analysis of motivations of the FLOSS community members again underlines the diversity and vividness of the community. As is quite typical for people who try out something new, at the level of reasons to join the community we observe a dominance of unclear motivations. Besides this, the political dimension of the FLOSS community clearly turned out to be another important factor in its attractiveness. The scope of the community apparently offers also opportunities to people with a strong professional background and a certain desire for material improvement or personal recognition. Besides this, dealing with software is of course a vital attractor of the community, too. Motivations that enable the community to persist are interest in learning and improving skills and ideological motivations rather than interest in new forms of collaboration or material motivations. Thus the FLOSS community turns out to be attractive enough to catch the fancy of very different people and to offer them opportunities for realizing their ideas, and it is powerful enough to integrate these differences in the course of time.

The fact that material motivations can be identified as a significant and distinctive motivation for joining the FLOSS community but dissolve as a motivation to continue in the community contradicts heavily with Lerner and Tirole's argument that the whole community can be explained by 'simple economics'. Community members do not strive for monetary and career concerns. Admittedly, a large number of the community members strive for personal improvement, but this aspiration is clearly directed towards skills improvement, not towards job improvements or higher income. One could argue that skills improvements are usually related to labour market and income opportunities, which we do not deny. But if we consider people's motivations to join and to contribute to the FLOSS community, we have to distinguish very clearly what these people have in mind and what they do not have in mind. The results of the FLOSS survey show unequivocally that the overwhelming majority of the community members do not relate their activities in the community directly to the labour market.

Overall the analysis has clearly confirmed our initial assumption that a variety of co-existing, sometimes complementary, sometimes contradictory motivations exist within the FLOSS community. The existence of diverse continuing motivational groups suggests that over time the community does not advance in a single direction, but that personal improvements and political objectives are the main determinants of the community as a whole, accompanied by a strong desire for software improvement and, less important but still vital, a wish to be recognized and acknowledged within the community.

NOTES

1. Instead of the code, vendors of proprietary software provide the users with only object or binary code, which can be read by the machine, but not by users.
2. This is obviously the line of argument behind the comments of Microsoft's managers Steve Ballmer (see http://linuxtoday.com/news_story.php 3?ltsn=2000–07–31–002–20-PS-BZ-MS) and Jim Allchin (see http://news.cnet.com/investor/news/newsitem 0–9900–1028–4825719-RHAT.html), both ascribing characteristics of communism and anti-Americanism towards free software and open source software.
3. The term 'free software' was popularized in the mid-1980s by the Free Software Foundation, which was founded by Richard Stallman (see www.fsf.org). The term 'open source software' was established in 1997/98 by the Open Source Initiative (see www.opensource.org).
4. There is a wide variety of such licence agreements, which may differ considerably in the strength and scope by which they require the users to make the source code available. For instance, Lerner and Tirole (2000, pp. 5–7) point out that the General Public License (GPL, also known as 'copyleft') requires the user not to impose any licensing restrictions on others, whereas the open source definition of the open source initiative emphasizes the users' freedom to make their own choices about their own software and refuses any compulsion to place restrictions on software in these licences. However, today the terms open source software and free software are largely used as synonyms and cannot be distinguished by specific licence agreements.
5. This is a summarizing interpretation of a number of documents of the Free Software Foundation (see http://www.fsf.org) and the Open Source Initiative (http://www.opensource.org) that explain the motivations and purposes of these two institutions. The breadth and depth of the material that is provided on these websites can only very limitedly be presented here, since the self-perception and presentation of these two organizations are not the focus of this chapter.
6. One of the best-known examples of the latter kind of images has been ironically adopted in Douglas Coupland's novel *Microserfs* (1995), which describes software developers (in general, not FLOSS developers in particular) as 'nerds'. According to Coupland's depiction, the typical software developer is male, hangs out at home (after

work in a software company), is interested only in software and information and communication technologies, has only software developers and engineers as friends, earns a relatively high income, and has a 16 to 20 hours 'working night' (enabled by Prozac). Obviously as a consequence of many of these features, a software developer is usually single.

7. Many observers think that FLOSS developers are young amateurs rather than professionals, which corresponds largely with the findings of the WIDI survey, whereupon students outnumber the proportion of professionals in the community. Others claim that the opposite is true and that the FLOSS community rather consists of professionals who work in traditional software areas. This point of view finds also support from empirical studies (Young 1999; Lakhani et al. 2002; Dempsey et al. 1999, 2002). The community members clearly incline to the latter conception and like to emphasize outstanding professionalism and experience as typical features of FLOSS developers (Bezroukov 1996; Raymond 1998b). The contradictions between the results of the different empirical studies are clearly due to dissimilarities in the methodological approaches and target groups of these studies and do therefore not allow a decision as to which kind of FLOSS developer is more typical for the community as a whole.

8. Based on a source code analysis that was conducted in parallel to the developer survey, the FLOSS team was able to identify a sub-sample of approximately 500 FLOSS developers and to crosscheck some of their answers to the survey by their documented contribution to software code (FLOSS Final report part IVa (Appendix); accessible online at http://www.floss.nl). This sub-sample provided a validated group of FLOSS developers, to which the other respondents could be statistically compared. This procedure validated that survey respondents represented close to a random sample of developers, rather than of the general population of the Internet.

9. WIDI stands for who-is-doing-it and was conducted by a group at the Technical University in Berlin. The results of the WIDI survey are accessible online at http://widi.berlios.de. The WIDI survey asked Free Software developers for their nationality, their residence, and some technological aspects and reached approximately 5600 persons. Compared to this survey, the FLOSS survey concentrated very much on motivations, orientations and economic aspects of the FLOSS scene, thus providing deeper insights into the functioning of this community. To fill in the FLOSS questionnaire required more time than to fill in the WIDI questionnaire, which explains largely the differences in the sample size.

10. The hacker survey was based on a pre-selection that focused on the more active members of the Open Source scene, thus reaching 660 persons. Consequently, the personal features of the BCG hackers, like age structure and occupational background of the respondents, deviate considerably from the personal features of the general FLOSS developer as it was revealed by WIDI and FLOSS. Results of the hacker survey are accessible online at http://www.bcg.com/opensource.

11. A Kolmogorov-Smirnov test confirmed a significant deviation from normal distribution (error probability $p < 0.001$).

12. This does not imply that programming can only be learnt in the course of higher educational attainment. However, higher educational degrees are an advantage for programming and thus for participating in the FLOSS community.

13. Paul David, Andrew Waterman and Seema Arora at Stanford: see http://www.stanford.edu/group/floss-us/

14. See the European Commission's Open Source Observatory at http://europa.eu.int/ida/

15. Roughly 23 per cent spend only two hours per week on this, 26 per cent expend 2–5 hours per week, and 21 percent spend 6–10 hours per week on developing Open Source/Free Software.

16. Related to the complete sample of the FLOSS survey, this extraordinarily active group provides 0.8 per cent of the respondents.

17. Overall, the socio-demographic factors explain only 3.9 per cent of the total variance regarding the patterns of time spent on developing FLOSS.

18. This is the reason why we did not offer a pre-formulated definition of 'project' in our online questionnaire and left it to the respondent's understanding of a project. A project can thus either be ascribed to a specific team or consortium, to the specific product or to oneself. Thus it may be possible, however not very likely, that *leading a project* could mean every individual effort to contribute to the production of a specific product without direct collaboration with other FLOSS developers.

19. A reprint of Kohn's article is accessible at http://www.gnu.org/philosophy/motivation.html

20. These studies are: Ghosh et al. (2002a); Lakhani et al. (2002); Hars and Ou (2001); Hertel et al. (2003).

21. 'Develop FLOSS at work' is selected by those who are paid by their employer for developing FLOSS during their usual working time. In contrast, 'job description does not include FLOSS development' means a more indirect way of being paid for FLOSS development at work, i.e. the boss does not know or care or require that the developer works with FLOSS.

22. However, many respondents insisted on a larger choice, therefore we did not restrict their responses technically in the online questionnaire. On average, each respondent named 3.3 reasons for starting in the FLOSS community and 3.8 reasons to continue participating in the community. The spread of the number of reasons uttered by the respondents increased from 1.95 for the initial motivation to 2.30 for the continuing motivation.

23. NB. The term 'initial motivational team' does not mean that members of this group belong to starters in the community. The term only describes a group within the FLOSS community that reported a certain set of motivations to join that could be distinguished from other groups with different initial motivations. The same applies to the term 'continuing motivational groups', which is not meant as a label for people who belong to the FLOSS community for a longer period. The initial motivation thus answers the question 'why did you join the FLOSS community?' (regardless of whether this was five weeks or five years ago), whereas the continuing motivation answers the questions 'why are you still in the FLOSS community?' (regardless of whether one belongs to the community for five weeks or for five years).

BIBLIOGRAPHY

Bezroukov, N. (1996), 'Portraits of open source pioneers', http://www.softpanorama.org/People/.

Bonnaccorsi, A. and C. Rossi (2002), 'Why open source software can succeed', Accessible online at http://opensource.mit.edu/papers/bnaccorsirossimotivation-short.pdf

Bonnaccorsi, A. and C. Rossi (2003), 'Altruistic individuals, selfish firms? The structure of motivation in open source software', http://opensource.mit.edu/ papers/bnaccorsirossimotivationshort.pdf

Butler, B., L. Sproull, S. Kiesler and R. Kraut (2002), 'Community effort in online groups: who does the work an why?', http://opensource.mit.edu/papers/butler.pdf

Castells, M. and P. Himanen (2002), *The Information Society and the Welfare State. The Finnish Model*, Oxford: Oxford University Press.

Ciborra, C.U. and R. Andreu (2001), 'Sharing knowledge across boundaries', *Journal of Information Technology*, **16**, 73–81.

Coupland, D. (1995), *Microserfs*, New York: Regan Books.

Dempsey, B.J., D. Weiss, P. Jones and J. Greenberg (1999), 'A quantitative profile of a community of Open Source Linux developers', http://ibiblio.org/orst/developro.html

Dempsey, B.J., D. Weiss, P. Jones and J. Greenberg (2002), 'Who is an open source developer? Profiling a community of Linux developers', *Communications of the ACM*, **45**, 67–72.

DiBona, C., S. Ockman and M. Stone (eds) (1999), *Open Sources: Voices from the Open Source Revolution*, Sebastopol, CA: O'Reilly.

Ettrich, M. (2000), 'Wer kodiert?', *iX*, 1, 112.

Feller, J. and B. Fitzgerald (2000), 'A framework analysis of the open source software development paradigm', *Proceedings of the 21st International Conference on Information Systems*, Brisbane, Queensland, Australia, pp. 58–69.

Feller, J. and B. Fitzgerald (2001), *Understanding Open Source Software Development*, London: Pearson.

Franke, N. and S. Shah (2001), 'How communities support innovative activities: An exploration of assistance and sharing among innovative users of sporting equipment', Sloan Working Paper No. 4164.

Garzarelli, G. (2002), *Open Source Software and the Economics of Organization*, http://econwpa.wxst.edu/eps/10/papers/030410304003.pdf

Ghosh, R.A. (1999), 'Cooking pot markets: an economic model for the trade in free goods and services on the Internet, *First Monday*, 3.

Ghosh, R.A. (2003), 'Understanding free software developers: Findings from the FLOSS study', Paper presented at HBS – MIT Sloan Free/Open Source Software Conference: New Models of Software Development, 19–20 June 2003, Cambridge, MA.

Ghosh, R.A., R. Glott, B. Krieger and G. Robles (2002a), 'Free/libre and open source software: survey and study, Part IV: Survey of developers', Maastricht: International Institute of Infonomics / MERIT.

Ghosh, R.A., G. Robles and R. Glott (2002b): 'Free/libre and open source software: survey and study, Part V: Source Code Survey', Maastricht: International Institute of Infonomics / MERIT.

Ghosh, R.A. and V.V. Prakash (2000), 'The orbiten free software survey', *First Monday*, 5.

Hars, A. and S. Ou (2001), 'Working for free? – Motivations participating in open source projects', in IEEE (ed.), *Proceedings of the 34th Hawaii International Conference on System Sciences* (HICSS-34), Volume 7, Washington: IEEE Computer Society.

Hertel, G., N. Niedner and S. Herrmann (2003), 'Motivation of software developers in open source projects: An internet-based survey of contributors to the Linux Kernel', Paper presented at HBS – MIT Sloan Free/Open Source Software Conference: New Models of Software Development, 19–20 June 2003, Cambridge, MA.

Himanen, P. (2001), *The Hacker Ethic and the Spirit of the Information Age*, New York: Random House.

von Hippel, E. and G. von Krogh (2002), 'Exploring the open source software phenomenon: Issues for organization science', Working Paper MIT.

Kohn, A. (1987), 'Studies find reward often no motivator', *Boston Globe*, 19 January.

Lakhani, K.R. and E. von Hippel (2000), 'How open source software works: "Free" user-to-user assistance', MIT Sloan School of Management Working Paper No. 4117.

Lakhani, K.R., B. Wolf, J. Bates and C. DiBona (2002), *The Boston Consulting Group Hacker Survey*, Release 0.73, in cooperation with OSDN, http://www.osdn.com/bcg/bcghacnersurvey-0.73.pdf

Lee, S., N. Moisa and M. Weiss (2003), 'Open source as a signalling device – an economic analysis', Working Paper Johann-Wolfgang-Goethe University.

Lerner, J. and J. Tirole (2000), 'The simple economics of open source', National Bureau of Economic Research Working Paper 7600.

Moon, J.Y. and L. Sproull (2000), 'Essence of distributed work: The case of the Linux kernel', *First Monday*, 5.

O'Reilly, T. (1999), 'Lessons from open source software development', *Communications of the ACM*, **42**, 33–7.

Ousterhout, J. (1999), 'Free software needs profit', *Communicaations of the ACM*, **42**, 44–5.

Raymond, E.S. (1998a), 'The cathedral and the bazaar', http://www.tuxedo.org/~esr/writings/cathedral-bazaar

Raymond, E.S. (1998b), 'Homesteading the noosphere', *First Monday*, 3.

Scacchi, W. (2002), 'Understanding the requirements for developing open source software systems', Working Paper MIT.

Searls, D. (1998), 'Betting on Darwin', *Linux Journal*, **52**, http://linuxjournal.com/issue/52.

Shah, S. (2003), 'Understanding the nature of participation and coordination in open and gated source software development communities', Paper presented at HBS – MIT Sloan Free/Open Source Software Conference: New Models of Software Development, 19–20 June 2003, Cambridge, MA.

Stallman, R. (1999), 'The GNU operating system and the free software movement', in C. DiBona, S. Ockman and M. Stone (eds), *Open Sources: Voices from the Open Source Revolution*, Sebastopol, CA: O'Reilly.

Stallman, R. (2002), *Free Software, Free Society: Selected Essays of Richard M. Stallman*, Boston: Free Software Foundation.

Suriya, M. (2003), 'Gender issues in the career development of IT professionals: a global perspective', http://www.gisdevelopment.net/mapasia/2003/papers/i4d/i4d002.htm.

Technopolis (2003), 'Benchmarking telecommunications and access in the information society', http://www.empirica.biz/sibis/files/WP5_No1_T_and_A_2pdf.

Torvalds, L. (1999), 'Interview with Linus Torvalds: What motivates free software developers?', *First Monday*, 3.

Torvalds, L. (2001), *Just for Fun: The Story of an Accidental Revolutionary*, London: Texere.

Wenger, E. (2000), 'Communities of practice: learning, meaning and identity', Cambridge: Cambridge University Press.

Wheeler, D.A. (2002), 'Why open source software / free software (OSS/FS)? Look at the numbers!', http://www.dwheeler.com/oss_fs_why.html.

Young, R. (1999), 'Giving it away: How Red Hat stumbled across a new economic model and helped improve an industry', in C. DiBona, S. Ockman and M. Stone (eds), *Open Sources: Voices from the Open Source Revolution*, Sebastopol CA: O'Reilly.

8. Technological change, job stress and burnout*

Bas Straathof and Rifka Weehuizen

8.1 INTRODUCTION

New technologies do not only lead to the destruction of some jobs and the creation of others, they also change the composition of existing jobs. According to a study of the US labour market by Autor et al. (2003) a shift has been taking place from routine to non-routine tasks. This shift has been concentrated in the rapidly computerizing industries and started in the 1970s. Spitz (2004) reports that the task composition of German jobs also has shifted towards non-routine activities. In a study of the UK, Green et al. (2003) find that the spread in computer usage has coincided with an increase in job skills, which is an additional indication that non-routine tasks become more and more prevalent.

Besides a change in the nature of work, the intensity of work has also changed. The *Third European Survey on Working Conditions 2000* (Paoli and Merllié 2001) states that the proportion of workers in the EU that report they work at 'high speed' a quarter of the time or more rose from 47 per cent in 1990 to 56 per cent in 2000. The proportion of workers reporting they face 'tight deadlines' a quarter of the time or more also increased: from 49 per cent in 1990 to 60 per cent in 2000. Using the surveys of 1990 and 1995, Green and McIntosh (2001) find evidence that the intensification of work has been stronger for jobs that involve the use of a computer.

The intensification of work does not appear to have left workers unaffected. Paoli and Merllié (2001, pp. 14–15) find that the proportion of workers facing tight deadlines (almost) all of the time that suffer from health problems is almost twice as large as for workers that (almost) never face tight deadlines. In particular, 40 per cent of the people facing tight deadlines report that they suffer from stress at least a quarter of the time against 21 per cent of the people who do not face tight deadlines. For 'overall fatigue' the

* We are grateful to Bas ter Weel and an anonymous referee. Their suggestions and support greatly helped improving this chapter. A previous version was presented at a MiMaMa seminar in December 2003 at the University of Maastricht.

numbers are 33 per cent against 18 per cent; for headaches they are 22 per cent against 11 per cent. The figures relating to 'working at high speed' are almost identical to the numbers for 'tight deadlines'.

These empirical observations suggest a relation between new technologies and the intensity of work and between the intensity of work and mental health. In this chapter we provide a theoretical framework that links technological change to mental health via its effect on the intensity of work. A better understanding of this relationship might turn out to be important to preserving the health and productivity of the workforce.

Various authors have discussed the effects of new technologies on the intensity of work. Green and McIntosh (2001), for example, argue that new technologies have raised the pressure on employees, thereby increasing the intensity of work. According to them, the pressure on employees might have risen for two reasons. First, competition has probably become fiercer because of globalization. Second, the pressure on employees might have increased because new technologies and management practices have led to a reduction of stoppage and wasted time as well as to a greater ability of managers to prevent 'shirking'.[1] Another reason for the intensification of work might have been a change in wage inequality. A more convex ('all-or-nothing') relationship between hours worked – or effort made – and career prospects provides a greater incentive for employees to work harder (Bell and Freeman 2001; Gregg 1994).

According to these authors new technologies either raise the intensity of work in ways that are exogenous to workers, or they alter the incentives of workers such that they choose a higher intensity. In this chapter we investigate a third possibility, namely, that it is not the technology itself that raises the intensity of work but rather the adjustment of a worker's effort that follows or anticipates the technology.

The contribution of this chapter is twofold. First, we propose a theoretical framework in which the intensity of work depends on the rate of technological change, while others seek to explain the intensity of work by the adoption of a specific technology. Second, we demonstrate how more rapid technological change can lead to a deterioration of mental health and a greater incidence of burnout. We discuss two similar models: in the first workers respond to their environment adaptively, in the second they have perfect foresight.

In both models, technological change reduces the price of machinery, say computers, relative to that of human labour. This change in relative prices causes entrepreneurs to automate a larger proportion of routine tasks. As a consequence, workers will be required to do fewer routine tasks and spend more time on non-routine activities.

The shift from routine to non-routine tasks affects a worker's fatigue. For routine tasks it is relatively easy to find out what pace of work is maximally sustainable (with manual labour, for example, you will know whether you have worked too hard at the end of the day, if not sooner). For non-routine tasks, the maximally sustainable level of effort is more difficult to assess. One non-routine task may, for example, require a different kind of effort from another. Also, non-routine tasks usually do not come in well-defined portions during a working day but arrive irregularly and with varying priority.

The employee in the adaptive model has to learn what level of effort has to be made on non-routine activities in order to reach a certain target level of production. If this target is too high, the employee starts accumulating fatigue and risks burnout. Burnout is accompanied by a period of absence from work and involves a permanent deterioration in the health of the worker, which causes a decline in his or her sustainable productivity. However, a production target that is unsustainable does not necessarily lead to burnout if the worker has some flexibility in setting his or her target. In the model, an employee has the possibility to make only gradual changes in the target level of production. This should reflect inertia in the allocation of tasks that is a character of complex organizations in which workers have their own responsibilities.

Technological change makes it difficult for workers to find their maximally sustainable level of production. The reason is that the rising degree of automation, which is induced by technological change, simultaneously raises the density of non-routine tasks and the level of production that the entrepreneur expects given the effective labour input of the employee. In a rapidly changing environment, fatigue accumulates more easily because there is less time to learn about sustainable production targets.

A positive relation between fatigue and technological change also exists in the second model with perfect foresight, albeit the underlying mechanism is different. In particular, technological change affects fatigue in two ways. First, it causes productivity growth, which induces workers to postpone some of their efforts. This has a downward effect on fatigue. The second effect works in the opposite direction. Technological change raises the intensity of work in the future. Workers therefore anticipate the intensification of their jobs by shifting some of their future effort to the present, at the expense of a higher level of fatigue.

Our work fits into the literature on decisions made by individuals about their education and health. The seminal contributions in this field by Becker (1962), Ben-Porath (1967), and later, Rosen (1976) were concerned with the accumulation of human capital. Although they use 'human capital' as a catch-all term for things like 'education, health, occupational choice, mobility, etc.' (Ben-Porath 1967, p. 352), their models are best suited to explaining a worker's investment in education. Grossman (1972) modified human capital theory with a focus on investment in health.[2] In his model, people can postpone their deaths by using health services that slow down the deterioration of their health status.

Like the authors mentioned above, we study the effect of an accumulatable factor – fatigue – on productivity. However, fatigue plays a role that is somewhat different from the role normally played by accumulatable factors. As fatigue cannot grow indefinitely, it can be considered to be similar to the 'inverse' of a depletable resource. Following this analogy a worker will end up with maximum fatigue at the end of his or her working life. We ignore the effects of a finite working life and focus on workers who have an infinite planning horizon. The consequence of this approach is that it is optimal to have a near-constant level of fatigue. Accumulation of fatigue does not arise as a long-term strategy.

The models presented in this chapter also bear some resemblance to the 'empirical' models of Karasek (1979) and Karasek and Theorell (1990). Karasek (1979) identified decision latitude and job demands as the two factors that determine the amount of 'unresolved strain' of a person. Workers with high job demands only tend to be dissatisfied with their jobs if they have insufficient control over them. Later Karasek and Theorell (1990) extended the model in order to account for learning and 'accumulation of strain'. Our model differs from the Karasek framework in three respects. First, in our model decision latitude refers to the flexibility a person has in terms of setting the target of production – 'control over demand' – while for Karasek decision latitude refers to the scope of a person's capability to cope with problems – 'control versus demand'. Second, our model explicitly takes into account technological change. Third, we offer a more detailed treatment of the dynamic aspects of worker behaviour.

The learning principles on which the model is founded are similar to those of the informal models of Kahneman (1973) and Hockey (1997). In the latter paper, a distinction is made between short-term and long-term decisions. Short-term decisions are adjusting the level of effort to a target, while long-term decisions are adjusting targets in response to unsustainable effort levels.

Another type of model has been constructed by Yaniv (1995). He focuses on the amount of overtime that is optimal for an employer. Overtime reduces labour costs per hour worked but at the same time it raises absenteeism due to burnout. Our model differs from that of Yaniv in two respects. First, we concentrate on the decisions made by the employee rather than those made by the employer. Second, our model incorporates the evolution in job characteristics due to technological change.

Borghans and Ter Weel (2004) consider the effects of a discrete automation decision: whether an employee gets a computer or not. A drop in the costs of using a computer – presumably caused by technological change – leads to a wider adoption of computers. The main difference with our approach to technological change is that we consider the impact on a worker of a gradual rather than discrete change in technology.

The chapter is organized as follows. The first model, in which workers behave adaptively, is introduced in section 2. The simulation results for this model are presented in section 3. Section 4 contains a variation on the model of section 2, but then with forward-looking workers. The chapter ends with some concluding remarks.

8.2   A MODEL WITH ADAPTIVE BEHAVIOUR

A firm produces a single good y and employs one person and k machines. The employee can perform both routine tasks l and non-routine tasks h. The routine tasks can also be performed by machines but routine labour and machinery are imperfect substitutes. Non-routine labour is complementary to both routine tasks and machines. Production takes place with constant elasticities of substitution (CES) and constant returns to scale:

$$y = \left[h^{\phi} + (l^{\mu} + k^{\mu})^{\frac{\phi}{\mu}} \right]^{\frac{1}{\phi}}$$

(8.1)

The parameter $\phi < 0$ ensures the complementarity of non-routine tasks with routine tasks and machines, the parameter $0 < \mu < 1$ determines the degree of substitutability between routine labour and machinery.

The entrepreneur chooses the amounts of routine and non-routine labour and machinery such that the profits of the firm are maximal. The optimization problem for given prices of output p_y and machines p_k and given wage rate w can be stated as

$$\max_{h,l,k} \left\{ p_y \left[h^{\phi} + (l^{\mu} + k^{\mu})^{\frac{\phi}{\mu}} \right]^{\frac{1}{\phi}} - w(h + l) - p_k k \right\}.$$

(8.2)

It follows directly from the first order conditions that $k/l = (w/p_k K)^{1/(1-\mu)}$. After somewhat more elaborate manipulation, the optimal ratio of non-routine to routine labour, or κ, can also be expressed as a function of w/p_k.

$$\kappa \equiv \frac{h}{l} = \left((w/p_k)^{\frac{\mu}{1-\mu}} + 1 \right)^{\frac{\phi(1-\mu)}{\mu(\phi-1)} + 1}$$

(8.3)

After substitution of l and k in the production function (8.1) the output of the firm becomes a linear function of the amount of non-routine tasks, given the price of machines and the wage rate.

$$y = \Gamma h \tag{8.4}$$

$$\Gamma \equiv \left[\left((w/p_k)^{\frac{\mu}{1-\mu}} + 1 \right)^{\frac{\phi(1-\mu)}{\mu(\phi-1)}} + 1 \right]^{1/\phi} \tag{8.5}$$

The Γ effectively indicates the technology that has been chosen for production.

The employee is paid according to the number of tasks that have been performed. Although the entrepreneur decides on the ratio of non-routine to routine tasks, the employee is free to choose the number of tasks to be performed. It is assumed that the optimal amount of machinery is available for every number of tasks chosen by the employee. From the perspective of the employee, non-routine tasks differ from routine tasks because the former require 'mental effort', m, and lead to fatigue, f. The number of non-routine tasks that are performed depends linearly on mental effort and on the level of fatigue.

$$h = \max\{m - \alpha f, 0\} \tag{8.6}$$

Here, α is a parameter that determines by how much productivity is affected by fatigue. During routine tasks the worker can recover from non-routine activities. In particular, ρ hours of m are compensated for during one hour of l. After one period of routine and non-routine activities, compensated mental effort equals

$$m - \rho l = m - \frac{\rho}{\kappa}(m - \alpha f) = \left(1 - \frac{\rho}{\kappa}\right)m + \frac{\alpha\rho}{\kappa}f. \tag{8.7}$$

In order to ensure that work is always tiring, it is required that $\rho < \kappa$. When mental effort is not fully compensated for during routine activities, it causes fatigue to accumulate.

$$f_t = \max\left\{ f_{t-1} - r_t + \left(1 - \frac{\rho}{\kappa}\right)m_t + \frac{\alpha\rho}{\kappa}f_{t-1}, 0 \right\}$$

$$= \max\left\{ \left(1 + \frac{\alpha\rho}{\kappa}\right)f_{t-1} - r_t + \left(1 - \frac{\rho}{\kappa}\right)m_t, 0 \right\} \tag{8.8}$$

Where r is the 'recovery capacity' of the worker. Every period r is subtracted from the fatigue accumulated in the current and previous periods. A person with a high recovery capacity is able to do a large number of non-routine tasks without experiencing a decline in his or her productivity. Sluiter et al. (2001) have found evidence of a negative relation between opportunities for recovery and health status under mildly stressing circumstances.

As a person cannot become infinitely tired there is a maximum to the fatigue a person can accumulate. If this maximum is reached the person experiences burnout, which leads to an abrupt change in behaviour. First of all, the employee goes on sick leave ($m = 0$) until the fatigue has disappeared ($f = 0$). Second, the recovery capacity of the person is damaged permanently. Burnout causes r to be reduced by the amount ω. Whether or not a person has burnout is signified by the dummy variable b, that equals one in case of burnout and zero otherwise. The conditions for burnout are illustrated in Figure 8.1.

Now we have specified the environment in which the employee has to work. He or she can adjust to the environment by changing his or her mental effort and by setting his or her aspired level of output, y^a. The employee gradually adjusts the effort made according to the rule:

$$m_t = \begin{cases} \max\{m_{t-1} + \beta(y^a_{t-1} - y_{t-1}), 0\} & \text{if } b_t = 0 \\ 0 & \text{if } b_t = 1 \end{cases} \qquad (8.9)$$

where β is a parameter. The employee changes the level of effort made to get closer to his or her aspired level of output. If production in the

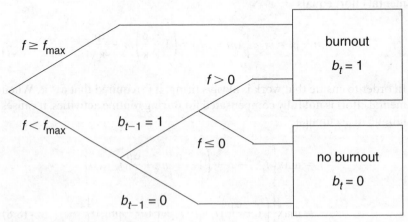

Figure 8.1   Conditions for burnout

previous period was above the aspired level then the worker will reduce his or her efforts, if production was too little he or she will work harder.

Besides changing their efforts workers may also alter their aspired level of production. If no fatigue is being accumulated while the aspired level of production already has been reached, the employees multiply their desired level of production by $\eta > 1$. Conversely, if fatigue accumulation does occur while the aspired level of production has not been reached, employees know that this behaviour is likely to be unsustainable and will start reducing their aspired level of production by dividing it by η. Furthermore, workers entering burnout will multiply their production target by $\gamma < 1$, knowing that the previous target has been unsustainable and that burnout has reduced their recovery capacity. Besides the worker, the entrepreneur can also change the aspired level of production. When the entrepreneur decides to use a different technology – a different mix of inputs – this will affect the production per hour worked and therefore the production target should be multiplied by Γ_t/Γ_{t-1} The decision rules governing the aspired level of production are summarized below.

$$
y_t^a = \begin{cases}
y_{t-1}^a \dfrac{\Gamma_t}{\Gamma_{t-1}} \gamma & \text{if } \Delta b_t = 1 \\[2ex]
y_{t-1}^a \dfrac{\Gamma_t}{\Gamma_{t-1}} \eta & \text{if } b_t = 0 \text{ and } y_{t-1}^a \le y_{t-1} \text{ and } \Delta f_{t-1} \le 0 \\[2ex]
y_{t-1}^a \dfrac{\Gamma_t}{\Gamma_{t-1}} \eta^{-1} & \text{if } b_t = 0 \text{ and } y_{t-1}^a > y_{t-1} \text{ and } \Delta f_{t-1} > 0 \\[2ex]
y_{t-1}^a \dfrac{\Gamma_t}{\Gamma_{t-1}} & \text{otherwise}
\end{cases}
\tag{8.10}
$$

8.3   SIMULATION RESULTS

The complexity of the model outlined above does not allow for a straightforward analytical solution and therefore we will have to rely on numerical simulation for the analysis of the model. In order to grasp the basic working of the model, we will start by having a fixed aspiration level for production ($\eta = \gamma = 1$). The worker is not allowed to vary the target and the entrepreneur is not allowed to change the technology of production. In this setting two events are possible. First, the aspired level of production might be feasible and sustainable given the worker's recovery capacity. In this case the worker will adjust his or her effort level, perhaps temporarily over- or undershoot the target level of production, reach the

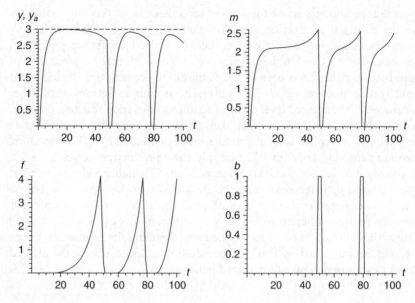

Figure 8.2   Fixed aspired production level

target, and then stick to the target with a constant level of mental effort and fatigue.

Second, the worker may not be able to sustain or even reach the aspired level of production. This situation is illustrated by Figure 8.2, which plots the actual (solid line) and aspired (dashed line) level of production against time, as well as mental effort, fatigue and b, the burnout dummy. [3] Initially the worker is able to achieve the production target but fatigue immediately starts accumulating. The adverse effect of fatigue on productivity causes the worker to exert him or herself more and more in order to stick to the target. In period 49 fatigue has reached a maximum and the person experiences burnout. After a few periods of rest, fatigue has disappeared and the person goes back to work. However, the permanent damage to the recovery capacity inflicted by the burnout makes it impossible to achieve the aspired level of production again. A second burnout follows quickly.

Let us next allow for flexibility in the aspired level of production while keeping technology constant. Simulation results with $\eta = 1.001$ and $\gamma = 0.9$ can be found in Figure 8.3. The other parameter settings are identical to those of the simulation of Figure 8.2. As soon as fatigue starts accumulating the worker begins adjusting his or her target downwards. Unfortunately, he or she is unable to reduce the target quickly enough and burnout is postponed rather than avoided. Burnout leads the worker to drastically

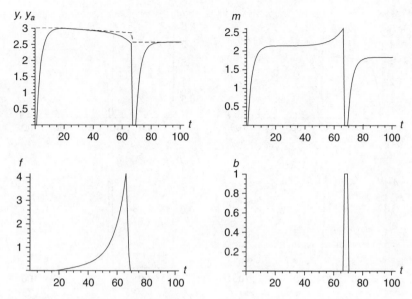

Figure 8.3   Flexible aspired production level

reduce his or her aspired level of production. In the situation depicted in Figure 8.3 the post-burnout production target proves to be sustainable and a second burnout is avoided. Flexibility in the aspired level of production thus postpones the first burnout and avoids the second and third burnouts completely.

The simulation illustrated by Figure 8.4 allows for gradual technological change. In particular, unskilled tasks are increasingly taken over by machinery – such as computers. This process of mechanization requires workers to increase their mental effort in order to keep up with the targets set by the entrepreneur. Although the worker is able to make the same adjustments to the target as before, he or she is not able to postpone burnout as long as in the situation without technological change. Mechanization has an adverse effect on the worker's mental health because the worker spends a larger part of his or her working day on non-routine activities, which makes him or her more susceptible to fatigue accumulation and burnouts.

A more complete picture of the functioning of the model is provided by Table 8.1, which contains simulation results for 27 parameter configurations. The configurations differ in three dimensions: recovery during routine work, ρ, flexibility in the aspired level of production, η, and the speed of mechanization, κ_t / κ_{t-1}. The first three columns of the table show the values for ρ, η and κ_t / κ_{t-1}, the fourth column contains the number of burnouts after

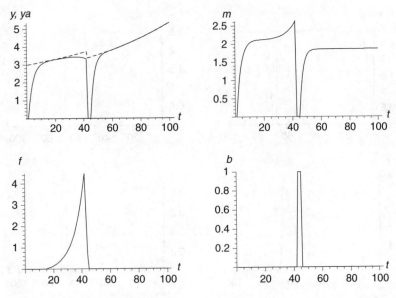

Figure 8.4   Technological change

100 periods and the fifth column shows the period in which the first burnout starts. For each combination of ρ and η, a higher rate of mechanization leads to more and earlier burnouts. Higher flexibility (η) has the opposite effect. The more flexibility workers have in choosing their targets, the lower the number of burnouts will be. Less interesting, when routine tasks allow for recuperation from non-routine tasks, fewer burnouts will occur.

8.4   A MODEL WITH PERFECT FORESIGHT

In the model presented above, workers try to reach their target by following a set of behavioural rules. These rules are adaptive in nature and do not guarantee an outcome that is optimal to the worker. In this section we show how workers would behave if they perfectly understood the situation they were in and would therefore be able to choose the amount of effort that maximized the present value of their production.[4] The primary purpose of the current exercise is to verify whether technological change reduces the optimum level of fatigue or not.

In contrast with the previous model, the worker no longer tries to achieve a target level of production in the current period, but maximizes the discounted value of production in all future periods.

Table 8.1   Simulation results

ρ	η	k_t / k_{t-1}	Number of burnouts	Period 1st burnout
0	1	1	2	28
0	1	1.01	2	28
0	1	1.03	4	27
0	1.001	1	1	29
0	1.001	1.01	1	28
0	1.001	1.03	2	27
0	1.01	1	1	50
0	1.01	1.01	1	48
0	1.01	1.03	3	41
0.05	1	1	1	49
0.05	1	1.01	1	40
0.05	1	1.03	1	33
0.05	1.001	1	1	67
0.05	1.001	1.01	1	43
0.05	1.001	1.03	2	34
0.05	1.01	1	0	—
0.05	1.01	1.01	0	—
0.05	1.01	1.03	2	94
0.1	1	1	0	—
0.1	1	1.01	1	90
0.1	1	1.03	1	46
0.1	1.001	1	0	—
0.1	1.001	1.01	1	94
0.1	1.001	1.03	3	49
0.1	1.01	1	0	—
0.1	1.01	1.01	0	—
0.1	1.01	1.03	2	94

$$\int_0^\infty y(\Gamma_t, h_t)\exp[-\delta t]\mathrm{d}t \qquad (8.11)$$

In order to keep the model as simple as possible, we assume that a worker never stops working and discounts his or her future output a constant rate δ. Notice that we have switched to continuous time. The discontinuous nature of burnouts in the adaptive model complicates our search for the optimal response of workers to technological change. For this reason, we assume that a worker will no longer experience a sudden drop in productivity when his or her fatigue exceeds a certain threshold. Instead, the worker will face a gradual, but possibly rapid, decrease in productivity as fatigue accumulates. For this purpose, equation (8.6) is replaced by a more general formulation.

$$h_t = m_t - \alpha f_t^\beta, \quad \beta > 1 \tag{8.12}$$

This formulation provides roughly the same incentives as the original discontinuous form in combination with the possibility of burnout. With both approaches a worker can be caught in a situation with low productivity that is due to overexertion in the past. (Note that β is defined in a different way from before.)

The accumulation of fatigue as given by equation (8.8) changes because of the nonlinear effect of fatigue on productivity.

$$\dot{f} = \left(1 - \frac{\rho}{\kappa}\right) m_t + \frac{\rho}{\kappa} \alpha f_t^\beta - r \tag{8.13}$$

A dot above a variable denotes the derivative with respect to time. The absence of burnout as a discrete effect brings with it that the recovery capacity, r, remains constant over time.

The optimization problem of the worker is to maximize (8.11) subject to (8.13) by choosing the optimal path of m. Solving this problem yields an expression for the path of fatigue that maximizes the present value of production.

$$f_t = \left(\frac{\delta - \hat{\Gamma}_t + (\rho^{-1}\kappa_t - 1)^{-1}\hat{\kappa}_t}{\beta\alpha}\right)^{\frac{1}{\beta-1}} \tag{8.14}$$

Variables wearing a hat are growth rates; details can be found in the Appendix. Transitional dynamics are absent because technically there are no restrictions on the value of m.

Three mechanisms affect the optimal level of fatigue. First, optimal fatigue depends positively on the discount rate. Workers are more inclined to overexert themselves when the future is less important to them. A similar effect, but operating in the opposite direction, is triggered by productivity growth. A positive rate of productivity growth, approximated by $\hat{\Gamma}$, reduces the optimal level of fatigue. Workers realize that they will be more productive in the future, which gives them an incentive to 'rest now and work later'.

The third effect is related to the future intensity of work. Workers choose higher fatigue if their jobs become non-routine more rapidly. The parameter ρ indicates that this effect depends on whether a worker is able to recover during routine tasks. If workers know in advance that there will be fewer opportunities for on-the-job recovery in the future, they have an incentive to shift part of their future effort to the present. Workers anticipate that their jobs will become tougher by working long hours today and gradually reduce their efforts as time proceeds.

It is also interesting to see what does not affect fatigue in equation (8.14). In particular, note that in the absence of technological change, fatigue no longer depends on the task composition of the job. The specific characteristics of a technology do not influence the mental health of a worker: it is the rate of technological change that matters.

Concluding, the optimally chosen level of fatigue is negatively affected by productivity growth, while time preference and the growing intensity of work have a positive effect. As technological change influences both productivity and job composition, its net effect on fatigue will depend on parameter settings and, through κ, on time itself. For large values of κ the work intensity effect will be small and, consequentially, the productivity growth effect will dominate.

8.5   CONCLUDING REMARKS

In this chapter we have presented two models that relate a worker's mental health to the rate of technological change. The first, adaptive, model shows that a high rate of technological change reduces the mental health of workers especially if they are not allowed or are not able to have a higher degree of control over their production targets. A cautionary note is in place here. The conclusion that increasing job control, task autonomy or flexibility is enough to avoid burnout in a rapidly changing environment is incorrect. Giving employees more control over their work may raise the amount of non-routine tasks they need to perform and may add to the problem rather than diminish it.

In the second model, workers with perfect foresight choose the optimal path of their fatigue. Now the effect of technological change on fatigue can be either positive or negative. It can be negative because workers will be more productive in the future, letting them postpone some of their effort. It can be positive because there will be fewer opportunities for on-the-job recovery in the future, making it more attractive for workers to work hard now and gradually reduce their efforts over time.

The models can be extended in several ways. For example, they can be used to assess the impact of the type of contract between employer and employee on health and productivity. The effects of (obligatory) disability insurance could also be taken into account. Additionally, the models can be incorporated in a general equilibrium framework with endogenous technological change. In such a framework, the rate of technological change might depend on whether the costs of burnouts are carried by employers or by, for example, the government.

This chapter illustrates that the relation between mental health and technology goes beyond the influence of individual technologies. We have shown that a succession of technologies that are harmless by themselves can nevertheless lead to a deterioration of mental health.

NOTES

1. For a case study on monitoring technologies see Hubbard (2000).
2. In an earlier paper Mushkin (1962) proposed that health care must be seen as an investment.
3. The other parameter settings are: $f_0 = 0$, $f^{max} = 4$, $m_0 = 0$, $y^a = 3$, $r = 2$, $\alpha = 0.2$, $\beta = 0.2$, $\omega = 0.1$, $\Phi = 2$, $\kappa = 1$, $\mu = 0.5$, $\rho = 0.05$.
4. It would be more accurate to let the worker maximize income and not production. The absence of a general equilibrium structure, however, prevents us from finding a solution for the wage rate. This problem is not very serious because in standard models of economic growth production workers receive a fixed share of the output.

REFERENCES

Autor, D.H., F. Levy and R.J. Murnane (2003), 'The skill content of recent technological change: An empirical exploration', *Quarterly Journal of Economics*, **118** (4), 1279–333.
Becker, G.S. (1962), 'Investment in human capital: A theoretical analysis', *Journal of Political Economy*, **70** (5, Part 2), 9–49.
Bell, L.A. and R.B. Freeman (2001), 'The incentive for working hard: explaining hours worked differences in the US and Germany', *Labour Economics*, **8** (2), 181–202.
Ben-Porath, Y. (1967), 'The production of human capital and the life-cycle of earnings', *Journal of Political Economy*, **75** (4, Part 1), 352–65.
Borghans, L. and B. ter Weel (2004), 'What happens when agent *T* gets a computer? The labor market impact of cost efficient computer adoption', *Journal of Economic Behavior and Organization*, **54**, 137–51.
Green, F., A. Felstead and D. Gallie (2003), 'Computers and the changing skill-intensity of jobs', *Applied Economics*, **35** (14), 1561–76.
Green, F. and S. McIntosh (2001), 'The intensification of work in Europe', *Labour Economics*, **8** (2), 291–308.
Gregg, P. (1994), 'Share and share alike', *New Economy*, **1** (1), 13–9.
Grossman, M. (1972), 'On the concept of health capital and the demand for health', *Journal of Political Economy*, **80** (2), 223–55.
Hockey, G.R.J. (1997), 'Compensatory control in the regulation of human performance under stress and high workload: A cognitive-energetical framework', *Biological Psychology*, **45** (1–3), 73–93.

Hubbard, T.N. (2000), 'The demand for monitoring technologies: The case of trucking', *Quarterly Journal of Economics*, **115** (2), 533–60.

Kahneman, D. (1973), *Attention and Effort*, Englewood Cliffs, NJ: Prentice Hall.

Karasek, R. (1979), 'Job demands, Job decision latitude, and mental strain: Implications for job redesign', *Administrative Science Quarterly*, **24**, 285–308.

Karasek, R. and T. Theorell (1990), *Healthy Work: Stress, Productivity, and the Reconstruction of Working Life*, New York: Basic Books.

Mushkin, S.J. (1962), 'Health as an investment', *Journal of Political Economy*, **70** (5, Part 2), 129–57.

Paoli, P. and D. Merllié (2001), *Third European Survey on Working Conditions 2000*, Luxembourg: Office for Official Publications of the European Communities.

Rosen, S. (1976), 'A theory of life earnings', *Journal of Political Economy*, **84** (4), 67.

Sluiter, J.K., M.H.W. Frings Dresen, A.J. Vander Beek and T.F. Meijman (2001), 'The relation between work-induced neuroendocrine reactivity and recovery, subjective need for recovery, and health status', *Journal of Psychosomatic Research*, **50** (1), 29–37.

Spitz, A. (2004), 'Are skill requirements in the workplace rising?', ZEW Discussion Paper 04–33.

Yaniv, G. (1995), 'Burnout, absenteeism, and the overtime decision', *Journal of Economic Psychology*, **16** (2), 297–309.

APPENDIX

The Hamiltonian associated with the optimization problem is given by

$$H = \Gamma_t(m_t - \alpha f^\beta)\exp[-\delta t] + \mu_t\left(\left(1 - \frac{\rho}{\kappa_t}\right)m_t + \frac{\rho}{\kappa_t}\alpha f_t^\beta - r\right). \quad (8.15)$$

The associated first order conditions are $\partial H_t/\partial m_t = 0$ and $\partial H_t/\partial f_t = -\mu_t$. From the first of these first order conditions follows a solution for μ.

$$\mu_t = \frac{-\Gamma_t\exp[-\delta t]}{1 - \rho/\kappa} \quad (8.16)$$

Differentiate with respect to time and substitute for μ in the second of the first order conditions to obtain a second solution for μ.

$$\mu_t = \frac{\beta\Gamma_t\alpha f_t^{\beta-1}\exp[-\delta t]}{\hat{\Gamma}_t - \delta - (\rho^{-1}\kappa_t - 1)^{-1}\hat{\kappa}_t + \beta\alpha f_t^{\beta-1}\rho^{-1}\kappa_t} \quad (8.17)$$

Equate both expressions for μ and solve for f to arrive at equation (8.14).

9. Some economics of digital content[*]

Wilfred Dolfsma

9.1 CONTENT INDUSTRIES

Content may be defined, by looking at the use of communication infrastructures such as the Internet, as the information exchanged that is not necessary to maintain the infrastructure itself. Content includes entertainment people seek, but includes personal exchanges of emails as well. I focus mostly on the information exchanged by people via the Internet that is unrelated to their professional activities. To give an indication of the extent to which the Internet is used for purposes other than 'functional' ones, observe Table 9.1 showing the most sought keywords.

Content is in large part the product of the (mostly) deliberate efforts of individuals and organizations to be creative, and content tends to be an information good. Information goods have properties that make them distinct from the goods exchanged on markets that generally figure in economic theories. Consumption by one person does not exclude in any way the consumption by others. In addition, and especially using ICT, an information good may be consumed by several (many) individuals at the same time without any of them having an experience that is diminished in any way. Information goods are, thus, non-excludable and non-rivalrous. Information, therefore, is a public good.

Economists argue that the market offers insufficient benefits for individuals and organizations to be creative, giving rise to a need for Intellectual Property Rights such as copyrights (Landes and Posner 1989). Copyright law is an intellectual property right such as patent law and trademark law. Copyright actually refers to a number of different though related rights to such works. It includes reproduction in various forms, recordings, broadcasting, translation into other languages, or – more controversially – adaptation, such as a novel into a screenplay. So-called 'neighbouring rights' have been added in recent years, preventing the public performance of a work without consent from and payment of royalty to the author. Unlike

* I would like to thank an anonymous referee and the editors for useful comments on an earlier draft of this chapter.

Table 9.1   The most popular search words

Gambling
Sex
Casino
Porn
Investing
Hardcore
Movie
Nude
xxx
Game

Source: www.keywordcity.com (25, September 2003).

patents that protect the idea for a new good or production process, copyright protects the specific way in which an idea is expressed; it protects 'original works of authorship'. If the same idea is expressed in ways that are sufficiently different, both expressions will be protected from imitation without infringing on each other. Copyright duration is longer, however, generally lasting for the life of the author plus 70 years. There is an overall increase in the duration for which copyrights provide protection. The Statute of Anne provided protection for 14 years (once renewable). Since 1993 in Europe and 1998 in the USA the term mentioned above holds. Copyright law restricts the commercial exploitation of a newly developed good to the person or organization that has developed it, or holds the rights in it. Music, movies, books, computer code but also fragrances for perfume for instance may all be protected under copyright law. 'Copyright industries' (OECD 1998) produce goods the exploitation of which can be limited under copyright law. Up to a point, the holder of the copyrights may choose not to exercise his or her rights. The work may be cited, and copies may be made by an individual for private, non-commercial purposes (referred to as 'fair use' or 'fair dealing'). One does not have to apply or register in order for one's creative work to be protected under copyright law, although having copyrighted work registered in some countries facilitates legal action against infringement. Content industries, media industries and copyright industries will, for the purpose of this chapter, be used as synonyms.

At present, one cannot understand the goings on in content industries without understanding the role copyrights play (Huygens et al. 2001; Klaes 1997). Firms producing and distributing works that are protected by copyrights typically rely on these rights; they allow them to weather downturns and they constitute de facto entry barriers. Examples of such 'original works of authorship', literary and artistic works in fixed form, include writing, music, drawings, dances, computer programs, and movies. In recent years databases have also come to be protected under copyright law (Maurer et al. 2001). Ideas, concepts, principles, algorithms and 'brute' facts are not included. The first time copyrights were formally enacted was in the English Statute of Anne (1709) in the UK, based on informal previous practice.

9.2 MEDIA, COPYRIGHTS AND TECHNOLOGY

Within the discipline of economics, a separate field of economics of information has emerged (Riley 2001), recently acknowledged when Akerlof, Spence and Stiglitz won the Nobel Prize in 2001. Information goods increasingly take a central place in economic reality, whether it be pure information goods, or the information component of physical goods. A number of goods that previously were inseparable from a physical object, now become or can be digitized. Certainly the emerging 'market' for digitized music has caught the attention over the past few years, shaking up as it did a sector in the economy that many people take a particular interest in, a sector that had also developed some degree of complacency. The Internet and other technical means of communicating and exchanging information allow for easier copying and distributing of information, in fact driving down marginal costs of such activities. This is in a way attractive for producers and distributors of information, but it also poses a threat. Others, particularly those who might otherwise have purchased the information, may now obtain it from other sources, possibly at greatly reduced prices. This would in many cases be an infringement of the copyrights held in such works. Developments in technology put pressure on the system of copyright law in previous decades as well by reducing the effort it takes to make copies (Burke 1996), but now the threat seems particularly acute.

Information and communication technology (ICT) very rapidly and substantially changes our economy and society (Freeman and Perez 1988). In times of changing techno-economical paradigms, it is not easy to make predictions. However, some comments can be made on the developments media will face in the future. Information goods have properties that make them distinct from the goods exchanged on markets that generally figure in economic theories, besides the ones related to their public good features discussed above. Information products are not subject to damage through use or as a result of copying. A clandestine party, and even a customer, can benefit from the economic advantages of having manufactured such a product by unlawfully acquiring and marketing it. The options for unlawful uses are many; the result of such arbitrage is a decline in the product's price. In addition, copies cannot be distinguished from the originals. For this reason, the price of the used, second-hand product does not alert the customer to the quality of the original. Second-hand markets no longer give the quality signals of the corresponding first-hand products (see Akerlof 1970). A third feature of information products is that they can easily be modified. One could primarily think of modifications due to market developments or based on customer preference. Uncertainty for consumers increases as the possibility to compare a product with others decreases. Providing demo versions does not completely solve this problem of information asymmetry that is inherent to information products, however. How should a customer judge the genuineness of a demo if he or she is not able to determine how representative the demo is? Problems of information asymmetry are difficult to solve, unless by recourse to the reputation of the firm selling the product. Reputation is thus a valuable asset for firms in markets for information goods. Reputation can be hard to attain – incumbent, well-endowed firms have an advantage in this regard as they have had time to prove they do not sell 'lemons'. Attempts at manipulating intermediaries are tempting, and seem to be an inevitable part of the industry. For the music industry they are particularly well known and even studied by economists (Coase 1979).

For these reasons larger firms producing content have an advantage. Their advantage is also due to the strong network effects in markets where information goods are exchanged (Shapiro and Varian 1999). Consumption or use of information goods by some makes it more attractive for others to also start consuming the good. Each additional member of the group increases the value to the existing members of being a part of the group, for example by using the information good. The product itself can be configured such that network effects are made better use of, for instance by playing into the social elements of consuming content.[1] Another option is to make the products technically or thematically compatible with complementary goods. Table 9.2 gives some insight into content and the entertainment markets.

Discussed, or at least mentioned, much more extensively is another characteristic of information goods. Information goods tend to have a distinct cost structure: creating a first issue involves high investment costs that are to a large degree sunk costs. Such costs need to be invested, but to the extent that they are sunk, cannot be recovered if the project fails; they are idiosyncratic to the product or project. Budgets for producing a movie, a computer game, or a piece of music have multiplied over the past years. Marketing budgets have increased even more, as the supply of content has grown and diversified; being noticed is more difficult. Costs already 'sunk' in the project, must not but often are considered in a decision about

Table 9.2   A glance at content/entertainment markets

	World	USA	Japan	UK	The Netherlands
Revenue music recordables (US$, m, 2002)	30 980.9	12 609	5 001	2 936	397.6
Music copyrights, gross royalties (US$, m, 2002)	6 626.78	1 940.42	759.64	669.73	176.57
Production long films (no.)		420[b]	238	78[d]	16[b]
Cinema, attendance (m)		63[d]	123[b]	114.6[d]	16[b]
Cinema, box office (US$, m)		5 250[d]	153 580[b]	384[d]	188[b]
Daily Newspapers, (no. titles, 1996)		1520	122	99	38
Books (no. titles)		(n.a.)	3 401[c]	2 853[c]	11 002[a]
Books, trade balance, (no. copies, 1997)		689 001	−145 195	855 714	−24 900
Radio receivers (/1000 inhabitants, 1997)		2116	956	1443	980
Television sets (/1000 inhabitants, 1997)		806	686	521	519
Leisure software (games, US$, m, 2000)	21.61	7.48	3.99	1.55	
Internet domains	31 987 198				
Information on the Internet (terabytes)	532 897				

Notes:
[a] 1993
[b] 1994
[c] 1996
[d] 1995

Sources: IFPI (2003); NMPA (2002); UNESCO (1999); Spectrum Strategy Consultants (2002); P. Lyman and H.R. Varian, "How much information', 2003. retrieved from http://www.sims.berkeley.edu/how-much-info-2003 on 10 December 2003.

whether or not to continue. If, against the economic logic, a firm investing in the creation of an information good decides to continue anyway, it may come to a position, when the product can be brought to the market, where it decides to try to generate whatever cashflow it can to at least recover variable costs and some of the fixed costs. The firm will thus cut prices, forcing other players in the field to adjust prices as well.

High initial investment costs and low marginal or variable cost are an important consideration for firms in designing their strategy. High investment costs, borne before the product developed or produced can be marketed, imply that firms run a risk. If the product does not find a (sufficiently large) market, such costs will not be recovered. The sunk cost effect will be especially strong for markets where information products are exchanged. Alternatively, competitors can easily imitate an information product. Intellectual Property Rights (IPRs) of various kinds, which legally protect the products of the intellect from being commercially exploited by or in the name of parties other than the creator/author, are only a partial protection from such imitation.

Legal protection is, however, only one element of what might be called the 'appropriability regime' of a product, determining the extent to which the innovative firm can appropriate the profits, or benefits more generally, associated with the product (Teece 1986). Another is the 'nature of technology', conceived broadly (see e.g. Dolfsma 2001). If, for instance, a (new) product must be produced using a new production process and is critically dependent on this process, the likelihood of imitation is diminished as process innovations need to be 'read' from a product. New contents are forms of product innovations. ICT enables the production and distribution of content; as such it facilitates process innovation. In addition, the production of new content depends on the tacit knowledge of the people involved, it is not so likely that the product can be imitated – one needs to be knowledgeable of previous content not only to be accepted by your peer producers of content, but also to be creative (Crane 1992; Shuker 1994). Links with other parties, such as in (r)etail, the media, or organizations in the business of live performances are important complementary assets (Vogel 1998), and often rely on personal contacts (Aksoy and Robins 1992; DeFillippi and Arthur 1998; Jones and DeFillippi 1996; Eberts and Norcliffe 1998). In the interactions between musicians and the staff responsible for production, tacit knowledge plays an important role as well (Gillet 1996). While ICT facilitates some of the technical aspects of the work of producers, these are not the critical capabilities that they have. What is critical is the way they relate to the musicians.[2] Contrary to expectations (Malone et al. 1989), ICT does not produce the perfect market from economists' textbooks (see Brynjolfsson and Smith 2000; Graham 1998; Dolfsma 1998). The ease of making versions of an information product gives competitors the opportunity to imitate cheaply but also gives the initial creator the possibility of catering to different audiences and thereby increasing the revenues from an innovation – I will elaborate on this now.

9.3 PRICE DISCRIMINATION AND PRODUCT DIFFERENTIATION

It is only recently that the Internet began to have an impact on society, an influence going beyond the confines of the universities and research laboratories where it had been in use for several decades. Still, the theoretical discussion that has preceded this section, as well as an understanding of the industry studied, does allow one to make some predictions.

As a number of observers have indicated (e.g. Varian 1996; Reinartz 2001) the Internet provides ample opportunity to collect information about consumers' preferences on the basis of which one might adjust the products one offers as a firm ('versioning'), but on the basis of which one might also charge different prices to consumers with differing willingness to pay. Such price discrimination has different forms:

- First-degree price discrimination means that the producer sells different units of output for different prices and these prices may differ from person to person. This is known as perfect price discrimination.
- Second-degree price discrimination means that the producer sells different units of output for different prices, but every individual who buys the same amount of the good pays the same price. Thus prices depend on the amount of the good purchased, but not on who does the purchasing. A common example of this sort of pricing is volume discounts.
- Third-degree price discrimination occurs when the producer sells output to different people for different prices, but every unit of output sold to a given person sells for the same price. This is the most common form of price discrimination, and examples include senior citizens' discounts, student discounts, and so on.

Conditions for price discrimination to hold include the availability of information to discriminate between (groups of) consumers, and the absence of arbitrage between the groups or individuals addressed. The Internet would now seem to offer the possibility of first-degree price discrimination. People's willingness to pay is easy to determine, while the (menu) costs for re-pricing goods on the Internet decrease. There is, of course, the possibility that people will be upset when they learn that identical products are sold on different terms. As consumers become more sophisticated about buying on-line, this objection might disappear (Reinartz 2001).

Important in evaluating price discrimination in welfare economic terms is Figure 9.1. The total area below the demand curve signifies the utility to society when such a product would be available free of charge. Assume

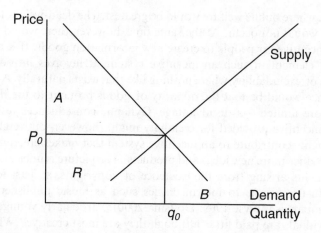

Figure 9.1   Price discrimination

a given price (P_0). Area R is the revenue accruing to the firms in this market. Areas A and B are, however, of greatest import in a welfare analysis. A is the so-called consumers' surplus; it is the price which some consumers would have been willing to pay for a product but, given the price prevailing in the market, did not have to pay. They can now spend it on something else. Area B is a dead-weight welfare (efficiency) loss, since the consumers here would like to have consumed the good, but the good is not offered at the price they are able or willing to pay.

Price discrimination means that some consumers pay a higher price, but not all. More consumers may be able to consume the good. Price discrimination on the Internet will most likely be combined with product differentiation, making it hard to asses the consequences; consumers may have to pay a higher price, but may at the same time obtain a product that more closely meets their preferences. It is likely that the first effect will be stronger than the latter. Since they need to make idiosyncratic investments, they are more dependent on this relationship than the firms are (see Williamson 1975). It is only after an initial period where consumers invest in a relationship by filling in questionnaires, surfing on a site, and answering questions that they may expect the benefits of tailored products. As such, they may become the victims of opportunistic behaviour on the part of the firm; they are locked in to a relation.

For pure information goods, marginal costs for producing an additional copy are or approach zero. Economic analysis would suggest that people should be able to obtain such a good at a price that equals marginal costs, a situation where public welfare would be greatest. The dead-weight loss of triangle *B* would not occur. At the same time, however, there would be no material incentive for people to create new information goods. IPR are an important element in such an incentive system. It involves introducing a measure of excludability where nothing like that exists naturally. A static consequence would be that the quantity of goods brought to the market will be more limited – a disadvantage. Dynamic consequences resulting from the incentive provided for creativity might, however, outweigh this. Do copyrights contribute to an incentive system that makes creative individuals produce more new ideas and products? The picture is unclear. Most of the benefits arising from the existence of copyrights, at least for the music industry, accrue to intermediaries such as music publishers and record companies (Towse 1999; Dolfsma 2000). Particularly younger creative individuals are paid little, although they are most creative.[3] Whether this points to an inherent need to be creative and express oneself, or to an (irrational) expectation that one will become one of the few stars in the system, cannot be determined more conclusively (Abbing 2002).

On electronic markets consumers continuously provide information about their preferences and their willingness-to-pay. Firms can and do make use of that information directly in altering the (bundle of) product(s) they offer, and the price they offer it for. Rather than the trial-and-error process of taking a new product to the market and waiting to see if there will be demand for it, firms now know (much) more about their customers who in fact become subcontractors, becoming relatively more dependent on suppliers of digital content than the other way around, even though the volatility of markets for content does limit the influence of providers.

9.4   CONTENT THAT BINDS

In emerging electronic markets consumers are flooded with information that they need to filter and qualify. Intermediaries are in a much better position to perform these tasks than consumers themselves. Not only will they be able to exploit economies of scale and scope in gathering and interpreting information about products available on the Internet, but they will be able to strike deals with upstream suppliers to consider their products and bring them to the attention of consumers. Intermediaries' position will depend on their reputation in both the market where they buy products (information, usually) from suppliers, and where they sell to final consumers. Consumers in their turn, will appreciate the selection of information done for them by these intermediaries and will be willing to pay for these services.

With the use of the preferences that consumers reveal by their implicitly or explicitly stated choices, the intermediaries that form the last chain before the consumers are able to construct detailed consumer profiles. Answers to questions, information about previous purchases, as well as clicking behaviour, constitute valuable information that intermediaries use to customize their products as well as their sales efforts. Since contemporary hardware and software have become increasingly sophisticated, information gathering and subsequent profiling on the basis of that can be automated to a significant degree. Consumer profiles that intermediaries are able to construct become increasingly focused on single individuals. Indeed, firms' overall strategies are increasingly informed by such considerations.[4] As consumers are, as such, increasingly involved in the production process itself – especially in the design and marketing aspects of it (if one can still legitimately distinguish between these aspects in cases such as these) – one may for that reason perceive of them as subcontractors to the intermediaries or suppliers (Dolfsma 2004a).

Consumers and intermediaries may both benefit from these developments in electronic markets. Consumers benefit because they can save time searching for the products they want and will even be offered items they might like but had not considered or known about until then, of a kind and quality that meet their preferences to higher degrees. Intermediaries will particularly benefit, however (Dolfsma 1998). They are crucial gatekeepers as they control an important funnel of attention that consumers rely on to determine the quality and value of information goods (see Crane 1992). It will be difficult for upstream suppliers to go around this bottleneck and reach consumers directly or establish their own intermediary. Intermediaries that have built up a reputation have an advantage over new entrants in that they have already established links with (potential) consumers.

Given that digital products can easily be reproduced and versioned, and do not deteriorate if used or copied (Whinston et al. 1997), customization of them is progressing and will continue to do so in the future. Consumers, however, need to convey information about themselves in order to secure these benefits of customization. However this information is conveyed, it means much more investment in terms of time and money on the part of consumers than on the part of intermediaries. Intermediaries will do much of the information gathering and classifying by the use of special software. The extensive databases that are thus built can subsequently be used to fine-tune marketing efforts and offer customers products that will meet their preferences in better ways. Related products in which some interest may have been expressed can also be presented. Firms such as Amazon generate additional revenues efficiently and add to the profiles that they already have of other, similar people. Since the cost of investing in a market relation between intermediary and consumer is much higher for the latter than for the former, and switching costs for a consumer are high, the investments of consumers can be considered as idiosyncratic investments in terms of transaction costs economics (Williamson 1975). These investments are idiosyncratic, because discontinuing the business relation in which investments were made and starting one with another intermediary means that the consumer has to enter afresh into a process of providing implicit or explicit information about his or her preferences to this new partner. Such investments make the party undertaking them dependent on the other party in the relation; the first party is locked into a relation. This second party may then use the leverage to extract higher rents from the relation.

Before making the investment, consumers may therefore need to be persuaded of the benefits they will reap from entering into such a relationship with an intermediary. Once this relationship has started, the costs involved in the investments made will prevent either party from abandoning it. If one party has invested idiosyncratically, this party will be in an unfavourable position. Rational consumers *may* be aware of this and decline to enter into such a relation. If no alternative firms are available that will not build and use profiles to their own advantage, even rational and knowledgeable customers may have to enter into such a relation. What is more, statements of firms on electronic markets to the effect that they will not use people's information have been violated before.[5] Olson's (1965) logic of collective action indicates that organizing many consumers to prevent firms from adopting the kind of policy discussed above will be insurmountably difficult. Customers are likely, in addition, to have to go without the benefits associated with such practices as well, however. When consumers are not rational and perfectly informed *homo economici*, but rather creatures of habit (e.g. Dolfsma 2002, 2004b), there is an additional reason why they will simply enter into a relation with an established, reputable firm and later find themselves in a subcontracting relation. Consumers generally are aware of their investment, and if they are not yet aware they will rapidly become so; their knowledge does not stop them, however, from participating in such a relationship. The potential benefits of decreased search costs and increased fulfilment of their needs may convince them that it is beneficial to initiate a relationship with a particular intermediary. Consumers may also appreciate it when they are pointed to different but related products. In addition, intermediaries in this early and immature state of many electronic markets have started to compensate (potential) customers for the personal and unique information they provide by answering questionnaires. This compensation takes the form of rebates or samples.

The balance of advantages and disadvantages for consumers and firms might be different for electronic markets. Why would intermediary firms necessarily be the parties that are likely to gain most? Even if they are to gain more than consumers, however, that gain may not be at the expense of Internet consumers. Total economic activity may expand due to developments in Internet markets. The additional consumer surplus may outweigh the deadweight loss that consumers suffer; in all the process may end up in a situation that is a Pareto improvement even when further welfare improvements would be possible. If this is the case, and if intermediaries take the bigger share of that market, the economic position of consumers need not deteriorate in absolute terms. Developments in electronic markets can increase the economic pie, even when they can change the distribution of the pie itself.

Furthermore, two countervailing forces are at play in electronic Internet markets that set limits to the degree to which intermediaries can wield their market power. One is the fact that communities that form in the virtual world – for instance, in discussion groups – may find it easier to organize themselves as they are not bound by geography and can more easily reach a critical mass. The likelihood that information about alternative intermediaries to turn to, or about (alleged) abuses by the intermediary with whom community members now deal, will spread round in the network or community is substantial. The background and sources of information at the disposal of each member of the community will probably differ significantly more than in traditional, physical markets. In network theory, this is known as the 'weak ties' argument, and for many different situations it has positive effects (see e.g. Granovetter 1995). Especially Rheingold (1994) believes that Internet communities will be an important countervailing power in the social and the economic realm. Jones (1995, 1998) provides empirical studies of Internet communities that present a more mixed perspective. Extant relations tend to persist, or tend to be reflected in relations on the Internet; power is not absent from the Internet, contrary to what many had expected. Whatever effect Internet communities have on the behaviour of firms depends on firms wanting to preserve their reputation.

A second tendency that will be observed as electronic markets develop and mature is an increased volatility in demand in these markets. New products altogether, or new variants of an existing product are likely to find their way to the market. These will partly be delivered by entrants into electronic markets in an attempt to establish a foothold in a particular market, but may also be launched by incumbents as a means of constructing barriers to entry and defending their own position in a market. Such practices by incumbents are already known for certain physical markets such as cereals, soaps, washing powders and detergents (see Scherer and Ross 1990) and will be copied and perfected in Internet markets.

Whether or not incumbents will succeed in maintaining their possibly dominant positions in electronic markets depends on how responses to their behaviour are perceived and acted on in the different Internet communities that are relevant to these firms. Internet communities have extended possibilities, in terms described by Hirschman (1970), to express their voice, while their members may not always be able to exercise the exit option because they are locked into a relation with an intermediary that they themselves have invested in heavily. How this works out in terms of the absolute and relative numbers of customers who remain loyal to an intermediary firm and the products it brings to a market is not clear. The effect may be that the position of a firm will become less secure than it is in physical markets, but that need not necessarily result in its position inevitably deteriorating. Entertainment industries provide examples of industries where a fundamental feature of business is an equivalently high degree of demand volatility. Still these industries tend to be dominated by a few large companies (see Vogel, 1998), because large, diversified firms can take advantage of such circumstances while small, single-product firms are very vulnerable. Relevant Internet communities consist of large numbers of consumers with diverse interests. As Olson had already argued persuasively in 1965, a small group of parties that has a well-defined interest often finds it easy to mobilize against such a large(r) group. In addition, as Internet communities allow for people to communicate anonymously, parties (firms) that have a specific interest may be able to introduce information in the community through individuals that pose themselves as independent. Sony Music has notoriously done so by persuading a reviewer of newly released music to write favourably about its music. Future developments will thus, of course, determine which of these tendencies will be stronger.

9.5   ORGANIZING PRODUCT INNOVATIONS

The ongoing existence of companies in the media industry is closely related to their capability not only to constantly develop new products, but also to target a large enough market with these products. The rate of success of new products in the media industry was already at a relatively low level of 10 per cent in the 1960s and 1970s (Peterson and Berger 1975), but it has even declined in the years thereafter: 95 per cent of music released nowadays does not even reach its break-even point. At the same time, of course, the thorough selection before actual release of songs involves substantial costs as well. However, the few media products that are actually profitable handsomely compensate for the non-profitable ones. The success rate of product innovations thus challenges the organization of media companies. Scale is important to survive failures, but a certain feeling for the market is equally important. The latter is notoriously difficult for large corporations.

Given the pressure, including illegal use, on information product markets, producers are driven to constantly launch new products. It is a certain way to stay ahead of – unlawful – competition. In addition, adapting products to every taste is a well-known strategy that was initially analysed by the economist Hotelling (1929) in the case of ice cream parlours alongside beaches. Possibilities to influence success of a certain song through effective marketing are there, but of limited use as consumers are not perfectly malleable nitwits.

The large incumbent players in the music industry – the 'majors' – control the most important complementary assets that allow them to maintain and even improve their position over long periods of time despite the uncertainty in the market. For decades the five majors have had a combined market share of 80 per cent (Table 9.3) – the music industry is no exception among the entertainment industries. Deep (financial) pockets, distribution capabilities and marketing expertise are what large existing corporations focus on – based on these capabilities, they are in the more advantageous position.

Next to this negative reason to increase the pace of product innovation, there are several positive reasons. It is important for businesses in the media industry to launch new products in order to be ahead of the competition and to make the most out of a certain market. Product life cycles have shortened, the fashion extent of the economy increases. Producing

*Table 9.3   The five major record
companies (% of sales, 2000)*

Global	
Universal	21.1
Sony	17.4
EMI	14.1
Warner – Time Warner	13.4
BMG – Bertelsmann	11.4
Independents	22.6

Source: Music Business International (MBI, 2000).

upgrades or versions of existing goods limits the costs of product innovation as initial costs have already been made.

If businesses learn that a smaller percentage of new products prove successful, they must be able to survive unsuccessful releases. The period for raising profits from the market will shorten. Success has to be generated through short, highly agile, intensive and sophisticated advertisement, but there are additional means to use. A proven strategy is that of building on previous success by creating 'platforms'. Platforms can remain internal to the genre. The star system in the music industry is an example of such a platform strategy. Star musicians releasing a new album have less chance of the new production being a flop. Platforms can also transcend genres: Britney Spears who 'writes' a book, or the Spice Girls who shoot a film are examples. Music proves to be a media product that can serve as a platform itself, but it can rely on other platforms as well. Stars featuring in a film increase the chances of success for that production. The soundtrack of a Disney film, made by Elton John, is an example of this. One should not be surprised that the influence of companies in the media industry is widespread. The result is that for entertainment industries economies of scope are important. Being present in related fields allows you to leverage a successful product in related fields or genres, as Table 9.4 indicates.

The importance of a thorough feeling for the market will increase, implying the need for a very flexible way of organizing a big firm (Storper 1989; Hakfoort and Weigand 2000). Major players in the entertainment indus-

Table 9.4   Economies of scope in entertainment industries

	Time Warner	Disney	Sony	Seagram	Bertels- mann	Viacom	Newscorp
Television, production	√	√	√	√	√	√	√
Film	√	√	√	√	√	√	√
Music	√	√	√	√	√	√	√
Publishing	√	√			√	√	√
Television, broadcasting	√	√			√	√	√
Cable television	√	√	√	√		√	√
Satellite television	√		√	√	√		√
Internet	√	√	√	√	√	√	√
Theme parks	√	√				√	
Retail	√	√			√	√	

Source: *The Economist* (1998) 'Wheel of Fortune – A survey of technology and Entertainment', 21 November.

tries thus seek agreements with smaller ones in order to take over talent that proved successful in local markets. Both players benefit from such an arrangement (Hesmondhalgh 1998). The kind of agreements that result are complex, offering a range of incentives to the players involved (Caves 2000).

9.6 SOME CONCLUSIONS

Content industries are in a genuine maelstrom at the moment. Many developments affect them, and many of those relate to what might be called the process of digitization or informatization. Much is expected from this process; its consequences are welcomed as well as feared. In this contribution it is argued that final consumers will not tend to come into direct contact with agents who have created (new) content. Intermediaries are indispensable.

Compiling extensive consumer profiles offers the possibility for unforeseen product differentiation and price discrimination by intermediaries in the content industries. Consumers will be implicated in the production of the goods and services provided, and should thus be perceived as subcontractors to firms producing content. Their idiosyncratic investments lock them into the relationship. Economies of scope are significant too, creating a necessity for providers of content to have a presence in related content markets in order to spread risks and maximize the benefits of a product as and when it turns out to be successful. If and when incumbent firms in the content industries use the favourable position they (still) find themselves in, there is no reason why they should not continue to prosper in the digital age, especially now that technical and legal measures have become available that enable these firms to lock their consumers even more firmly into their content providers as subcontractors.

NOTES

1. See Mitchell (1997), Frith (1996), Stahl (1997) and Dolfsma (2004b).
2. On the relation between innovation and trust or 'culture' more generally, see e.g. O'Reilly and Tushman (1997).
3. On this particular point, as well as on the issue of motivation of individuals and the role of material incentives generally, see Frey (1997).
4. A good, and some would say notorious, example is Microsoft (see *Financial Times*, 31 December 2001 'Microsoft's direct connection to the customer').
5. Despite the public outcry that this has sometimes evoked, such action may not be illegal. Firms on electronic markets can have their customers sign 'click-wrap' contracts, which many never read, that contain clauses that allow them to alter their policy in relation to privacy without the consent of their extant customers.

REFERENCES

Abbing, H. (2002), *Why are Artists Poor? – The Exceptional Economy of the Arts*, Amsterdam: Amsterdam UP.

Akerlof, G.A. (1970), 'The market for "lemons": Quality uncertainty and the market mechanism', *Quarterly Journal of Economics*, **84**, 488–500.

Aksoy, A. and K. Robins (1992), 'Hollywood for the 21st century', *Cambridge Journal of Economics*, **16**, 1–22.

Brynjolfsson, E. and M.D. Smith (2000), 'Frictionless commerce? A comparison of internet and conventional retailers', *Management Science*, **46**, 563–85.

Burke, A.E. (1996), 'How effective are international copyright conventions in the music industry?', *Journal of Cultural Economics,* **20**, 51–66.

Caves, R.E. (2000) *Creative Industries – Contracts between Art and Commerce*, Cambridge, MA: Harvard University Press.

Coase, R.H. (1979), 'Payola in radio and television broadcasting', *Journal of Law and Economics*, **22**, 269–328.

Crane, D. (1992), *The Production of Culture – Media and the Urban Arts*, Newbury Park, CA: Sage.

DeFillippi, R.J. and M.B. Arthur (1998), 'Paradox of project-based enterprise: The case of film making', *California Management Review*, **40**, 125–39.

Dolfsma, W. (1998), 'Internet: An economist's utopia?', *Review of International Political Economy*, **5**, 712–20.

Dolfsma, W. (2000), 'How will the music industry weather the globalisation storm?', *First Monday*, 5.

Dolfsma, W. (2001), 'Metaphors of knowledge in economics', *Review of Social Economy*, **59** (1), 79–91.

Dolfsma, W. (2002), 'The mountain of experience: How people learn in a complex, evolving environment', *International Journal of Social Economics*, **29**, 675–84.

Dolfsma, W. (2004a), 'The logic of collective consuming: Consumers as subcontractors on electronic markets', *International Journal of Social Economics*, **31**, 832–39.

Dolfsma, W. (2004b), *Institutional Economics and the Formation of Preferences: The Advent of Pop Music*, Cheltenham, UK and Northampton, MA, USA: Edward Elgar.

Eberts, D. and G. Norcliffe (1998), 'New forms of artisinal productions in Toronto's computer animation industry', *Geographische Zeitschrift*, **86**, 120–33.

Freeman, C. and C. Perez (1988), 'Structural crises of adjustment, business cycles and investment behaviour', in G. Dosi, C. Freeman, R. Nelson, G. Silverberg and L. Soete (eds), *Technical Change and Economic Theory*, London: Pinter.

Frey, B. (1997), *Not Just for the Money*, Cheltenham, UK and Lyme, USA: Edward Elgar.

Frith, S. (1996), *Performing Rites: On the Value of Popular Music*, New York: Oxford University Press.

Gillet, C. (1996), *The Sound of the City*, 2nd edn, New York: Da Capo.

Graham, S. (1998), 'The end of geography or the explosion of place? Conceptualizing space, place and information technology', *Progress in Human Geography*, **22**, 165–85.

Granovetter, M. (1995), *Getting a Job*, Chicago, IL: The University of Chicago Press.

Hakfoort J. and J. Weigand (2000), *Magazine Publishing – A Quiet Life? The Dutch Market for Consumer Magazines*, Den Haag, Centraal Planbureau, available at *http://www.cpb.nl/nl/pub/werkdoc/120/cm/*.

Hesmondhalgh, D. (1998), 'The British dance music industry', *British Journal of Sociology*, **49**, 234–51.

Hirschman, A.O. (1970), *Exit, Voice and Loyalty*, Cambridge, MA: Harvard University Press.

Hotelling, H. (1929), 'Stability in competition', *Economic Journal*, **39**, 41–57.

Huygens, M., C. Baden-Fuller, F.A.J. Van Den Bosch and H.W. Volberda (2001), 'Co-evolution of firm capabilities and industry competition: Investigating the music industry, 1877–1997', *Organisation Studies*, **22**, 971–1011.

International Federation of the Phonographic Industry (IFPI) (2003), *The Recording Industry – World Sales, 2002*, April.

Jones, C. and R.J. DeFillippi (1996), 'Back to the future in film: Combining industry and self-knowledge to meet the career challenges of the 21st century', *Academy of Management Executive*, **10**, 89–103.

Jones, S.G. (ed.) (1995), *Cybersociety*, Thousand Oaks, CA: Sage.

Jones, S.G. (ed.) (1998), *Cybersociety 2.0*, Thousand Oaks, CA: Sage.

Klaes, M. (1997), 'Sociotechnical constituencies, game theory, and the diffusion of compact discs', *Research Policy*, **25**, 1221–34.

Landes, W.M. and R.A. Posner (1989), 'An economic analysis of copyright law', *Journal of Legal Studies*, **18**, 325–63.

Malone, T., J. Yates and R. Benjamin (1989), 'The logic of electronic markets', *Harvard Business Review*, 166–70.

Maurer, S., P.B. Hugenholtz and H. Onsrud (2001), 'Europe's database experiment', *Science*, **294**, 789–90.

Mitchell, T. (1997), 'New Zealand music on the Internet: A study of the NZPOP mailing list', *Perfect Beat*, **3**, 77–95.

Music Business International (2000), *World Directory 2000*, London: MBI.

National Music Publishers' Association (NMPA) (2002), *International Survey of Music Publishers Revenues, 2001*, 12th ed, New York: NMPA.

OECD (1998), *Content as a New Growth Industry*, Paris: OECD.

Olson, M. (1965), *The Logic of Collective Action*, Cambridge, MA: Harvard University Press.

O'Reilly, C.A. and M.L. Tushman (1997), 'Using culture for strategic advantage: Promoting innovation through social control', in M.L. Tushman and P. Anderson (eds), *Managing Strategic Innovation and Change*, New York: Oxford University Press.

Peterson, R.A. and D.G. Berger (1975), 'Cycles of symbol production: The case of popular music', *American Sociological Review*, **40**, 158–73.

Reinartz, W.J. (2001), 'Customising prices in online markets', *European Business Forum*, **6**, 35–41.

Rheingold, H. (1994), *The Virtual Community*, London: Secker & Warburg.

Riley, J.G. (2001), 'Silver signals: Twenty-five years of screening and signaling', *Journal of Economic Literature*, **39**, 432–78.

Scherer, F.M. and D. Ross (1990), *Industrial Market Structure and Economic Performance*, Boston, MA: Houghton Mifflin.

Shapiro, C. and H.R. Varian (1999), *Information Rules. A Strategic Guide to the Network Economy*, Boston, MA: Harvard Business School Press.

Shuker, R. (1994), *Understanding Popular Music*, London: Routledge.

Spectrum Strategy Consultants (2002), *From Exuberant Youth to Sustainable Maturity – Competitiveness Analysis of the UK Games Software Industry*, London: Department of Trade & Industry.

Stahl, G. (1997), 'Citing the sound: New Zealand indie rock in North America', *Perfect Beat*, **3**, 60–76.

Storper, M. (1989), 'The transition to flexible specialisation in the US film industry', *Cambridge Journal of Economics*, **13**, 273–305.

Teece, D.J. (1986), 'Profiting from technological innovation: Implications for integration, collaboration, licensing and public policy', *Research Policy*, **15**, 112–3.

Towse, R. (1999), 'Copyright and economic incentives: An application to performers' rights in the music industry', *Kyklos*, **52**, 369–90.

UNESCO (1999), *Statistical Yearbook*, Paris: UNESCO.

Varian, H.R. (1996), 'Differential pricing and efficiency', *First Monday*, 1.

Vogel, H.L. (1998), *Entertainment Industry Economics*, Cambridge: Cambridge University Press.

Whinston, A.B., D.O. Stahl and S.-Y. Choi (1997), *The Economics of Electronic Commerce*, Indianapolis, IN: Macmillan.

Williamson, O.E. (1975), *Markets and Hierarchies: Analysis and Antitrust Implications*, New York: Free Press.

10. How computerization has changed the labour market: A review of the evidence and a new perspective*

Lex Borghans and Bas ter Weel

10.1 INTRODUCTION

The use of computer technology at work has increased dramatically over the past decades from about 20 per cent in the early 1980s to more than 70 per cent at the beginning of the new millennium. This increase in the adoption and use of new technology is likely to have changed the labour market in many dimensions.[1] With respect to wages it has been found that computer users earn substantially higher wages than non-users, with wage premiums up to levels as high as 20 per cent. It is however not clear whether this observed premium is a reflection of the returns to (computer) skills, the result of unobserved heterogeneity between computer users and non-users, or whether there are other sources underlying these wage differentials.[2] Computer technology is particularly used by the more highly educated workers, suggesting skill advantages play a crucial role in adjusting to and using new technologies. Hence, adoption of computer technology is easily connected to changes in the wage structure. On the other hand, looking at the present use of computer technology, it is hard to understand why more highly educated workers have an advantage in using for example a PC compared with less highly educated workers. Related to this observation is the

* The chapter has benefited from discussions with Daron Acemoglu, Joshua Angrist, David Autor, Eli Berman, Harrie Borghans, Allard Bruinshoofd, David Card, Andries de Grip, Hans Heijke, Hugo Hollanders, Lawrence Katz, Francis Kramarz, Alan Krueger, Geoff Mason, Richard Murnane, Luc Soete, John Temple and Bruce Weinberg. We also would like to thank two anonymous referees for a number of useful comments on an earlier draft. We would like to thank several people and institutions for providing us with the data. The data about Germany, the German Qualification and Career Survey, were collected by IAB (Institut für Arbeitsmarkt- und Berufsforschung der Bundesanstalt für Arbeit) and BIBB (Bundesinstitut für Berufsbildung) and were made available for research by the Zentralarchiv für Empirische Sozialforschung, Universität zu Köln. The UK data were made available by the Data Archive (British Social Attitudes Survey), and by Francis Green (Skills Survey of the British Workforce). CPS data about the USA were made available by the NBER. This research is supported by the Netherlands Organisation for Scientific Research (NWO).

issue of the trend towards skill upgrading over the past decades. Is it really true that skill upgrading is the result of differences in computer skills between workers? Investigations of patterns of computer use over the life cycle have been concerned with the notion that older workers might be less able to work with computer technology and end up being unemployed. However, figures suggest that the patterns of computer technology use over the life cycle have been surprisingly flat.

While most observers agree that computer technology has changed the workplace to a considerable extent, there is no consensus with regard to how this change has occurred. This chapter reviews the most important developments in the economic literature on the impact of computer technology on the labour market and provides a framework to understand how computer technology has changed the labour market by developing and making use of a threshold model of technology diffusion. The focus of the model is to explain wage differentials between computer users and non-users, the secular trend towards upgrading of skill requirements, and the wage developments over time experienced by many OECD countries. It demonstrates that wage differentials between computer users and non-users are consistent with the fact that computer technology is first introduced in high-wage jobs because of cost efficiency. This stands in sharp contrast with the view that computer use increases wages. In fact, it reverses the causality of the relationship between computer technology and wages. In addition, the framework reveals that skill upgrading in jobs where computer technology is introduced occurs because of a re-emphasis on non-routine job activities or tasks. It also shows that neither differences in computer skills nor skills complementary to using computer technology are needed to explain wage differentials between computer users and non-users and to explain skill upgrading. Finally, the framework predicts a changing wage structure over time, which is consistent with the changes in the wage structure in the OECD countries over the past decades.

The chapter is in five sections. Section 10.2 presents information about the extent of computer technology use at work in a number of countries and discusses the trends over time. It also describes the development of wages, and particularly wage differentials between computer users and non-users, over time and relates these observations to the adoption of computer technology. Section 10.3 reviews previous empirical studies and discusses the suggestive evidence presented in this body of empirical work. Section 10.4 presents a threshold model of technology diffusion to provide a new perspective on the computerization of the labour market in which the empirical evidence can be reconciled and consistently explained. Section 10.5 concludes.

10.2 TRENDS IN COMPUTER TECHNOLOGY USE AND WAGE DIFFERENTIALS

Table 10.1 summarizes the incidence of using computer technology for different categories of workers in Britain, Germany and the United States in the mid-1980s and late 1990s. Computer technology use in the mid-1980s is lower in Germany and Britain than in the United States. However, by 1997 the levels of computer use in Germany and Britain are higher. Differences in these figures might of course be the result of different wordings of the questions in the survey, but comparisons with other sources of information about computer technology usage suggest that such effects are likely to be of a small magnitude.[3] The most important message from the numbers in the table is that although computer use at work is increasing over time, the patterns of use among various labour-market groups are very similar in

Table 10.1 Percentage of workers in age, educational level and gender categories using computer technology at work in Britain, Germany and the United States

	Britain		Germany		United States	
	1985	1997	1985	1997	1984	1997
All workers	19.3	69.2	19.3	56.2	24.3	52.5
Age:						
20–29	21.2	67.8	18.4	50.8	24.8	47.8
30–39	24.0	71.6	22.0	57.6	27.9	54.3
40–49	13.7	71.9	19.3	58.3	23.2	55.5
50–60	17.1	63.0	13.8	56.6	18.4	50.6
Educational level:						
< High school	12.0	40.2	4.3	23.8	5.1	12.6
High school	28.2	55.1	18.4	50.5	19.2	36.9
Some college	31.5	75.1	25.6	76.9	30.6	53.2
College or higher	45.9	95.5	33.6	87.6	42.4	71.2
Gender:						
Men	24.1	69.2	18.6	54.4	21.6	43.6
Women	14.9	69.1	21.0	60.5	29.6	55.6

Note: Data about computer technology use in Germany refer to the Länder of the former West Germany only. German data are taken from the *German Qualification and Career Survey*. Information about Britain stems from the *British Social Attitudes Survey* for 1985 and the *Skills Survey of the Employed British Workforce* for 1997. Data on computer use in the United States are based on the 1984 and 1997 October Supplements to the *Current Population Surveys*.

relative terms. Computers are predominantly used by the more highly educated, but there is also a considerable group of less highly educated workers whose jobs involve the use of computer technology. In contrast to what is often expected, the highest rate of computer technology use at work is not found in the youngest age group (20–29): workers in the age group 30–39 or 40–49 are the most frequent users of computer technology and the oldest group of workers does not seem to suffer to a large extent from the adoption and diffusion of computer technology.[4] What is also interesting to observe is that women are generally more likely to use computer technology at work than men, especially in the United States.[5]

There have been many other authors who have investigated the use of computer technology for a number of different countries. Examples are Reilly (1995) who used the *General Segmentation Survey* for Canada; Asplund (1997) used the Finnish labour force survey; Entorf and Kramarz (1997) and Entorf et al. (1999) explored the French labour force survey; Miller and Mulvey (1997) applied the *Survey of Training and Education* in Australia; Oosterbeek (1997) used information from the *Brabant Survey* to study computer use in the Netherlands; and Sakellariou and Patrinos (2000) described computer technology use among higher education workers in Vietnam using the *Higher Education Tracer Study* in that country. All studies reported an increasing pattern of computer technology use over time. For the United Kingdom, Bell (1996) used a different data source called the *National Child Development Study* and Chennells and Van Reenen (1997) and Haskel and Heden (1999) applied different waves of the British *Workplace Industrial Relation Surveys* to assess computer use at work. The results are comparable to the ones we present for the United Kingdom in Table 10.1. Hamilton (1997) used the *High School and Beyond Survey* for the United States and found similar computer use figures to the ones presented in Table 10.1 using the *Current Population Surveys*.

The adoption of computer technology has coincided with relatively large changes in the wage structure, mainly increasing wage inequality since the early 1980s, in many OECD countries. These trends have been carefully documented by, for example, Katz and Murphy (1992), Freeman and Katz (1995), Gottschalk and Smeeding (1997), Autor et al. (1998), Berman et al. (1998), Gottschalk and Joyce (1998), Machin and Van Reenen (1998), Katz and Autor (1999), Hollanders and Ter Weel (2002) and Acemoglu (2003). Table 10.2 takes a more modest approach by simply presenting the log wage differentials between computer users and non-users for Germany and the United States, in the 1980s and 1990s. What is clear from these numbers is that the wage differential between computer users and non-users is substantial, accelerating from the 1980s to the 1990s and levelling off somewhat towards the late 1990s. These numbers are consistent with the

Table 10.2   *Log wage differentials between computer using and non-using workers in age, educational level and gender categories in Germany and the United States*

	Germany				United States			
	1979	1985	1992	1997	1984	1989	1993	1997
All workers	0.137	0.236	0.271	0.292	0.264	0.309	0.349	0.352
Age:								
20–29	0.121	0.102	0.068	0.113	0.194	0.203	0.215	0.210
30–39	0.133	0.183	0.230	0.239	0.262	0.301	0.329	0.331
40–49	0.235	0.321	0.330	0.350	0.286	0.323	0.362	0.366
50–60	0.138	0.343	0.372	0.363	0.299	0.380	0.315	0.457
Educational level:								
< High school	0.137	0.226	0.231	0.220	0.224	0.270	0.307	0.230
High school	0.098	0.166	0.161	0.176	0.149	0.137	0.179	0.178
Some college	0.159	0.217	0.220	0.244	0.187	0.193	0.219	0.193
College or higher	0.041	0.133	0.162	0.217	0.164	0.206	0.234	0.225
Gender:								
Men	0.161	0.264	0.294	0.316	0.322	0.383	0.417	0.411
Women	0.142	0.191	0.226	0.280	0.284	0.318	0.353	0.364

Note: Data about computer technology use in Germany refer to the Länder of the former West Germany only. For Germany we use the *Qualification and Career Survey* of the German Federal Institute for Vocational Training (BIBB) and the Federal Employment Service (IAB). Data on computer use and wages in the United States are based on the 1984, 1989, 1993 and 1997 October Supplements to the *Current Population Surveys*.

evidence presented in the recent literature and suggestive to linking rising wage inequality to the computerization of the labour markets. The same trends seem to hold for all groups considered and the patterns are strikingly similar for Germany and the United States, despite the fact that the labour markets in these countries are often seen as examples of a highly institutional labour market and a labour market in which wages are determined by demand and supply. The German labour market structure would induce less wage dispersion among workers, which would be translated in a lower wage differential between those who use computer technology at work and those who do not. Apparently the wage differentials between computer users and non-users originate from other sources.

The figures presented in Tables 10.1 and 10.2 suggest that computer use is higher among more highly educated workers and is associated with higher wages. In the next section we review the most prominent approaches to explain the relationship between wages and computer technology use.

10.3 A REVIEW OF THE EVIDENCE

Different authors have used different data sources to assess the impact of computerization on labour-market outcomes. We distinguish three different levels of aggregation by separately discussing papers that have applied individual level data and firm data and studies that have used data at the occupational or industrial level.

10.3.1 Individual Level Data

An important contribution to the debate concerning the effects of computer technology on wages has been made by Krueger (1993). His initial approach is to augment a standard cross-sectional earnings function to include a dummy variable indicating whether an individual i uses a computer at work:

$$\ln W_i = \alpha + \beta_i X_i + \gamma_i C_i + \varepsilon_i, \tag{10.1}$$

where C_i represents a dummy variable that equals one if individual i uses computer technology at work, and zero otherwise; $\ln W_i$ is the log of the hourly wage of worker i; X_i represents a vector of observed characteristics; and α is the intercept.

Table 10.3 reports the coefficients of estimating equation (10.1) for the United States using the October Supplements to the 1984, 1989, 1993 and 1997 *Current Population Surveys*. Inclusion of several covariates in the wage equation suggests that computer users earn substantially higher wages than non-users and that the coefficient is relatively stable over time, ranging from 15.5 to 21.3 per cent. The studies for other countries mentioned in the previous section obtain generally similar results. Inclusion of only a dummy variable for using a computer at work leads to wage differentials ranging from 30.2 per cent in 1984 to 42.2 per cent in 1997. Similar wage differentials between computer users and non-users are obtained for the German and British data shown in the previous section.

Although it seems clear that computer users earn more than non-users, the figures presented in Tables 10.1 and 10.2 suggest that it is important to understand the effect of computer use on the relationship between earnings and education. A rather simple but straightforward test is to examine equation (10.1) first without computer use and then comparing these coefficients

Table 10.3 *OLS regression estimates of the effects of computer technology use on pay in the United States, 1984–1997 (dependent variable: ln hourly wage (standard errors in brackets))*

	1984	1989	1993	1997
Uses computer technology	.145 (.009)*	.153 (.009)*	.150 (.009)*	.144 (.010)*
Years of education	.058 (.002)*	.070 (.002)*	.070 (.002)*	.072 (.002)*
Experience	.026 (.001)*	.025 (.001)*	.027 (.001)*	.032 (.002)*
Experience squared/100	−.043 (.003)*	−.039 (.003)*	−.045 (.003)*	−.059 (.004)*
Black	−.090 (.011)*	−.087 (.011)*	−.066 (.011)*	−.076 (.012)*
Part-time job	−.212 (.010)*	−.150 (.011)*	−.188 (.010)*	−.160 (.012)*
Female	−.189 (.013)*	−.197 (.013)*	−.132 (.013)*	−.173 (.015)*
Married	.134 (.012)*	.142 (.012)*	.151 (.012)*	.123 (.013)*
Union member	.244 (.010)*	.224 (.010)*	.238 (.011)*	.201 (.013)*
Occupational dummies	Yes	Yes	Yes	Yes
Industry dummies	Yes	Yes	Yes	Yes
Regional dummies	Yes	Yes	Yes	Yes
Adjusted R^2	.409	.412	.417	.381

Note: * is significant at the 5 per cent level. All data are taken from the October Supplements to the *Current Population Survey* in the relevant years. The regression equation also included dummies for living in a small or medium-sized area and female*married.

with the ones reported in Table 10.2. In doing so, it turns out that the returns to a year of education without inclusion of the computer use dummy variable are 0.076 (0.001) in 1984, 0.091 (0.002) in 1989, 0.092 (0.001) in 1993 and 0.092 (0.001) in 1997 (standard errors in brackets). In other words, the rate of return to education increases by 1.5 percentage points between 1984 and 1989 if the computer dummy is excluded from the regression equation. If for 1984–1989 the computer dummy is included, the return to education increases by 1.1 percentage points. This implies that almost 30 per cent of the increase in the return to education can be attributed to the rise in computer use over the period 1984–1989. The validity of such an exercise is doubtful because for the other years in the sample the returns to education remain stable while the use of computers increases. In particular, this argument poses two problems. First, if computer technology increases the demand for skilled workers, this can raise the wages of all skilled workers relative to unskilled workers, regardless of whether they actually use computer technology at work. Second, if something else changes the demand for skilled workers, it may also change the relationship between education and computer use. Hence, controlling for computer use might lead to attributing wages effects to computer use, even if the actual force were something else.

An alternative way to analyse the differentials in computer use by different educational groups is to add a (computer use * years of education) dummy. If the coefficient is positive it indicates that more highly educated workers gain more from computer technology use than less highly educated workers. However, the coefficients for this variable are all insignificant at the 5 per cent level. The coefficients are (standard error) 0.001 (0.001) for 1984, 0.006 (0.003) for 1989, 0.002 (0.002) for 1993 and −0.003 (0.003) for 1997. These results, although drawn from a simple framework, suggest that more highly educated workers do not seem to benefit more – in terms of wages – from computer technology use than less highly educated workers.

Krueger (1993) has analysed the returns to various uses of computers included in the CPS for the United States in 1989. He runs a wage regression including the usual suspects and the following specific tasks (coefficients and standard errors in brackets): word processing (.017 (.012)), bookkeeping (−0.058 (0.013)), computer-assisted design (0.026 (0.020)), electronic mail (0.149 (0.016)), inventory control (−0.056 (0.013)), programming (0.052 (0.031)), desktop publishing or newsletters (−0.047 (0.021)), spread sheets (0.079 (0.015)), sales (−0.002 (0.016)). What is striking about these results is that relatively straightforward computer tasks, such as the use of electronic mail, yield the highest wage premium (16.0 per cent) and that the advanced use of computer technology, such as computer programming, yields an insignificant wage premium of only 5.3 per cent. Given the fact that tasks such as programming most likely involve computer skills and the use of email, in relative terms, does not, these results suggest that the computer wage premium might not reflect returns to computer skills.[6]

In addition, most contemporary computer usage concerns emailing and word processing and related activities. This is not exactly the type of specialist knowledge that would only be available among high-skilled workers. Many less highly educated and intermediately educated workers use computers at work (e.g., Table 10.1). Bresnahan (1999) and Handel (1999) show that it is therefore not likely that the demand for more highly educated workers is caused by the need for high-skilled workers to operate computers. In particular many secretaries and typists use PCs intensively. This does not seem to indicate that the use of new technology primarily requires sophisticated computer skills.

A major drawback of the data used by Krueger and many others is that only information about computer use is available and no information about the actual computer skills. Computer skills have been measured only indirectly in the literature as some kind of 'computer ability' (Bell, 1996) or 'computer knowledge' (DiNardo and Pischke, 1996 and Hamilton, 1997). Bell uses data from the UK *National Child Development Study*. DiNardo and Pischke utilize data from the *West German Qualification and Career Survey* conducted by the Federal Institute for Vocational Training. In this data information on both 'computer use' and 'computer knowledge' is available. Hamilton uses variables from the 1986 *High School and Beyond Survey* indicating whether an individual has ever used software packages or has used a computer language to program. These three studies find support for the thesis that a number of particular computer skills are rewarded in the labour market while others are not.

Based on data from their 1997 *Skills Survey of the British Workforce*, Green and Dickerson (2004) differentiate four levels of sophistication of computer use: advanced, complex, moderate and straightforward. The higher the complexity of computer use, the higher the wage premium. There is similar information about writing and maths. In addition, the data include the respondents' self-assessed effectiveness of the use of computer technology, writing and maths. The scale of this variable, which we interpret as a worker's skill on this task, is constructed from the answer to the following question: 'If your job involves using . . . are you able to do this effectively?' The answers are always, nearly always, often, sometimes and hardly ever.[7] The relationship between the specific writing, maths and computer tasks and wages might result from the skills needed to perform these tasks, but is also likely to reflect unobserved heterogeneity associated with these tasks, indicating that some tasks are more common in jobs with higher earnings than others. Here we are not interested in investigating the relationship between the tasks workers perform and their wages, but in the effects of skills on wages. However, we have to take into account that, as a result of experience, the performance of every specific task will increase the related specific skills, even if they would not be rewarded in the labour market. To distinguish empirically between skills that really matter and skills that are obtained as a by-product of the tasks a worker carries out, we regress the effects of skills on wages given the tasks of a worker:[8]

$$\ln W_i = \alpha + \beta_i X_i + \gamma_1 u_i^1 + \gamma_2 u_i^2 + \gamma_3 u_i^3 + \gamma_4 u_i^4 + \varphi_1 s_i^1$$
$$+ \varphi_2 s_i^2 + \varphi_3 s_i^3 + \varphi_4 s_i^4 + \varepsilon_i \qquad (10.2)$$

Table 10.4   OLS regressions for the effect of writing, math and computer skills on pay (dependent variable: log hourly wage (standard errors in brackets))

	Writing	Maths	Computer
Use:			
Straightforward	.105 (.054)	.059 (.055)	.211 (.044)*
Moderate	.100 (.053)	.219 (.055)*	.472 (.077)*
Complex	.169 (.051)*	.186 (.051)*	.554 (.130)*
Advanced	–	–	−.204 (.470)
Skill:			
Straightforward	−.020 (.011)	−.014 (.013)	−.013 (.014)
Moderate	.039 (.013)*	.002 (.013)	−.039 (.023)
Complex	.031 (.011)*	.025 (.012)*	−.043 (.036)
Advanced	–	–	.183 (.123)
Adjusted R^2	.321	.299	.343

Note: * is significant at the 5 per cent level. All data are from the 1997 *Skills Survey of the Employed British Workforce*. For writing the following categories apply: straightforward is filling in forms, moderate is writing short documents with correct spelling and grammar, and complex is writing long documents with correct spelling and grammar. For maths, straightforward is adding and subtracting numbers, moderate is performing calculations, and complex is advanced mathematics. For computer use, straightforward means tasks such as printing etc., moderate is e.g. using a word processor or email program, complex is e.g. using a computer to perform statistical analyses, and advanced is e.g. computer programming and developing software. For writing and maths only three levels of sophistication of use exist in the data.

where s_i^x, $x = 1, \ldots, 4$ equal the skills levels for workers who apply writing, maths and computers at the different levels of sophistication and u_i^x, $x = 1, \ldots, 4$ equal the use variables. Now, the parameters $\varphi_1, \ldots, \varphi_4$ represent the effects of increased skills, conditional on the level of sophistication at which writing, maths or computers are being used. The results of this exercise are given in Table 10.4, which only reports the coefficients on the use and skills variables.

The regression results show that the skills to write both long and short documents have a significant and positive effect on wages. A 1-point increase on the skill scale adds 3–4 per cent to the worker's wage.[9] The difference between these skills is not statistically significant, however. These regression results for writing skills suggest that there are no large differences between the skills involved in writing long or short documents. The effect of the ability to fill in forms is not significantly different from 0. The regression results reported in the second column of Table 10.4 show that there are no labour-market returns for the most straightforward maths skills such as adding and subtracting when keeping the level of sophistication of use constant. In addition, there are no returns to skills for calculations using decimals, percentages or fractions. This implies that although the use of this form of maths seems to be typical for higher paid workers, the skill in itself does not appear to be scarce and is not rewarded in terms of wages. Only the ability to apply advanced mathematical procedures has a significant labour-market return of some 2.5 per cent for a 1-point increase on the skills scale, which is somewhat lower than the returns to writing skills. Hence, for most mathematical applications there seems to be a coincidental correlation (unobserved heterogeneity) between the group of workers who use such mathematical applications (and for whom this is important) and their wages. Only for advanced mathematical procedures there seems to be a significant effect of skills on wages. Finally, the estimates reported in the final column of Table 10.4 suggest that computer skills are not important in explaining the wage differentials between computer users and non-users and that these wage differentials are in all likelihood caused by other factors.[10] Only the point estimate for computer skills at the highest level of sophistication of computer use is positive, and the level of significance comes close to 10 per cent, indicating that increases in computer skills might have a substantial effect on the wages of computer programmers and related occupations using computers at the advanced level.[11]

A number of researchers interpret Krueger's computer wage premium as an indicator of the fact that the introduction of computer technology in the workplace increases wages, that is, computer technology is regarded as a 'treatment'. An employee who is given a computer to use sees his or her wages go up, while an identical employee from an imaginary control group who is not given such a computer will not receive this wage rise. The reasoning is that computer technology increases productivity and that the employee will subsequently have this productivity increase reflected in his or her wages. If we assume that there is competition in the labour market, it is not clear why workers with similar capabilities would not be rewarded similarly. In other words, there is no reason for an employer to pass on the benefits of increased productivity to the employee.[12] Chennells and Van Reenen (1997), Entorf and Kramarz. (1997) and Entorf et al. (1999) studied a panel of employees who started to use computers during the research period. They found that employees who started to use computers did not receive significantly higher wages than the group who did not start to use computers. Entorf et al. concluded that employees with the largest – unobservable – computer talent are selected by the company to use computers. Haisken-DeNew and Schmidt (1999) found similar results for computer usage in a German panel. Bell (1996), on the other hand, did find a considerable wage increase for computer usage. His study, however, covered a much longer period than the aforementioned analyses. A study by Entorf and Kramarz (1997) shows that employees who use computers annually experience a wage increase that is about 1 per cent greater than average. They interpret this as the market value of the computer experience that individuals have acquired. It is debatable, however, whether this interpretation is correct. After all, the findings could also indicate that it is not the computer usage of each individual worker, but the increased market value of the group as a whole that influences wages. Nevertheless, figures ranging from 15 to 20 per cent higher wages seem odd when moving from a cross-sectional to a longitudinal or panel approach to analyse the data over time.

10.3.2 Firm Level Approach

The idea that the computer wage premium should be regarded as an appreciation of an individual's computer skills implies that only those who actually use a computer will obtain higher wages. A study by Doms et al. (1997) shows that the computer wage premium is unlikely to be an individual, but rather a company-related effect. They find that companies that work with advanced technology, such as computer technology, pay their employees more. It is irrelevant whether employees use the technology or not, they will nevertheless receive a wage premium. Furthermore, it is remarkable that in particular managers who do not themselves use the most advanced technology, receive the highest wage premium from the firm's adoption of advanced technologies. The interesting results from this study are appealing but it is not clear why wages in technologically more advanced firms are generally higher.

In an effort to try a deeper analysis of the results obtained by Doms et al. (1997), a number of studies have focused on understanding the productivity effects from computer technology adoption. Handel and Gittleman (1999) use cross-sectional data from the United States to analyse the effects of high performance measures on the average wages paid by firms. They do not find a significant correlation and interpret this result accordingly. A problem with this conclusion might be that only the average wages within a firm are observed and no information about the quality (education, experience, etc.) of the workers is available. Eriksson (2001) uses Danish data and finds a positive correlation between new organizational designs and high performance measures and the level of education of the firm's workforce. Bauer and Bender (2004) analyse German establishment data in the mid-1990s and obtain a positive correlation between new organizational practices and the wages for, more highly educated workers. Bertschek and Kaiser (2004) obtain similar results for the level of productivity in

German firms. Greenan and Mairesse (1999) find similar results for France. Cappelli and Neumark (1999) investigate the effects of the implementation of high performance measures on both employers and employees in the period 1977–1996 for a panel of US firms. Their estimates suggest that firms gain from the adoption of innovative forms of workplace organization because the productivity of their workers is enhanced. However, when taking into account the costs of the workers the beneficial productivity effect disappears because adopting firms hire more highly educated and more expensive workers. The net effect on the firm's efficiency is almost negligible. These findings suggest that the decision of firms to carry out organizational and technological changes is not based on random events. Firms weigh the costs against the benefits and decide on adoption, so the use of advanced technologies, the demand for different types of workers, organizational structures and revenues can be different between firms, but the differences in terms of profits are relatively minor.

A number of other studies have used firm level data to address the relationship between technological change and the demand for labour more explicitly. Keefe (1991) looks at whether the introduction of numerical control machines led to changes in the demand for skills in the United States in the 1970s and 1980s. His findings suggest that the demand for highly educated labour in 57 different occupations did not increase following the adoption of numerical control machines. Related to this study is a set of four case studies on the demand for labour in large banks. Groot and De Grip (1991) for a large Dutch bank, and Levy and Murnane (1996), Hunter et al. (2001) and Autor et al. (2002) for different US banks analyse the effects of automation on the demand for labour and the composition of the bank's labour force. Their findings suggest that the adoption of different types of computer equipment has led to a number of new tasks that are in general performed by more highly educated workers. In addition, automation of routine activities is observed, which induces workers to focus more on non-routine job tasks. Fernandez (2001) considers the retooling of a large chocolate factory in the United States. His estimates show that computerization has led to upgrading in most occupations, but sometimes jobs have become less advanced and require less skilled workers. However, the overall pattern suggests a higher demand for educated workers.

Finally, a number of studies have analysed the interplay between firm productivity, organizational changes and the demand for labour. The most important studies were carried out by Black and Lynch (2001, 2004) and Bresnahan et al. (2002) for the United States, and by Caroli and Van Reenen (2001) for the United Kingdom and France.

Black and Lynch (2001) analysed the impact of the way in which a firm is organized, ICT and human capital investments on productivity in almost

700 firms in the period 1987–1993 (Black and Lynch, 2004, updated this study and found basically the same results). The authors used data from the *Educational Quality of the Workforce National Employers Survey* (EQW-NES) of 1994 in which, next to the standard demographic information, information about total quality management, benchmarking, the diffusion of computer technology within firms and conditions of employment is available. This database has been merged into the *Longitudinal Research Database* to construct a panel of firms. The performance of a simultaneous analysis of organization, workforce and technology is important because a particular way of organizing the production process associated with a higher level of productivity might have been complemented with the hiring of more highly educated workers. In such a case the effects attributed to organizational changes or the adoption of innovative work practices might be the result of the employment of more highly educated workers only. Black and Lynch follow the companies in the period 1987–1993 to catch the effects of changing capital and labour stocks. A major limitation of their study is that the configuration of the organization within each firm is only observed in 1994, so they need to assume that the organization of work remained constant in the 1987–1993 period. There are at least two potential problems with this assumption. First, it is not possible to control for the correlation between observed firm characteristics and the organizational form. A counter argument is that because of the short time period this is not necessarily a big problem. Second, other studies have shown that especially the period 1985–1995 is characterized by a large number of organizational changes that are most likely correlated with the adoption of computer technologies (e.g., Osterman, 2000). Nevertheless, Black and Lynch (2001, 2004) conclude that the effects of organizational changes on the firm's productivity have been relatively small. They also find that the use of computer technology is associated with higher levels of productivity.

Bresnahan et al. (2002) investigate to what extent innovations in areas such as computer technology, complementary changes in the organization of work and the development of new products or services have induced skill upgrading in the United States. To do so, three different data sources were merged: a panel database in which information about ICT and capital is available for the period 1987–1994; *Compustat* data about production in this period; and a cross-sectional survey performed by the authors in 1995/1996 from which information regarding the firm's organization and employees is available. Organizational changes were measured in terms of the use of modern forms of workplace organization, such as the extent to which a firm is working with self-managing teams, whether there is room for employee voice, the extent to which team building is stimulated, and the space workers have to develop themselves further. In the survey a firm's human capital is evaluated by the manager on the basis of an evaluation of the skills and level of education of the firm's workforce and the mix of different occupations within the firm. In addition, there is information available about the training and screening of employees. This procedure results in a database including around 300 large US firms. The authors estimate production functions, which suggest a strong correlation between ICT investments, the level of human capital and modern workplace organization. This result is consistent with the individual level studies, which suggest a secular trend towards upgrading when computer technology is being adopted (or is being invested in). In addition, the implementation of ICT in the production process yields productivity gains as large as 40 per cent when this implementation is complemented with organizational amendments.[13] The crucial factor in being able to estimate these kinds of production functions is that the authors have to assume that it is highly coincidental which managers have implemented the optimal strategy and which have not. The possibility that certain firms changed their organization earlier because the cost–benefit assessment was positive compared to firms that changed later is not excluded in this analysis. If firms decide rationally, and with making mistakes, on their strategy the analysis only explains the optimal relationship between labour demand and organizational change instead of a causal relationship between the two.[14] The same assumption is at the bottom of the analyses of Cappelli and Neumark (1999), Black and Lynch (2001, 2004) and Caroli and Van Reenen (2001). Furthermore, the effectiveness of the form of organization is measured in terms of revenues instead of profits. Firms adopting a strategy of employing more highly educated workers or more capital-intensive inputs are likely to perform better in such an analysis, but the profitability is not necessarily higher.

Caroli and Van Reenen (2001) analyse British and French data to see whether there is skill-biased organizational change independent of the effect of computer technology on the demand for labour. They define organizational change as the way in which the production process is being decentralized. Their paper offers a simple framework to understand the pros and cons of decentralization. The advantages are that the costs of communication are reduced, the organization is better able to adjust to external events and is more flexible, the monitoring of workers is easier and the level of productivity will be increased because workers will be more satisfied when working in a more decentralized environment. The disadvantages of decentralization are the risk of replication of activities, the occurrence of mistakes that will be noticed relatively late in the production process, the loss of economies of scale due to specialization and a possible reduction of the individual worker's efficiency. Along the lines of this framework the assumption is made that more highly educated workers both reduce the costs of decentralization and raise the benefits. The main reasons for this to occur are that more highly educated workers are better at communicating and more efficient in dealing with (a lot of) information. Next to that the costs of training are lower for highly educated workers and they are better able to work autonomously. Finally, these workers like diversified work more than less highly educated workers. If skill-biased organizational change is present this will be manifested as follows: organizational change leads to skill upgrading; lower wages for more highly educated workers in a certain area (region) have a positive effect on the extent of organizational changes; and firms employing relatively more highly educated workers will actualize higher revenues when they adjust their organization of work.

The estimated coefficients suggest that decentralization of work reduced the demand for less highly educated workers in both France and the United Kingdom in the late 1980s and early 1990s. In addition, firms present in regions with lower relative wages for highly educated workers are more likely to reorganize their workplace to upgrade their workforce. A third finding is that decentralization is more effective in firms already employing a larger share of more highly educated workers. Overall the results suggest a complementary relationship between the demand for more highly educated workers and decentralization, independent of the adoption of computer technology. Nevertheless, there is also an independent effect of computer technology adoption on skill upgrading, which is consistent with the other studies in this area. The likely conclusion from this study is that both technological and organizational changes have an impact on labour demand, but that it is not the complementarity between these forces that determines skill upgrading in France and the United Kingdom.

10.4 A NEW PERSPECTIVE

To obtain a greater understanding of the importance of the introduction of computer technology for the labour market, we study how computers are used and in what way the activities of workers and the organization within the company adapt to this. An essential characteristic of computer technology is that it supports workers in their activities. To determine the influence of computer technology on the way in which a job is carried out, assume a worker has to perform two tasks – task a and task b. Assume further that these tasks are highly interrelated and that computer technology is able to take over task a, but not task b.[15] Although the nature of and the required skills for the tasks may differ greatly, the interrelationship of the activities makes it impossible to separate the tasks into two different jobs, which would have enabled the appointment of two individuals, each of whom would be best qualified for one of the tasks.[16] Finally, assume that task *a* is a routine task and that task *b* is a non-routine job activity.

From this simple setup, we explore two questions. First, when will firms decide to buy computer technology for a particular worker? Second, how will jobs change when computer technology is implemented?

10.4.1 When to Adopt Computer Technology

The efficiency of the production process increases when an individual is able to carry out tasks faster as a result of computer technology. The time gained may relate to the work that is computerized or to the work that cannot be taken over by the computer. If task *a* is automated, the time required to carry out the task itself is replaced by the time that is required to operate the computer. The largest gain can therefore be achieved if task *a* can easily be computerized and the user is able to handle the computer effectively. In principle, the activities that cannot be computerized will continue to take as much time as before. It is also possible, however, that the introduction of computer technology makes it possible to carry out task *b* more efficiently. This reflects the possibility that technology and labour are complementary. Accountancy might be a good example of an occupation in which task *b* gains from such a complementary relationship. Accountants today need not do their calculations by means of mental arithmetic or use a notebook to check a company's books. They will use computers and spreadsheet applications to add up numbers, divide figures, and so on. Accountants can now concentrate entirely on analysing and checking (by means of the computer) the accuracy of the figures and detect any errors or fraud more quickly if the figures are incorrect. If the complementarity of the two tasks is high, task *b* (the analysis) will also be completed in less time.

There are three points of view with respect to the employment effects of computer usage representing extreme examples of this conceptual framework. In the view that expects computers to take over the work of human beings, work consists merely of task *a* that can be automated and there is little or no time required to operate the machine. As it is in particular the less highly educated workers who perform such tasks, they are the first to fall victim. The second view states that work consists only of task *a*, but that computer skills are so important that keeping computers running requires a great deal of time and specific skills. As it is expected that more highly educated workers have such skills (or adapt more easily to new technology), they will be the ones who carry out this computer work. Lastly, there is a view in which complementary skills determine the value of computer usage. Here the task to be automated is marginal and there is not much time to be gained. The advantage should then be obtained from increased efficiency of the complementary tasks (task *b*).

It is interesting to see that even when computer skills are not important and there are no complementarity advantages to be gained, the introduction of computer technology can nevertheless achieve time gains without the work disappearing completely. In this case, the employee need only carry out task *b*, while the computer takes over task *a* completely.

A firm will only decide to introduce computer technology if the costs involved match the time that can be gained.[17] Time gained in the production process is translated into a productivity increase and constitutes savings on labour costs. It is therefore attractive to acquire computer technology if the costs of the setup are lower than the wages that must be recovered. In addition to the amount of time saved, the wages of the worker involved will determine whether computer technology will be beneficial to the firm. This appears to be true even when the wages are not a proper reflection of productivity. If various institutional factors cause the wages in a particular occupational group to be relatively high compared to other occupational groups, *ceteris paribus*, computer technology will be introduced more rapidly. The mechanism that determines when computer technology is introduced at the workplace therefore depends on the wages earned by individuals rather than the computer skills or complementary skills of these workers.

This observation reverses the causality between wages and computer technology adoption suggested by previous studies. Even when we correct for personal characteristics and job characteristics, wage fluctuations explain the probability of individuals adopting computer technology. Hence, the observation that more highly educated workers have adopted computer technology earlier on and that their incidence of computer technology use is higher does not seem to be a reflection of their higher level of education or skills, but is more likely to be the result of their higher wages.

Another result we can derive from our setup is that the less relevant the technology is for the job, the greater the wage difference must be to make its purchase profitable. This is consistent with the results of Krueger, who finds that relatively trivial tasks, such as emailing and word processing, have a great impact on wages. If a manager and an assistant spend an equal amount of time on the same task, and they are both equally good at it, then the benefits of computerization will compensate the costs more easily in the case of the manager.

Productivity differences may emerge, however, because an individual is capable of producing products of greater value or higher quality, but these may also arise because one person is able to carry out the work faster than another. Just like higher wages indicate greater speed of working, investments in computer technology will be made less easily. After all, in the case of faster workers there is less time to be gained by computers taking over the work.

Following this line of reasoning, we can state that when the costs of computer usage are reduced further, the introduction of the computer will become profitable for other jobs too. If the costs were reduced to zero, all jobs in which the introduction of computer technology could result in time gain, would do so. If the possible applications and efficiency of computer technology increase further, the group of jobs in which useful application is possible will also grow. If the costs are reduced sufficiently and the areas of application increase, eventually almost every worker will probably use computer technology.

For a large part, the costs of the introduction of computer technology do not depend on the number of employees in a company or department who make use of the technology, but follow on from the development and implementation in the company or department as a whole. As people must be able to work together within a department, it will often be difficult to allow some workers to use computer or communication systems and not others. As a result, it is to some extent not the individual wages, but the average wages of the department in which one works that affect the decision whether or not to adopt computer technology.[18]

10.4.2 Productivity, Demand and Wages

The introduction of computer technology leads to productivity increases. In terms of our framework, these are equal to the relative time gain achieved in the production process as a result of the computerization of task a. If the total production volume remains the same, the demand for employees in this profession will decrease by a similar percentage. Production costs decrease less, because the decreasing wage costs are offset by the increasing costs for the use of computer technology. In addition to this immediate reduction of the demand for labour as a result of productivity increases, the lower cost price per unit of product will lead to an increase in demand for the product concerned and hence indirectly to higher demand for the labour involved. Eventually, the effect on employment depends on the size of the two effects. If demand is characterized by high price elasticity, efficiency improvements may lead to an increase in the demand for labour and this will create an upward pressure on wages.[19] If we assume that computer technology is introduced in particular among the more highly educated workers, there will only be skill-biased technological change if this elasticity is sufficiently large, that is, an improvement in the position of the more highly educated workers in relation to the position of the less highly educated. In addition, if the costs of computer usage have decreased to such an extent after some time that computer technology is introduced in all jobs in which time can be gained, these demand effects are equally likely to occur among less highly educated workers. Eventually, the effect of computer technology on the demand for labour through this route, seems ambiguous and it is not likely that we will find the main explanation for long-term skill-biased technological change here.[20]

10.4.3 Skills and Education

We have argued that even if computer skills play no role and there is no complementarity in which certain skills come into their own better because of the use of computers, the adoption of computer technology can nevertheless be explained, and it is plausible that workers with high wages are the first to make use of computer technology. Even without an explicit role for computer skills and complementary skills, the value of different skills in the labour market will start to shift as a result of the adoption and diffusion of computer technology. After all, the structure of the work is shifting, making the skills that promote productivity in the remaining work more important, whereas the importance of the skills that were required for the work that is now done through computer technology will decrease.

The education and qualification requirements set by an employer for a particular job, can be regarded as a balance between the higher wages that must be paid for a more highly educated employee and the additional productivity that such an employee may provide. In a job in which a more highly educated employee adds little to productivity compared with a less highly educated employee, educational requirements will therefore not easily be raised. It seems reasonable to assume that a more highly educated worker will yield productivity benefits in particular in those activities that cannot easily be automated.

Before computer technology was introduced, increasing educational requirements meant that highly paid workers would also do work in task *a* in which they were no better than workers with a lower educational background. This acted as a restraint on the qualification requirements that were set. After the introduction of computer technology, activities such as task *a* no longer play a role. Even if the highly educated worker is not more adept at carrying out the computerized task *a*, it may be expected that employers will increase their educational requirements, because the importance of task *b* increases. Groot and De Grip (1991) were among the first to show that the introduction of computer technology leads to higher educational requirements. By comparing various branches of a large Dutch bank, which introduced *front office* and *back office* automation at different moments in time, they were able to show that automated branches did indeed increase their educational requirements.[21]

This shift in the importance of tasks also constitutes a possible cause of skill-biased technological change. Whether it is a high-skilled job or a low-skilled job, after the introduction of computer technology we may expect a gradual increase in the educational requirements of the job concerned. Within each job, it is not a change from requiring an unskilled worker to an academic, but as an aggregate these demand shifts will change the employment structure as a whole. It can be expected that this effect is much more likely to lead to skill-biased technological change than the previous possible effects. After all, shifts in demand can be both to the advantage and to the disadvantage of the more highly educated, while this increase in educational requirements within a particular job almost always moves in the same upward direction.

10.4.4   Is Work Becoming More Complex or More Standardized?

Just as an employer may consider which educational level to demand for a particular job, he or she may also vary the nature of the product by putting greater emphasis on task *a* that can be computerized, or instead on task *b* that cannot be computerized. The choice of the product to manufacture will depend on the costs and benefits of the various combinations. If a product is standardized, it is likely that a greater part of the work will be routine and capable of being automated. The costs will drop, but the value of the product will also decrease. On the other hand, more tailor-made work will be required for a greater amount of work that is difficult to automate. This will lead to higher costs, but will probably also make the product more valuable. The product actually manufactured is therefore determined by the balance between these factors. The introduction of computer applications will also upset this balance.

On the one hand, as we have indicated above, the routine part of the work becomes cheaper as a result of the introduction of computer technology. This will give rise to a tendency to standardize the product. On the other hand, complementarity will also increase the productivity of non-routine work. If this latter effect dominates, there would be a renewed trend to supply more tailor-made products. The eventual changes in the product will therefore depend on the cost savings in the routine part on the one hand, and the achieved complementarity advantages on the other.

10.5   CONCLUDING REMARKS

The adoption and rapid diffusion of computer technology have drastically changed the labour market. Many tasks have been computerized and many workers are able to work more efficiently. As a result, the labour market is also affected to a great extent by computer technology in PCs, but also in other ICT applications. Further diffusion of new computer technology is likely only to increase the importance of computers and computer-related technology.

In this chapter we have discussed the way in which people work together with computer technology. On the basis of this analysis of the interaction between worker and machine, we have shown which workers use computer applications, what influence this has had on the content of their work, and what the implications are for the demand for various types of labour. Considered from the current view on the effects of computer technology on employment, our findings shed new light on the relationship between computer technology and the labour market. It is true that new computer techniques are initially used more by more highly educated than by less highly educated workers, but this is often used to arrive at the conclusion that special computer skills are needed to be able to use this new technology. Our results suggest that the primary aspect is not the high educational level but the high wage that explains the earlier adoption of computer technology in these groups. For workers with high wages, a small increase in productivity results in greater cost savings. As computer technology becomes cheaper and more interesting applications emerge – we expect – almost everybody will come into contact with computer technology at the workplace. Because these new applications are meant to support people in their work, the use of this new technology will create few problems with regard to skills.

This does not mean that nothing has changed. The use of computer technology has increased productivity in many occupations. On the one hand, this has decreased the demand for the category of labour concerned, but on the other hand the lower production costs also decrease the production price, which in turn increases demand. As a result of such processes, the importance of certain activities will increase while that of others will decrease. As we expect that eventually both the more and the less highly educated will use computer applications in their work, and these production increases may have both a positive and a negative effect on demand, a long-term effect on relative wages is not expected.

As ICT applications take over work from human beings, the importance of various types of skills will undergo major changes in the near future. On the basis of the new production options, employers will reconsider the product range that their companies supply and the working methods used.

In certain circumstances, we expect that there will be more tailor-made products, while under other conditions there will be greater standardization of products. Some will benefit from the shift in the importance of skills on the labour market, while others will suffer disadvantages. Again, we do not expect that this process will be clearly to the advantage of the more highly educated, because it is not only the value of skills relating to cognitive intelligence that will increase.

The third effect of greater penetration of computer technology is that individuals at work are able to concentrate more on those activities that constitute the essence of their profession. Many secondary tasks will be taken over by the new technology. This means that employers will tend to increase the required qualifications within the various professions. After all, the costs of higher wages will be compensated by the fact that less time is lost on tasks in which these skills are not used. It is in particular this argument that gives rise to the expectation that the demand for more highly educated workers will continue to grow. This form of skill upgrading, however, is unlikely to lead to a situation in which there is no work for the less highly educated and an increasing scarcity of more highly educated workers, resulting in a threatening digital split of society. The gradual nature of these shifts means that in the time to come, almost everybody will study longer and will need to spend a little more energy on increasing and maintaining knowledge levels in order to be able to continue functioning properly on the labour market.

Finally, it cannot yet be predicted how exactly the labour market will further change as a result of the adoption and diffusion of computer technology. This depends to a large extent on the applications that are still to be developed, while the response to these developments may be very complex. It seems therefore of great importance to carefully monitor developments in the labour market, because only then will it become clear in time in which direction the labour market is moving. This demands different perspectives in research and hence also a new type of (experimental) data collection, with much greater emphasis on the nature and content of the work, the required competences, and the available knowledge and skills of workers. Such an instrument would serve both research and policymaking. To be able to follow labour-market developments adequately in the future, we will need to develop the tools used to measure skills, and researchers will need to have the possibility to test their insights in the developments on the labour markets against real-life situations. For policymakers, such instruments may constitute the basis for policies in the field of education and training enabling them also to keep a finger on the pulse in a knowledge-based economy.

NOTES

1. Katz and Autor (1999), Katz (2000), Acemoglu (2002), Aghion (2002), Card and DiNardo (2002) and Autor et al. (2004) provide useful overviews of the body of literature on the computerization of the labour market.
2. Microsoft interpreted the observed wage differential as a premium for using a PC. In the early 1990s they used the computer wage premium in an advertising campaign to suggest that using Microsoft software yields wage gains up to 20 per cent.
3. A different problem with this information is that the use of computer technology is measured by the direct use of (personal) computers by workers. While this measure is incomplete and misses workers who use devices with embedded microprocessors, it does reflect a particularly prevalent form of computer technology that has been important in both the production process and in facilitating modern forms of communication within most firms.
4. The relationship between age and computer use at work is addressed at length in Borghans and Ter Weel (2002) for Britain, Weinberg (2002) and Friedberg (2003) for the United States and Aubert et al. (2004) for France.
5. Weinberg (2000) has explained this observation by arguing that jobs which previously required a great deal of physical strength and stamina have been transformed into more women-friendly jobs after the introduction of computer technology. Also computers seem to be more heavily used in occupations in which women are particularly present.
6. Entorf and Kramarz (1997) and Entorf et al. (1999) report similar findings but attribute such results to unobserved heterogeneity. Doms et al. (1997) examine the use of advanced technologies by firms. They distinguish between plants using less than 4 technologies, plants using 4 to 6, 7 to 8, 9 to 10, 11 to 13 and plants using more than 13 technologies. Their results suggest a monotonically increasing relationship between technology use and the educational level of the workforce. Finally, Haisken-DeNew and Schmidt (1999) show that in Germany no computer wage premium can be obtained when they control for unobserved heterogeneity. See also a recent study by Lang (2001) for an interpretation of the premium.
7. Borghans and Ter Weel (2005) offer an elaborate discussion of the robustness of this skill measure. See also Spenner (1985) for an assessment of the robustness of self-assessed skills.
8. See Borghans and Ter Weel (2004a) for a more formal treatment and derivation of the underlying theoretical structure.
9. The finding of DiNardo and Pischke (1997) that a worker who uses a pen earns more than the average worker, can therefore be understood as a return to writing skills. Of course, not every worker who uses a pen will earn more, but within the group of pen users there is a large fraction of people who have to write short or long documents and whose skills to do so are rewarded in the labour market. Trivial skills involving a pen have no returns.
10. If computer skills are important in the labour market and the spread of computer technology has made them a scarce commodity, it can be expected that employers will try to ensure that anyone who has such skills does work in which they are important. DiNardo and Pischke (1996), however, show that in Germany it is not the case that all those who possess computer skills are working in jobs in which computer technology is used. On the other hand, quite a large number of people have jobs in which computers are used, even though they have no computer skills. Also, people who use computers at work frequently switch to jobs in which computers are not used.
11. The fact that the coefficient is not significant at the 5 per cent level might also be due to the rather small number of people in the sample using computers at the advanced level.
12. To deal with this problem, Gould et al. (2001) and Aghion et al. (2002) argue that workers differ in their adaptability to new technology as a result of random shocks or

luck, and Violante (2002) argues that workers are matched to jobs based on unobserved quality differentials.

13. Darby and Zucker (1999) and Gale et al. (2002) found similar results for Japanese and US biotech companies and a cross-section of about 3,000 US firms, respectively.

14. Bresnahan et al. (2002) were concerned about this criticism and try to make their assumption credible in their section 5.

15. Autor et al. (2003) and Spitz (2003) offer related theoretical considerations of modelling the way in which computer technology has changed the work from routine to non-routine tasks.

16. Borghans and Ter Weel (2004b) consider a case where it is possible to split the tasks into different jobs. They derive that it is profitable to do so if the wage differential between workers carrying out the tasks is relatively large, the coordination costs are low, if skilled (unskilled) workers have a comparative advantage in skilled (unskilled) tasks and if the task that is handled by computer technology is a relatively time-consuming one.

17. Autor et al. (1998) and Borghans and Ter Weel (2003) calculate that the average annual rent of computer technology for a US worker in the late 1990s was about $6,500. This figure exceeds 20 per cent of the average US worker's annual wage. These are the cost for the entire deal (i.e., hardware, software, maintenance, furniture, etc.).

18. Borghans and Ter Weel (2004b) formally show that the decision to adopt computer technology for the department or firm as a whole is determined by the average wages in the department or firm. The mechanism explored for individual workers remains the same though.

19 This is only a partial effect on wages. Because computer technology will change the demand for a variety of professions, and wage changes in one submarket may affect other submarkets, it is difficult to get an overview of the final effects in a general balance.

20 Borghans and Ter Weel (2003) develop a more formal technology diffusion model in which these effects are shown to be consistent with the wage structures of the United States and Germany since the 1970s.

21. Doms et al. (1997) and Autor et al. (1998) find similar 'upgrading' effects for the United States. Levy and Murnane (1996), Fernandez (2001) and Autor et al. (2002) carry out case studies for US firms and derive similar results.

BIBLIOGRAPHY

Acemoglu, D. (2002), 'Technical change, inequality, and the labor market', *Journal of Economic Literature*, **40** (1), 7–72.

Acemoglu, D. (2003), 'Cross-country inequality trends', *Economic Journal*, **113** (485), F121–F49.

Aghion, P. (2002), 'Schumpeterian growth theory and the dynamics of income inequality', *Econometrica*, **70** (3), 855–82.

Aghion, P., P. Howitt and G.L. Violante (2002), 'General purpose technology and wage inequality', *Journal of Economic Growth*, **7** (4), 315–45.

Allen, S.G. (2001), 'Technology and the wage structure', *Journal of Labor Economics*, **19** (2), 440–83.

Asplund, R. (1997), 'Are computer skills rewarded in the labour market? Evidence for Finland', Working paper, ETLA.

Aubert, P., E. Caroli and M. Roger (2004), 'New technologies, workplace organization, and the age structure of the workforce: Firm level evidence', Working Paper, CREST-INSEE.

Autor, D.H., L.F. Katz and M.S. Kearney (2004), 'US wage and consumption inequality trends: A re-assessment of basic facts and alternative explanations', Working Paper, MIT/Harvard/Wellesley.

Autor, D.H., L.F. Katz and A.B. Krueger (1998), 'Computing inequality: Have computers changed the labor market?', *Quarterly Journal of Economics*, **113** (3), 1169–213.

Autor, D.H., F. Levy and R.J. Murnane (2002), 'Upstairs, downstairs: Computers and skills on two floors of a large bank', *Industrial and Labor Relations Review*, **55** (3), 432–47.

Autor, D.H., F. Levy and R.J. Murnane (2003), 'The skill content of recent technological change: An empirical exploration', *Quarterly Journal of Economics*, **118** (4), 1279–333.

Bauer, T.K. and S. Bender (2004), 'Technological change, organizational change, and job turnover', *Labour Economics*, **11** (3), 265–91.

Bell, B.D. (1996), 'Skill-biased technical change and wages: Evidence from a longitudinal data set', Working paper, Nuffield College.

Berman, E., J. Bound and Z. Griliches (1994), 'Changes in the demand for skilled labor within US manufacturing industries', *Quarterly Journal of Economics*, **109** (1), 367–98.

Berman, E., J. Bound and S. Machin (1998), 'Implications of skill-biased technological change: International evidence', *Quarterly Journal of Economics*, **113** (4), 1245–79.

Bertschek, I. and U. Kaiser (2004), 'Productivity effects of organizational change: Microeconomic evidence', *Management Science*, **50** (3), 394–404.

Black, S.E. and L.M. Lynch (2001), 'How to compete: The impact of workplace practices and information technology on productivity', *Review of Economics and Statistics*, **83** (3), 434–45.

Black, S.E. and L.M. Lynch (2004), 'What's driving the new economy? The benefits of workplace innovation', *Economic Journal*, **114** (493), F97–F116.

Borghans, L. and B. ter Weel (2002), 'Do older workers have more trouble using a computer than younger workers?', *Research in Labour Economics*, **21**, 139–73.

Borghans, L. and B. ter Weel (2003), 'The diffusion of computers and the distribution of wages', Working paper, Maastricht University.

Borghans, L. and B. ter Weel (2004a), 'Are computer skills the new basic skills? The returns to computer, writing and math skills in Britain', *Labour Economics*, **11** (1), 85–98.

Borghans, L. and B. ter Weel (2004b), 'What happens when agent *T* gets a computer? The labor market impact of efficient computer adoption', *Journal of Economic Behavior & Organization*, **54** (2), 137–51.

Borghans, L. and B. ter Weel (2005), 'Do we need computer skills to use a computer? Evidence from the UK', Working paper, Maastricht University.

Bresnahan, T.F. (1999), 'Computerisation and wage dispersion: An analytical reinterpretation', *Economic Journal*, **109** (464), F390–F415.

Bresnahan, T.F., E. Brynjolfsson and L.M. Hitt (2002), 'Information technology, workplace organization, and the demand for skilled labor: Firm-level evidence', *Quarterly Journal of Economics*, **117** (1), 339–76.

Cappelli, P. and D. Neumark (1999), 'Do "high performance" work practices improve establishment-level outcomes', NBER Working Paper 7374.

Card, D. and J.E. DiNardo (2002), 'Skill-biased technological change and rising wage inequality: Some problems and puzzles', *Journal of Labor Economics*, **20** (4), 733–83.

Caroli, E. and J. Van Reenen (2001), 'Skill-biased organizational change? Evidence from a panel of British and French establishments', *Quarterly Journal of Economics*, **116** (4), 1449–92.

Chennells, L. and J. Van Reenen (1997), 'Technical change and earnings in British Establishments', *Economica*, **64** (256), 587–604.

Darby, M.R. and L.G. Zucker (1999), 'Local academic science driving organizational change: The adoption of biotechnology by Japanese firms,' NBER Working Paper 7248.

DiNardo J. and J.-S. Pischke (1996), 'The return to computer use revisited: Have pencils changed the wage structure too?', NBER Working Paper 5606.

DiNardo J. and J.-S. Pischke (1997), 'The return to computer use revisited: Have pencils changed the wage structure too?', *Quarterly Journal of Economics*, **112** (1), 291–303.

Doms, M., T. Dunne and K.R. Troske (1997), 'Workers, wages and technology', *Quarterly Journal of Economics*, **112** (1), 253–90.

Entorf, H., M. Gollac and F. Kramarz (1999), 'New technologies, wages and worker selection', *Journal of Labor Economics*, **17** (3), 464–91.

Entorf, H. and F. Kramarz (1997), 'Does unmeasured ability explain the higher wages of new technology workers?', *European Economic Review*, **41** (6), 1489–509.

Eriksson, T. (2001), 'How common are the new compensation and work organization practices and who adopts them?', Working Paper, Aarhus School of Business.

Fernandez, R.M. (2001), 'Skill-biased technological change and wage inequality: Evidence from a plant retooling', *American Journal of Sociology*, **107** (2), 273–320.

Freeman, R.B. and L.F. Katz (eds) (1995), *Differences and Changes in Wage Structures*, Chicago: The University of Chicago Press.

Friedberg, L. (2003), 'The impact of technological change on older workers: Evidence from data on computers', *Industrial and Labor Relations Review*, **56** (3), 511–29.

Gale, H.F., T.R. Wojan & J.C. Olmsted (2002), 'Skills, flexible manufacturing technology, and work organization', *Industrial Relations*, **41** (1), 48–79.

Gottschalk, P. and M. Joyce (1998), 'Cross-national differences in the rise in earnings inequality: Market and institutional factors', *Review of Economics and Statistics*, **80** (2), 489–502.

Gottschalk, P. and T.M. Smeeding (1997), 'Cross-national comparisons of earnings and income inequality', *Journal of Economic Literature*, **35** (3), 633–87.

Gould, E.D., O. Moav and B.A. Weinberg (2001), 'Precautionary demand for education, inequality, and technological progress', *Journal of Economic Growth*, **6** (4), 285–315.

Green, F., and A. Dickerson (2004), 'The growth and valuation of computing and other generic skills', *Oxford Economic Papers*, **56** (3), 371–406.

Greenan, N. and J. Mairesse (1999), 'Organizational change in French manufacturing: What do we learn from firm representatives and from their employees?', NBER Working Paper 7285.

Groot, L. and A. De Grip (1991), 'Technological change and skill formation in the bank sector', *Economics of Education Review*, **10** (1), 57–71.

Haisken-DeNew, J.P. and C.M. Schmidt (1999), 'Money for nothing and your chips for free? The anatomy of the PC wage differential', Working paper, Deutsches Institut für Wirtschaftsforschung.

Hamilton, B.H. (1997), 'Returns to computer skills and black–white wage differentials', Working paper, John M. Olin School of Business.

Handel, M.J. (1999), 'Computers and the wage structure', Working paper, Jerome Levy Economics Institute.

Handel, M.J. and M. Gittleman (1999), 'Is there a wage payoff to innovative work practices?', Working Paper, Jerome Levy Economics Institute.

Haskel, J. and Y. Heden (1999), 'Computers and the demand for skilled labour: Industry- and establishment-level panel evidence for the UK', *Economic Journal*, 109 (462), C68–C79.

Hollanders, H. and B. ter Weel (2002), 'Technology, knowledge spillovers, and changes in employment structure: Evidence from six OECD countries', *Labour Economics*, 9 (5), 579–99.

Hunter, L.W., A. Bernhardt, K.L. Hughes and E. Skuratowicz (2001), 'IT's not just the ATMs: Technology, firm strategies, jobs, and earnings in retail banking', *Industrial and Labor Relations Review*, 54 (2), 402–24.

Katz, L.F. (2000), 'Technological change, computerization, and the wage structure', in E. Brynjolfsson and B. Kahin (eds), *Understanding the Digital Economy*, Cambridge, MA: MIT Press, pp. 217–44.

Katz, L.F. and D.H. Autor (1999), 'Changes in the wage structure and earnings inequality', in O.C. Ashenfelter and D. Card (eds), *Handbook of Labor Economics*, Amsterdam: North-Holland, pp.1463–555.

Katz, L.F. and K.M. Murphy (1992), 'Changes in relative wages, 1963–1987: Supply and demand factors', *Quarterly Journal of Economics*, 107 (1), 35–78.

Keefe, J.H. (1991), 'Numerically controlled machine tools and worker skills', *Industrial and Labor Relations Review*, 44 (3), 503–19.

Krueger, A.B. (1993), 'How computers have changed the wage structure: Evidence from microdata, 1984–1989', *Quarterly Journal of Economics*, 108 (1), 33–60.

Lang, K. (2001), 'Of pencils and computer use', Working paper, Massachusetts Institute of Technology.

Levy, F. and R.J. Murnane (1996), 'With what skills are computers complements?', *American Economic Review*, 86 (2), 258–62.

Machin, S. and J. Van Reenen (1998), 'Technology and changes in skill structure: Evidence from seven OECD countries', *Quarterly Journal of Economics*, 113 (4), 1216–44.

Miller, P.W. and C. Mulvey, (1997), 'Computer skills and wages', *Australian Economic Papers*, 36 (1), 106–13.

Oosterbeek, H. (1997), 'Returns from computer use: A simple test on the productivity interpretation', *Economics Letters*, 55 (2), 273–7.

Osterman, P. (2000), 'Work reorganization in an era of restructuring: Trends in diffusion and effects on employee welfare', *Industrial and Labor Relations Review*, 53 (2), 179–96.

Reilly, K. (1995), 'Human capital and information: The employer size-wage effect', *Journal of Human Resources*, 30 (1), 1–18.

Sakellariou, C. and H. Patrinos (2000), 'Labour market performance of tertiary education graduates in Vietnam', *Asian Economic Journal*, 14 (2), 147–65.

Spenner, K.I. (1985), 'The upgrading and downgrading of occupations', *Review of Educational Research*, 55 (1), 125–54.

Spitz, A. (2003), 'IT capital, job content and educational attainment', Discussion Paper no. 03–04, Centre for European Economic Research.

Violante, G.L. (2002), 'Technological acceleration, skill transferability and the rise in residual inequality', *Quarterly Journal of Economics*, **117** (1), 297–338.

Weinberg, B.A. (2000), 'Computer use and the demand for female workers', *Industrial and Labor Review*, **53** (1), 290–308.

Weinberg, B.A. (2002), 'Experience and technology adoption', Working paper, Ohio State University.

11. ICT and optimal unemployment benefits when Pissarides meets Dixit–Stiglitz*

Thomas Ziesemer

11.1 INTRODUCTION

Information and communication technology (henceforth abbreviated to ICT) has changed life considerably in several areas. Here we emphasize just two of them, the goods market and the labour market. Autor (2001) has discussed the effects of ICT on the US labour market extensively, and Ziesemer (2003) describes the impact on the European labour market and some of the goods market effects. We briefly summarize both now. In the 1980s public employment services improved data banks and search techniques by introducing computer-aided job search. In the 1990s this was extended to include the use of the Internet. In short, search technologies in the labour market have been improved. In the goods market, computers first allowed for just-in-time systems and more recently the Internet has been used to reduce the bureaucracy of firms and to provide advertisements for cars, both reducing fixed costs, facilitating the buying of intermediates and thereby reducing variable costs.

In economic theory the improvements in labour market search can be captured as a gain in the efficiency of a matching function as used in Pissarides' (2000) model. The reduction in variable costs and increase in fixed costs through the use of the Internet can be captured as technological substitution[1] in the Dixit–Stiglitz (1977) model. Therefore we present in section 11.2 a brief summary of a synthesis of the models by Pissarides and Dixit–Stiglitz as developed in Ziesemer (2003) for the market equilibrium. In this chapter we look also at the central planner's optimum and compare it to the market equilibrium with a special emphasis on the effects of ICT, monopoly power and bargaining power. The economy as modelled in this

* I am grateful to Bas ter Weel and two anonymous referees for useful comments and to Marcel Jansen for urging me to try this in his reaction to one of the related papers. Responsibility is entirely mine.

way has only one instrument to approach the (x-best) optimal market equilibrium, that is, unemployment benefits.

If individuals are risk averse the motive for unemployment compensation is insurance for income uncertainty. If the insurance is very large there may be a moral hazard problem, which requires the design of an insurance scheme in a way that balances the desire for insurance and the risk of moral hazard (see Karni 1999). Unemployment benefits did decrease in the recent past, because there seemingly was a political dominance of views that emphasized the moral hazard problem, and unemployment benefits have since been reduced. At least in the Netherlands this has led – together with other measures undertaken – to a degree of labour market tightness that some[2] seem to perceive as inefficient. Sufficiently high unemployment benefits can avoid this. Rather then being justified as an insurance mechanism they can be considered as a Pigovian correction mechanism, a subsidy that may be, in principle, either positive or negative.[3]

In this chapter we try to find the impact of ICT, bargaining power and monopoly power on x-best optimal unemployment benefits and on three market imperfections: search externalities, monopoly prices and variety externalities.[4]

The major contribution of the chapter from the point of view of economic theory is as follows. The central planner's optimum has two local optima because the utility function has increasing marginal utility from variety. If unemployment benefits are determined such that the optimum tightness and unemployment rates are achieved, we get x-best multiple, unique or no equilibria if worker bargaining power is above, at (Hosios', 1990, condition) or below that of the elasticity of matching with regard to vacancies. Quantity and variety cannot be optimal because hiring costs are covered by household production.

From the point of view of economic policy the major result is that ICT justifies higher unemployment benefits under unique and multiple equilibria. Lower monopoly power and worker bargaining power decrease optimal benefits in the high unemployment equilibrium, but increase them in the low unemployment equilibrium with the opposite effect on tightness. The impact on all market imperfections is discussed extensively in the respective sections on the pure market equilibrium, the central planner's optimum and the x-best equilibria.

In Ziesemer (2003) we discussed the impact of ICT on the market equilibrium, which is restated here in sections 11.2 and 11.3, and in this chapter we contribute the analysis of welfare effects. We derive the central planner's optimum and discuss the effects of ICT on the optimum in section 11.4. In section 11.5 we discuss conditions for the optimality of x-best market equilibria. In section 11.6 we discuss the effects of changes in ICT, monopoly and bargaining power on x-best optimality of equilibria. Section 11.7 summarizes and concludes.

11.2 THE MODEL[5]

11.2.1 Trade in the Labour Market

From the Pissarides (2000) model we use the matching function $mL = Tm(uL, vL)$, where L is the labour force, that is the total number of employed and unemployed workers, u is the unemployment rate, v is the rate of vacancies and mL is the number of matches produced by this function. T is an efficiency parameter or the level of productivity in the matching process. When computers enter the labour intermediation process or when job-search websites appear on the Internet, T is assumed to go up.[6] The function is assumed to be increasing in both arguments; it is concave and linearly homogeneous. Defining labour market tightness as $\theta \equiv v/u$, and dividing the matching function by vL yields $q(\theta) = Tm(u/v, 1)$ as the probability (Poisson arrival rate) of a firm finding a worker for a vacancy and $\theta q(\theta) = Tm/u = Tm(1, v/u)$ as the probability of an unemployed worker finding a job. Both these probabilities are enhanced by a change in ICT. By implication, the expected duration of a vacancy, $1/q(\theta)$, is reduced by technical progress in the matching function and the same holds for the expected time an unemployed worker needs to find a job. We assume that the technical change is neutral. If it were augmenting $uL(vL)$, this would mean would it work as if there were relatively more (less) unemployed people from which the employers could choose rather than a greater number of vacancies from which workers could choose. Instead, we assume that both these effects are equally strong because a computer search is equally accessible for both; firms can afford computer equipment and unemployed workers can use those of public libraries or labour intermediaries. These public facilities may even provide some help in using the computer equipment.

A shock is a percentage rate s at which $(1 - u)L$ employed workers lose their job by assumption in every period. Therefore, $s(1 - u)L$ workers go from a job into unemployment every period. On the other hand, $\theta q(\theta)uL$ unemployed workers are expected to find a job each period. The change in the rate of unemployment then is:

$$\dot{u} = s(1 - u) - \theta q(\theta)u \qquad (11.1)$$

A labour market steady state equilibrium is defined as a situation where the numbers of workers going into and out of unemployment are equal and expectations turn out to be true, $s(1 - u)L = \theta q(\theta)uL$. When all other variables are constant, technical progress in the matching function increases the right-hand side of this equation, thus contributing to a quicker process of bringing workers out of unemployment. Solving this equation for u yields the Beveridge or UV curve:

$$u = \frac{s}{s + \theta q(\theta)}, \quad \partial u/\partial s > 0, \; \partial u/\partial \theta < 0. \text{[7]} \tag{11.1'}$$

An increase in $\theta q(\theta)$ by increasing T, therefore reduces u for a given tightness ratio. Multiplying equation (11.1') by θ yields an equation for the vacancy rate because $u\theta = uv/u = v$, so that

$$v = \frac{s}{s/\theta + q(\theta)}, \quad \partial v/\partial s > 0, \; \partial v/\partial \theta > 0. \tag{11.1''}$$

An increase in $q(\theta)$ by increasing T, for a given tightness ratio, therefore reduces v.

Equations (11.1') and (11.1'') are drawn in the lower right quadrant of Figure 11.1.

11.2.2 Households and Workers

Households are assumed to have love-of-variety preferences of the CES type,

$$y = \left[\int_{i=0}^{n} c_i^\alpha \, di \right]^{\frac{1}{\alpha}},$$

with $0 < \alpha < 1$, on a continuum of goods with index i, ranging from zero to n, the (integral measure of the) number of firms.[8] It is well known that this specification of preferences leads to a constant elasticity of the inverse demand function, $\alpha - 1$, and to relative demand for goods independent of the income earned by employed or unemployed persons. One can show that the inverse price elasticity is $\alpha - 1$. All results henceforth are steady-state results.

Technologies are defined by $l_i = f + ax_i$, with $a, f > 0$. The left side represents demand for labour to produce good i, f is the fixed part and ax_i is the variable part of labour demand, where x_i is the output of a firm. As all goods are assumed to be identical in the utility function and in production technology, their prices and quantities will be the same.

Total labour demand is $nl_i = n(f + ax_i)$. Equating this to the employment $(1-u)L$ yields $(1-u)L = nl_i = n(f + ax_i)$. Solving the latter equation we find the rate of unemployment linked to the number of firms as:

$$u = (L - nl_i)/L = [L - n(f + ax_i)]/L \tag{11.2}$$

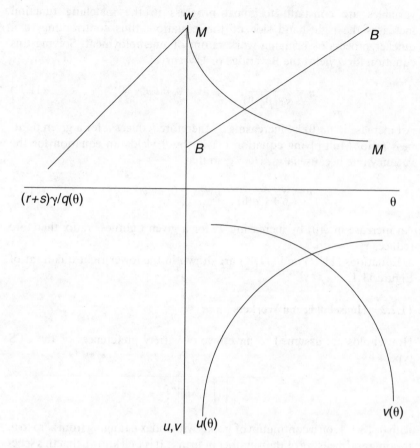

Figure 11.1   The market equilibrium of the model

Present-discounted value of the firm's expected profits, which has a current value of zero in every period in equilibrium, is defined in nominal terms as:

$$\pi_i = \int_{\tau=0}^{\infty} e^{-rt} \{p(x_i)x_i - W(f + ax_i) - p\gamma V_i\}\,dt \qquad (11.3)$$

where W is the nominal wage rate and real hiring costs for vacancies, γV_i, are made nominal by multiplying their real value by the price. The assumption is that *nominal* hiring costs are given from the labour market; monopoly pricing then has no impact on the value of hiring costs. The firm maximizes profits as defined in equation (11.3) through choice of the quantity x and the number of vacancies V_i using the dynamic concept of the large firm from Pissarides (2000, Chapter 3). The dynamics come from the fact that the firm can post a number of V_i vacancies, which increase employment with probability $q(\theta)$ and costs $p\gamma V_i$. On the other hand, the firm loses workers sl_i. The expected change in employment then is $l_i = q(\theta)V_i - sl_i$. From $l_i = f + ax_i$ and $dl_i = adx_i$ we get the corresponding change in the quantity as

$$\dot{x}_i = \frac{q(\theta)V_i}{a} - s\left(\frac{f}{a} + x_i\right)$$

The current value Hamiltonian for each firm's decision problem then is:

$$H = p(x_i)x_i - W(f + ax_i) - p\gamma V_i + \lambda[q(\theta)V_i/a - s(f/a + x_i)]$$

The first-order condition for the number of vacancies determines the value of the co-state variable as marginal hiring costs:

$$\partial H/\partial V_i = -\gamma p + \lambda q(\theta)/a = 0, \quad \text{or} \quad \lambda = \gamma pa/q(\theta)$$

The other canonical equation is

$$-\partial H/\partial x = -\{p'x + p - aW - \lambda s\} = \dot{\lambda} - r\lambda$$

Insertion of λ from the previous first-order condition and setting its change equal to zero in the steady state, and noticing that the price elasticity $p'x/p = \alpha - 1$ this latter first-order condition yields:

$$p\alpha = a[W + p(r+s)\gamma/q(\theta)] \tag{11.4}$$

In the steady state the change of employment also must be zero and therefore we get the number of vacancies as a function of the quantity produced:

$$V_i = s(f + ax_i)/q(\theta) \tag{11.5}$$

The solution for the quantity and the tightness ratio will be derived below.

11.2.3 Wages

Linking equation (11.4) to standard considerations on Nash bargaining about rents from expected income of employed and unemployed workers, and the values of jobs, J, and vacancies through $J = \gamma/q(\theta) = (\alpha/a - w)/(r + s)$ yields:

$$w_j = (1 - \beta)z + \beta\left(\frac{\alpha}{a} + \theta\gamma\right) \tag{11.6}$$

The first term indicates that higher unemployment benefits, z, increase the extent to which wages exceed the unemployment benefits by a factor β, the bargaining power of workings in the Nash bargaining process. The last term indicates that workers participate in the hiring costs saved on occupied jobs compared to vacancies. The second to last term is net revenue per worker. In both, workers participate according to their bargaining power. This equation is drawn as the *BB* curve in the upper right quadrant of Figure 11.1.

11.3   THE EQUILIBRIUM SOLUTION: EXISTENCE AND UNIQUENESS

Equations (11.1′)–(11.6) – with the index j dropped because we are considering the general equilibrium now – determine the six variables of the model when goods produced serve as numéraire ($p = 1$): V_i, u, n, x, θ and w. Inserting (11.5) for the number of vacancies into (11.3), equations (11.3), (11.4) and (11.6) can be solved for x, w and θ; then (11.1′) determines u and (11.2) determines n. Insertion of wages per worker from (11.4) and the number of vacancies into the current profit function contained in (11.3) allows us to solve for the zero-profit[9] equilibrium quantity:

$$x = \frac{\left[\dfrac{\alpha}{a} - \dfrac{r\gamma}{q(\theta)}\right]f}{1 - \alpha + \dfrac{ar\gamma}{q(\theta)}}, \quad \partial x/\partial\theta < 0 \tag{11.7}$$

For the case of no hiring costs, $\gamma = 0$, this is exactly the quantity that appears in Dixit–Stiglitz models; the larger the hiring costs the lower is this quantity. Using equation (11.7) we can calculate the labour demand per firm as:

$$l_i = f + ax_i = \frac{f}{1 - \alpha + \dfrac{ar\gamma}{q(\theta)}}, \quad \partial l_i/\partial\theta < 0$$

Both output and labour demand depend negatively on hiring costs via the probability $q(\theta)$ because an increase in the tightness ratio increases expected marginal hiring costs. Each firm knows that it will be separated from the worker with probability s, resulting in sl_i separations, and can fill a vacancy with probability $q(\theta)$. A flow equilibrium of the firm – allowing it to keep the labour demand that allows it to produce the profit-maximizing output level – then requires that expected separations equal expected hiring, $sl_i = q(\theta)V_i$. The number of vacancies the firm will post to satisfy its labour demand, l_i, then are calculated from this equilibrium flow condition as:

$$V_i = f[s/q(\theta)]/[1 - \alpha + ar\gamma/q(\theta)] \tag{11.8}$$

The equilibrium output quantity of the model is directly dependent on the labour-market parameters r and γ and indirectly on all those having an impact on the tightness ratio stemming from Pissarides' part of the model (unemployment compensation z, hiring costs γ, unemployment rate u, vacancies v, separation rate s, power parameter β and interest r; see below) and also via ICT in the matching process because this leads to a higher value of q for any given θ. Clearly, this result is due to the fact that the firm's part of the Dixit–Stiglitz model is changed by adding hiring costs (per vacancies actually filled) to the wage rate: these terms, the wage and the expected hiring costs constitute marginal costs and therefore have an impact on the quantity, the employment and the vacancies posted.[10]

Using (11.7) to replace x in (11.2), we get:

$$n = L(1 - u)\frac{1 - \alpha + ar\gamma/q(\theta)}{f} \tag{11.2'}$$

This is a function $n(\theta)$. A higher tightness ratio increases expected hiring costs, decreases the firm size and the unemployment rate, and therefore increases the number of firms. Aggregate output can be found by multiplying the solutions for the output and the number of firms, equations (11.7) and (11.2'): $nx = (1 - u)L[\alpha/a - r\gamma/q(\theta)]$. Although there are internal economies of scale at the firm level, aggregate output has constant returns in the size of the economy L, and employment $L(1 - u)$ for a given tightness ratio. An increase in the marginal value product of labour, $d\alpha/a > 0$, increases nx directly because it appears in the numerator but will be shown below to have an indirect impact on the tightness ratio, hiring costs and the unemployment rate.

Using the result for the number of firms from equation (11.2'), we can calculate the *total* number of vacancies from equation (11.8) as $vL = nV_i =$

$n(s/q)l_i = (s/q)L(1-u)$. Cancelling L and dividing by $(1-u)$ yields $v/(1-u) = s/q = \theta u/(1-u)$.

> *Proposition 1*: The equilibrium quantity and employment of the firm, the total number of firms and vacancies as well as aggregate output of the modified Dixit–Stiglitz model are all dependent on marginal hiring costs, which link it to the labour market variables via the tightness ratio.

To solve the system the next steps serve to arrive at a second equation – besides (11.6) – relating the real wage and the tightness ratio. Dividing (11.4) by the price and solving for the real wage yields:

$$w = \frac{\alpha}{a} - \frac{r+s}{q(\theta)}\gamma \qquad (11.4')$$

Larger hiring costs $(r+s)\gamma/q(\theta)$ imply lower wages according to (11.4') as in Pissarides' model when interest is given. Equation (11.4') is drawn as a function $w(\theta)$ in the upper right quadrant of Figure 11.1, indicated as the *MM* curve. The *MM* curve is rotated downward by increases in r, s and γ, and shifted downward by decreases of α/a. It is also drawn in the upper left quadrant of Figure 11.1 with wages as a function of hiring costs.

The intersection of lines *BB* and *MM* determines the wage and the tightness rate in the upper right quadrant, and hiring costs in the upper left quadrant. Given the rate of tightness thus determined, the solution for the rates of unemployment and vacancies can be found in the lower right quadrant.

The effect of ICT in matching is to rotate the *MM* curve upwards and to move the Beveridge curve towards the horizontal axis. ICT in production moves the *BB* curve and the *MM* curve upwards. It can be shown (see Ziesemer 2003, propositions 5–7) that unemployment goes down, and tightness and real wages go up. The implications for the market imperfections discussed in the introduction are as follows. The probability of finding a job has increased and so has the probability of filling a vacancy if the direct effect of ICT in matching is larger than the indirect effect of an increase in the tightness ratio. This is a Pareto improvement leading to more vacancies, unless the indirect effect of increased tightness on finding a worker is dominant. For workers the situation has improved. The impact on variety remains unclear as can be seen from equation (11.2'). The direct effect of ICT in production and matching reduces variety. The increase in tightness and employment increases variety. The degree of monopoly is unchanged and the impact on quantities is as unclear as that on variety, because tightness works against the other effects.

Equations (11.4) and (11.6) are two functions $w(\theta)$. Equating (11.4) and (11.6) we get:

$$\alpha = a\left[z + \frac{1}{1-\beta}\frac{r+s}{q(\theta)}\gamma + \frac{\beta\gamma\theta}{1-\beta}\right] \tag{11.9}$$

The left side is marginal revenue and the right side is marginal cost. In Figure 11.2 both functions are drawn; here, the left side is denoted as *MR* and the right side as *MC*. *MC* is increasing in θ and may have a negative second derivative in θ.[11]

The *MC* curve starts at az if $\theta = 0$ and $\lim_{\theta \to 0} q = \lim m(1/\theta, 1) = \lim m(\infty, 1) = \infty$; otherwise it starts above az. As θ goes to infinity the *MC* curve also goes to infinity. Thus the *MC* curve either intersects once or not at all. Therefore we have a unique or no equilibrium.

Proposition 2: The existence of a unique equilibrium is guaranteed if $z < \alpha/a$. This implies a positive equilibrium value for the tightness ratio $v/u = \theta$. The fixed cost parameter f and the size of the economy, L, have no impact on the value of $v/u = \theta$.

If, however, $z \geq \alpha/a$, the tightness ratio is zero, there are no vacancies and unemployment is 100 per cent according to equation (11.2). With no output, z cannot be paid, therefore this cannot be an equilibrium situation.

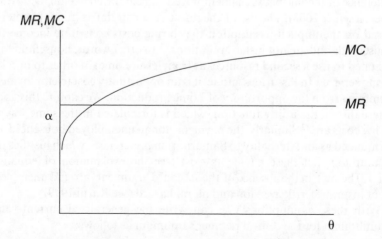

Figure 11.2   Determination of the tightness ratio θ of the market equilibrium

11.4   THE CENTRAL PLANNER'S OPTIMUM WITHOUT BARGAINING CONSTRAINTS

In order to find the optimum unemployment compensation we need to derive the central planner's optimum. We assume that a hypothetical, benevolent central planner optimizes the utility function (with discount rates equal to interest rates as usual in this type of model):

$$\int_{\tau=0}^{\infty} e^{-r\tau} \left\{ \left[\int_{i=0}^{n} c_i^{\alpha} di \right]^{1/\alpha} + zu - \theta u\gamma \right\} Ld\tau,$$

subject to the dynamics of the unemployment rate according to equation (11.1), and the resource constraint for labour:

$$(1-u)L - n(f+ax) = 0. \tag{11.10}$$

Both functions need some explanation. The firms' budget, with $x = c_i L$, is $npx - Wn(f+ax) - p\gamma V_j n = 0$. In order to have the resource constraint compatible with the budget constraints we have to assume that the households have a budget $W(1-u)L + p\gamma nV_i - npc_iL = 0$ assuming absence of capital income. Then adding up these budgets yields the resource constraint (11.10). The implicit assumption here is that firms buy hiring services from all households equally and pay the hiring costs to the households. As this is going to employed and unemployed households alike, it would drop out from the difference of income between unemployed and employed persons as zu does (see Ziesemer 2003). The use of the resource constraint as in this chapter is based on the implicit assumption that hiring costs constitute income for households and are not just evaporations.[12] In other words, households are assumed to use a second resource (as from leisure time) in order to provide hiring services. In Pissarides' model it is an opportunity cost to employment stemming from the opportunity of home production. We capture this as an externality in the utility function, which is formulated in the same way as hiring costs are.[13] Similarly, the payments for an unemployed household are formulated as an externality to Samaritarian preferences, which justifies the assumption that these payments exist (see the explanation of equation (11.13) below), in the absence of the standard arguments around unemployment insurance, risk aversion and moral hazard (see Karni 1999).

With these assumptions one can write the generalized current-value Hamiltonian for the central planner's optimum as follows:

$$H = n^{\frac{1}{\alpha}} x + zuL - \theta u\gamma L + \lambda[(1-u)L - n(f+ax)] + \mu[s(1-u) - \theta q(\theta)u]$$

The first-order conditions then are the following.

$$\frac{\partial H}{\partial x} = n^{\frac{1}{\alpha}} - \lambda na = 0 \tag{11.11}$$

$$\frac{\partial H}{\partial n} = \frac{1}{\alpha} n^{\frac{1}{\alpha}-1} x - \lambda(f + ax) = 0 \tag{11.12}$$

$$-\frac{\partial H}{\partial u} = -\{zL - \theta\gamma L + \lambda(-L) + \mu[-s - \theta q(\theta)]\} = \dot{\mu} - r\mu \tag{11.13}$$

$$\frac{\partial H}{\partial \theta} = -\gamma uL + \mu[-q(\theta) - \theta q]u = 0 \tag{11.14}$$

$$\lim_{t \to \infty} e^{-rt} u\mu = 0 \tag{11.15}$$

From these first-order conditions we will derive a condition that is comparable to equation (11.9) of the market equilibrium, which determines the tightness ratio there. Equation (11.11) balances the marginal utility of quantities of the goods to the marginal production costs. Equation (11.12) balances the positive marginal love-of-variety effect of the number of products and the resource value of the labour used per variant or firm. From (11.11) and (11.12) we can find the optimal quantity at its Dixit–Stiglitz value:

$$x = \frac{\alpha f}{(1 - \alpha)a} \tag{11.16}$$

This optimal quantity is larger than that from the equilibrium according to equation (11.7) because – from the point of view of the central planner – hiring costs should play no role as what is a cost to the firm is an income to households that is not really drawing on resources but rather is an externality. Insertion of the optimum quantity into the resource constraint yields the optimal number of firms as a function of the rate of unemployment:

$$n(u) = (1 - u)L(1 - \alpha)/f \tag{11.17}$$

For any given unemployment rate the number of firms is smaller than in the market equilibrium because the quantity is larger, which is the opposite of what one would expect on the basis of the variety externality alone.

Equation (11.13) has on the left-hand side the marginal costs of more unemployment compensations paid and the reduction in hiring costs externalities, the impact of the lower amounts of resources available if the

unemployment rate is higher, and decreasing separations and increases in
the number of jobs found (for a given tightness ratio) – in short, the marginal costs and benefits of higher unemployment, which determine the
change in the (negative) shadow price of unemployment. In particular,
there are fewer separations and more inflow into employment, and lower
hiring costs under a higher unemployment rate. If z alone rather than zu
were in the welfare function of the planner, z would not appear at all in the
first order condition. If they do not appear in the first-order conditions of
the central planner's optimum, there is no justification to have them in the
model for the equilibrium. In other words, the way benefits are introduced
in the central planner problem shows what the justification is to have them
in the market equilibrium. Writing a parameter before this term in the
welfare function and discussing the effects of varying it are neglected for
reasons of length of the chapter. In the Pissarides model these are
Samaritarian preferences. Equation (11.14) balances the increase in hiring
costs and the increased chance of a worker to find a job. Solving (11.14) for

$$\mu = \frac{\gamma L}{-q - \theta q} = \frac{\gamma L}{-q(\theta)[1 - \eta(\theta)]} < 0, \text{ with } 0 < \eta = \frac{-\theta q'}{q} < 1,$$

and (11.11) for the value of resources, $\lambda = \frac{1}{a} n^{\frac{1}{\alpha} - 1}$, and inserting them into
(11.13) yields

$$-zL - \theta \gamma L + \left(\frac{1}{a} n^{\frac{1}{\alpha} - 1}\right)(-L) + \frac{\gamma L}{-q(1 - \eta)}[-s - \theta q(\theta)] = \dot{\mu} - r \frac{\gamma L}{-q(1 - \eta)}$$

For a constant μ and cancellation of L a slight rearrangement yields

$$\frac{1}{a} n(u(\theta))^{\frac{1}{\alpha} - 1} - z = \frac{r + s + \eta \theta q(\theta)}{q(1 - \eta)} \gamma \qquad (11.18)$$

Equation (11.18) will serve to establish conditions for the existence of an
optimum and then can be compared to equation (11.9) of the market equilibrium. $n(u)$ in (11.18) indicates that n depends on u according to (11.17);
moreover, u depends on the tightness ratio, θ, according to (11.1′).
Subsequent insertion of these equations yields

$$\frac{1}{a}\left[\frac{1}{\dfrac{s}{\theta q(\theta)} + 1} L \frac{1 - \alpha}{f}\right]^{\frac{1}{\alpha} - 1} - z = \frac{r + s + \eta \theta q(\theta)}{q(1 - \eta)} \gamma \qquad (11.19)$$

11.4.1 Existence and Multiple Steady States

The following analysis is summarized in Figure 11.3. As q goes from infinity to zero while the tightness ratio goes from zero to infinity, the right-hand side of (11.19) is zero when tightness is zero (the assumption that the matching function is Cobb-Douglas is sufficient for this result)[14] and has a positive but decreasing slope because the curvature must be the same as in Figure 11.2. The right-hand side is drawn as *RS* in the upper right quadrant of Figure 11.3. The left-hand side of equation (11.18) is a function of n, which we draw in the upper left quadrant of Figure 11.3. For the case where $\alpha = 0.5$, this is a linear function of n. For lower (higher) values of α it has an increasing (decreasing) slope. n itself is a function of u according to (11.17). This is drawn in the lower left quadrant of Figure 11.3. Finally, the Beveridge curve is drawn in the lower right quadrant of Figure 11.3. The crucial point for existence and uniqueness is whether or not the left-hand side of (11.18) intersects the right-hand side when the left-hand side

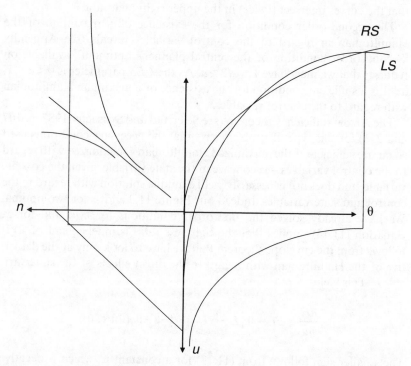

Figure 11.3   The central planner's local optimum with the lower unemployment rate is better

is mapped into the upper right quadrant. This can be done point wise in the following way. Fix a value of the tightness ratio. Take the corresponding value of u in the lower right quadrant and the corresponding value of n in the lower left quadrant. Then take the value of the left-hand side function in the upper left quadrant, use it as a coordinate of the vertical axis and combine it with the value of the tightness ratio from which the procedure started. This gives the first point of the left-hand side. Proceeding in the same way for each value of the tightness ratio we get the LS curve in the upper right quadrant. It starts from $(-z)$ and is upward sloping with a decreasing slope, at least if the function has a value of α in the neighbourhood of 0.5. The LS curve has an upper bound when tightness goes to infinity, whereas the RS curve continues to grow. The RS curve therefore starts and ends above the LS curve, hence it will either be tangential or intersect not at all, or twice, as drawn in Figure 11.3. For any given unemployment benefit z this requires either that the economy is sufficiently productive in the sense of having a high marginal product of labour, $1/a$, or low hiring costs γ, which make the right-hand side small enough, in order to make sure that the curves intersect (twice) in the upper right quadrant.

The second-order condition for the existence of a maximum of the Hamiltonian in regard to the control variables reveals (see Appendix 'Second-order condition of the central planner's optimum', available on request) that we must have $1 + \alpha/2 > a$. As the CES parameter is $0 < \alpha < 1$, $a \leq 1$ is a sufficient condition for the existence of a maximum Hamiltonian with regard to the control variables.

The Arrow sufficiency theorem (see Seierstad and Sydsaeter 1987, p. 107 and 231) for this type of problem says that the necessary conditions used so far are sufficient if the maximized Hamiltonian – maximized with regard to the control variables – is concave in the state variable, given the co-state variable, and does not necessarily yield a unique solution with regard to the control and state variables. Indeed our Figure 11.3 allows for two optima. We have already solved the first-order conditions for $n(u)$ and for x. Equation (11.14) implies that the tightness ratio is independent of u. It follows from the envelope theorem that we have to look only at the derivative of the Hamiltonian with regard to the direct effects of the state variable u. This yields:

$$\frac{\partial H}{\partial u} = zL - \theta\gamma L - \lambda L + \mu[-s - \theta q(\theta)] < 0$$

The smaller sign follows from (11.13) for a constant μ, which is negative according to equation (11.14). The second derivative of the maximized Hamiltonian with regard to the state variable u is

$$\left(\frac{\partial^2 H}{(\partial u)(\partial \theta)}\right)\frac{\partial \theta}{\partial u} = 0$$

As the tightness ratio is independent of the unemployment rate according to (11.14) and depends only on μ, the second derivative is zero. The maximized Hamiltonian is a linearly falling function of the rate of unemployment. The Arrow sufficiency theorem then says that the necessary conditions are sufficient.

As the necessary conditions do not produce a unique optimum we have to clarify which of the two intersection points in the upper right quadrant has larger welfare. As the Hamiltonian is convex in the number of varieties (its second derivative is positive), the welfare with the larger number of varieties must be higher as far as the first part of the Hamiltonian is concerned. This leads to a lower unemployment rate and in turn to a higher value of the maximized Hamiltonian if $z < \theta\gamma$ (sufficient), where the inequality also holds for higher values of θ. By implication, in the upper right quadrant of Figure 11.3 the intersection point with the higher tightness ratio is the global optimum.

Proposition 3: In the central planner's welfare maximization of a Pissarides–Dixit–Stiglitz economy with hiring costs, which is constrained by the production technology, the (matching function or) unemployment dynamics may lead to two local optima if the marginal product of labour is sufficiently large or hiring costs are low, because the utility function is convex in the number of products. The global optimum is the one with the larger variety, lower unemployment rate and larger tightness ratio.

11.4.2 Comparative Static Analysis of the Central Planner's Optimum

Unlike the market equilibrium, the central planner's optimum depends on the size of the economy. It enhances the left-hand side of equation (11.19) and therefore the *LS* curve in Figure 11.3. The reason is that it enhances variety, which in turn enhances the shadow price of the labour resources.

ICT can be described as technical progress in production and matching (see Ziesemer 2003 for an extensive illustration of the arguments). In production, an increase in fixed costs, $df > 0$, is assumed to generate a decrease in the variable labour requirement, $da < 0$, and increases the probability of filling a vacancy for any given tightness ratio, $dq > 0$, for example through Internet search. This latter effect shifts the *RS* curve down and increases tightness. An increase in fixed costs shifts the *LS* curve down and decreases the tightness ratio, whereas the decrease in the variable labour requirement shifts the *LS* curve up and increases the tightness ratio.[15] If the increase in fixed costs does not dominate – as it should not for the effects outweighing the costs – optimal unemployment falls. Moreover, it follows from (11.19) that an increase in the separation rate and in the unemployment benefits decreases the tightness ratio. Both shift the *LS* curve down in Figure 11.3. These results can be summarized as follows.

> *Proposition 4*: Increases in labour force size and ICT, and decreases in the separation rate and unemployment benefits decrease the optimal rate of unemployment in the central planner's optimum.

11.5   CONDITIONS FOR THE X-BEST OPTIMALITY OF THE MARKET EQUILIBRIUM

As the quantity of the firm differs in equilibrium from its optimal value as can be seen from a comparison of equations (11.7) and (11.16), we cannot have a first-best optimum. However, the tightness ratio and the unemployment rate could reach their first-best levels.

Comparison of equations (11.9) and (11.18) immediately shows that in the Pissarides–Dixit–Stiglitz model the Hosios condition $\beta = \eta$ *alone* is not sufficient for an optimum. An optimal tightness ratio and unemployment rate require that equation (11.9) equals (11.18) or (11.19). If Hosios' condition holds this requires (to see this bring a and z in (11.9) to its left-hand side and compare the left-hand sides of (11.9) with that of (11.18) and (11.19)):

$$\alpha = [n]^{\frac{1}{\alpha}-1} = \left[(1-u)L\frac{1-\alpha}{f}\right]^{\frac{1}{\alpha}-1} = \left[\frac{1}{\frac{s}{\theta q(\theta)}+1}L\frac{1-\alpha}{f}\right]^{\frac{1}{\alpha}-1} \quad (11.20)$$

This result, say θ^*, only provides an equation guaranteeing that equilibrium and x-best optimum coincide if Hosios' condition holds. The question is, how this optimal tightness ratio, θ^*, can be brought about. The unemployment benefit is the obvious candidate for this. From the point of view of the market equilibrium this is a Pigovian policy instrument, but from the point of view of the central planner it is a political preference, because we put it as a Samaritarian preference into the welfare function used by the central planner. When determining it in order to make equilibrium and optimum coincide with regard to the tightness and unemployment rates, we do not only determine the value of the instrument but also endogenize the preference of the central planner. The values that make x-best optimum and the market equilibrium identical under the Hosios condition are called z^*, θ^* and u^*.

If the rate of unemployment is optimal, the corresponding first-best number of firms is lower than the number of firms in the market equilibrium, which follows from comparison of (11.2) and (11.17) at an optimal unemployment rate u^*. In market equilibrium, variety is above its optimal level if tightness and unemployment rates are at their first-best value.[16] Therefore we are dealing with x-best market equilibria only.

The rates of unemployment benefits and tightness that make the market equilibrium an x-best optimum can be found by use of (11.9) and (11.19) as two equations for the determination of z^* and θ^*. They are drawn in Figure 11.4 where (11.9) is labelled the *EE* curve and (11.19) is labelled the *CC* curve. In order to understand the curvature we restate the equations with z on the left-hand side:

$$z = \frac{\alpha}{a} - \left[\frac{1}{1-\beta} \frac{r+s}{q(\theta)} \gamma + \frac{\beta\gamma\theta}{1-\beta} \right] \tag{11.9'}$$

$$z = \frac{1}{a} \left[\frac{1}{\dfrac{s}{\theta q(\theta)} + 1} L \frac{1-\alpha}{f} \right]^{\frac{1}{\alpha}-1} - \frac{r+s+\eta\theta q(\theta)}{q(1-\eta)} \gamma \tag{11.19'}$$

In line with the curvature of the *RS* curve in Figure 11.3 we can say that the curve for (11.9') starts at α/a and then falls at decreasing rates. The first term on the right-hand side of (11.19') is the *LS* curve in Figure 11.3 without

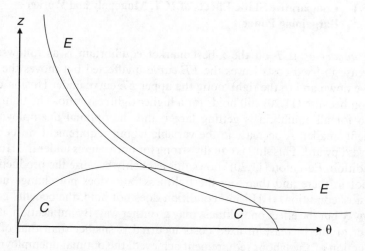

Figure 11.4   Unique or multiple x-best equilibria

the z-term and the second, subtracted term is the *RS* curve of Figure 11.3, both starting at the origin. By implication, the right-hand side of (11.19′) is a curve with an inverted u-shape. Both curves are drawn in Figure 11.4. The market equilibrium curve *EE* is drawn twice; the upper curve is tangential to the *CC* curve and yields a unique tightness and benefit value. This is in accordance with equation (11.20), which has been derived under Hosios' condition and has a unique solution for the tightness ratio. However, if worker bargaining power is larger than the matching elasticity, the falling market equilibrium curve *EE* has a lower position and we get two intersection points, one with high tightness and low benefits and the other with low tightness and high benefits.[17] The possibility for multiple equilibria appears in the literature only under increasing returns in the matching function (see Pissarides 2000, pp. 135 and 142). Here it is due to the increasing marginal utility with regard to the number of variants. This property leads to two local optima in the central planner's optimum and to a u-shaped relation between benefits and tightness when benefits are endogenous.

Proposition 5: The absence of hiring costs from the resource constraint makes a first-best equilibrium impossible. The Hosios condition is insufficient to achieve an x-best optimum unless the tightness and unemployment rate are at the optimal level, which implies that the number of firms is above the optimal level. If unemployment benefits ensure the first-best tightness and unemployment rates, x-best equilibrium is unique with regard to tightness and benefits if Hosios' condition holds. If worker bargaining power is higher (lower) there are multiple (no) equilibria because of increasing marginal utility with regard to variety.

11.5.1 Comparative Static Effects of ICT, Monopoly and Worker Bargaining Power

The impact of ICT on the x-best market equilibrium is as follows: an increase in fixed costs leaves the *EE* curve unaffected but moves the *CC* curve down and to the right along the upper *EE* curve under Hosios' condition because (11.20) still holds for a higher tightness ratio. The tightness ratio for all equilibria is getting larger and the optimal unemployment benefit smaller. A decrease in the variable labour requirement shifts both curves upward. This shift is equally strong for both curves under the Hosios condition. Equation (11.20) shows this explicitly because the productivity is not in there and therefore the tightness ratio does not change under Hosios' condition. If Hosios' condition does not hold, the benefits go up anyway but the effect on tightness may go either way. By implication, if the effect of the increase in fixed costs incurred is smaller than that of the reduction of the labour requirement achieved, the optimal unemployment benefit goes up as tightness does anyhow. This special result shows that

Pissarides' suggestion that compensations should be formulated as functions proportional to productivity is highly plausible, and de-linking of technical change and benefits is not.

If Internet search enhances the probability of filling a vacancy for a given tightness ratio, both curves go up and increase the optimal unemployment benefit. But if the Hosios condition holds, the *CC* curve goes up more strongly and to the left and therefore, perhaps surprisingly, decreases the optimal market-tightness ratio, because, according to (11.20), the x-best number of firms and the unemployment rate are fixed under the Hosios condition and therefore the last expression is kept constant after an increase in matching productivity by a lower tightness ratio.

In other words, technical change in matching decreases unemployment in the pure market equilibrium of Figure 11.1 (see Ziesemer 2003), but the latter should be constant in an x-best equilibrium when Hosios' condition holds according to (11.20), which can be ensured in the market equilibrium through a higher unemployment benefit. The only positive net effect of ICT on x-best unemployment under Hosios' condition comes from the increase in fixed costs, as can be seen from (11.20). This increases employment and the tightness ratio, increases the probability of finding a job and decreases the probability of filling a vacancy unless it is outweighed by this effect of fixed costs. In other words the search externalities are changed in favour of workers. Variety is unchanged according to (11.20) unless monopoly power on the left-hand side changes, but ICT does nothing here. Reduction of unemployment through the fixed costs effect in (11.20) therefore must increase firm size in terms of employment and output. The monopolistic imperfection therefore seems to be reduced in terms of output and employment per firm, but not in terms of the parametrically given mark-up, which is the exact measure of the monopolistic imperfection. In short, ICT leaves the variety and the monopoly externality unchanged and shifts the search externality in favour of workers under Hosios' condition and increases benefits also in the case of multiple equilibria.

If bargaining power of workers is increased (decreased) the *EE* curve shifts down (up), the equilibria move further apart (towards each other). If bargaining power falls too low, the x-best equilibria may vanish. It is not possible then to set benefits at a level that generates optimum tightness, but rather at any benefit level the market equilibrium tightness will be larger than the optimal one. This is a cost of having weak worker bargaining power.

If the degree of product differentiation and monopoly, $1/\alpha$, is increasing, the *EE* curve is going down and the *CC* curve is going up. If this effect is strong enough – as α approaches zero – the optimal unemployment benefit is becoming negative at the equilibrium with larger tightness. Such a policy may lack credibility when capital markets become imperfect at negative benefits, and force policy to choose the equilibrium with positive benefits and relatively low tightness. At this higher equilibrium the effect of a decrease in the CES parameter is to increase benefits and to decrease tightness.

> *Proposition 6*: x-best unemployment benefits are increased through ICT in production and matching. Larger worker bargaining power and increasing of monopoly power make the two equilibria drift apart. The tightness ratio is increased by ICT in production, and decreased through ICT in matching.

This result is interesting with regard to the fact that lower bargaining power, more competition and higher marginal productivity are major features of recent developments in European industrial countries (see Blanchard and Giavazzi 2003). Moreover, the Internet seems to improve the matching process. It is not clear then in which direction optimal unemployment benefits go: ICT suggests they should go up, lower bargaining power suggests they could go down only if the economy is in the equilibrium with higher unemployment, and the same holds for reduction of monopoly power. At the equilibrium with larger employment, benefits should go up if monopoly and bargaining power are going down. In short, ICT and reductions in power may point to opposite directions for optimal unemployment benefits in response to these changes. Probably real-world unemployment compensation was decreased because the belief in moral hazard problems was dominant, at least in the Netherlands. It is unclear as to how far it has been recognized that this may drive hiring costs above the optimum and unemployment benefits below it when the x-best equilibria do not exist and market equilibrium has a higher tightness than the optimum. For the USA in turn the changes in power are less relevant, whereas the changes in ICT are similar. By implication this would bias the argument of this chapter in favour of higher unemployment benefits in the USA whereas those for Europe are less obvious. If countries like the Netherlands, Austria and Switzerland are perceived to be in the high employment equilibrium, there benefits should go up with the modern trends in order to keep tightness optimal.

11.6   CONCLUSION

ICT affects the pure market equilibrium, and also the first-best equilibrium. However, only an x-best equilibrium can be achieved. ICT and changes in competition and bargaining power affect the three imperfections of the x-best equilibria. First, the unemployment has search externalities. ICT enhances the probability of a worker finding a job under Hosios' condition, because the unemployment rate is decreased through the increase in fixed costs of production. The probability of filling a vacancy is enhanced if the increased technological efficiency in the search technology is not out-weighed by the effect of fixed costs on the tightness ratio. If so, ICT in the search technology yields a Pareto improvement with regard to search exter-nalities. However, the optimal x-best policy requires enhancing the unem-ployment benefits, which would partly remove the employment effects. Second, monopolistic firms have prices that differ from marginal costs, and also the quantity differs from its optimum. The mark-up can change only exogenously and is not affected by ICT. Third, the variety externality expe-rienced by households indicates in the first instance that variety is lower than optimal. However, it is above its optimal value in the presence of hiring costs for given first-best (un-) employment. It could be changed by higher or lower employment though. In the market equilibrium ICT has an unclear impact on variety because the direct effect of ICT in production and matching decreases variety, but the indirect effect via tightness and hiring costs decreases variety. In the x-best equilibrium variety does not react on ICT or changes in worker bargaining power but only on changes in the degree of monopoly, if Hosios' condition holds.

The current political trend to decrease unemployment benefits in spite of strong labour market tightness (in some countries even in recessions) may make hiring costs inefficiently large and firms inefficiently small and lead to excess variety. ICT increases optimal unemployment benefits, whereas reductions in monopoly power and worker bargaining power decrease optimal benefits in the equilibrium with high unemployment but not in that with low unemployment. There is no support for the de-linking of benefits and technical change.

NOTES

1. The chapter does not discuss endogenous technical progress, but rather uses steady states with zero growth rate. We also do not discuss any skill-bias in technical change. Moreover, it is not our ambition to explain comparative labour market features. See, e.g., Acemoglu (2002) and Mortensen and Pissarides (1999) on these issues. On all of these issues we would not try to limit the explanation to technical change but rather include international trade, oil price shocks and high interest and education policies under con-ditions of international capital and labour movements.
2. 'I hope to see such a low unemployment never again', said Teulings, 'This was really unsustainable. . . . The labour market is structurally tight', *Volkskrant* 12 April 2003.
3. A negative benefit would be a punishment, which would have the effect of reducing the unemployment income and the negotiated wage when the punishment appears as a neg-ative opportunity income.
4. We do not consider risk aversion and moral hazard problems but only general equilib-rium effects of labour market tightness, in particular in regard to ICT.
5. Subsections are titled as in Pissarides (2000). The search part is explained in greater

detail there. This section is based on Ziesemer (2003). We drop many details of the explanation, which can be found there.

6. An implicit assumption here is that the additional hits from the Internet are not all useless. In this sense, mismatches have to be decreased by the Internet as well and the increase in the number of hits – cleaned for mismatches – has to leave us with an increased number of matches per unit of time.

7. This result requires that $q + \theta q' > 0$, because in order to make u fall with θ, θq must increase with θ. As $\theta q = Tm(1, v/u)$ as derived above this merely requires that the second derivative of the matching function is positive. Therefore it does depend on the linear homogeneity assumption but not on the Cobb-Douglas form. In (11.1″) both terms in the denominator are falling in the tightness ratio, which therefore has a positive impact on the share of vacancies.

8. By implication we only consider the case of a large number of firms in which no strategic behaviour takes place.

9. Note that if the sum of all present-discounted profits is zero, in a steady state with all terms in the profit function constant – except for time in the discount factor – it follows from carrying out the integration that current profits have to be zero.

10. It can be shown that this part drops out if the firm is myopic and does not take into account that it will lose workers through separation, which will require it to incur search costs again.

11. To get a negative second derivative of the MC curve it is sufficient to assume that the matching function is of the Cobb-Douglas type.

12. If hiring costs were just evaporations, which do not reach the households (analogous to Samuelsonian iceberg costs) the resource constraint could be derived from the budget constraints only in a form that would contain also the hiring costs. If used in that form from equation (11.2) onwards, we would get a different result than those before proposition 1, and they would ultimately contradict equation (11.1′). The assumption of evaporation is therefore not compatible with the principle of having resource constraints consistent with those obtained by adding up budget constraints.

13. An alternative to this procedure may be to formulate a second sector for hiring services. In this case one would need a non-arbitrage condition saying that working in production should earn as much as working in hiring services.

14. Petrongolo and Pissarides (2001) evaluate the empirical literature on matching functions and come up with the conclusion that the Cobb-Douglas form with constant returns to scale is indeed a good approximation.

15. Note that in case of a unique optimum for an almost linear LS curve the comparative static effects would be those corresponding to the other local optimum, with fairly counterintuitive results.

16. Note that it follows from (11.20) that the integral measure of the number of firms is below unity.

17. Even the left one has to be to the right of the maximum of the CC curve, because the optimum in Figure 11.3 is reached to the right of the maximal vertical difference of LS and RS for any z.

REFERENCES

Acemoglu, D. (2002), 'Technical change, inequality, and the labor market', *Journal of Economic Literature*, **40**, 7–72.

Autor, D.H. (2001), 'Wiring the labor market', *Journal of Economic Perspectives*, **15**, 25–40.

Blanchard, O. and F. Giavazzi (2003), 'Macroeconomic effects of regulation and deregulation in goods and labor markets', *Quarterly Journal of Economics*, **118**, 879–907.

Dixit, A. and J.E. Stiglitz (1977), 'Monopolistic competition and optimum product diversity', *American Economic Review*, **67**, 297–308.

Hosios, A.J. (1990), 'On the efficiency of matching and related models of search and unemployment', *Review of Economic Studies*, **57**, 279–98.

Karni, Edi (1999), 'Optimal unemployment insurance: A survey', *Southern Economic Journal*, **66**, 442–65.

Mortensen, D.T. and C.A. Pissarides (1999), 'Unemployment responses to "skill-biased" technology shocks: The role of labour market policy', *Economic Journal*, **109**, 242–65.

Petrongolo, B. and C.A. Pissarides (2001), 'Looking into the black box: A survey of the matching function', *Journal of Economic Literature*, **39**, 390–431.

Pissarides, C. (2000), *Equilibrium Unemployment Theory*, Cambridge, MA: MIT Press.

Seierstad, A. and K. Sydsaeter (1987), *Optimal Control Theory with Economic Applications*, Amsterdam: Elsevier North-Holland.

Ziesemer, T. (2003), 'Information and communication technology in matching and production', *Journal of Economics*, **79**, 263–87.

12. Unleashing animal spirits: Investment in ICT and economic growth*

Eric J. Bartelsman and Jeroen Hinloopen

12.1 INTRODUCTION

The EU countries lag well behind the US in the intensity with which the business sector uses ICT as a factor of production. Further, businesses in the EU produce relatively lower quantities of ICT goods and services, on average. This chapter discusses various possible explanations for the lag in ICT investment for economic performance. A model is developed that links ICT investment to competitive pressure and makes predictions about co-movement of ICT investment and indicators of market dynamics. The empirical results point to a significant effect of the regulatory environment on the share of ICT in total investment spending.

It may seem that policy concerns about ICT and the economy should have disappeared along with the New Economy-hype and the overvaluation of ICT-related stocks. However, despite the precipitous drop of the NASDAQ, the technologies being developed and deployed continue to have the potential to alter the economic landscape in years to come. New Economy pundits claim that use of improved information and communications technology (ICT) not only increases the quality and variety of consumer goods and producers' durable equipment, but also reduces the cost of transactions between many economic agents. Further, the use of ICT may increase the efficiency of the innovative processes taking place within industrialised economies. The potential benefits will accrue to economies with firms that continue to invest in and successfully adopt the new information and communications technologies.

In the EU, policy makers are worried about performance in the area of ICT. As witnessed by the statistical material available, the rate at which EU countries adopted ICT is quite mixed, and the ICT share of investment is

* We are grateful to anonymous referees and the editors for their comments and assistance.

lower than in the US in all EU countries. Furthermore, aggregate economic outcomes, as measured by GDP growth or the unemployment rate, are also mixed and weaker on average than in the US. At the Lisbon summit of 2000, EU policy makers banded together and called for measures to cata-pult Europe into first place within a decade. Strategies were developed to enable Europe 'to become the most competitive and dynamic knowledge-based economy in the world . . . with more and better jobs and greater social cohesion'. The main strategies stated for reaching this goal were 'better policies for the information society', structural reform for competi-tiveness, and an appropriate macroeconomic policy mix. The EU has launched the transition to the knowledge-based economy with due consid-eration for the role of ICT. To accomplish the transition EU policy makers are asking the following question: What can be done to boost ICT uptake in the EU? Before attempting an answer to this question, the chapter reviews answers provided in the literature on the following questions: (1) How important is ICT for an economy? (2) Is ICT uptake lower in the EU than in the US?; (3) If so, what are the causes of a low ICT share in total investment?

The evidence provides a reasonable case that ICT contributes less to the economy in the EU than in the US. This is true for production of ICT goods and services and, more important for policy, for benefits of accu-mulated investment in ICT assets in ICT-using industries. Quite a few reasons have been put forward by policy makers for the low rates of ICT investment in the EU (EC 2001). The costs of implementing ICT-related investments may be higher, for example owing to scarcity of adequately educated workers or sources of venture funding. And the benefits of ICT investments may differ across countries because market conditions result in different price and quantity outcomes for successful innovators. We claim that lack of competitive pressure in general, and restrictive employment protection in particular, are among the main causes for retarding incentives to invest in ICT by firms in the EU.

To answer the above questions, section 2 starts with a review of the recent empirical literature relating ICT and economic performance from both a micro and a macro perspective. The production of ICT goods and services contributes a significant amount to the increase in output in the US, but much less so in most EU countries. The use of ICT capital as a production factor is becoming more important for economic growth, both because growth rates of ICT capital are high and because the installed base has been increasing. Because ICT investment continues to be lower in the EU than in the US, the contribution of ICT capital services to economic growth is lower as well. The empirical evidence on the economic effects of ICT is complemented by a story that describes how the benefits of ICT use may go beyond the direct contribution to growth from ICT capital services, providing further reasons for policy intervention to boost ICT adoption.

The main contribution of the chapter is to explore how the regulatory setting may contribute to low ICT uptake. Section 3 introduces a model that relates competitive pressure to incentives for early uptake of a risky technology such as ICT. In the model, the share of firms investing in a risky technology in an attempt to acquire a more efficient production process increases as competitive pressure becomes more intense. In the model competitive pressure also has implications for changes in productivity, market shares of successful firms and other indicators of economic dynamics at the micro level. In section 4 we turn to empirical evidence and estimate the link between ICT investment as a share of total investment and indicators of competitive pressure and market dynamics. The estimates confirm the significant effect that restrictions on resource reallocation have on firms' propensity to invest in ICT.

12.2   EVIDENCE ON ICT AND ECONOMIC IMPLICATIONS

Since the advent of computers a half-century ago, the price/performance ratio has been declining at a breakneck pace. The price deflator for a broad measure of ICT investment goods in the US, as measured by US Bureau for Economic Analysis (BEA), has been falling relative to that of total investment (Figure 12.1).[1] In the 1960s, Licklider and Taylor (1968) looked back at two decades of improvements and foresaw continuation of the doubling of technical performance characteristics of IT every two years. With incredible foresight, they described most of the features of our present interconnected world, although they did warn that the telecom monopoly would constitute a major bottleneck. Observing the impressive technical improvement in computing at the end of the 1980s, well into the microcomputer revolution, Solow (1987, p. 36) in his famous quote, wondered why 'We see computers everywhere except in the productivity statistics.'

12.2.1   Micro-level Evidence

Not until five years later did economists start to see that which Solow had not, namely improvements in productivity related to ICT use. Using firm-level data, Brynjolfsson and Hitt (1994, 2003) and Lichtenberg (1995), found that the returns to firm-level IT investment were high. In fact, their estimates of the rate of return to computer investment seem implausibly high, even considering the short lifespan of computer capital. Similarly,

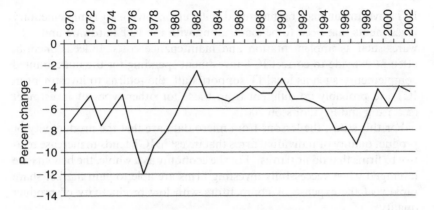

Source: Bureau of Economic Analysis (2002), Tables 5.3.3 and 5.3.5, lines 1 and 10.

Figure 12.1 Annual change in deflator for information processing equipment and software relative to deflator for total private fixed investment

early research for European firms also displays a productivity-boosting effect of IT capital, or of the use of automated production equipment (Entorf and Kramarz 1998; Bartelsman et al. 1998; Crepon and Heckel 2001). For non-manufacturing firms, McGuckin and Broersma (2003) find that in the Netherlands trade sector, IT investment does not provide a supra-normal return. Similarly, for a panel of German service firms, Licht and Moch (1999) find that IT use has effects on service quality but not on measured productivity. Overall, at the firm level in manufacturing, IT use seems to be correlated with quality, success, profitability, and productivity of firms; in the services sector returns to firms do not seem excessive (for a more recent review, with evidence from more countries, see OECD 2003). The evidence across studies does not point to any significant differences in the impact of IT usage on firms between those in the EU and those in the US.

The evidence from micro-level studies cannot be used to extrapolate the effect of ICT on output for the economy as a whole. First of all, the firm-level results show private returns, which may deviate from social returns because the benefits of the investment may not be fully appropriable by the firm, but may spill over to other firms or to consumers. In a competitive market place, the benefit from innovations will to a large extent end up in consumer surplus. Next, the private returns include the business stealing effect, namely the 'value' extracted from the firm whose market share has been poached by the successful innovator.[2] Finally, the private return to

ICT investment may be measured with error, owing to complementary investments that need to be made along with the ICT hardware and software, such as implementation and maintenance costs. Indeed, once an attempt is made to correct ICT investment spending for the unaccounted complements, such as local IT support staff, the returns to investment in ICT are probably no different from those for other types of investment (see Yang and Brynjolfsson 2001).

For this study, the lessons from micro data are that the productivity or product quality of individual firms that invest in ICT tends to increase relative to firms that do not invest. For the economy as a whole, the benefits are leveraged when successfully investing firms are able to gain market share rapidly at the expense of competitors with low productivity or product quality.

12.2.2   Sectoral and Macro Evidence

From the micro level, we step up to a higher level of aggregation. What is the role of ICT for individual sectors or for the economy as a whole? The first cut at an answer is to treat ICT like any other good or service. If statistical agencies maintain up-to-date hierarchical descriptions of commodities, products, and industries with enough detail, they could produce all indicators from national accounts for the sub-category ICT. In other words, we would have statistics on production by firms or establishments in ICT industries and services, we would know final demand for ICT products or services, we would know investment in ICT asset types by industry and we would have information on employment of workers in ICT-producing firms, in ICT-related occupations, or with ICT educational background, or a combination of the three.

Unfortunately, statistical agencies in many countries find themselves catching up with the information needs of the information age. Researchers have taken to collecting and harmonising their own indicators in an attempt to make cross-country comparisons. The best non-official source for this information is Van Ark et al. (2002, 2003), where official sources are stitched together with analysis and assumptions. The best official source is the OECD (see databases referenced in OECD 2003), which also provides much of the material underlying the work of Van Ark.

A first view of the role of ICT comes from the production accounts. Figure 12.2 shows the percentage of GDP in the non-agricultural business sector emanating from ICT goods and service producing sectors, as published in OECD (2003). The disparity in ICT intensity of production across countries is quite significant. The US is a large producer of ICT, but falls behind Ireland and Finland. The rest of the EU lag behind. In Finland and

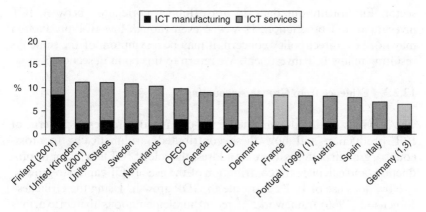

Source: OECD (2003).

*Figure 12.2 Value added produced by ICT sectors as percent of
non-agricultural business sector output*

Ireland, it is especially the magnitude of the ICT manufacturing sector that
results in their position at the top. Although most EU countries show an
increase in the ICT share of production over time, the gap with the US does
not seem to be closing.

Using value added data by industry, the direct contribution to GDP
growth from changes in ICT output can be computed. This mechanical
'shift-share' exercise, performed by Van Ark et al. (2002), reveals that in the
US the ICT manufacturing sector contributed 0.5 percentage points to the
4.6 per cent annual average growth rate of real GDP for the period
1995–1998. In contrast, leaving aside Finland with a contribution of 0.8
percentage points, the direct contribution of the ICT manufacturing sector
to GDP was less than 0.2 percentage points in Europe. Likewise, only in the
US and Finland did the ICT sector contribute substantially to the acceleration in GDP growth from first half to the second half of the 1990s,
although the contribution from ICT services in the Netherlands increased
as well.

Establishing that the size of the ICT-producing sectors varies across
countries, and that the contribution to aggregate output growth is relatively
low when a country has a small share of fast-growing ICT producers, does
not lead directly to any policy recommendations. Possible market failures
requiring policy action would occur if production of ICT goods provided
spillovers to other local ICT producers, or to users of ICT goods and
services. For example, it might be more costly to adopt ICT because local
production of these goods increases the absorptive capacity of the business

sector. Empirically our data do not exhibit a correlation between ICT investment and production. However, even though low ICT production may not be a direct policy concern, it may be a symptom of the same ills resulting in low ICT investment. We return to this point in section 5.

12.2.3   Evidence from Growth Accounting

The previous section documented cross-country differences in patterns of ICT production and how these contributed, arithmetically, to cross-country growth patterns. Here we address the role of ICT as a factor of production, and calculate the contribution of the use of ICT capital to growth.

How does use of ICT contribute to GDP growth? Using the Griliches–Jorgenson (1966) framework, or recent implementations thereof, various authors have calculated the contribution of capital services delivered by accumulated ICT capital goods. The growth accounting method is straightforward: output is produced by employing the services of various productive inputs. A cost-minimising firm hiring factors of production will do so until the marginal cost of each factor equals the factor's marginal product. In the accounting framework, all revenue is accounted for as payments for factor inputs. Under these conditions, the growth rate of output equals a weighted average of the growth rates of factor inputs plus the growth unaccounted for, or TFP. Total factor productivity (TFP) thus remains the measure of our ignorance, that part of growth that is unaccounted for by explicit resource expenditures of firms.

To find the contribution of ICT capital to aggregate growth, a service flow is created for the component assets of ICT capital, and for the aggregate of all other types of capital. In the US statistical system, current and historical cost investments for 13 types of ICT assets presently are published (BEA 2000), while the remaining capital comprises about 45 different asset categories. These data are provided also for roughly 60 disaggregated sectors for the period 1929 through 2000. In most EU countries, no official data exist until recently for ICT investment as a whole at the macro level, let alone for component assets at the sectoral level for longer periods. The studies mentioned below thus had to rely on non-official statistics and imputations as data sources for many countries.

Figure 12.3 shows an indicator of ICT investment as a share of total nominal non-residential investment spending, as published by OECD (2003). The shares show great variation, with the US leading the pack, followed by the UK, with the main EU countries closing the list. Another version of this indicator, but with annual observations, was graciously supplied to us by van Ark (2002) and is used as the variable to be explained in the empirical work in Section 4.

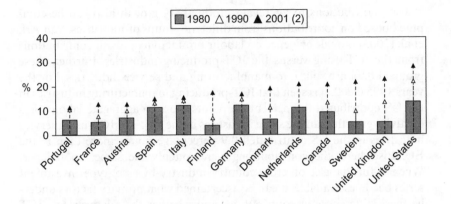

Source: OECD (2003) (data for 2001 are from 2000 for some countries, see source for details).

Figure 12.3 ICT investment as a share of total non-residential investment

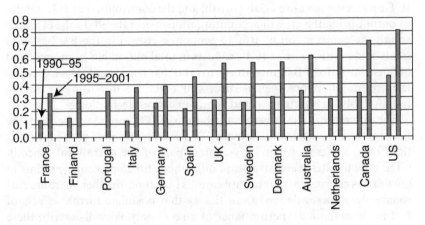

Source: OECD (2003).

Figure 12.4 Contribution of ICT capital use to GDP growth

From Figure 12.4, it can be seen that the contribution of the services of ICT capital to output growth, as published by OECD (2003), is largest in the US. This is also true for alternative computations, for example whether calculated by Colecchia and Schreyer (2001), or Daveri (2002). Furthermore, in the US, the UK, Denmark and Finland the contribution of ICT capital accelerated from the early to the late 1990s.[3]

The contributions to aggregate productivity growth also can be computed based on contributions from different groups of industries. Van Ark et al. (2003) provide evidence on labour productivity growth contributions from the ICT-using versus the ICT-producing industries. Further, these grouped data are split into manufacturing and service industries. For the years 1995–2000, it is seen that ICT-producing manufacturing industries in the US contributed 0.5 percentage points more to aggregate labour productivity growth than the same industries in the EU. The ICT-using service industries in the US contributed 0.9 percentage points more than in the EU. Elsewhere, the contributions were roughly the same, on balance. When a full dataset of cross-country industry-by-asset-type investment series becomes available, it can be ascertained what primary factors underlie these differences in contribution, and whether the relatively low ICT investment in the EU is more pronounced in the ICT-using sectors.

12.2.4   ICT Investment and Economic Welfare

In the previous sections we documented the arithmetic contribution of the ICT-producing sector to GDP growth, and the contribution of ICT capital to output using the growth accounting framework. Based on the evidence so far, the contribution of ICT to economic growth in the EU has been small because the share of ICT products in total output has been small and because the ratio of ICT investment to GDP has been small. The EU countries, overall, have not been as successful as the US in putting to use the rapidly evolving information and communications technologies.

The difference in the growth contribution of ICT capital use between the EU and the US seems small, around 0.25 percentage points per year during the 1990s, and can explain only a small part of the overall difference in GDP growth rates. Yet a structural difference of 0.25 percentage points in growth has enormous welfare implications over time. Further, there are reasonable hypotheses derived from theory that postulate further effects of ICT investment on the performance of an economy. We will describe these hypotheses where the adoption of ICT leads to a temporary increase in TFP growth, and the possibility of a permanent increase in TFP growth.

The use of ICT possibly has implications beyond the direct returns flowing to firms that make use of its services in production. The technology increases the efficiency of communication and information processing throughout the economy, which has a potential effect of lowering transactions costs, and increasing the productivity of knowledge workers. We will discuss these two effects of ICT use in turn.

Overall, lower costs of communications and better processing of information allow more efficient matching of supply and demand in many markets. Further, many new markets become feasible because the transactions cost wedge is no longer prohibitive. The benefits show up not only in increased productivity in production processes that involve logistics-intensive supply chains, but also increased utilisation rates of many production factors, such as hotel rooms or airline seats. As ICT diffuses throughout the economy, more and more markets will function more efficiently, leading to a gradual shift to a higher level of productivity.

Another implication of lower transactions costs may be that as markets become more transparent customers more readily switch to competing suppliers. The implication of this possible change in market structure for the incentive to invest in ICT will be discussed in section 3.

The second potential effect of increased ICT usage is the increase in efficiency of the knowledge production process. Knowledge-creating activities typically benefit from an increase in efficiency with which information is gathered and processed. Researchers have more data at their disposal and can process these data much more efficiently. ICT, in addition, allows researchers to carry out their research in a way that was unthinkable only a few years ago. A good example is the Human Genome project. It was immense computing power that enabled the researchers to actually map each individual human gene. Further, managers of large R&D portfolios, for example at software or pharmaceutical concerns, can use ICT to track competing R&D projects, and selectively prune, weed and nurture them to provide better overall performance (see Cockburn et al. 1999).

The diffusion and absorption of newly developed knowledge is an important input into further knowledge creation. Because of ICT it is much easier to disseminate new knowledge and to absorb it. And in the literature it is common to suppose that the efficiency of the knowledge creation process is enhanced by an increase in diffusion and absorption intensity (see Romer 1989; Jones and Williams 1998 and Eaton and Kortum 1999). Indeed, the development of the World Wide Web by CERN was first initiated in order to speed up and broaden the dissemination of new knowledge.

In standard endogenous growth models, an increase in the efficiency of knowledge production will permanently boost TFP growth rates, all else being equal.

While many of the above hypotheses concerning links between ICT and TFP growth have not yet found empirical support, they are appealing enough to lead one to think that the 0.25 percentage point lag in ICT capital contribution calculated in growth accounts is a lower bound on the gains to be had by boosting ICT investment in the EU. Furthermore, one need not even appeal to external effects or wedges between private and social returns to ICT investments made by firms to make a case for policy to boost ICT in the EU. If the ICT uptake of business firms is low because expected private returns are suppressed by restrictive policies, then a careful re-balancing of the policy trade-offs may lead to welfare improvements.

12.3 COMPETITION, ICT INVESTMENT AND MARKET DYNAMICS

The main point of this section is to construct an analytical device to explore the relationship between competitive environment and investment in risky technologies, such as ICT. In the model developed below, the competitive environment is taken to influence the conduct of firms. Firms take into account each other's behaviour and make simultaneous decisions regarding entry, investment, and output quantity or price. Aggregate output, prices, market structure, investment in a risky technology (ICT) and productivity growth are outcomes of the model, given assumptions about product demand, the costs of investment and the effect of successful investment on the firm-level marginal cost of production. The competitive environment is modelled with a parameter that describes what a firm believes will be the reaction of its competitors to its actions. Building on recent theoretical insights we show that this parameter is a genuine measure for competitive pressure. The model then allows predictions to be made about investment in risky technology, as well as predictions about reallocation of market shares and distributions of productivity.

12.3.1 A Model of Competition and Risky Technology

The representative industry is populated by profit maximising firms that pay a fixed entry fee e in order to produce with the default relatively inefficient technology such that marginal costs are c_H. On entry the i-th firm could invest an additional fixed amount F_i in order to have a chance to acquire a more efficient production technology that yields a reduction in marginal cost to $c_L < c_H$. We assume F_i to be uniformly distributed on the interval $[\underline{F}, \bar{F}]$. This heterogeneity in fixed investment costs could be caused by variety of sources, such as differences in access to capital or skilled labour. Successful acquisition and implementation of a new technology occurs with probability φ, conditional on making the investment F_i.

The demand side of our model captures the notion that competition takes place among firms producing similar, substitutable, goods and that substitutability between different groups of goods is more limited than within groups. In particular we choose a demand function for our representative industry where the expenditure share on goods from that industry is independent of the price level, although the revenue share of a firm in that industry may respond sharply to competition. Formally, the inverse demand curve for the industry is $p = aQ^{-1}$ where Q is aggregate production of the n firms active in the industry. This formulation is useful when trying to build a model that captures micro-level features as well as macro outcomes, for example as in Klette and Kortum (2002). In their model, expenditure shares for each type of differentiated goods are constant, but within each type, the best producer captures the full market. Our model can be thought of as an extension that allows the market shares for each type to be split among producers with different costs, but as a simplification because it abstracts from the interactions between the different groups or types of goods.

The advantage of this demand formulation when modelling the effects of competition is that the demand elasticity facing the aggregate suppliers in a market does not vary with number of competitors or level of technology. With a linear demand curve, monopolists operate on the elastic portion of the demand curve, giving them an added incentive to gain a cost reduction through innovation (see e.g. Hinloopen 1997). Similarly, when prices are low and many suppliers are already active, demand is inelastic, reducing incentives for innovation. With a model where the substitution elasticity of demand for differentiated products is used as an indicator of competitiveness, the 'love-of-variety' or scale effect clouds the results related to competition (see e.g. Blanchard and Giavazzi 2003 and results from Aghion et al. 2005). With our demand specification, we consider the effect of competitive pressure within an industry on the incentives of firms to invest in a risky technology, while abstracting from the change in aggregate expenditures on products in the industry owing to changes in competition and technology.

To capture the notion of competitive pressure within the industry in our model we introduce the following conjectural derivative (see Hicks 1935):

$$\lambda = \frac{\partial Q_{-i}}{\partial q_i} \tag{12.1}$$

The parameter λ, which varies from -1 to 1, captures the belief of firms as to the change in output of all other firms in the industry in response to a change in their own output. Positive values of λ correspond to (believed) cooperative behaviour of all rival firms: if firm i lowers its production it conjectures that total production of all other firms will drop as well. Likewise, negative values of λ reflect (believed) competitive behaviour of rivals: if firm i lowers its production it believes that total production of all other firms in the industry will increase.[4]

Specific values of λ correspond to well-known market types. If $\lambda = 0$, each firm maximises its profits assuming all other firms keep their production level constant, the well-known Cournot conjecture, while the industry acts collectively as a monopolist if $\lambda = 1$. Indeed, the lower is λ the more competitive is the industry.

We thus propose λ to be our indicator for competitive pressure. Boone (2001) specifies four conditions that have to be met for an indicator to be a genuine measure for this competitive pressure. The idea behind these four criteria is that an increase in competitive pressure highlights efficiency differences between firms. In particular it must be that (1) there is a limit value of the indicator such that firms are not affected by competitors' actions, (2) if competition becomes more intense profits of the least efficient firm fall, (3) if competition becomes more intense profits of the most efficient firm increase, provided that this most efficient firm uses a technology that is superior enough (i.e. efficient) to the technology used by the next most efficient firm, and (4) if competition becomes more intense profits of all firms fall if all firms use the same production technology. It is straightforward to show that in our model λ meets the Boone criteria (see Part B of the Appendix).[5]

In Part A of the Appendix the equilibrium of the model is presented in detail. This is determined through the interaction of profit maximising firms, given technology, the market demand curve, and a zero expected profit condition determining entry, exit and risk investment.

12.3.2. Investment in New Technology

Because of the analytical complexity of the model we resort to numerical simulations in order to illustrate comparative statics. Given the parameter λ, the fixed entry costs, e, the distribution of costs to innovate, $[\underline{F}, \bar{F}]$, the chance of being successful ϕ, and the marginal costs of successful and unsuccessful firms c_L and c_H, the fraction of firms undertaking innovative activities is determined along with the number of firms and the output levels of high and low cost firms.

Figure 12.5 shows how the fraction of firms undertaking innovation, α, varies with intensity of competition, λ, for different values of the marginal costs of successful innovators. Free entry and exit determines the equilibrium number of firms. For the value of the other parameters chosen, the fraction of innovators increases monotonically with the intensity of competition. The fraction of firms attempting to innovate increases as the difference between c_L and c_H increases. With other choices of exogenous parameters, flat spots occur at high λ and $\alpha = 0$, or low λ and $\alpha = 1$.

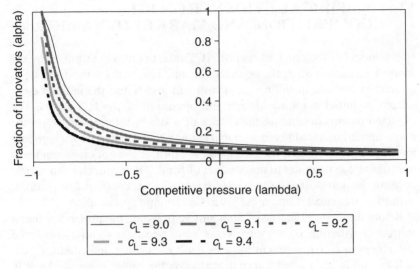

Note: Simulation with $a = 50$, $e = .5$, F in $[0,2]$, $\varphi = .2$, $C_H = 10$.

Figure 12.5   Share of innovating firms

12.3.3 Implications for Market Shares and Productivity

We can consider the effect of a change in competitive pressure on productivity growth for the industry as a whole. To compute productivity growth we have to introduce a time dimension into our model. It is assumed that only technology c_H exists prior to some initial date. At that point, the possibility of undertaking the risky investment falls out of the sky like manna from heaven. An investment may or may not bear fruit in the ensuing period.

The model predicts that aggregate productivity increases both because productivity increases within firms that are successful innovators, and because successful firms gain market share at the expense of unsuccessful ones. The market share of successful innovators shows a similar relationship to competitive intensity as the share of innovators.

Note that the output growth of firms that are successful in adopting the innovation is higher with more intense competition, and therefore also with increases in the share of firms attempting innovation. By contrast, even though the share of firms attempting innovation increases if the fixed cost distribution, $[\underline{F}, \bar{F}]$, shifts to the left, the growth in output of those firms that are successful does not increase relative to high-cost firms. This feature provides a path for distinguishing the effects of investment costs on adoption rates from the effects of competitive intensity.

12.4   EMPIRICAL EVIDENCE ON ICT, COMPETITION, AND MARKET DYNAMICS

In the model in the previous section, ICT investment is determined by the costs of investing and by the expected returns. The costs are the direct costs of purchasing and installing the investment goods and the indirect costs related to initial planning, design and operation of the ICT assets. The expected returns depend on the chance of a successful innovation, on the mark-up and on the difference in market size between firms with high and low costs. In the model, the parameter λ captures the notion of competitive pressure as it applies to the conduct of firms. The parameter was shown to move the mark-up and the market-size incentives in opposite directions, with the latter effect dominating given the demand specification.

Before discussing the role of competitive pressure, the possibility that a shifted distribution of resource costs across countries causes observed differences in ICT investment must be dealt with. First, information technology goods are traded internationally, so the direct price of the ICT investment goods should not vary significantly around the globe. However, the inputs that are complementary to the investment good may differ in price across countries. Evidence on the skill-bias of technology backs up the assertion that the availability of ICT-ready workers may be a bottleneck for rapid investment. We use an indicator of years of education as a measure of worker skills, which may not properly capture the ability of workers to use ICT capital. Recent work using linked employer–employee data (e.g. Abowd et al. forthcoming) may improve our understanding of worker heterogeneity and technology adoption. The run-up in wages for computer professionals in the US in the late 1990s does point out that the US did not have unlimited supply of complementary workers.[6] Another issue that resonates with EU policy makers, is the supposed shortage of 'entrepreneurs'. Empirically, it is difficult to find an exogenous measure of 'entrepreneurial supply' that does not reflect differences in regulations on entrepreneurship.

Financing conditions also may affect the total cost of an ICT investment. As a first approximation, international capital markets and fully mobile capital set a common interest rate. However, even if local capital market conditions differ, the ratio of ICT investment to total investment would not be strongly affected. For the same reason differences in corporate tax rates, although a hot policy discussion in the EU, should not affect ICT investment intensity. A more important source of variation in investment costs arises because much of the activity in ICT takes place in firms that do not have access to traditional capital markets and must rely instead on alternative sources of funds, such as venture capital. We find a significant effect of an index of availability of venture capital on ICT investment, but consider the role of venture capital to remain an open area for further research. In a review of the importance of the financial system for growth, Rajan and Zingales (2001) are unwilling to anoint the financial sector of any particular OECD country as the optimal model for promoting growth, and find positive features in different countries. Availability of venture capital is shown in Figure 12.6.

So far, no research has shown that differences in costs of investing in ICT explain much of the difference in ICT intensity in the EU, although we do find a significant role for the venture capital indicator in some specifications. Fortunately, the model provides a means of distinguishing a shift in the distribution of investment costs from a shift in the competitive pressure parameter. If investment costs differ across countries, but competitive pressure plays no role, then adoption rates of ICT will be correlated with costs, but not with indicators of reallocation. On the other hand, if investment costs do not vary, but competitive intensity differences are driving the differences in innovation, then ICT uptake would be correlated with resource reallocation to successful firms.

The model shows how the expected profit from a risky innovative investment increases as competitive pressure increases. The increase in profit occurs because the increase in market share that the low-cost producer achieves when competitiveness increases is not fully offset by a reduction in mark-up. It should be noted that this increased incentive for investment

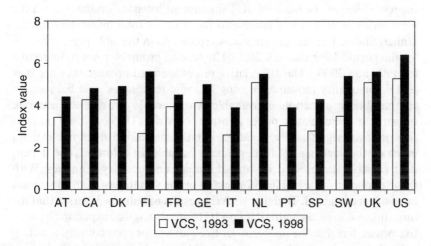

Source: World Economic Forum (1993, 1998).

Figure 12.6   Availability of venture capital

happens whether or not actual profitability of the investment is positive, but occurs based on the difference in outcomes between undertaking the investment or not. So, for example the investments made by banks for cash dispensers were necessary to retain market share, and did not demonstrably add to the bottom line. However, the benefits greatly flowed to consumers, in the form of consumer surplus.

In the simple specification in the next section, we attempt to explain the movement of ICT investment as a share of total investment, across countries and over time, by time-series of ICT asset prices relative to other investment goods and cross-country indicators of competitive pressure. Following this, we add two indicators that proxy for ICT investment costs not captured by the relative deflator, namely an indicator of venture capital availability and the number of years of schooling. Finally, we use information on market dynamics to distinguish the path of competition versus investment costs in a two-equation model. Unfortunately, owing to data availability, these estimates could only be made for a subset of the countries.

12.4.1　ICT Investment Intensity and Competition

The first set of results, presented in Table 12.1, shows parameters of a regression, with the ratio of nominal investment in ICT assets to total nominal gross fixed capital formation for 13 OECD countries as the dependent variable. The share of ICT in investment is expected to increase as the relative price of ICT assets declines. The first column of Table 12.1 shows the regression of the panel of ICT investment intensity on the (log of) the price index of ICT assets relative to the price of total investment for the United States. The first group of rows (panel A) in the table present results for the period 1991 through 2000. The second group of rows show results for 1995 and 2000.[7] The US relative prices are used because they are corrected for quality movements using hedonic techniques, and because no comparable information is available which would provide an accurate measure of these relative prices in other countries. The coefficient on relative prices is significantly negative, but the regression does not explain much of the variance of the dependent variable. In column 2, the dependent variable is regressed on time dummies and country dummies. With these 'explanatory' variables, 97 per cent of the variance of ICT investment intensity is explained. Together with the results of column 3, we see that the time dimension of the panel data on ICT intensity is well explained by relative prices, but that the intercept, or fixed effect, for each country is not.

In the next four columns of the table, the ICT investment share is explained by relative ICT prices, one of the hierarchically defined product market regulation indicators, and the employment protection indicator.

Table 12.1 ICT intensity regression results

Dependent variable: ratio of ICT to total investment	1	2	3	4	5	6	7	8	9	10
PANEL A										
Rel. P_{ICT} deflator	-2.79		-2.79	-2.48	-2.51	-2.52	-2.52	-1.60	-2.48	-2.61
t-stat	3.7		12.1	5.2	5.4	5.4	5.5	2.9	5.2	6.0
Prodreg					-1.36					
t-stat					2.1					
ADM						-.91				
t-stat						2.7				
BSTART							-.76			
t-stat							3.3			
BSTART2								-1.18		
t-stat								3.1		
EPL				-2.71	-2.45	-2.42	-2.38	-2.33	-2.72	-1.88
t-stat				13.8	10.5	10.8	11.0	10.1	11.0	7.7
EDU									.00	
t-stat									.1	
VCS										1.54
t-stat										5.2
dummies	–	c, t	c	–	–	–	–	–	–	–
R^2	.10	.92	.92	.64	.65	.66	.67	.66	.64	.70
130 Obs.										
PANEL B										
Rel. P_{ICT} deflator	-2.99		-2.99	-2.50	-2.57	-2.58	-2.59	-1.2	-2.54	-2.67
t-stat	1.5		6.6	2.0	2.1	2.1	2.2	.8	2.0	2.3

Table 12.1 (continued)

Dependent variable: ratio of ICT to total investment	1	2	3	4	5	6	7	8	9	10
Prodreg					−1.71					
t-stat					1.1					
ADM						−1.09				
t-stat						1.3				
BSTART							−1.09			
t-stat							2.0			
BSTART2								−1.3		
t-stat								1.5		
EPL				−3.08	−2.74	−2.72	−2.59	−2.64	−2.93	−2.32
t-stat				6.5	4.9	5.0	5.5	4.8	4.9	3.9
EDU									−1.6	
t-stat									.4	
VCS										1.39
t-stat										2.0
dummies	–	c, t	c	–	–	–	–	–	–	–
R²	.08	.98	.98	.68	.70	.70	.73	.71	.68	.73
26 Obs.										

Notes:
Dependent variable: Nominal ICT investment/Total investment, source Van Ark et al. (2002).
Countries: Austria, Canada, Denmark, Finland, France, Germany, Italy, Netherlands, Portugal , Spain, Sweden, UK, USA.
Time: Panel A, 1991–2000; Panel B, 1995–2000.
Regressors: P_{ICT} , authors' calculations from BEA data; Prodreg, ADM, BSTART, BSTART2, EPL: Nicoleti et al. (1999); EDU, VCS: OECD and World Economic Forum, made available by Gust and Marquez (2004).

Information on competition comes from the OECD International Regulation Database. This database is an impressive collection of country responses to a set of more than a thousand questions on the state of regulation in labour and product markets (see Nicoleti et al. 1999). Figure 12.7 presents some indexes for product market regulation. The indicators are built up hierarchically from the underlying questions in steps. The final index of product market regulation (PRODREG) is a weighted average of sub-indexes of state control, barriers to entrepreneurship, trade restrictions, economic regulation and administrative regulation (ADM). The index of barriers to entrepreneurship and administrative regulation in turn are made up of more detailed indexes, and both contain the indicator for administrative burdens on startups (BSTART). A second indicator on administrative burdens, generated by the World Economic Forum (1993, 1998), is available for two time periods. The employment protection legislation index is also built up from responses to individual questions, split into rules affecting regular contracts (EPL) and those affecting temporary contracts.[8] The EPL indicator is available for 1990 and 1998.

As shown, the employment protection indicator is always significantly negative and explains much of the variance of investment. Adding an indicator of product market regulation does not add much to the overall fit. In general, the more narrowly the indicator is focused on regulation of startups, the more significant is the effect.

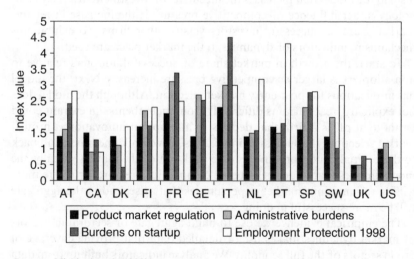

Source: Nicoletti et al. (1999b).

Figure 12.7   Indicators of product and labour market regulation

Finally, columns 9 and 10 in Table 12.1 add indicators of investment costs to the specification with employment protection legislation. The number of years of schooling has no significant effect, although in a specification without the regulatory indicator it does show up positively. The indicator of the venture capital availability (World Economic Forum 1993, 1998) has a significant positive effect, adds a bit to the variance of ICT investment intensity explained, over that with EPL alone. Further, inclusion of the venture capital indicator reduces the magnitude of the effect of regulation by about 20 per cent.

Because the explanatory variables do not vary much over time, if at all, the cross-country vector of these indicators is merged into the country-by-time investment data.[9] The statistical significance of these indicators may be overstated using OLS, as described by Moulton (1986). As a robustness test, the regression is estimated for the 13 countries and two time periods. The columns represent the same specifications as in the top group of rows, and the results are qualitatively very similar, although only the startup regulations remain significant in regressions that also include EPL.

12.4.2 The Role of Market Dynamics

The model makes predictions about differences at the firm level and in the aggregate resulting from differences in competitive pressure. The mechanism in the model that increases the incentive for investment in a risky technology under influence of competitive pressure is the increase in relative market share of successful investors versus other firms. To exhibit this mechanism, indicators of dynamics in the market place are used.

To start, the growth in market share of successful adopters relative to non-adopters is larger as competitive pressure increases. Next, the model has implications for post-entry market selection. Although the model does not explicitly treat entrants differently from incumbents, an entrant could be thought of as a firm that decides to attempt an innovation. Through market selection, the successful innovators grow, while the others fall back to their initial conditions, in this case back out of the market. Finally, the model implies that under heightened competitive pressure, firms are more willing to jump into market opportunities that arise, and in the aggregate will be more successful in doing so.

The empirical evidence we use to build aggregate or sectoral indicators of market dynamics makes use of detailed data that provide coverage of broad sectors of the full economy. We analyse indicators built up from data on production and employment at individual firms over time. Correlations between these indicators and investment intensity should strengthen the evidence that the mechanism of increased incentives through easy resource reallocation drives ICT investment intensity.

12.4.3   Dynamics at the Firm Level

For a group OECD countries, sectoral time-series indicators have been created using firm-level business registries and surveys. The data have been constructed under auspices of the OECD Economic Department by researchers in each country using confidential micro data from national statistical offices (see Bartelsman et al. 2003b, and Barnes et al. 2001). The data portray firm demographics (firms' size distribution, entry and exit rates of firms, and chances of survival), the evolution of employment, the distribution of productivity across firms, and the contribution to sectoral productivity growth from resource reallocation. While the exploration of these rich data has just started, a few surprising stylised facts have already emerged that are relevant to the story in this chapter.

Preliminary exploration of the OECD dataset on firm dynamics indeed has revealed that the process is more complex than looking at entry and exit statistics alone (see OECD Economic Outlook 2000). The distance from an entrant to the average incumbent size is sizeable, as is the post-entry growth of surviving firms. This last is shown in Figure 12.8: the rows show the rate of growth of employment in a cohort of firms over five years following their entry, for manufacturing and services as well as ICT goods producers

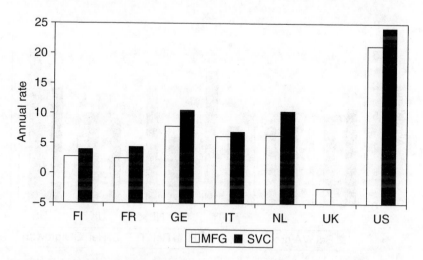

Source: Bartelsman et al. (forthcoming).

Figure 12.8   Employment growth over 5 years of entry cohort

and ICT service producers. The growth rate for the actual survivors would be even larger; the data in the figure show the total employment in surviving firms, divided by the employment in all firms that entered five years earlier. In the regression explaining ICT investment intensity, we use the five-year employment growth of surviving entrants for the service sector (5yrEmp).

The next dynamics indicators are derived from longitudinal production statistics in the various countries. Using a tightly coordinated methodology, researchers with access to such micro-level panel datasets ran the same computer code to generate indicators of productivity and market dynamics. Although the underlying sampling methodology of the micro data may vary across countries, many features of the produced indicators, such as method of deflation, outlier correction, definitions of productivity, and so on, were identical (see Bartelsman and Barnes 2001 for a description of the methodology and an overview of the indicators produced). For example, in making comparisons of total factor productivity (TFP) across countries for a particular sector, they were able to impose the same production function parameters, based on average expenditure shares across countries, on all the firms in any country for that sector. Using the micro data, means of certain variables were created for each quartile of the cross sectional distribution of that variable for a particular year and a particular country. In Figure 12.9 for example, the mean growth of value added in the bottom quartile of firms by value added for total manufacturing, is subtracted

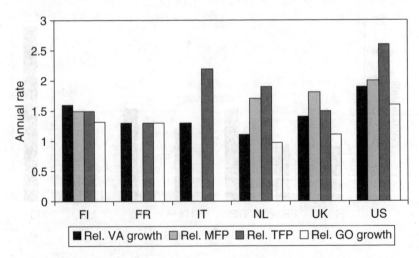

Source: Bartelsman et al. (forthcoming).

Figure 12.9   Indicators of micro-level dynamics

from the growth at the top quartile.[10] The next two indicators show levels of productivity in the top quartile of the productivity distribution compared to the bottom quartile. The productivity measures are TFP (deflated gross output per aggregate unit of capital/labour/materials) and MFP (here defined as deflated value added per aggregated unit of capital/labour). The TFP indicators show how the distribution of TFP growth of firms in an industry may be wider in certain countries than in other. For the purpose of our model, this indicator would increase if the percentage of firms adopting the new technology was initially small, then increased to cover a full quartile of firms. The indicator of the relative growth in output of fast and slow growing firms does tell us more about the flexibility of resource reallocation and is affected by an increase in the share of ICT adopters only if this is caused by more competition. Therefore the regressions use the growth of value added or gross output in the fastest quartile of firms relative to the slowest quartile (Q4/Q1 VA, Q4/Q1 GO, respectively).

12.4.4 Empirical Evidence on Dynamics and ICT

Table 12.2 shows some results from a two-equation model of ICT investment. The first equation looks very similar to those presented in Table 12.1, except that the effects of the competition indicators are split. Product market regulation is taken to affect the mark-up. The resource reallocation incentive for investment is proxied by the dynamic indicator showing how quickly the fastest growing firms gain market share relative to slow (or negative) growth firms. Finally, the equation includes indicators for cost, in this case the relative ICT investment price and the venture capital indicator.

The second equation explains the dynamic indicator as a function of employment protection legislation. Because employment protection rules make it costly for firms to shed workers, and make firms reluctant to add employees for current needs in the face of an uncertain future, lax EPL is expected to lead to a wider distribution in output growth among firms. Also, EPL will reduce the desire of entering firms to attempt to grow rapidly. The costs of investment do not play a role in this equation.

In the second equation, the model predicts a negative sign on the coefficient of EPL. In the first equation, venture capital should receive a positive sign and relative ICT prices a negative sign. The dynamic indicator is a proxy for the ease of resource reallocation, which provides a positive incentive to ICT investment in the model. Finally, the coefficient on product market regulation may be ambiguous. In the model, mark-ups increase with regulation, but resource reallocation becomes more difficult.

Table 12.2   ICT intensity and market dynamics

2-equation	Dyn 1		Dyn 2		Dyn 3	
System 3SLS	Eq 1	Eq 2	Eq 1	Eq 2	Eq 1	Eq 2
	ICT_shr	Q1/Q4,GO	ICT_shr	5yrEmp	ICT_shr	Q1/Q4 VA
Rel. P_{ICT}	−2.47		−3.28		−2.48	
t-stat	1.9		3.0		1.3	
BSTART	−2.96		−1.04		−.33	
t-stat	3.5		1.5		.3	
VCS	1.16		−.89		.99	
t-stat	1.4		.9		.8	
Dyn. var	.12		.66		.13	
t-stat	2.9		3.9		2.4	
EPL		−10.87		−5.25		−17.60
t-stat		2.1		4.2		3.8
No. OBS	10	10	12	12	12	12
R^2	.88	.35	.90	.64	.63	.60

Notes:
Two-equation model, eq 1: ICT intensity, eq 2: dynamics variable dyn 1, dyn 2, or dyn 3. Dynamics variables; 1: Average gross output growth in top quartile of firms relative to bottom quartile (Fin, Fra, Neth, UK, US). 2: Employment growth in entrant cohort over 5 years, service sector (Fin, Fra, Ger, Ita, Neth, US). 3: Average value added growth in top quartile of firms, relative to bottom quartile (Fin, Fra, Ita, Neth, UK, US); Regressors: see notes for Table 12.1.

To the extent the latter effect is fully captured by the dynamics indicator, the coefficient on regulation in the first equation should be positive. However, the quality of the proxy may be such that the regulatory indicator picks up the effect of reallocation as well, possibly resulting in a negative sign.

The equations are estimated for five or six countries for which the dynamics indicators are available. The regressions presented in Table 12.1 have also been run for the relevant subsets of countries with similar results to all 13 countries, but the results are not presented here. Table 12.2 shows the results of the system of equations for three dynamics indicators. As may be seen, EPL is significantly negative for all three dynamics indicators. The dynamics indicator used on the left-hand side of equation two shows up with a significant positive sign when included as an explanatory variable in the first equation in all three cases. The venture capital indicator always has a positive sign, but is only slightly significant in one of the cases. Overall, the results of the system do not contradict the prediction made by the model.

12.5 CONCLUSIONS

The Lisbon Council identified the 'transition to the Knowledge-based Society' as an important path to economic progress. To underscore the importance of this transition, the National Reports on Structural Reforms submitted by EU member states to the Economic Policy Committee will contain information on the production and use of ICT, on its economic impact, and on policy measures taken to speed up its adoption. Much statistical work is presently being undertaken to construct comparable data on production and use of ICT and its impact on firms, workers and households. Until such time as these coherent and comparable data become available, it seems premature to draw strong policy conclusions.

Nonetheless, based on the available cross-country indicators, the intuition as highlighted by the model, and the empirical results, an evaluation can be made of generic areas of policy. First, policy should be aimed at reducing costs of investing in ICT by stimulating the further development of factors that are complementary to ICT up-take by business. Next, policy should be aimed at increasing the expected benefits of firms that invest in ICT, particularly by ensuring that demand-side wishes for better price/quality of goods and service are translated rapidly into market share gains by innovative supplying firms.

Another area identified in our empirical work as affecting ICT investment is the availability of financing. In a truly integrated EU market, no local rules or national idiosyncrasies in regulation or supervision should affect the availability of venture capital funding. Only the quality of fundable projects should affect the price of available funding.

Much of the literature on national innovations systems is aimed at improving the supply conditions of inputs necessary for innovation, and can be used as a guideline to find further ideas for enhancing availability of skilled labour and financial capital. Also, recommendations are to be found on how the innovations system can be set up to improve availability of existing (international) knowledge to local researchers in order to increase the efficacy of their efforts. In our model, this can be thought of as a means of increasing the probability that an innovative investment is successful. Indeed, a country that increases this probability will have higher ICT uptake, all else being equal. Unfortunately, in much of the analysis, it is never made clear why these knowledge spillovers would not be available to researchers with proper incentives to innovate. In our opinion, this supposed supply problem will probably disappear once the complementary inputs are available and the demand for innovation is allowed to function adequately.

The model is very explicit about the role of competitive pressure in product markets on the incentives for ICT uptake. In particular, having a market environment that selects firms that produce efficiently or firms that provide a good price–quality balance to their customers, may be the least-cost method to boost uptake of risky technologies. Product market regulations that limit entry or reduce the ability of customers to make informed choices should thus be removed, as shown by our econometric results.

The empirical results point to a significant role for employment protection legislation. As expected, hiring and firing costs reduce the distribution of output growth rates of firms in an industry. This in turn reduces the incentive for firms to invest in innovative activities because relative market share gains of successful innovators are reduced. Of course, this does not imply that all innovation is stifled. In fact, gradual upgrading of the workforce, of the production process, and of product quality, may well become the trajectory of choice for firms in countries with strong EPL. In terms of our model, this means investing in innovations where the probability of technological success is high and predictable. If competitors also innovate, the need for large market share shifts is reduced. With limited product market competition, the mark-up will be high enough to cover the investment cost as well. Although we are not able to provide empirical evidence as yet, such a path of innovation may lead to productivity and output growth rates that on average do not lag much over the long run, but will lead to a sustained gap in productivity levels over countries where firms push forward the technology frontier with risky investment.

NOTES

1. It should be noted that the sharp deceleration in ICT prices of the mid-1990s has ended, and price declines have now reverted to the historical pattern.
2. Nordhaus (2002) provides a breakdown of how the rewards to productivity improvements accrue to consumers, workers, and stockholders.
3. While most accounts show an acceleration of the ICT contribution to output between the first and second half of the 1990s in the US, some do not. See, e.g., Meijers and Hollanders (2003).
4. The specification in equation 12.1 is static in nature, although the notion of a conjectural derivative is inherently dynamic. As shown by Dockner (1992), Lapham and Ware (1994) and Cabral (1995) however, the outcomes of dynamic models are mimicked by static specifications including conjectural derivatives.
5. Note that the result of our model regarding the share of firms investing in risky technology as λ declines, is not the reason that λ fits the Boone criteria. If there were no technological choice in our model, but exogenous differences among firms in cost structures (the history of cost structures in Boone's model), then the four conditions that have to apply for λ to adequately represent intensity of competition still hold.
6. Using US CPS data from 1977 through 1999, authors' calculations show the premium for ICT-related occupations to rise from around 20 per cent to over 30 per cent after 1994. The premium was calculated in a standard wage regression, controlling for education, experience, industry, gender, part-time work and year effects.

7. The regulatory indicators that are available in two separate years are used as a proxy for the closest year, i.e., the 1993 value of the startup burden indicator is used for 1995, and the 1998 value for 2000.
8. When both EPL indicators are included in the regression, the temporary contracts have an insignificant effect on ICT investment. In the results presented we use the indicator for permanent contracts. All the results hold for the aggregate EPL index as well, although with a looser fit.
9. For the regressors with two observations, the first datapoint is used for that year and all prior years, the second datapoint for all ensuing years, and a moving weighted average for the years in between.
10. Actually, Figure 12.9 shows the average value of this indicator over a five-year period ending in 1997 (or earlier in some countries).
11. The second-order condition requires that $Q^H_{-i} > \lambda q^H$, where $Q^H_{-i} = Q - q^H = n(1 - \alpha\phi)q^L + (n\alpha\phi - 1)q^H$.
12. The second-order condition states that $Q^L_{-i} > \lambda q^L$, where $Q^L_{-i} = Q - q^L = (n(1 - \alpha\phi) - 1)q^L + n\alpha\phi q^H$.
13. In particular, the stability conditions require that $|-(1 - \alpha\varphi)[1 \pm a(1 + \lambda)/\sqrt{D^L}]/\alpha\varphi| < 1$, and $|-\alpha\varphi[1 \pm a(1 + \lambda)/\sqrt{D^H}]/(1 - \alpha\varphi)| < 1$.

BIBLIOGRAPHY

Abowd, J., J. Haltiwanger, J. Lane, P. Lengermann, R. Jarmin, K. McCue, K. McKinney and K. Sandusky (forthcoming), 'The relationship between human capital, productivity, and market value: Building up from micro evidence', in C. Corrado, J. Haltiwanger and D. Sichel (eds), *Measuring Capital in the New Economy*, Chicago: The Chicago University Press.

Aghion, P., N. Bloom, R. Blundell, R. Griffith and P. Howitt, (2005), 'Competition and innovation: An inverted U relationship', *Quarterly Journal of Economics*, **120**(2), pp. 701–28.

Barnes, M., J. Haskell and M. Maliranta (2001), 'The sources of productivity growth: Micro-level evidence for the OECD', mimeo.

Bartelsman, E.J. and M. Barnes (2001), 'Comparative analysis of firm-level data: A low marginal cost approach', mimeo, November.

Bartelsman, E J., A. Bassanini, J. Haltiwanger, R. Jarmin, S. Scarpetta and T. Schank (2004), 'The spread of ICT and productivity growth: Is Europe really lagging behind in the new economy?', in D. Cohen, P. Garibaldi and S. Scarpetta (eds), *The Information Economy: Productivity Gains and the Digital Divide*, Oxford: Oxford University Press, pp. 1–140.

Bartelsman, E.J. and M.E. Doms, (2000), 'Understanding productivity: Lessons from longitudinal micro data', *Journal of Economic Literature*, **38**(3), pp. 569–94.

Bartelsman, E.J., George van Leeuwen and Henry R. Nieuwenhuijsen (1998), 'Adoption of advanced manufacturing technology and firm performance in the Netherlands', *Economics of Innovation and New Technology*, **6**(4), pp. 291–312.

Bartelsman, E J., S. Scarpetta, and F. Schivardi (forthcoming), 'Comparative analysis of firm demographics and survival: Micro-level evidence for the OECD countries', *Industrial and Corporate Change*.

Bassanini, A. and Ekkehard Ernst (2001), 'Labor market institution, product market regulation, and innovation', *OECD Economics Department*, November.

Blanchard, O. and F. Giavazzi (2003), 'Macroeconomic effects of regulation and deregulation in goods and labor markets', *Quarterly Journal of Economics*, **118** (3), pp. 879–907.

Boone, J. (2001), 'Intensity of competition and the incentive to innovate', *International Journal of Industrial Organization*, **19** (5), pp. 705–27.

Broersma, L., R.H. McGuckin and M.P. Timmer (2003), 'The impact of computers on productivity in the trade sector. Explorations with Dutch microdata' *De Economist*, **151** (1), pp. 53–79.

Brynjolfsson, E. and L. Hitt (1994), 'Computers and economic growth: firm-level evidence', MIT Sloan School Working Paper, no. 3714.

Brynjolfsson, E. and L. Hitt (2003), 'Computing and productivity: Firm-level evidence', *Review of Economics and Statistics*, **85** (4), pp. 793–808.

Bureau of Economic Analysis (2002), *Survey of Current Business* (data release).

Cabral, L.M.B. (1995), 'Conjectural variations as a reduced form', *Economics Letters*, **49** (4), pp. 397–402.

Cockburn, I., R. Henderson and S. Stern (1999), 'The diffusion of science-driven drug discovery: Organizational change in pharmaceutical research', NBER Working Paper 7359, September.

Colecchia, A. and P. Schreyer (2002), 'ICT invesment and economic growth in the 1990s: Is the United States a unique case? A comparative study of nine OECD countries', *Review of Economic Dynamics*, **5** (2), pp. 408–42.

Crepon, B. and T. Heckel (2001), 'Computerisation in France: An evaluation based on individual company data', *Review of Income and Wealth*, **48** (1), pp. 77–98.

Dockner, E.J. (1992), 'A dynamic theory of conjectural variations', *Journal of Industrial Economics*, **40** (4), pp. 377–95.

Eaton, J. and S. Kortum (1999), 'International technology diffusion: Theory and measurement', *International Economic Review*, **40** (3), pp. 537–69.

Entorf, H. and F. Kramarz (1998), 'The impact of new technologies on wages: Lessons from matching panels on employees and on their firms', *Economics of Innovation and New Technology*, **5** (2–4), 165–97.

European Commission (2001), *Annual Report of the European Policy Committee*, Brussels.

Griliches, Z. and D.W. Jorgenson (1966), 'Sources of measured productivity change', *American Economic Review*, **56** (2), 50–61.

Gust, C. and J. Marquez (2004), International comparisons of productivity growth: The role of information technology and regulatory practices', *Labour Economics*, **11** (1), pp. 33–58.

Hicks, J.R. (1935), 'Annual survey of economic theory: The theory of monopoly', *Econometrica*, **3** (1), pp. 1–20.

Hinloopen, J. (1997), 'Subsidizing cooperative and noncooperative R&D in duopoly with spillovers', *Journal of Economics*, **66** (2), 151–75.

Jones, C.I. and J.C. Williams (1998), 'Measuring the social rate of return to R&D', *Quarterly Journal of Economics*, **113** (4), pp. 1119–35.

Klette, T.J. and S. Kortum (2002), 'Innovating firms and aggregate innovation', NBER Working Paper, No. 8819.

Lapham, B. and R. Ware (1994), 'Markov puppy dogs and other animals', *International Journal of Industrial Organization*, **12** (4), pp. 569–93.

Licht, G. and D. Moch (1999), 'Innovation and information technology in services', *Canadian Journal of Economics,* **32** (2), 363–83.

Lichtenberg, F.R. (1995), 'The output contributions of computer equipment and personnel: A firm-level analysis', *Economics of Innovation and New Technology*, **3** (3–4), 201–17.

Licklider, J.C.R. and R.W. Taylor (1968), 'The computer as a communication device', *Science and Technology*, April.

Merjers, H. and H. Hollanders (2003), 'Sources of growth: measuring the knowledge based economy', MERIT-In Fonomics Research Memorandum, No. 2003–029.

Moulton, B.R. (1986), 'Random group effects and the precision of regression estimates', *Journal of Econometrics*, **32** (3), pp. 385–97.

Nicoletti, G., S. Scarpetta and O. Boylaud (1999), 'Summary indicators of product market regulation with an extension to employment protection legislation', Economics Department Working Paper, No. 226.

Nordhaus, W.D. (2002), 'Productivity growth and the new economy', *Brookings Papers on Economic Activity*, 2, pp. 211–65.

OECD (2000), A New Economy? The Changing Role of Innovation and Information Technology in Growth, Paris: OECD.

OECD (2003), 'ICT and Economic Growth: Evidence from OECD Countries, Industries and Firms, Paris: OECD.

Rajan, R. and L. Zingales (2001), 'Financial systems, industrial structure, and growth', *Oxford Review of Economic Policy*, **17** (4), pp. 467–82.

Romer, P. (1990), 'Endogeneous technological change', *Journal of Political Economy*, **98** (5), pp. s71–s102.

Solow, R.M. (1987), 'We'd better watch out', *New York Times*, Book Review Section, 12 July, p. 36.

Van Ark, B., R. Inklaar and R.H. McGuckin (2003), 'ICT and productivity in Europe and the United States. Where do the differences come from?', The Conference Board Working Paper EPWP 03–5.

Van Ark, B., J. Melka, N. Mulder, M.P. Timmer and G. Ypma (2002), *ICT Investment and Growth Accounts for the European Union, 1980–2000*, Research Memorandum, GD–56. Growth and Development Centre.

World Economic Forum (1993), World Competitiveness Report 1993.

World Economic Forum (1998), Global Competitiveness Report 1998.

Yang, S. and E. Brynjolfsson (2001), 'Intangible assets and growth accounting: Evidence from computer investments', mimeo.

APPENDIX

A Model Equilibrium

Denoting firm-level profits by π, a firm i wants to invest in an attempt to acquire and implement the more efficient technology if the following holds:

$$\pi^H \leq \varphi \pi^L + (1 - \varphi)\pi^H - F_i, \qquad (12A.1)$$

or

$$F_i \leq \bar{F} \equiv \varphi(\pi^L - \pi^H), \qquad (12A.2)$$

where $\phi \in [0,1]$ is the probability of a successful innovation, where superscripts refer to the level of marginal cost and where $\bar{F}$ is the threshold cost level at which firms are indifferent between making the investment or not. The fraction of firms that attempts to adopt the new technology, α, is then equal to:

$$\alpha = \frac{1}{\bar{F} - \underline{F}} \int_{\underline{F}}^{\bar{F}} g(z)dz, \qquad (12A.3)$$

where $g(t)$ is the uniform probability density function. The fraction of firms that in equilibrium actually produce with the new technology thus equals $\varphi\alpha = \vartheta(\bar{F} - F)/(\bar{F} - \underline{F})$. In order for the market to exist we assume that $a > c_H > c_L$. The price-elasticity of demand is taken to be constant in order not to create perverse market size effects due to increased efficiency of production. In particular, $p = aQ^{-1}$, with $Q = \Sigma_{i=1}^{n}q_i$. If firm i has not invested in the efficiency-enhancing technology it maximises:

$$\pi_i^H = (p - c_H)q^H \qquad (12A.4)$$

over q_i, yielding:[11]

$$q^H = \frac{B^H - \sqrt{D^H}}{A^H}, \qquad (12A.5)$$

where $B^H = a[1 + \lambda - n(1 - \alpha\varphi)] + 2n^2c_H\alpha\varphi(1 - \alpha\varphi)q^L$, $A^H = -2n^2c_H(1 - \alpha\varphi)^2$, and $D^H = a^2[n(1 - \alpha\varphi) - (1 + \lambda)]^2 + 4an^2c_H\alpha\varphi(1 - \alpha\varphi)(1 + \lambda)q^L$. On the other hand, profits of a firm that has successfully adopted the new technology equal:

$$\pi_i^L = (p - c_L)q^L. \qquad (12A.6)$$

Maximising these over q^L gives as reaction function:[12]

$$q^L = \frac{B^L - \sqrt{D^L}}{A^L}, \qquad (12A.7)$$

Where $B^L = a[1 + \lambda - n\alpha\varphi] + 2n^2c_L\alpha\varphi(1 - \alpha\varphi)q^H$, $A^L = -2n^2c_L\alpha^2\varphi^2$, and $D^L = a^2[n\alpha\varphi - (1 + \lambda)]^2 + 4an^2c_L\alpha\varphi(1 - \alpha\varphi)(1 + \lambda)q^H$. In Figure 12.A1 reactions functions (12A.6) and (12A.7) are drawn for specific parameter values such that the concomitant stability conditions are also met.[13]

Entry and exit of new firms takes place to ensure that the expected profitability of firms in the market is zero. Because in the monopolistically

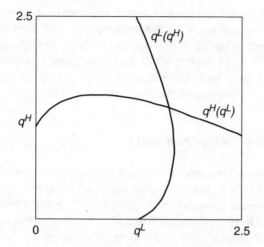

Figure 12.A.1   Reaction functions for a stable equilibrium ($a = 50$,
$\lambda = -1/4$, $n = 2$, $\alpha = 1/2$, $C_L = 10$, $C_H = 11$, $\varphi = 0.5$)

competitive model we have fixed marginal cost and mark-ups, the arbitrage condition, $\pi_i^H = e$, ensures that the quasi-rents cover the fixed entry fee e.

Solving for the number of firms that comprise the market, as a function of the equilibrium fraction of investors and the output levels of both types of firms, yields:

$$n = \frac{\alpha q^H}{[\alpha\varphi q^L + (1 - \alpha\varphi)q^H](e + c_H q^H)} \qquad (12A.8)$$

Note that equations (12A.3), (12A.5) and (12A.7), together with the arbitrage condition, jointly determine the equilibrium of the model. As this equilibrium is not tractable analytically we have to resort to numerical simulations for examining the comparative statics of the model.

B λ as a Measure of Competitiveness

Before we proceed we should check whether our proposed competitiveness measure is indeed a measure for competition. In particular the following must hold: (1) there exist a value of λ such that local monopolies emerge, (2) a decrease in λ lowers the profits of those firms using the inefficient technology, (3), a decrease in λ increases the profits of those firms using the efficient technology, provided that the difference between c_H and c_L is 'large enough', and (4), a decrease in λ lowers the profits of all firms if they all use the same technology. We consider these four conditions in turn.

The limiting value of λ that corresponds to the lowest intensity of competition is 1. In that case all firms act jointly as one monopolist. If $c_H > c_L$, we must have that $\partial \pi^H / \partial \lambda > 0$. There exists a value $d > 0$ such that if $c_H - c_L > d$ we must have that. $\partial \pi^L / \partial \lambda < 0$. If $c_H = c_L$ we must have that $\partial \pi / \partial \lambda < 0$.

C An Extension Towards Productivity

The model allows for a straightforward extension incorporating the notion of productivity. In particular, define productivity as $\tau_j = c_j^{-1}$, for $j = L, H$. Initially, aggregate productivity is given by c_H^{-1}, being equal to firm-level productivity. However, there is a fraction of firms that tries and succeeds in acquiring and implementing the more efficient production technology. Accordingly, aggregate productivity is a share-weighted average of firms with high and low costs (i.e. low and high productivity), with the shares being a firm's expenditures divided by the industry expenditure inputs:

$$\bar{\tau} = \frac{(1 - \alpha\varphi)q^H c_H \tau_H + \alpha\varphi q^L c_L \tau_L}{(1 - \alpha\varphi)q^H c_H + \alpha\varphi q^L c_L} = \frac{(1 - \alpha\varphi)q^H + \alpha\varphi q^L}{(1 - \alpha\varphi)q^H c_H + \alpha\varphi q^L c_L}. \tag{12A.9}$$

13. The impact of ICT investment on knowledge accumulation and economic growth*

Adriaan van Zon and Joan Muysken

13.1 INTRODUCTION

Ever since Solow's observation that computers are everywhere except in productivity data, people have been concerned about the apparent inability of ICT to live up to its productivity promises. However, the wide scope for application of ICT, specifically in data and signal processing, and more generally in organising and streamlining the way we do business and live our lives, suggests that ICT is essentially a general purpose technology (GPT). The GPT literature has provided a compelling story of why, after the advent of a drastic innovation, productivity growth may seriously fall behind expectations. In fact, most GPT papers suggest a slump in growth after the arrival of a technological breakthrough because of the redirection of R&D efforts needed to extend the new technology to make it more profitable to be adopted by its prospective users (Helpman and Trajtenberg, 1998; Greenwood and Jovanovic, 2000; David, 2000). It should not come as a big surprise then that it takes time before the full impact of ICT on productivity growth may be felt, since there are all kinds of adjustment problems to be dealt with first (Kiley, 1999). But now there is evidence that the impact is indeed building up, certainly so in the US (Oliner and Sichel, 2000; Stiroh, 2002), even though the measurement of total factor productivity (TFP) and the contribution of ICT is fraught with difficulties – see Jorgenson (2001) for a survey.

The question that immediately arises is: through which mechanisms would ICT in fact be able to influence productivity growth, and how important would each of these mechanisms be? There are five main candidates for such mechanisms, of which the first two are widely discussed. The first is that the ICT sector itself experiences both high output growth and

* We would like to thank Bas ter Weel and two anonymous referees for their constructive comments.

high productivity growth levels, and may function as an 'e-motor' of growth through its forward and backward linkages with the rest of the economy. For instance, Gordon (1999, 2000) has claimed that the productivity growth in the ICT sector indeed results in corresponding productivity growth in the rest of the economy, partly through spill-overs. However, the overall growth effect is limited because the ICT sector itself is relatively small.

Therefore, the second mechanism is also important. The non-ICT sectors use ICT goods and services to facilitate their production processes, and by doing so are able to increase productivity – see among others Bartelsman et al. (1998), Oliner and Sichel (2000, 2002), Nordhaus (2001) and Baily and Lawrence (2001). However Oliner and Sichel (1994) had claimed at an earlier date that expectations regarding the productivity effects of ICT use were exaggerated because of the relatively small proportion of ICT equipment in total equipment. Meanwhile, Moore's law and the ongoing price-drop in ICT equipment apparently have led to an increase in the ICT intensity in user industries (Jorgenson, 2001), that is, to ICT capital deepening and the labour productivity increases this entails.

The three other mechanisms through which ICT influences productivity growth have received much less attention in the literature. The third mechanism is that ICT improves the market process as such, and enables more flexible organisation of productive activities both at the micro- and at the macro-level. Borenstein and Saloner (2001) emphasise that this also holds for the labour market and this point has also been raised by Harris (1998) and Autor (2001) who have stressed the role of the Internet in promoting the (virtual) mobility of skilled labour, thus improving productivity at the aggregate level. A related point is raised by de Groot (2001), who claims that more efficient communication allows firms to concentrate on their core business and so to lower their fixed costs.

The fourth mechanism is that ICT becomes more productive the more users of ICT there are because of the network features usually associated with it. This notion has been corroborated recently by Meijers (2003), who found convincing empirical evidence that the contribution of ICT to productivity growth does go beyond its direct contribution as an ordinary factor of production, just like 'normal' capital. Meijers shows that his TFP measurements for a limited number of EU countries indicate a positive relation between TFP growth and the growth in ICT capital that includes software. This result is in line with the claim by Brynjolfsson and Hitt (2000) and van Leeuwen and van der Wiel (2003) that econometric estimations of the impact parameters estimated for ICT capital significantly outweigh the cost shares of ICT capital in total costs. The latter shares are the standard weights used in measuring the contribution of ICT growth to output growth.

Finally, the fifth mechanism recognises that ICT is instrumental in facilitating the creation of knowledge that can be used to produce new things or to produce old things more efficiently, and so extend the 'growth base' of the economy (Stehr, 1999; Bartelsman and Hinloopen, 2005).

In order to be able to analyse productivity growth, we need a framework that is as complete and consistent as reasonably possible, hence it must at least be able to accommodate the mechanisms mentioned above. As far as we know, such a framework does not exist. The purpose of this chapter then is to formulate such a framework in which all mechanisms and their potential interactions can be identified explicitly. Such a framework would also allow the formulation of a set of simultaneous econometric relations that, in principle at least, enables the actual measurement of the contribution to productivity growth of the individual mechanisms, just like a more ad hoc TFP measurement framework would do. However, we leave that for further research and concentrate on the structural model behind the measurement framework.

Its potential use as a measurement framework suggests that it may be worthwhile to stick as closely as possible to the standard framework of TFP measurement. This leads us to follow a neo-classical production function approach that explicitly allows for the effects of capital deepening, but also allow for the spill-over effects associated with ICT capital use, while acknowledging that the 'true' source of productivity growth is ultimately linked to (the productivity of) knowledge accumulation.[1] Therefore, we extend the Lucas (1988) model with ICT capital, both in final output production (to cover the first two mechanisms[2]), but also in the accumulation of knowledge (the fifth mechanism). The third and fourth mechanisms are covered through the introduction of spill-overs, which we limit to those originating from knowledge accumulation.[3]

In order to find out more about the importance of the different mechanisms as sources of growth, we concentrate on the steady state growth properties of this set-up, rather than using the framework as a growth accounting device. The latter would entail a refocus on transitional dynamics, which enormously complicates the analysis.[4] We try to find out which parameters are decisive in defining the steady state level of output growth. In addition, we want to find out how spill-overs arising from knowledge accumulation influence macroeconomic growth performance for different degrees of internalisation of these spill-overs. Interestingly, we find that in the case of completely internalised spill-overs (i.e. the social planner solution) the possibility of a multiple equilibria steady state growth situation arises, where the highest growth equilibrium does not necessarily represent the maximum welfare equilibrium. We also find that welfare increases with the size of the spill-over parameters. This suggests that it may be worth-while to define education policies aimed at raising the computer-literacy of the population, in order to improve the spill-over potential of ICT use in knowledge accumulation in general.

The remainder of this chapter is organised as follows. In section 2 we present the extended Lucas (1988) model, while section 3 is devoted to discussing the steady state growth results with and without knowledge spill-overs. Finally, section 4 contains some concluding remarks.

13.2   THE MODEL

We assume that total consumer utility of a representative consumer con-sists of the present value of an infinitely long stream of consumption of final output, as given by the standard Constant Intertemporal Elasticity of Substitution (CIES) utility function:

$$U = \int_0^\infty e^{-\rho t} \cdot \frac{C(t)^{1-\theta} - 1}{1 - \theta} \, dt \quad \theta, \rho > 0 \tag{13.1}$$

In equation (13.1), U represents total utility, $C(t)$ is the flow of consump-tion at time t, ρ is the subjective rate of discount, and $1/\theta$ is the elasticity of substitution between flows of consumption at different points in time.

Output Y is produced using three different inputs – physical capital K_y, ICT capital K_{iy} and human capital services $h \cdot L_y$. Labour used in final output production L_y is measured in man-years per year and h is an index of the human capital content of a man-year, further referred to as know-ledge per worker. The production structure can be described by a linear homogeneous Cobb-Douglas production function:

$$Y = A'(h \cdot L_y)^\alpha (K_{iy})^{\beta_y} (K_y)^{1-\alpha-\beta_y} \quad 0 \le \alpha, \ \beta_y \le 1 \tag{13.2}$$

It should be noted that A' in equation (13.2) represents total factor pro-ductivity, while α and β_y are the partial output elasticities of labour (meas-ured in efficiency units) and ICT capital used in final output production.

Like Lucas (1988), we assume that the growth rate of knowledge per worker is proportional to the time spent on schooling:

$$h = \delta_h' \cdot h \cdot L_h / L \tag{13.3}$$

where a dot over a variable denotes the time-derivative of that variable. Moreover, L is the total labour force measured in man-years per year and

$L_h = L - L_y$ is the total number of man-years spent in accumulating knowledge. The parameter δ'_h represents the productivity of the knowledge accumulation process. Equation (13.3) states that knowledge per worker will grow at a rate that is proportional to the relative amount of time spent per person on accumulating knowledge.

13.2.1 ICT as a General Purpose Technology: Its Impact on Productivity

As we mentioned in the introduction, we would like our model to emphasise that information and communication technologies enhance knowledge accumulation in general, which is a process that may lead to knowledge spill-overs. This is an important aspect of the general purpose nature of ICT. It is also for that reason that we distinguish between physical capital and ICT capital in production.

The impact of ICT equipment on knowledge accumulation can be modelled by assuming a positive influence of the ICT capital intensity on this process. We implement this by postulating:

$$\delta'_h = \delta_h \cdot (K_{ih}/(h \cdot L_h))^{\beta_h} = \delta_h \cdot \mu_{ih} \quad \delta_h > 0, \ 0 \le \beta_h < 1 \qquad (13.4)$$

where K_{ih} is the amount of ICT capital (both hardware and software) used in knowledge accumulation and δ_h and β_h are parameters. Moreover, μ_{ih} is a direct indicator of the ICT capital intensity of the knowledge accumulation process, and it is implicitly defined by the equivalence between the right-most part of (13.4) and its middle part.

The spill-overs of ICT as a general purpose technology follow from the notion that using ICT capital, while accumulating knowledge, generates experience that can be used to handle the ICT capital stock in the final output sector more productively – see the fifth mechanism mentioned in the introduction. One can implement this in the production function by postulating ICT capital augmenting 'technical change', and in turn linking the associated 'augmentation factor' to ICT capital use in knowledge accumulation. This notion of ICT augmentation is easy to include in the Cobb-Douglas production function (13.2) by redefining A' as follows:

$$A' = A(K_{ih}/(h \cdot L_h))^{\sigma \cdot \beta_y} \quad \sigma \ge 0 \qquad (13.5)$$

where σ is a spill-over parameter. If $\sigma = 0$, there are no spill-overs from knowledge accumulation to the productivity of the final output sector and A' is equal to total factor productivity A. However, for $\sigma > 0$, equation (13.5) states that, next to total factor productivity, ICT capital augmenting technological change will occur due to spill-over effects. This also allows ICT capital to be a source of growth through capital deepening, as is observed in Jorgenson (2001). Actually, σ can be seen as an indicator of the quality of the match between ICT use in education and in final output production. By adapting the way in which ICT is used in education to the computer literacy needs in final output production, it is possible to have more spill-overs for the same resources spent in education. In the context of our model this would boil down to having a higher value of σ, ceteris paribus.

The specification of A' also has the advantage that if $\beta_y = 0$, spill-overs have zero productivity effects in final output production, which seems to be a logical requirement because, generally speaking, if one does not use computers, computer literacy will not matter. This also emphasizes the ICT capital augmenting nature of the spill-over effects.

Substitution of (13.5) and (13.4) into (13.2) and (13.3), respectively, gives rise to equations (13.6) and (13.7):

$$Y = A(h \cdot (L - L_h))^\alpha ([K_{ih}/(h \cdot L_h)]^\sigma K_{iy})^{\beta_y} (K_y)^{1-\alpha-\beta_y} \qquad (13.6)$$

$$\hat{h} = \delta_h (K_{ih}/(h \cdot L_h))^{\beta_h} \cdot L_h/L \qquad (13.7)$$

where a 'hat' over a variable name denotes its instantaneous proportional rate of growth.

With respect to the macroeconomic budget constraint we assume, for reasons of simplicity, that the various types of capital are made up, one-for-one, out of consumption forgone.[5] Furthermore, we ignore depreciation in order to keep the model as simple as possible.[6] We therefore have:

$$\dot{K}_y = v_y \cdot (Y - C) \quad v_y \geq 0 \qquad (13.8A)$$

$$\dot{K}_{iy} = v_{iy} \cdot (Y - C) \quad v_{iy} \geq 0 \qquad (13.8B)$$

$$\dot{K}_{ih} = (1 - v_y - v_{iy}) \cdot (Y - C) \quad v_y + v_{iy} \leq 1 \qquad (13.8C)$$

where v_y and v_{iy} are the volume shares of investment in physical capital and investment in ICT capital by the final output sector in total investment (including investment in ICT capital by the knowledge generating sector), respectively. These investment shares are endogenously determined in the model. Finally, $Y - C$ is total final output not used for consumption purposes, but for investment purposes.

13.3   STEADY STATE GROWTH: AN ANALYTICAL SOLUTION

The model developed so far is too complicated to obtain a closed form solution, except for the case of steady state growth. As a consequence we will focus on steady state growth situations for the remainder of this chapter.

Following Lucas (1988), we concentrate on the social planner solution of the model described in section 2. This implies that the Hamiltonian function with state variables h, K_y, K_{iy} and K_{ih}, as given by:

$$H = e^{-\rho t}(C^{1-\theta} - 1)/(1 - \theta) + \lambda_h \cdot \dot{h} + \lambda_{Ky} \cdot \dot{K}_y + \lambda_{Kiy} \cdot \dot{K}_{iy} + \lambda_{Kih} \cdot \dot{K}_{ih} \quad (13.9)$$

(where $\lambda_{Ky}, \lambda_{Kiy}, \lambda_{Kih}$ and λ_h are the corresponding co-state variables), is maximised with respect to its control variables C, L_y, v_y, v_{iy}, subject to the constraints implied by equations (13.6), (13.7) and (13.8A) – (13.8C).

In the Appendix we show that the solution to this problem can be summarised in two relationships between ICT capital intensity μ_{ih} and the fraction of time spent on knowledge accumulation, that is, $\ell_h = L_h/L$, which we will use to derive the equilibrium growth rate in the steady state. The first relationship is called the 'labour allocation relation', since it is derived from the first order conditions describing the optimal allocation of (labour) time between producing output and knowledge:[7]

$$\mu_{ih} = \cfrac{\rho}{\delta_h \ell_h \left[\cfrac{\alpha(1 - \beta_h)}{(\alpha - \sigma\beta_y)\ell_h + \beta_y\sigma} - \theta \right]} \quad (13.10)$$

The second relationship is called the 'capital allocation relation', since it is obtained from the first order conditions describing the allocation of capital over the production of output and knowledge:[8]

$$\mu_{ih} = \left(\left[1 + \left(\frac{1}{\ell_h} - 1 \right) \cdot \frac{\beta_y\sigma}{\beta_h\alpha} \right]^\alpha \left[1 - \beta_h - \theta\ell_h - \frac{\beta_y\theta\sigma}{\alpha}(1 - \ell_h) \right] \frac{\xi}{\rho} \right)^{-\beta_h/(\beta_y\sigma - \alpha)}$$

$$(13.11)$$

where $\xi = (\beta_h\alpha)^\alpha(1 - \beta_h)^{-(1+\alpha)}(1 - \alpha - \beta_y)^{1-\alpha-\beta_y}\beta_y^{\beta_y}$. We elaborate on the nature of these relations below.

Unfortunately, combining (13.10) and (13.11) does not provide a closed form solution for ℓ_h in terms of the parameters of the growth system for $\sigma > 0$. However, when we ignore spill-over effects, hence assume $\sigma = 0$, the system can be solved directly as we will show first.

13.3.1   The Solution Without Spill-overs

The model is simplified considerably if spill-overs are assumed to be absent, since in equations (13.10) and (13.11) all terms containing σ will vanish. For $\sigma = 0$, the labour allocation relationship (13.10) is reduced to:

$$\mu_{ih} = \frac{\rho}{1 - \beta_h - \ell_h \theta} \frac{1}{\delta_h} \qquad (13.10')$$

This relation between ℓ_h and μ_{ih} as given by (13.10') remains positive when the impact of ICT capital on knowledge accumulation is ignored, that is, when $\beta_h = 0$, because essentially it represents the relation between ℓ_h and capital intensity in production. Figure 13.1 presents the labour allocation relation in the μ_{ih}, ℓ_h plane in the northeast quadrant. The graph for (13.10') is a convex upward-sloping function of ℓ_h. It has a positive intercept at $\mu_{ih} = \rho/((1 - \beta_h)\delta_h)$, and a vertical asymptote at $\ell_h = (1 - \beta_h)/\theta$.

For $\sigma = 0$, the capital allocation relationship (13.11) becomes:

$$\mu_{ih} = \left(\frac{\rho}{1 - \beta_h - \ell_h \theta} \frac{1}{\xi} \right)^{-\gamma} \qquad (13.11')$$

with $\gamma = \beta_h / \alpha$ and $\gamma < 1$ since presumably $\beta_h < \alpha$.[9] For the parameter set we have chosen (see section 4), we find that ξ^γ decreases starting from unity when β_h increases from a value of zero, but quickly rises above unity again.[10] The graph for (13.11') represents μ_{ih} as a concave downward sloping function of ℓ_h in the μ_{ih}, ℓ_h plane of the northeast quadrant of Figure 13.1. The function has a positive intercept, which lies above unity for plausible values of the parameters,[11] and reaches a value of zero at $\ell_h = (1 - \beta_h)/\theta$. When $\beta_h = 0$ the relationship is a horizontal line at $\mu_{ih} = 1$.

The point of intersection of the labour allocation relation (13.10') and the capital allocation relation (13.11') represents the unique equilibrium allocation of labour time ℓ^*_h in the absence of knowledge spill-overs.

The northwest and southeast quadrants in Figure 13.1 contain a 45-degree line. The southwest quadrant represents an iso-growth field. Iso-growth lines further away from the origin denote higher rates of steady state growth. An iso-growth line can be obtained by solving equation (13.7) for ℓ_h in terms of μ_{ih}, for given values of $\hat{h}$. The iso-growth line corresponding to a growth rate $\hat{h}^*$ would therefore be given by:

$$\ell_h = \hat{h}^*/(\delta_h \mu_{ih}) \qquad (13.12)$$

The point of intersection between (13.10') and (13.11') in the northeast quadrant then translates into the choice of a specific iso-growth line, hence

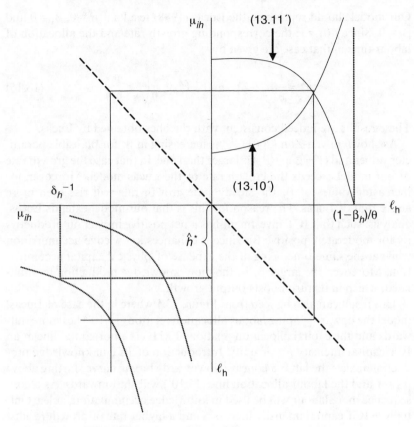

Figure 13.1   The steady state

a steady state growth rate. The value of that growth rate can be obtained by calculating the value of ℓ_h for $\mu_{ih} = 1/\delta_h$ in accordance with (13.12), in which case we would have $\ell_h = \hat{h}^*$, as shown in Figure 13.1.

The resulting steady state growth rate is given by:

$$\hat{h}^* = \frac{1}{\theta}[(1 - \beta_h) \cdot \delta_h \cdot f(\beta_h) - \rho] \text{ with } f(\beta_h) = (\xi/\delta_h)^{\frac{\gamma}{1+\gamma}} \quad (13.13)$$

and the corresponding allocation of labour time ℓ^*_h is given by:

$$\ell^*_h = \frac{1}{\theta}\left[1 - \beta_h - \frac{\rho}{\delta_h f(\beta_h)}\right] \quad (13.14)$$

Our model should reproduce the Lucas (1988) results if $\sigma = 0$, $\beta_y = 0$ and $\beta_h = 0$. Since $f(0) = 1$, the corresponding growth rate and the allocation of labour time in that case are given by:

$$\hat{h}^* = \frac{1}{\theta}[\delta_h - \rho] \quad \text{and} \quad \ell^*_h = \frac{1}{\theta}\left(1 - \frac{\rho}{\delta_h}\right) \tag{13.15}$$

These results are indeed consistent with the ones obtained by Lucas.

As shown in van Zon (2001), $\hat{h}^*$ is increasing in β_h for plausible parameter values and $(1 - \beta_h) \cdot f(\beta_h)$ is larger than one. In that case the growth rate of our model exceeds the growth rate of the Lucas model. Moreover, for increasing values of β_h the steady state growth rate will rise even more above that of Lucas. The reason for this is that our model extends Lucas' analysis, such that ICT investment has a net positive impact on productivity for moderately positive β_h, since it enhances knowledge accumulation while at the same time being at the expense of physical capital accumulation. Moreover, the larger β_h is, the more knowledge production is stimulated, which in its turn boosts output growth.

This result can also be seen from Figure 13.1 where in the case of Lucas' model the upward-sloping labour allocation relation (13.10') lies more outwards and the capital allocation relation (13.11') is a horizontal line at an ICT capital intensity μ_{ih} of unity. Introduction of ICT in knowledge production makes the latter a concave downward-sloping curve starting above $\mu_{ih} = 1$ and the labour allocation line (13.10') will shift inwards. As a consequence more labour will be used in knowledge accumulation, at least initially,[12] ICT capital intensity increases and a higher rate of growth results.

13.3.2   Including Spill-overs: The Market Solution

The general solution of the model presented in equations (13.10) and (13.11) takes all potential spill-over effects fully into account. It is often called the social planner solution (Barro and Sala-i-Martin, 1995, 2.4) since this is typically the result a benevolent social planner would obtain.[13] As such it is contrasted with the market solution, where by their very nature external effects are ignored.[14] In our model this implies that under the decentralised market system the participants would not take into account that employing ICT capital might have spill-over effects on human capital accumulation.[15]

For the solution of the model this implies that the terms containing σ all vanish in the labour allocation relation (13.10), which effectively means that it is the same as for the 'no spill-overs' case, and can be replaced by equation (13.10'). The intuition is that labour is allocated while ignoring the possible spill-over effects from a more efficient capital use. However, since the ICT capital stock does become more efficient – although that is perceived to be an exogenous event – the ICT capital intensity will increase relative to the capital intensity of production in the final output sector.

In terms of the northeast quadrant of Figure 13.1 the capital allocation relationship for the 'external spill-overs' case will therefore be above that associated with the 'no spill-overs' case, while the labour allocation relation will not shift. This implies that the rectangle that links the point of intersection in the northeast quadrant in the 'external spill-overs' case actually contains that of the 'no spill-overs' case, and so the corresponding iso-growth curve must lie further from the origin than in Figure 13.1. Consequently, the ICT capital intensity of knowledge accumulation, the labour time spent on knowledge accumulation and, therefore, the steady state growth rate[16] in the 'external spill-overs' case exceed those in the 'no spill-overs' case.

Turning to the analytical solution, we also obtain for the capital allocation relation an equation that is similar to that of the 'no spill-overs' case, but in equation (13.11') the exponent $\gamma = \beta_h/\alpha$ should be replaced by $\chi = \beta_h /(\alpha - \beta_y\alpha)$. Since we assume $\beta_y.\sigma < \alpha$,[17] we find $\chi > \gamma$. Therefore, using equations (13.13) and (13.14) we find that the steady state growth rate $\hat{h}*$ and corresponding allocation of labour time $\ell*_h$ are now given by:

$$\hat{h}* = \frac{1}{\theta}\left[(1 - \beta_h)\cdot\delta_h\cdot g(\beta_h) - \rho\right] \quad \text{with} \quad g(\beta_h) = (\xi/\delta_h)^{\frac{\chi}{1+\chi}}$$

$$\ell*_h = \frac{1}{\theta}\left[1 - \beta_h - \frac{\rho}{\delta_h g(\beta_h)}\right] \qquad (13.16)$$

Compared to the situation of absence of spill-overs discussed above, we then find a higher growth rate and more labour time spent on knowledge allocation, since $g(\beta_h) > f(\beta_h)$ when $\chi > \gamma$. That a higher growth rate is obtained when including spill-overs is a logical consequence of the fact that the use of ICT capital in knowledge allocation does make its use in production more productive too, even though the market participants do not take this external effect into account in their decision making.

13.3.3 The Social Planner Solution

In the social planner case, the solution of the model is given by equations (13.10) and (13.11), with $\sigma > 0$. Turning first to equation (13.10), we notice that for $\sigma > 0$ the denominator declines relative to the 'no spill-overs' case, which implies an upward shift in the labour allocation relationship compared to Figure 13.1. Moreover, the relationship becomes U-shaped, since from equation (13.10) we see that the denominator approaches infinity when ℓ_h tends to zero. So, apart from a vertical asymptote on the right-hand side,[18] the μ_{ih}-axis itself becomes a vertical asymptote.

From equation (13.11) we see that the impact of $\sigma > 0$ on the capital allocation relationship is that the μ_{ih}-axis becomes a vertical asymptote too. However, inspection of equation (13.11) also shows that the capital allocation function remains a decreasing function in the μ_{ih}, ℓ_h plane of the northeast quadrant of Figure 13.1, since $\beta_y \cdot \sigma < \alpha$, and it still intersects with the ℓ_h-axis at the vertical asymptote of the labour allocation relationship.

Given the highly non-linear nature of equations (13.10) and (13.11) nothing definite can be said about the solution in an analytical way. Since the labour allocation relationship is U-shaped, it may have two points of intersection with the capital allocation relationship, allowing for multiple equilibria, but it may also lie above the capital allocation relationship, which implies that no social planner equilibrium can be obtained. Therefore, in order to develop a notion of the basic characteristics of the steady state in the social planner case, we will perform some numerical experiments.

13.4. STEADY STATE GROWTH: A NUMERICAL SOLUTION

The parameter set we use in our simulations is presented in Table 13.1. These were chosen on a priori grounds, since little or no information is available with respect to them. However, these parameters values are close to the values used by Lucas (1988), and so are the outcomes. An exception is the intertemporal elasticity of substitution, which is rather high in comparison with Lucas, that is, $1/\theta = 2$, but this value ensures the existence of a unique steady state.[19] In addition to this, the Lucas model does of course not contain any investments in ICT, hence the parameters β_h and β_y are chosen on a priori grounds, but in such a way that outcomes are still in line with Lucas' results and broadly in line with Oliner and Sichel (2000). The corresponding steady state values for $\sigma = 0$ are $\hat{h}^* = 0.0188$, $l_h^* = 0.2534$, and $\mu_{ih}^* = 1.3502$. Note that the allocation of time to knowledge accumulation is roughly in line with our 'back of the envelope' requirement that with an 'active' lifetime of roughly 60 years (divided into roughly 15 years of education, and 45 years of labour services), approximately 25 per cent of a person's time should be spent on knowledge accumulation.

Table 13.1   The 'basic' parameter set

Parameter	Value	Parameter	Value	Parameter	Value
θ	0.5	β_h	0.2	ρ	0.05
α	0.7	β_y	0.2	δ_h	0.055

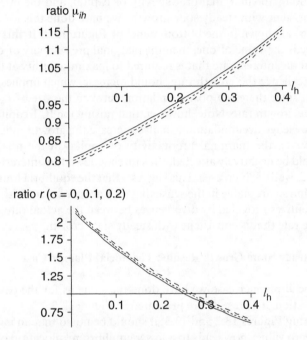

Figure 13.2   Simulation results for the market solution

13.4.1   Steady State Growth Results: The Market Solution

In order to show how the steady state depends on the spill-over parameter σ, we start with presenting the case of the market solution for different values of σ, using the parameter set as given by Table 13.1.[20] Figure 13.2 presents the ratio of (13.10′) and (13.11′) as a function of l_h, although in (13.11′) the exponent γ should be replaced by χ. A value of this ratio equal to 1 ensures that (13.10′) and (13.11′) are equal, as we should have in the steady state.

The solid line in Figure 13.2 corresponds with σ = 0, while the dotted line corresponds with σ = 0.1, and the 'striped' line with σ = 0.2. The horizontal line corresponds to a value of the ratio of ICT capital intensities equal to 1.

The points of intersection of the three curves with this horizontal line therefore correspond to equilibrium allocations of labour time between final output generation and human capital generation. As one should expect from the discussion on the market solution – see equation (13.16) above – we find indeed that the optimal allocation of labour time towards knowledge accumulation ℓ^*_h increases with σ.

An alternative way of looking at the steady state solution is by calculating the ratio of the marginal productivity of capital, and the interest rate that is consistent with steady state growth. We have done this for different values of σ, as shown in the bottom panel of Figure 13.2. If this 'interest ratio' exceeds the value of one, then the marginal productivity of capital is larger than the interest rate that is required to maximise utility at the given growth rate, hence the growth rate should increase, which implies a larger input of ℓ_h since there is a positive relation between the size of ℓ_h and the steady state growth rate. Note, however, that raising the ICT capital intensity of knowledge accumulation can also increase the growth rate. In both cases, however, the marginal productivity of capital in the final output sector would be negatively affected, thus forcing down the 'interest ratio' in Figure 13.2, while ℓ_h increases. This suggests that the equilibria found in the market solution are stable in the sense that they are consistent with the economic incentives provided by divergences between the actual rate of interest and the rate that is consistent with steady state growth.

13.4.2   Steady State Growth Results: The Social Planner Case

For the social planner case we have done the same as for the case of the market solution. The results are presented in Figure 13.3.

Comparing Figures 13.2 and 13.3, it should be noted that an increase in σ to non-zero values now leads to a lower equilibrium allocation of labour time between knowledge accumulation and final output production, because the internalisation of the spill-overs favours employment in final output production in two different ways. First, because the perceived opportunity costs of learning have risen, and second, because the reallocation of labour time this entails strengthens the spill-over effect, since the ICT capital intensity of knowledge accumulation will rise, ceteris paribus. The results suggest that the minimum of the U-shaped labour allocation relationship lies below the capital allocation relationship for low values of σ, such that the system then has multiple equilibria, that is, a high and a low growth allocation of labour time – compare the situation with $\sigma = 0.1$. However, when σ increases further, the high growth allocation of labour towards final output generation increases. Since schooling activities now have positive spill-overs to final output production, the opportunity cost of spending

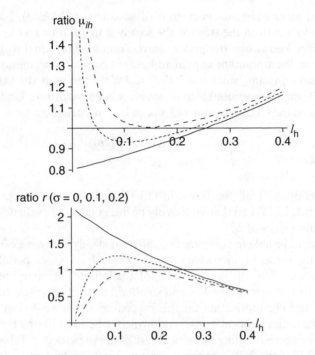

Figure 13.3   Simulation results for the social planner's solution

time on schooling has risen. This is due to the fact that when σ increases, the labour allocation relationship shifts upwards faster than the capital alloca- tion relationship does. As a consequence, for higher values of σ there may be no steady state solution at all – compare the situation with σ = 0.2.

Following the same reasoning as above in the market solution case – see. Figure 13.2 – we notice from the right-hand panel of Figure 13.3 that in the case of two equilibria, the social planner would be inclined to select the high-growth equilibrium when comparing the marginal productivity of capital and the interest rate consistent with optimum growth. The question that automatically arises, is whether the high-growth equilibrium is also the highest 'present value of utility' equilibrium. In order to answer this ques- tion, we provide the numerical results regarding total ('net') utility we have calculated for the various spill-over regimes.

13.4.3   Steady State Growth Welfare Results

In order to calculate welfare results, we disregard transitional dynamics and simply compare the two steady states under consideration, assuming that all capital stocks per efficiency unit of labour (i.e. $K/(h.L)$), have their optimum values from the start of the steady state (at time $t = 0$), and that the stock of knowledge per person starts from a value equal to 1. In the steady state, the amount of capital and output per efficiency unit of labour will remain constant, since both K, Y and h will grow at the same rate. Moreover, the proportional rate of saving s is constant too. Under these assumptions the CIES function (13.1) can be rewritten as:

$$U = \int_0^\infty e^{(h(1-\theta)-\rho)t} \frac{((1-s).(Y/h))^{1-\theta}}{1-\theta} \, dt \qquad (13.17)$$

In the steady state all the terms in (13.17) are constant, except for the antilog, and (13.17) can therefore easily be integrated and evaluated for the equilibrium values of l_h.

In order to be able to compare two different steady states, we can simply subtract the present utility value of the initial capital stock per efficiency unit of labour from the present value of the infinite consumption stream obtained from equation (13.17), and so obtain the 'net present value of the steady state'. The motivation for this procedure is that we do not want to include the initial physical capital endowment when comparing the welfare results. The corresponding numerical results are presented in Table 13.2.[21]

In Table 13.2, the 'NPV', entries correspond to the 'net present value of the steady state', while G_h and L_h correspond to the steady state growth rate, and to the amount of labour time used in knowledge accumulation, respectively. The postfixes 'low' and 'high' refer to the low- and high-growth equilibria associated with the social planner case. For the other spill-over cases the results are listed only under 'high', since the associated equilibria are unique.

Table 13.2 allows a number of conclusions to be drawn. First, the welfare results in the 'no spill-overs' case are lower than that of the market

Table 13.2   Comparative steady state results

	No spill-overs	Market solution	Social planner	Market solution	Social planner	Market solution	Social planner
σ	0.00	0.05	0.05	0.10	0.10	0.15	0.15
Lh low	–	–	0.0224	–	0.0487	–	0.0829
Lh high	0.2535	0.2580	0.2444	0.2626	0.2292	0.2673	0.2048
Gh low	–	–	0.0023	–	0.0050	–	0.0083
Gh high	0.0188	0.0192	0.0190	0.0196	0.0186	0.0201	0.0176
NPV low	–	–	45.999	–	47.014	–	47.950
NPV high	44.2257	44.715	44.949	45.223	45.831	45.748	46.924

solution, which in turn are lower than that of the social planner. Spill-overs contribute therefore positively to welfare, and the more they are taken into account, the higher the (minimum) welfare effects will be. Second, in the social planner case, we find that as σ increases the corresponding net present values increase as well, both for the low growth equilibria and the high growth ones. Third, and perhaps contrary to our a priori notion that higher growth represents higher utility, we notice that for a given value of the spill-over parameter σ, the low-growth equilibrium is associated with the highest net present value. Fourth, this suggests that, from a welfare point of view and if left on its own, the economy described in this chapter will tend to 'overaccumulate', because the social planner would always want to have the economy settle at the lower growth rate.

13.5 SUMMARY AND CONCLUSION

In this chapter we have extended the Lucas model by incorporating the notion that there may be a positive link between the production and use of ICT and productivity growth at the aggregate level. We do this by introducing ICT capital as a separate production factor in the production of final output and in the accumulation of knowledge – the latter ultimately drives growth. This enables us to identify explicitly a number of transmission mechanisms for the growth effects emanating from the ICT sector. One mechanism is the growth of the ICT sector itself that, through its backward linkages with the rest of the economy, would also promote growth there. The literature suggests, however, that this mechanism is of minor importance, so we have not explicitly introduced an ICT producing sector in our model. However, the forward linkages of the ICT sector to the rest of the economy have become more and more important as mechanisms for growth. The use of ICT in the final output sector gives rise to several potential growth transmission channels. First, significant productivity increases in the ICT sector may reduce prices of ICT services equally significantly, thus leading to the substitution of ICT for other factors of production, hence ICT capital deepening. Second, the network features of ICT may generate productivity spill-overs between the various sub-sectors of the economy, but also between human capital accumulation activities and final output production. Finally, human capital accumulation itself may become much more productive through ICT capital deepening. Especially the latter link provides a direct entry-point for ICT investment to influence growth performance.

Although the model essentially allows us to specify a consistent and relatively complete framework that would arable us to actually measure the contribution of each mechanism, we have not done so here, because that would entail the inclusion of explicit transitional dynamics, which would complicate the analysis enormously. Instead, we have focused on the structural features underlying the steady state endogenous growth properties of our model, in which growth is not so much caused by ICT investment, but certainly strengthened by it. We conclude that for reasonable parameterisations of the model, a positive link between ICT investment and economic growth does indeed exist.

We study this positive link between ICT investment and economic growth under three different spill-over regimes: one without any spill-overs from knowledge accumulation to final output production, and two others where these spill-overs do exist. In the latter case these spill-overs are either external, representing a decentralized market process, or internalised, as in the case of a benevolent social planner. From numerical simulation experiments we find that welfare is positively affected, the stronger these spill-overs are, but also the more these spill-overs are internalised. In addition to this, we find that under a system of decentralised decision making, the economy will consistently tend to overaccumulate in comparison to the social planner solution.

We find that in the case of the benevolent social planner, with internalised knowledge spill-overs, the economy may face a multiple equilibria steady state growth situation. The social planner will select the low-growth equilibrium, but due to its unstable nature there is an inherent tendency to move towards the non-optimal, high-growth equilibrium in which all types of capital are overaccumulated, including ICT capital.

In both the social planner case and the decentralised market solution we find that welfare is higher, the larger the spill-over effects are. This suggests that there is room for policy intervention to try to increase the impact on growth of these spill-over effects, for instance through education policies that increase computer literacy.

NOTES

1. After all, since the advent of endogenous growth theory we 'know' that the sole source of growth is knowledge accumulation.
2. Since its direct impact is relatively small, we do not distinguish a separate ICT sector in our analysis.
3. It is straightforward to include spill-overs originating from the use of ICT capital in the final output sector too, in a similar way as Lucas has done with respect to the use of human capital in final output production. Since it complicates matters without generating fundamentally new insights, we disregard these spill-overs in this chapter.
4. Nonetheless, just recently we have been able to formulate an extended version of the model that contains the transitional dynamics and that generates the same steady state results as the steady state version of the model.

5. By doing so, we neglect a further source of growth, namely productivity improvements in the ICT-producing sector itself. But in order to take this into account we would have to revert to a three-sector model, rather than the two-sector model we have here. At this exploratory stage, we are more interested in the direct growth effects of ICT investment, than the 'second order' growth effects through induced ICT substitution that Jorgenson and Stiroh (1999) focus on.

6. One might be inclined to think that the limited lifetime of ICT investment provides a rationale for treating ICT as a non-accumulating input. However, in our view this limited lifetime indicates a very high rate of technological progress that makes replacement of ICT equipment attractive before it has become physically obsolete. Hence, this limited lifetime may be interpreted as a result of rapid capital accumulation.

7. More specifically, the constraints underlying (13.10) are those with respect to the optimum allocation of labour at any moment in time, as well as those with respect to the optimum allocation of human capital over time, conditional on the constraints that describe the efficient sectoral allocation of capital but also the efficient allocation of capital over time.

8. More specifically, equation (13.11) can be derived from the relation between the interest rate and the growth rate of human capital (see AppendixA, equation (13A.6B)), and the definition of the real interest rate as the marginal product of capital in terms of the production function, next to the definition of the growth rate of h itself as given by (13.7), all under the condition of an efficient allocation of capital at each moment of time and also over time.

9. Given the nature of the Cobb-Douglas production structure this seems a plausible assumption.

10. We come back to this later on.

11. See section 4.

12. For implausible parameters, outside the realm of section 4 below, less labour may be used.

13. Lucas (1988) dubs this the 'optimal solution', which he contrasts with the 'equilibrium solution' obtained in a decentralised market system.

14. Since there are no external effects in the absence of spill-overs, there is no difference between the social planner solution and the market solution in the previous subsection.

15. We implement this by treating the ICT capital intensity of knowledge accumulation in the spill-over term of equation (13.6) as if it were an exogenously given number in deriving the first order conditions of the Hamiltonian problem. Once these conditions are derived, this number is replaced again by its definition in terms of the variables of the system, and the consequences of these revised first order conditions for steady state growth are evaluated.

16. See equation (13.3B).

17. Given the nature of the Cobb-Douglas production structure, the assumption $\beta_y < \alpha$ seems plausible.

18. At a value $\ell_h = [\alpha(1 - \beta_h) - \theta_\sigma \beta_y]/[\alpha\theta - \theta_\sigma \beta_y]$.

19. It ensures that the vertical asymptote in the northeast quadrant of Figure 13.1 lies at a value of $\ell_h > 1$.

20. We focus here on the spill-over parameter since this is a crucial parameter in our analysis. Van Zon (2001) shows that the sensitivity of the results to changes in the other parameters is rather modest.

21. More information on the procedure that is followed to obtain these results is presented in van Zon (2001).

22. Note that in the absence of spillovers (i.e. $\sigma = 0$), equation (13.11') requires the capital/effective labour ratios in both sectors to be proportional, with factor of proportion $\alpha\beta_h/((1 - \alpha - \beta_y)(1 - \beta_h))$.

23. Note that the re-specification of the productivity parameters in equations (13.5) and (13.4) also allows these parameters to be constant in the steady state.

REFERENCES

Autor, D.H. (2001), 'Wiring the labor market', *Journal of Economic Perspectives*, **15** (1), 25–40.

Baily, M.N. and R.Z. Lawrence (2001), 'Do we have a new e-conomy', NBER Working Paper, no. 8243.

Barro, R.J. and X. Sala-i-Martin (1995), *Economic Growth*, New York: McGraw-Hill.

Bartelsman, E.J. and J. Hinloopen (2005), 'Unleashing animal spirits: Investment in ICT and economic growth' in L. Soete and B. ter Weel (eds), *The Economics of the Digital Society*, Cheltenham, UK and Northampton, MA, USA: Edward Elgar.

Bartelsman, E.J., G. van Leeuwen and H. Nieuwenhuijsen (1998), 'Adoption of advanced manufacturing technology and firm performance in the Netherlands', *Economics of Innovation and New Technology*, 291–312.

Borenstein, S. and G. Saloner (2001), 'Economics and Electronic Commerce', *Journal of Economic Perspectives*, **15**, 3–12.

Brynjolfsson, E. and L.M. Hitt (2000), 'Beyond computation: Information technology, organizational transformation and business practices', *Journal of Economic Perspectives*, **14**, 23–48.

David, P.A. (2000), 'Understanding digital technology's evolution and the path of measured productivity growth: Present and future in the mirror of the past', in Erik Brynjolfsson and Brian Kahin (eds), *Understanding the Digital Economy*, Cambridge, MA: MIT Press, pp. 49–98.

Gordon, R.J. (1999), 'Has the "New Economy" Rendered the Productivity Slowdown Obsolete?', Manuscript, Northwestern University, 12 June.

Gordon, R.J. (2000), 'Does the "New Economy" Measure Up to the Great Inventions of the Past?', *Journal of Economic Perspectives*, **14**, 49–74.

Greenwood. J. and B. Jovanovic (2000), 'Accounting for growth', Rochester Center for Economic Research Working Paper, no. 4677.

Groot, de H.L.E. (2001), 'Macroeconomic consequences of outsourcing: An analysis of growth, welfare and product variety', *De Economist*, **149**, 53–79.

Harris, R.G. (1998), 'The Internet as a GPT: Factor market implications', in E. Helpman (ed.), *General Purpose Technologies and Economic Growth*, Cambridge, MA and London: MIT Press, pp. 145–66.

Helpman, E. and M. Trajtenberg (1998), 'A time to sow and a time to reap: Growth based on General Purpose Technologies', in E. Helpman (ed.), *General Purpose Technologies and Economic Growth*, Cambridge, MA and London: MIT Press, pp. 85–119.

Jorgenson, D.W. (2001), 'Information technology and the US economy', *American Economic Review*, **91**, 1–32.

Jorgenson, D.W. and K.J. Stiroh (1999), 'Productivity growth: Current recovery and longer-term trends', *American Economic Review*, **89**, 109–15.

Kiley, M.T. (1999), 'Computers and growth with costs of adjustment: Will the future look like the past?', Finance and Economic Discussion Series Paper, 1999–36, Federal Reserve Board.

Leeuwen, G. van and H.P. van der Wiel (2003), 'Relatie ICT en productiviteit: Een analyse met Nederlandse bedrijfsgegevens', CPB memorandum, no. 57.

Lucas, R.E. (1988), 'On the mechanics of economic development', *Journal of Monetary Economics*, **22**, 3–42.

Meijers, H. (2003), 'ICT and network effects: A macro economic approach', paper prepared for the conference ICT Clusters and City Dynamics: Does Policy Matter, Dublin Castle, 5–6 March.

Nordhaus, W. (2001), 'Productivity growth in the new economy', NBER Working Paper, no. 8096.

Oliner, S.D. and D.E. Sichel (1994), 'Computers and output growth revisited: How big is the puzzle?', *Brookings Papers on Economic Activity*, 273–317.

Oliner, S.D. and D.E. Sichel (2000), 'The resurgence of growth in the late 1990s: Is information technology the story?', *Journal of Economic Perspectives*, 14, 3–22.

Oliner, S.D. and D.E. Sichel (2002), 'Information technology and productivity: Where are we now and where are we going to?', Federal Reserve System, Finance and Economics Discussion Series, 2002–29.

Stehr, N. (1999), 'The productivity paradox: ICTs, knowledge and the labour market', in J. la Mothe and G. Paquet (eds), *Information, Innovation and Impacts*, Boston, MA: Kluwer Academic Publishers, pp. 255–72.

Stiroh, K.J. (2002), 'Information technology and the US productivity revival: What do the industry data say?', *American Economic Review*, **92**, 1559–76.

Zon, A.H. van (2001), 'ICT-investment, knowledge accumulation and endogenous growth', Merit Research Memorandum, no. 2001–38.

APPENDIX

The Hamiltonian function with state variables h, K_y, K_{iy} and K_{ih}, and control variables C, L_y, v_y, v_{iy} is given by:

$$H = e^{-\rho t}(C^{1-\theta} - 1)/(1 - \theta) + \lambda_h \cdot \dot{h} + \lambda_{Ky} \cdot \dot{K}_y + \lambda_{Kiy} \cdot \dot{K}_{iy} + \lambda_{Kih} \cdot \dot{K}_{ih}$$

$$= e^{-\rho t}(C^{1-\theta} - 1)/(1 - \theta) + \lambda_h(\delta_h \cdot (K_{ih}/(h \cdot (L - Ly))^{\beta h} \cdot ((L - Ly)/L) \cdot h +$$

$$\lambda_{Ky} \cdot v_y \cdot ((K_{ih}/(h \cdot (L - Ly))^{\beta_y \sigma}(h \cdot L_y)^\alpha (K_{iy})^{\beta y}(K_y)^{1-\alpha-\beta y} - C) +$$

$$\lambda_{Kiy} \cdot v_{iy} \cdot ((K_{ih}/(h \cdot (L - Ly))^{\beta_y \sigma}(h \cdot L_y)^\alpha (K_{iy})^{\beta y}(K_y)^{1-\alpha-\beta y} - C) +$$

$$\lambda_{Kih} \cdot (1 - v_y - v_{iy}) \cdot ((K_{ih}/(h \cdot (L - Ly))^{\beta_y \sigma}(h \cdot L_y)^\alpha (K_{iy})^{\beta y}(K_y)^{1-\alpha-\beta y} - C)$$

$$(13.A.1)$$

where $\lambda_{Ky}, \lambda_{Kiy}, \lambda_{ihy}$ and λ_h are the corresponding co-state variables, and where we have used equations (13.6), (13.7) and (13.8A) – (13.8C) to arrive at (13.A.1).

It is easy, although somewhat tedious, to show that by setting the derivatives of the Hamiltonian with respect to the control variables equal to zero, one obtains:

$$\lambda_{Ky} = e^{-\rho t}C^{-\theta} \tag{13A.2A}$$

$$\lambda_{Ky} = \lambda_{Kiy} = \lambda_{Kih} \tag{13A.2B}$$

$$\lambda_h = \lambda_{Ky} h^{\alpha + \beta_h - \sigma\beta_y - 1} K_{ih}^{\beta_y \sigma - \beta_h} \cdot K_{iy}^{\beta_y} \cdot K_y^{1 - \alpha - \beta_y} \cdot L(L - L_y)^{\beta_h - 1 - \sigma\beta_y} \cdot L_y^{-1 + \alpha} \cdot$$

$$(L\alpha + L_y(\sigma\beta_y - \alpha))/((1 - \beta_h)\delta_h) \tag{13A.2C}$$

The right hand side of equation (13A.2A) is equal to marginal utility, that is, the utility that would be lost if one allocated one unit of output to capital formation instead of consumption. So, equation (13A.2A) states that an optimum path cannot be improved on by shifting output from consumption to investment, or vice versa, because of the interpretation of the co-state variables as the shadow prices of the corresponding state variables. Equation (13A.2B) states that a marginal unit of investment in the three different capital stocks should generate the same return, otherwise total utility could be improved by shifting capital from the low return investment opportunities to the high return investment opportunities. Equation (13A.2C) states that on an optimum path, the two uses of labour hours (i.e. production of final output, and production of (more) future final output through knowledge accumulation) should generate the same return, in terms of total utility.

The shares of investment in the three different capital stocks can now be obtained by combining the dynamic constraints:

$$\dot{\lambda}_j = -\frac{\partial H}{\partial K_j} \quad \forall j = y, iy, ih \tag{13A.3}$$

with the time derivatives of equation (13A.2B). The latter simply imply that the derivatives of the Hamiltonian with respect to the various capital stocks should be the same. This results in:

$$K_{iy} = K_y \frac{\beta_y}{1 - \alpha - \beta_y} \tag{13A.4A}$$

$$K_{ih} = K_y \frac{((L - L_y)\alpha\beta_h + L_y\beta_y\sigma)}{L_y(1 - \alpha - \beta_y)(1 - \beta_h)} \tag{13A.4B}$$

Equation (13A.4A) requires the efficient use of ICT capital and physical capital in final output production, since the capital stock ratio given by (13A.4A) is the ratio that maximises effective capital (i.e. $K^e = K_{iy}^{\beta_y} \cdot K_y^{1 - \alpha - \beta_y}$) for a given budget in terms of consumption forgone. The other capital stock ratio given by (13A.4B) depends on the allocation of labour over its two different uses. This is because the capital stocks here have totally different functions: in knowledge generation, the ICT capital intensity of learning has a positive impact on the productivity of the learning process, hence on the growth rate of output for a given allocation of labour, while an increase in the capital intensity in final output production only has a level effect. Because changes in the allocation of labour also have a growth effect, it is not surprising that the allocation of labour turns up in the link between both types of capital stocks.[22]

Because the capital/effective labour ratios remain constant in a situation of steady state growth for a fixed allocation of labour (as it is the case in the Lucas, 1988 model), it follows immediately from equations (13A.4A) and (13A.4B) that the growth rates of the various capital stocks are the same too.[23] This result can be used in combination with equations (13.8A) – (13.8C) to obtain the values of the volume shares of ICT and non-ICT investment, as given by equations (13A.5A) and (13A.5B) below:

$$v_{iy} = \frac{L_y(1 - \beta_h)\beta_y}{L\alpha\beta_h + L_y(1 - \alpha - \beta_h + \beta_y\sigma)} \qquad (13A.5A)$$

$$v_y = \frac{L_y(1 - \beta_h)(1 - \alpha - \beta_y)}{L\alpha\beta_h + L_y(1 - \alpha - \beta_h + \beta_y\sigma)} \qquad (13A.5B)$$

The distribution of investment over its three different uses depends on the actual allocation of labour, for the same reasons as before. Note that an increase in L_y by a given percentage, increases the numerators of (13A.5A) and (13A.5B) more than the denominators, hence the investment share of capital used for final output production would rise, and that for knowledge production would fall, as one would expect, since an increase in L_y would raise the marginal productivity of the other factors used in final output production.

Steady state growth requires the marginal productivity of capital to remain constant for an increasing capital stock. Since we have used a linear homogeneous Cobb-Douglas production function, this requires output and capital to grow at the same rate. Together with the conclusion that the various stocks of capital should all grow at the same rate, this leads to the conclusion that output itself (hence the various capital stocks) should grow with the growth rate of h. However, a constant growth rate of output that is equal to the growth rate of the capital stock implies that the saving rate is constant too. Therefore, the propensity to consume, being equal to one minus the saving rate, must also be constant. But then the growth rate of consumption is equal to the growth rate of output. Consequently, on an equilibrium path the growth rate of consumption is given by equations (13A.2A) and (13A.3), the latter for $j = y$, giving:

$$\hat{\lambda}_{Ky} = -\frac{\partial Y}{\partial K_y} = -r \qquad (13A.6A)$$

$$\hat{C} = \hat{Y} = \hat{h} = (-\hat{\lambda}_{Ky} - \rho)/\theta = (r - \rho)/\theta \qquad (13A.6B)$$

where r is the real rate of interest, that is, the marginal productivity of physical (and ICT) capital in the final output sector.

Equation (13A.2C), as well as the steady state growth requirement, that is, the equality of the growth rates of output, the various capital stocks and human capital per head (as given by (13A.6B)), and equation (13A.6A) can be used to arrive at the conclusion that:

$$\hat{\lambda}_{Ky} = \hat{\lambda}_h = -r \qquad (13A.7)$$

Using the definition $\hat{\lambda}_h = (\hat{\lambda}_h/\hat{h}) \cdot \hat{h}$, where the terms within brackets are substituted for by using equations (13A.3) and (13.7), and substituting (13A.7) we find:

$$\hat{h} = r \frac{(L - L_y)\alpha + L_y \beta_y \sigma}{\alpha L(1 - \beta_h)} \qquad (13A.8)$$

Equation (13A.8) provides the second relation between $\hat{h}$ and the real interest rate r (equation (13A.6B) being the first, together with the requirement that $\hat{C} = \hat{h}$). By equating (13A.8) and (13A.6B) one arrives at a relation between r and L_y:

$$r = \frac{L\alpha(1 - \beta_h)\rho}{L\alpha(1 - \beta_h - \theta) + L_y \theta(\alpha - \beta_y \sigma)} \qquad (13A.9)$$

Equation (13A.9) can be substituted back into (13A.8) to arrive at a relation between $\hat{h}$ and L_y, which, in combination with (7), allows us to arrive at the following relation between μ_{ih} and $\ell_h = L_h/L$ (where we have substituted $L_h = L - L_y$), which we will use to derive the equilibrium growth rate in the steady state:

$$\mu_{ih} = \frac{\rho}{\delta_h \ell_h \left[\dfrac{\alpha(1 - \beta_h)}{(\alpha - \sigma\beta_y)\ell_h + \beta_y \sigma} - \theta \right]} \qquad (13A.10)$$

Finally, in order to obtain the equilibrium growth rate, we must first find an independent relation between the same variables. That relation can be obtained from equation (13A.6A) by substituting for K_y and K_{iy} in the marginal productivity of capital, while making use of equations (13A.4A), (13A.4B) and (13.7). In that case we obtain a relation between μ_{ih}, r and ℓ_h, which in combination with (13A.9) results in an additional relation between μ_{ih} and ℓ_h:

$$\mu_{ih} = \left(\left[1 + \left(\frac{1}{\ell_h} - 1 \right) \cdot \frac{\beta_y \sigma}{\beta_h \alpha} \right]^{\alpha} \left[1 - \beta_h - \theta \ell_h - \frac{\beta_y \theta \sigma}{\alpha} (1 - \ell_h) \right] \frac{\xi}{\rho} \right)^{-\beta_h / (\beta_y \sigma - \alpha)}$$

$$(13A.11)$$

where $\xi = (\beta_h \alpha)^{\alpha} (1 - \beta_h)^{-(1+\alpha)} (1 - \alpha - \beta_y)^{1 - \alpha - \beta_y} \beta_y^{\beta_y}$.

14. A digital society for us all: 'old' and 'new' policy reflections*

Chris Freeman and Luc Soete

14.1 INTRODUCTION

> The 1990s have witnessed a great proliferation of reports and papers on Information and Communication Technologies (ICTs) . . . The objective of this report is not to add one more document to this already over-subscribed field. Rather, it is to transcend this discussion from the outset, by making a separation between data and information, and by distinguishing between the notion of information and the need for knowledge. It is necessary to separate out the transmission of data from communication between people, and the acquisition of knowledge. Most present-day telecommunication systems are still systems of transmission of data. In this report, we focus our attention on ways in which information can be converted into useful knowledge, so that the 'information economy' may become a 'knowledge-based economy'. The underlying ICTs provide the potential for great increases in productivity and many new and improved products and services. However, history shows that the ability to convert this potential into actual gains in productivity and improvements in living standards and quality of life depends on a prolonged process of learning and institutional change. (HLEG, 1996, p. 1)

These are the first, introductory sentences of a policy report written 10 years ago by the two of us as part of a so-called European 'High-Level Expert Group' (HLEG) on the social and economic implications of the information society. The report written in 1995 and entitled 'Building the European information society for us all' was published by the European Commission in January 1996 and was meant to redirect the policy concerns of the then responsible European policy makers from a sheer unilateral focus on the technological[1] and regulatory[2] aspects of the convergence of computer and telecommunications technologies, towards the broader social and economic aspects of the diffusion of new information and communication technologies. In contrast to the then main policy concerns, it addressed some of the broader macroeconomic growth, distribution and

---

* We would like to thank the referees and Bas ter Weel for useful comments on an earlier version of this chapter.

employment issues, as well as many of the social and organisational aspects of the information society, the then 'buzz word' for the digital society referred to in this book.

Ten years would appear, certainly when looking at a set of radical, general purpose technologies such as ICTs, to be a long period. From a policy perspective, it might even appear to be an eternity. None of the policy players, such as the then European commissioners Mr Bangemann and Mr Flynn are still there. Many of the civil servants in charge at that time at the European Commission have moved to other divisions, dealing with other policy issues. We though are still there. It seemed hence appropriate to 'revisit', 10 years later, at the end of this book containing a wide and rich variety of 'new' economic insights, the many policy implications of the 'old' information society. In doing so we will limit ourselves to the social, employment and work related policy implications of information and communication technologies. The original EU report dealt with a wide variety of potentially relevant policy topics from regional growth and agglomeration aspects, to implications for health, education, skills, the media, democracy and the quality of life.

The fact that policy reports remain suspiciously topical, even when dealing with at first sight radical new technologies such as ICTs, might of course seem odd. Yet, after reflection, it appears that there are many good reasons why this should not really be surprising.

First and foremost, there is a natural tendency, particularly with respect to policy studies, to have a shortened 'policy' memory span. Most policy reports are relatively quickly forgotten, except when they are widely off the mark.[3] Combined with the other natural tendency: to have a shortened technology 'history' span, there will be an inherent trend to duplicate policy advice. To paraphrase Keynes: 'policy makers new to the job, who believe themselves to be quite exempt from earlier policy advice, are usually the slaves of some defunct EU policy report'.

Second, there is a desire particularly in the over-politicised advanced world to direct policy interests to new phenomena, even if those latter have barely made any impact, or are as yet only part of a future imaginary world. This certainly has been the case with the set of digital ICTs at the heart of this book. The limited 'real', widespread availability of many of these technologies as opposed to the science fiction versions represented in movies, in prototypes, or in the early commercial versions for sophisticated beta users, was characteristic of the 1980s and 1990s. As a consequence the speed of diffusion as well as the broader social and economic impact of many new ICTs applications have often been overestimated – one may think of the paperless office or videophone. By contrast, other, sometimes more simple applications (mobile telephony, sms messaging) have taken off and diffused much more rapidly than ever expected. In the same way that *The Economist* magazine once talked about 'the mystery of growth', one may talk about 'the mystery' of successful ICT applications. For policy reports such differences in the rates of diffusion are often by and large irrelevant. There is more concern not to miss out on possible relevant policy areas, less about a correct timing, even though the differences in the speed of diffusion might well be related to the existence of inappropriate policy frameworks.

Third, and to some extent as a direct consequence of the previous point, there is a strong pendulum trend in policy advice. Certainly with respect to the impact of new technologies on employment growth and displacement, policy concerns seem to re-emerge with each new rise in unemployment and disappear from public debate with each reduction. Over the past 25 years we have ourselves witnessed at first hand this sheer natural, cyclical policy interest. Our first main joint publication on the topic of technology and employment was in 1982, in the midst of the severest post-war EU employment and growth crisis. Entitled *Unemployment and Technical Innovation* (Freeman et al., 1982), it received a lot of attention and was widely publicised. As a result, we were even asked by a private firm (IBM) to prepare a detailed report, published in 1985, on the employment implications of information technologies (Freeman and Soete, 1985). Our second major joint publication on the topic was published in 1987 during a phase of European growth recovery and entitled *Technical Change and Full Employment* (Freeman and Soete, 1987). It passed more or less unnoticed, even though it provided a much more in-depth macro and sector analysis of the underlying structural changes. Finally, our third and last joint major publication on this topic, entitled *Work for All or Mass Unemployment: Computerised Technical Change in the 21st Century* was published in 1994 at the start of the new economy growth boom (Freeman and Soete, 1994). It was particularly noted for its strongly argued case on the significance of the computer technological revolution – 'the biggest juggernaut in history' – but far less for what it had to say about the likely employment and unemployment implications. In short, the timing of policy advice seems to be of the utmost importance.

This seems a good reason to revisit the employment policy part of a '10-year old' policy report. In the following two sections we reproduce some of the most relevant parts of the report dealing explicitly with employment, organisational change and the future of work. At the end of each section, we reflect on those policy conclusions '10 years after'.

14.2   THE INFORMATION SOCIETY AND EMPLOYMENT, 1995[4]

The concerns about the employment and distributional implications of the diffusion of information and communication technologies are, as has been emphasised in many reports, not based on any historical precedents. There is large potential for the growth of completely new forms of employment in the Information Society (IS). New core ICT-intensive sectors are forming the basis of new industries, notably the multimedia-based industry, which is likely to be a high value, high skill sector with considerable labour intensity. On a positive note, therefore, there is clear potential for new knowledge-rich forms of employment to emerge, which could create highly satisfying employment. The prospect of new occupations based on information services that reinforce creative, collaborative, communal and caring aspects of work, is strong and should be an area that policies seek to build up, not only because jobs with these attributes are socially desirable, but also because in many cases these innovative services will form the basis of the emerging information economy in Europe, and thus also a major component of its competitive advantage.

However, we also feel bound to raise the question to what extent new technologies represent a threat to employment, a subject that has been at the centre of polemic debates among economists and sociologists for the last 200 years. What brings these concerns about the IS back to the forefront, despite the reassuring historical analogies and macroeconomic compensation arguments, are the particular features and characteristics of the new ICTs underlying the IS. We emphasise five, each of which has been insufficiently addressed in the present policy debate and warrants more research.

14.2.1   The IS and the Jobs of the Future

The use of new ICTs is likely to lead to major changes in employment in Europe, especially in the service sectors and particularly in those sectors and occupations hitherto largely 'protected' from automation or 'informatisation'. These service sectors, which today account for more than 60 per cent of total employment in the EU, have traditionally been 'sheltered' from international competition and have acted as the main absorber of employment displacement in manufacturing and agriculture. Furthermore, it was the public service sector that was the almost exclusive creator of new employment opportunities in the EU employment boom over the second half of the 1980s.

Many of the new employment opportunities created in the IS are likely to be in the private service sector, with the continuing growth of ICT-based

services and information-intensive services such as multimedia software
and systems development, professionalised consulting services and so on.
It is the likely impact on public service sector employment that raises the
biggest issues of concern. Some traditional public services, such as public
administration, are by nature informationally intensive. In addition, some
public services are most subject to deregulation and liberalisation. There
are thus likely to be substantial transitional and adjustment problems with
many jobs facing the threat of rationalisation.

These problems will be complex and hard to tackle from a policy perspective, not least because of the striking disparity between the amount and
quality of statistical information and economic analysis on productivity
growth and employment trends in manufacturing as compared to the lack
of analysis of trends in service employment, their link to productivity
growth, and impact on overall competitiveness.

14.2.2   New 'Regulation' for New Employment and Growth

Both the overall macroeconomic climate and the regulatory institutional
environment are of utmost importance in creating the appropriate conditions for rapid diffusion and use of new information products and services
and as a consequence new employment creation. The Expert Group is concerned that on both accounts these conditions are not at present being fulfilled in the EU and that the European ICT industry, both manufacturing
and services, is at a major disadvantage in developing new demand opportunities for information products and services.

First, in so far as the dramatic decrease in the cost of obtaining data and
information with new ICTs can be compared with a macroeconomic disin-
flationary effect – an 'oil shock in reverse'[5] – the question can be raised
whether our present statistical methods for assessing 'inflation' are still
appropriate. There is at least a suspicion that, with the growing proportion
of consumption being devoted to 'information-intensive' goods and services with rising quality characteristics, current inflation estimates over-
value 'money illusion' and are unlikely to pick up real aggregate price trends
of the emerging IS. Little is known about the size of this issue, even less
about its macroeconomic consequences.

Second, the proposed changes in the appropriate regulatory framework
as presented in the present move towards liberalisation of the national
European telecom operator markets do not sufficiently take into account
both the speed and the scope of the required regulatory reform. The emergence of new markets for information services requires not just a more competitive framework, deregulation and open access, but also the development
of new institutions setting out the rules of such new markets, including

those governing property rights, security, privacy, and so on. At the same time, and as the case of the Internet illustrates, the speed of change goes well beyond the 'controlled' liberalisation process pursued at the moment in Europe, and involves a much more dramatic 'creative destruction' process, with a completely new communication pricing structure.

Furthermore, the IS will internationalise the communications media industries, the production of media content, editorial matter and the cultural industries in general. Traditionally, these industries operate and are largely controlled at national level because of longstanding concerns about the effect of communications industries on national sovereignty and security, democracy and censorship. In the IS the communications sector is becoming more 'commodified', with information being packaged and distributed internationally. In order to reinforce the growth and profitability of this sector, it is necessary that anti-trust laws, which regulate the sector at national level, should not be in contradiction in different countries.

14.2.3 Deregulation and Existing Jobs

Regarding the rationalisation effects that follow the introduction of ICTs, there are two main areas of concern to which we wish to draw attention. First, a major cost of the programme of telecommunications liberalisation that is currently under way will be the loss of jobs in some parts of the monopoly service providers and potential erosion of the social protection of workers in these industries. Second, in the public sector, especially in public administration, the ICTs provide an opportunity to offer direct services to citizens in the form of on-line services. This could lead to rapid rationalisation of the front offices of the government, with an ensuing loss of jobs.

Established telecommunication service providers are often hindered in their attempts to compete with the new private firms on two main grounds. New entrants can try to 'cherry pick' the high value added areas of the telecommunications market, while the established provider must continue to guarantee USP. The new entrants can also take advantage of their fresh start through operating very flexible industrial relations regimes, with perhaps lower levels of worker protection and working conditions than have been established over the years in the public sector telecommunication providers. The pressure will therefore be on the established providers to raise competitiveness challenges through a radical restructuring of the workforce to lower wage costs and raise productivity. This process, while inevitable, should be made as smooth as possible through engaging the support and cooperation of workers.

Public administration has traditionally been an employment-rich sector, aiming to serve citizens directly in their towns and villages, which has led to the proliferation of administrative offices offering different levels of service in different places. ICTs now allow direct on-line access to many such services from the home. This could lead to a gradual rationalisation of such offices dealing with a large number of routine or paper form filling tasks. In the IS many offices could close, leading not only to the loss of many front-office jobs but also to government becoming more remote and impersonal.

14.2.4   The Social Distribution of Jobs in the IS

ICTs are informational technologies. As they develop they lead to increased memorisation, speed, manipulation and interpretation of data and information. Their development will increasingly make possible the 'codification' of large parts of the skills required of people in the workplace. At the same time new forms of 'tacit' knowledge and skills become ever more important. An increasing number of routine skills have already become totally codifiable. As large parts of present day employment involve such routine tasks, there is increasing concern about the distributional employment impact of the IS. Furthermore, confronted with the accompanying widespread use of various forms of information and computer technologies, 'skill mismatches' are likely to be of a much more pervasive and general nature, raising questions about the inherent 'skill bias' of new ICTs. These distributional concerns justify the particular importance paid to the labour market functioning in the IS and education and training. Here we raise the broader macroeconomic issue about whether and how to develop appropriate 'redistribution' policies.

Such policies address more generally the question of how governments will be able to continue to raise funds in an increasingly information-based world in which value is generated through systems and global networks, rather than through clearly identifiable material production and exchange. There is a need to refocus the many debates and discussions on work and income within the context of the emerging IS and to consider how governments can marshal the funds to pursue such 'redistribution' policies. The HLEG shares the view that there might be a need for a new tax base, more closely associated with information exchange, such as in the case of a 'bit tax'.[6] Such a tax, preferably introduced on a worldwide basis so as to avoid distortions, could possibly be used to alleviate some of the distributional issues raised above.

14.2.5   Jobs and Globalisation

The possibility of ICTs to codify information and knowledge over both distance and time not only brings about more global access, it also enables firms/organisations to relocate the sort of routine activities that can be codified and thus also internationally traded. ICTs contribute in other words to economic transparency and, in so far as they bring to the forefront the cost advantages of alternative locations, to international capital mobility and international 'outsourcing' of particular activities. While the benefits to the world as a whole of such a more transparent, borderless world, are undisputed, there is concern about the worldwide distribution of those benefits.

For the poorest, most peripheral countries/regions there is concern that they may become excluded. For the richer, technologically leading countries/regions, there is concern about the increasing erosion of the monopoly rents associated with innovation, and their implications for employment and wages. Here we raise some of the broader macroeconomic implications of the shift towards a borderless capital mobile world.

National welfare systems, which already face considerable pressures of increased demand in a time of budgetary constraint, are further challenged both by the global dimensions of the IS and its association with new, more flexible forms of work organisation. First, in most EU countries, the financing of the national social security system and, more generally, the welfare state has been closely linked to employment through the contributions of employers and employees. This close national-level relationship is becoming increasingly hard to sustain, given the heightened international mobility of capital and investment in the globalised and economically transparent IS. National administrations face choices between international competitiveness and/or the long-term sustainability of the national welfare system. Second, there are trends towards new forms of work organisation in the IS such as part-time or fixed-term contract work. Such changes challenge the edifice of traditional welfare systems, which, typically, were constructed in periods of much lower unemployment, younger demographic profiles and much more stability in employment patterns. From the point of view of both financing the welfare system and encouraging more flexible working patterns, reforms to the present social security systems are urgently needed.

However, the international growth and employment implications of the emerging IS do not stop at the borders of the European Union. The notion of the emergence of a 'global' IS, in a world in which approximately half the population has no access to public telephony, is somewhat of a misnomer. The huge present day concentration of access to global information infrastructure and use of ICT equipment in the industrialised world also illustrates, however, the huge potential for catching-up for the 'other' countries.

14.3 THE DIGITAL SOCIETY AND EMPLOYMENT, A 2005 REVISIT

As was noted in the HLEG report, the relationship between new technologies and employment has been the subject of a long tradition in economics. For the sake of simplicity one may today distinguish between four separate historical phases of economic and political debate. The first debate, probably the most 'classical' in its origins, took place during the economic depression of the 1930s. The main contributors included Hansen, Kaldor, Weintraub and Neisser (e.g. see Freeman and Soete, 1994 for an overview). Many of the issues and concerns raised by these authors sound very familiar today, particularly in the context of the notion of increasing returns in current 'new' growth models (e.g. Aghion and Howitt, 1992; already initiated by Young, 1928). The second, more neo-classical inspired debate focused mainly on the post-war United States and the fear of 'automation'. In the 1960s, levels of unemployment were higher in the United States than in Europe, and many politicians blamed technological change. As a result, a National Commission on Automation was appointed and produced the famous massive six-volume report (US National Commission, 1966), with celebrated contributions from among others Bob Solow. The third debate, which began in the late 1970s, was particularly dominant in Europe. It focused on the emergence of the cluster of computer-based communication, information and automation techniques associated with microelectronics, which appeared at first glance to have great labour-displacing implications (e.g. David, 1991 and Katsoulacos, 1984). The fear that these displacement effects might dominate the compensating job creation effects for quite some time recalled in many ways the classical debate. Again it appeared to be a reflection of the times: there was the emergence of a set of 'revolutionary' new technologies on the one hand and growing and persisting high unemployment in Europe on the other. The final, most recent, debate focused much more on the global aspects of ICT and the possible erosion of employment and high living standards in advanced countries. It was this debate of which the HLEG report formed part.

Despite the controversial nature and the intensity of the old debates, the relationship between technology and employment at least from a closed macroeconomic perspective, appears today relatively straightforward. Either the introduction of new technologies leads to more efficient production processes, reducing costs by saving on labour, capital, materials, energy, or any other factor of production, or it leads more directly to the development of new products that generate new demand, or both. In either case, more welfare will be created; in the first scenario through more efficient production combinations that liberate scarce input resources; and in the second case by satisfying new wants. The extent to which this higher welfare or increased productivity feeds back into employment growth depends on the extent to which, and the pace by which, firms succeed in translating productivity gains into lower prices and new investment, and consumers respond to lower prices in terms of greater demand. The job losses that might follow the introduction of a new labour-saving process, for example, will thus become compensated by the job creation associated with the output growth following the decline in prices, by additional employment creation in other sectors, particularly the new technology-supplying sector, and by the possible substitution of labour for capital following the downward wage adjustment that clears the labour market. As long as there are unsatisfied needs in the economy and as long as labour and product markets are sufficiently flexible, technological change, even in the form of new labour-saving production processes, does not reduce aggregate employment but generates higher growth rates and more jobs.

Most of the controversies that dominated the economics literature on this issue over the last decades have centred on the automatic nature of the various compensation effects described above. Since the functioning and flexibility of product markets depends in part on the firm's monopoly power, the degree of economies of scale and various other factors influencing prices, many contributors have questioned the way in which cost reductions are effectively translated into lower prices and are likely to lead to more output growth. Similar questions can be raised with respect to employment growth and the functioning of labour markets; they range from downward wage flexibility to the many mismatches typical of (heterogeneous) labour markets. In either case, it is less technology itself that is at the centre of the debate than the pace and clearing function of the product and labour markets.[7] The relevant policy issues therefore fall primarily under the heading of improving the functioning of product and labour markets.[8]

The more recent contributions that were at the core of the concerns reflected in the HLEG report focus more explicitly on the international 'open economy' framework within which most of these compensation mechanisms operate today. As a result, the relatively straightforward linkages between technology, productivity growth, and job creation mentioned above are more complex. The trade, but also the effects of international spillovers of technology on productivity growth (OECD, 1996) or of international capital mobility, make it much more difficult to identify the key links between the introduction of a new technology and the ensuing domestic employment impact. Many of the concerns about the global implications of technological change for employment relate to these international compensation mechanisms and to the way that gains from technological change are distributed internationally. In the gloomy vision of some popular writers: 'wages in the most advanced economies are being eroded owing to the emergence of a global market-place where low-paid workers compete for the few jobs created by footloose global corporations' (Rifkin, 1995, p. 15). The globalisation of industry and services casts a radically new light on the interaction between technology and employment in an open economic framework characterised by low transport and communication costs.

While it is still generally agreed that in a 'world' economic framework, input-saving technical change leads, through increases in productivity, to higher welfare, wages, and growth and thus generates new employment, the impact on individual countries is much more complex and is based on a broad range of macroeconomic and microeconomic adjustment mechanisms (e.g. Berman, 2000). This is especially true because positive and negative effects do not coincide either in time or in space: adjustment takes time, and the industries and types of workers that will benefit from technical change are different from the ones that lose from it. At the same time, the premium placed on the role of knowledge and on the acquisition of skills in this global environment implies that international differences in the pattern of employment and unemployment depend increasingly on the capacity of national economies to innovate, enter new, unregulated 'service' areas and/or absorb new technology more rapidly.

Viewed from this perspective, the policy analysis presented in the HLEG report appears, not surprisingly, as relevant today as it was 10 years ago. Global competitive pressures have only increased and the impact of ICTs on the international tradability of services has affected many service sectors hitherto sheltered from international competition. But the report also drew attention to issues that at the time were insufficiently recognised by policy makers as being key to both international competitiveness and long-term employment growth. Thus the report by the HLEG, as one of the first policy advising groups, focused on the crucial role of the diffusion of ICT in the public sector raising on the one hand substantial employment 'adjustment' problems, while on the other hand being a key factor in raising the long-term competitiveness of the European member countries. At the time, the focus was primarily, practically solely, on the private sector. Over the last 10 years it is only fair to say that under the name of e-government a widespread number of government services have been gradually transformed to use digital service delivery (e.g. tax services, customs, social services, passports). In most European countries this process is as yet still far from complete. Furthermore many other typically information intensive services such as the health sector have been struggling with privacy and security problems (such as in the case of patients' medical records), so that the diffusion has been much slower than originally thought. The deregulation and liberalisation of network services such as public utilities has, with the exception of the telecommunication sector itself, barely taken off. Viewed in retrospect, one should acknowledge that here too the speed of the likely diffusion of ICT was overestimated.

By contrast, there is little doubt that the 'global' competition dimension has significantly rekindled, as expected, the policy debate about the long-term employment implications of digital technologies. Current policy discussions about the continuous outsourcing and off-shoring of both industrial and information intensive service activities, including R&D, probably top the list of employment concerns today. At the same time, there is an impression that the full scope of new job opportunities associated with ICTs has been insufficiently realised in Europe.

On the employment loss side, the fears of a significant displacement of employment from the public sector, including the old state telecom monopolies, towards the private sector seems in retrospect exaggerated. The European national telecom incumbent firms have generally speaking succeeded well in their step-wise transition towards a liberal, privatised environment. The new mobile communications opportunities have been instrumental in allowing for such successful adjustment, the rapid growth in demand for such services having enabled the terrestrial telecom operating companies to gain access to large cash flows to carry out their own internal adjustment.

More broadly, the shift in policy concerns over the last 10 years highlights the temporary nature of the technology–employment policy concerns. Over the last 10 years, many million jobs were created in the European Union. At the same time the total working population increased substantially, of which immigration accounted for the largest part. Over the next 10 years, the balance between the number of elderly people withdrawing from the active labour force and the new cohorts of youngsters entering the labour force will turn negative. The policy concern will then shift from lack of job opportunities and employment displacement towards labour shortages and productivity growth. As such labour shortages translate themselves into labour market frictions, they are likely to lead to much stronger incentives for increased labour participation than active labour market policies ever achieved in the 1990s. They are also likely to raise wages for those labour-intensive activities, high and low skilled, which can not easily be automated or transferred abroad: nursing and other health caring activities, and personalised service activities. As a result of such increasing labour shortage pressures, there could well be a further leap in household activities based on insourcing and automation at home.

In short, it appears clear that the employment concerns of the introduction of new technologies need to take fully into account the supply side of the equation. That side is likely in Europe to show a declining trend, bringing again to the forefront the many opportunities to save time and labour through more effective use of the new digital ICTs.

We now turn back 10 years to some of those organisational and future of work aspects of ICTs as they were discussed in the 1995 report.

14.4   ORGANISATIONAL CHANGE AND THE FUTURE OF WORK, 1995

The rapid rate of globalisation of production and competition, partly brought about by new ICTs, has put new demands on firms, organisations and employees. Such increased pressure for change has often been identified with a demand for an increase in flexibility at work and at home. It is this feature that leads to downsizing of large firms and the growth of many different forms of networking with small firms. These organisational and managerial changes are likely to have major consequences for the world market, although the assessment of the scale and impact of the new flows of investment and trade associated with ICT-based production and services is far from adequate. The IS is likely to have major impacts on intra-firm relationships through intensified competition and the need for accelerating innovation and rapid adjustment to new market trends. As a result there will be a further search for organisational structures and methods that are more flexible and innovative – 'lean' production, outsourcing, industrial networks – whereby big highly integrated organisations tend to be divided into more independent units.

A number of issues can be raised here: first, internal restructuring issues within firms and other organisations; second, external restructuring issues and in particular various new forms of networking; third the changing nature of work; and fourth the balance between work and time.

14.4.1   ICTs and Internal Restructuring: Towards the 'Flexible' Firm

Innovations in ICTs continue to occur with remarkable rapidity and frequency. Also, they are unprecedented flexible technologies, with the same technical system being used to create a wide range of continually upgraded and highly differentiated products. It is for these reasons that the most constant feature of production in the IS is likely to be change. Such unending change allows for the possibility to put in place new work practices and structures of organisation. Many existing organisations reflect the more stable operating conditions of the recent past. Functional boundaries between the departments in organisations have often been created which can be barriers to rapid and flexible innovation and change. In particular, hierarchical bureaucracies were established to enable consistent decision making and control. With the shift towards the existence of immediate electronic information flows, many people are now questioning the need for hierarchical organisations in which middle management mainly deals with routinised filtering of information and highly codified decision making. Many such routine activities can be devolved to workers with access to decision support systems on-line information. ICTs can be used within traditional structures or lead to new patterns of work and management. ICTs do not, however, determine the future. It is their use that allows for new patterns of work and management.

In other words, new ICTs will allow enterprises to introduce more flexible systems of coordination and management – the so-called flexible 'firm' – both in the private and the public sector. However, such new systems require major changes in practice and culture among both workers and management. Any technical or organisational innovation which substantially alters the way people work will be risky for enterprises. A clear cost advantage cannot always be identified, especially in the short term, and there is likely to be resistance from workers and managers alike, who are accustomed to existing work practices. In such cases, some may be deterred from taking the risk of innovating, preferring instead to learn from the (sometimes costly) mistakes of others.

Managers may also be rightly cautious about innovations that alter systems and procedures which currently deliver an acceptable level of performance, compared to entering an unknown realm in which there is great uncertainty about how to successfully complete the process of change, how long it will take, and so on. Increasingly, also, it is seen that with ICTs there are no 'turnkey' solutions. The very flexibility of the technologies means that they must be embedded in the social organisation of the workplace in order to achieve a competitive combination of productivity, performance and quality.

The new ICTs are an important factor in the restructuring of hierarchical layers; they are also a restructuring factor of certain distribution channels. For instance, through the possibility of guaranteeing direct contact between the enterprise and the client (telemarketing and teleshopping) and between the public administration and the user (administration at a distance), new ICTs might also bring about the reorganisation of certain traditional activities (shops and counters).

14.4.2 The IS and 'External' Restructuring: The Growth of Networking

There is a well-documented trend towards greater externalisation of services and production. As far as services are concerned, there is little doubt that the increasing 'outsourcing' of service activities has been a major factor behind the growth of the service sector. On the one hand, there has been a growth of highly specialised professional services, such as advertising, informatics support and management consultancy. On the other hand, many externalised services are in relatively routine and lower skilled areas such as catering, cleaning and security.

As far as production is concerned, many large organisations have undertaken major programmes of rationalisation and downsizing. Much attention has been on re-establishing a focus on the core business, so non-core activities have often been hived off. In addition, many larger firms now use sub-contracting chains of producers of goods and services to provide a more flexible ensemble of suppliers to meet their need to respond rapidly to changes in the level and type of demand.

ICTs are one of the major factors behind this 'external' flexibility. ICTs contribute to a greater rate of change and uncertainty in the business-operating environment, thus making the use of a more flexible configuration of production resources more attractive. ICTs may also contribute to the development of outsourcing through electronic integration of inter-firm links. In essence the transaction costs of finding appropriate suppliers in the market place are reduced through such inter-firm networks. Automated billing settlement systems can directly lead to lower cost and more efficient trading, but the integration of information systems between firms also blurs the boundaries which divide them, leading to more of a partnership relationship than an arm's length trading relationship.

ICTs certainly make networking and outsourcing more likely and attractive for firms. There are also good economic reasons why firms will increasingly seek to outsource production. While such outsourcing might imply higher quality and the use of highly skilled specialised workers, we have some concern that one of the reasons for the growth of outsourcing is the lower wage rates and working conditions in the sub-contractor organisations. There is undoubtedly a potential that major firms, particularly multinationals, may be attracted by the idea of using sub-contracting to avoid what they consider to be high levels of social costs in the core businesses in their home regions.

In addition, we are concerned that the rapid growth of single-person and micro-businesses may imply a form of self-employment in which employees are given a stark choice between redundancy and selling their labour back into the firm on a freelanced, piecework or other casualised basis. As we note below, there have been fears that some forms of home-based telework might fall into this pattern, where workers are denied the protection of the status of employee but are in effect on contract to only one client.

ICTs are only one factor behind the drive towards 'outsourcing'. By permitting easier management of the international and inter-organisational coordination of flows of goods and services, however, they make it much more feasible. The extent to which ICTs really reinforce such effects is not established. To our knowledge no definitive studies have been carried out. Rather, it seems that, as with so many features of the emerging IS, there are choices about how ICTs are used, for better or worse. Thus we are concerned that the promotion of the benign aspects of the IS should be promoted over approaches which are not favourable to the pay, security and conditions of workers.

14.4.3 The Changing Notion of Work

In its most extreme vision, the increasing use of ICTs makes it possible to bring work back to the home. It is as if work can be returned to the local community or even placed back into the home environment, as it was in the days before the industrial revolution. These changes could be significant, if they ever become widespread, as urbanisation has totally changed the concept of home and village, from its origins when most people lived in agricultural communities to the model of house and neighbourhood as a small domestic maintenance unit. The changes in social relationships associated with a shift of the workplace back to the home could be substantial. Such changes have clearly both positive and negative dimensions. On the one hand, there is a possibility that more people can integrate their private and work lives more satisfactorily. On the other hand, there is a greater chance that work duties will interrupt the flow of family activities by impinging on the space, time and attention spans of the household. Also, such changes have many social and economic consequences. With home-based teleworking, for instance, the employee is expected to invest in his or her workspace, but in return avoids the costs associated with commuting. With teleworking, traditional remuneration methods based on time at work will need to be adjusted. It is essential for the social partners to negotiate new systems of remuneration, which can avoid a return to some of the injustices associated with 'piecemeal' wages. However, whatever the remuneration system, teleworking will require from the worker certain self-discipline in the capacity to distinguish professional from family activities.

The ways in which these changes will impact on the cohesiveness of the family unit are not clearly understood, nor are the psychological pressures. For instance, could the impact on the family be an increase in quarrelling and divorces? And how will it be possible for information workers to concentrate in the midst of family life?

These examples of home teleworking are just the extreme examples of the types of issues that could become apparent if workplaces are less often seen as outside the home and neighbourhood. With the 'go anywhere' technologies of the Digital Societies, many traditional boundaries of space and time are blurred.

14.4.4 The IS and Working Time

The notion of working time will also change as ICTs pervade all work-places. Relatively few workers will be ICT technicians. A larger number of workers will be expected to operate or work with these technologies, while almost all workers will experience changes in the pace and rhythm of work as a result of the influence of new ICTs on organisations.

As a result we expect two key types of change. First, many workers will be expected to work over a more extended working week. This is not to say that they will work longer hours, but rather that the old regular shift patterns or the reliable '9 to 5' work pattern is less and less likely to be the norm in the future. Second, work will become more abstract in nature. Information work is brainwork requiring conceptual and analytical skills rather than being based on intuitive skills or physical actions.

At the same time, the high rate of innovation in the Digital Society will undoubtedly lead to a high rate of obsolescence of ICT systems. This will drive managers to seek highly intensive utilisation of their capital stock, in order to reinforce competitiveness. In essence, this will lead to extended plant operating hours, especially in the manufacturing industries, but also increasingly in the technologically intensive service sector. Extended operating hours for capital inevitably mean more extensive working times for workers. In other words, there is more and more evening, night and weekend work – with the attendant adverse health risks associated with shift work patterns for workers, especially older ones.

By the same token, as we noted above, there is a trend in the IS towards more volatility of demand associated with the increased rate of technological change and a much tighter integration of demand and supply. In zero inventory systems there is not much opportunity for matching work flows to the needs of workers. Rather, they must be there when the demand exists and not otherwise. Firms are increasingly using variable working hours to deal with such fluctuations.

14.5 ORGANISATIONAL CHALLENGES IN THE DIGITAL SOCIETY, A 2005 REVISIT

Even more than in the previous section on employment, the policy concerns dealing with ICTs and organisational change as expressed in the HLEG report appear strikingly valid today. In Chapter 10 by Borghans and ter

Weel in this volume, more detailed attention is paid to the aspects dealing with the presumed 'skill bias' of the use of ICTs. We limit our critical revisit here to some of the organisational aspects and changes in the nature of work following the widespread diffusion of ICTs over the last 10 years.[9]

Undoubtedly, as has been amply illustrated over the last 10 years, ICTs have dramatically facilitated and accelerated various kinds of networking arrangements at both the inter-firm and the intra-firm level. The potential for radical changes in the organisational set-up of firms has been an intrinsic feature of the new digital technologies. At the same time though, and despite the wave of creative organisational de- and reconstruction which took place in the 1990s in the ICT industry itself, it seems worthwhile noting today that these many forms and novel opportunities of re-subcontracting various parts of production, of design and service activities, or their transfer to exchange agreements with other independent firms, did not really weaken the role of the large multinational firm in most other sectors.

Today, it even seems reasonable to express some scepticism about the notion that the 'network' has been displacing the large firm as the basic unit of economic organisation in our economies. Whereas over the last 10 years many economists and sociologists emphasised the role of small and medium-sized firms in the new digital economy and the huge new opportunities offered to them by the Internet, after the financial dotcom collapse the emphasis has to some extent swung back to demonstrating the advantages of the large global firm. In the ICT industry itself, ICTs did of course weaken, sometimes even destroy, the old monopolistic power positions of the large, national state monopolies, as in the case of telecommunication discussed in the previous section. This did facilitate the rapid development of many new services, new firms and new technologies, particularly in the mobile communication segment. However, neither privatisation nor de-regulation led to the disappearance of large oligopolistic firms. On the contrary, if there is one sector characterised by very large firms and an increasingly oligopolistic industry structure it is the ICT sector itself.

By contrast, with respect to the future of work and working time, the policy relevant changes associated with the use of ICTs might well have been underestimated. The central feature of the Digital Society, which probably received insufficient attention in the HLEG report, might well be the emergence of a more mobile information society. The impact of communications technologies on the reduction in the costs of distance was of course well known and the notion of the 'death of distance' had subsequently been popularised in a striking way by Frances Cairncross (1998, for updates see http://www.deathofdistance.com) but the full implications in terms of changes in behaviour had only been analysed with respect to the rather traditional boundaries of work with, for example, telework, and other home or leisure activities. But such a notion of a mobile information society appears too narrow and too much based on the notion of physical distance and the particular new digital broadband technological opportunities of physical terrestrial wired communication networks. In a broader sense though, mobile communication represents much more the ultimate form of reachability. Physical access to the infrastructure of the network is no longer necessary; communication can effectively take place from any location, anywhere. It is this additional dimension of communication, 'reachability', which explains the originally unexpected boom in mobile telephone communication in the 1990s. It is also mainly from this perspective that the technological developments in the area of communication technology differ from previous breakthroughs in the area of network technologies, such as electricity. Apart from being dependent on the much higher capital costs of the various 'network stations', an electricity network is also much more dependent on high quantities of energy loss over its own network. In other words, distance continues to be an important cost factor in such a network so that it is extremely unlikely that there will ever be a worldwide electricity web such as the Internet, or a mobile electricity network beaming down megawatts of energy to individual users.

The behavioural implications of the mobile IS were barely studied 10 years ago, yet once the notion of 'reachability' is incorporated into economic transactions some obvious implications emerge – first with respect to production and distribution and in particular the physical mobility of goods, services and persons, second with respect to consumption. In the first case, through better tracking, as well as quick and easy 'reachability' of the physical goods and persons on the move, whether on the road, at sea or in the air, ICTs will enable better utilisation of transport vehicles and transport infrastructures. Mobile communication appears in this sense a complementary technology to existing distribution and transportation systems. While the term e-commerce seemed to imply a process of substitution of physical commerce, ICTs are instead increasing the efficiency of the distribution and transport delivery systems through a reduction in delivery time and transport costs, and better usage of transport equipment and infrastructure. Such use of ICT to increase the rate of return to the existing infrastructural space, as in the case of transport systems, will enter decreasing returns once the physical and safety limits of the existing infrastructure are reached. The only possible way ICTs can push those limits further will be through more radical mobile communication applications allowing ultimately the 'blind' movement of vehicles (or persons) through sensor technologies interacting with 'smart' surroundings, on roads but also in the home. In this sense, the next challenge for future applications of mobile person–machine interaction lies in the replacement of the eye–hand coordination that is essential in, for example, driving, by communication technologies: effectively allowing a blind person to drive.

At the consumption end, mobile communication technologies also offer interesting opportunities as a complementary technology. The rapid diffusion of mobile phones and mobile equipment over the last decade can at least partly be explained by the increasing time and the growing uncertainties with respect to travelling (congestion delays) most commuters and individuals have been confronted with. The 'reachability' of others has rapidly emerged as a new consumer need. From this perspective, the growing demand for mobile communication corresponds, as did the motor car in the previous century, to an individual need for freedom. And whereas in the twentieth century it was the individual freedom to bridge physical distance, exemplified by the ownership of a private motor car – 'the machine that changed the world' in the words of the famous MIT study on the motor car industry (Womack et al., 1990) – today it is rather the individual freedom to communicate over physical distance, exemplified by the mobile phone, that represents this new freedom.

14.6   CONCLUSIONS

At the time of writing of the EU HLEG policy report we noted that 'a large proportion of public opinion' appeared, 'sceptical about the new opportunities offered by the Information Society and even fearful about the job losses, employment displacement and work insecurity associated with a future Information Society (HLEG, 1996, p. 82).' We claimed that this lack of public support was primarily a reflection of the 'technology dominated' nature of the European IS policy debate. The last 10 years have certainly changed public awareness of the importance of ICTs. The use of computers, be they mainframe, laptops, or hand computers, of the Internet and of mobile communication is today a normal, fully integrated feature of our societies. The actual final convergence between the old information technology symbol, the computer, and the old communication technology symbol, the telephone, is taking place before our eyes. At the same time the digital skills acquired at work have been further exercised at home and vice versa. The Information or Digital Society is a reality today, even though it is still characterised by further radical changes.

As argued 10 years ago, the emergence of such an Information Society is first and foremost an endogenous process. 'The technology in itself', we argued 'is neither good nor bad. It is the use which human beings make of any technology which determines both the nature and extent of the benefits.' We were, we insisted:

> attempting to put forward a more balanced approach to a future IS vision, in which societal 'embeddedness' plays a central role. Such interdependence with the social and societal dimension is in the first instance based on economic arguments. Without any doubt, new ICTs provide tremendous opportunities for new growth and employment creation; for a more efficient use of inputs, not just of labour but also of energy, materials and capital, contributing to a potentially, more sustainable development path; for higher income and more broadly higher welfare; for more decentralised organisation forms, whether on the shop floor or in terms of work sharing; for more consistent regional and urban development patterns; for individual enrichment as well as more democratic decision making. All of these opportunities for higher economic and productivity growth crucially depend on congruence between the technological, economic and social dimensions. None is predetermined. Thus, just as in the case of industrial and commercial enterprises where the adoption of new technologies will be the subject of cautious analysis and rarely be based on speed only, so too should the societal adoption of new technologies be based on policy debate and on the search for measures necessary to achieve an economically and socially integrated IS. (HLEG, 1996, p. 83)

A conclusion that is still as valid today as it was 10 years ago. But we also claimed that:

> in the future there could be different models of Information Societies, just as today we have different models of industrialised societies. They differ in the degree in which they avoid social exclusion and create new opportunities for the disadvantaged. A strong ethos of solidarity should also characterise the European Model of the Information Society. This is not an easy goal to achieve since the traditional structures of the welfare state will have to undergo substantial changes. (p. 84)

Compared to the radical transformations the digital technologies have brought about in the organisation of production, of work, of the distribution of goods and services, in consumption, in leisure, and in activities in the home, the institutional changes in Europe's welfare systems have been piecemeal at best. Only in some of the smaller Scandinavian countries has the more rapid diffusion of ICTs been accompanied by significant adjustments in the flexibility of social welfare systems. The case made 10 years ago in favour of an active rather than passive concept of solidarity remains hence as valid as ever.

To conclude let us repeat the four features of such an active solidarity we choose to emphasise:

> First and foremost, it is essential to view the IS as a 'learning society' . . . putting the central emphasis on the learning society, rather than the IS per se, provides

a more positive route forward for the IS debate. In particular, the more appropriate emphasis on learning illustrates that, although access to the information super-highway is and will continue to be important, it is insufficient to ensure the rapid development of a knowledge-based economy.

Second, as information is assuming a much more important position in our lives, a crucial additional characteristic of a human IS is that people should be in control of the information, rather than it being used to control them. There are observable trends towards the individualisation of various aspects of life: individual contracts of employment, targeted benefits, consumer profiling, personalised health care, individualised insurance planning and so on. There are obvious advantages in terms of effectiveness of such systems in that, it will be possible to make services really responsive to individual needs – but there are also major risks in terms of the invasiveness of such systems and the likely reductions in social solidarity. Third, human activities (work, leisure, contacts with administrations, banks, etc.) will occur more and more through the intermediary of telecommunication networks. These activities will be increasingly based on representations of reality (that is, abstract and virtual images of reality), rather than reality itself. There are significant advantages to this evolution such as, for example, faster delivery of products and services, fewer accidents and, perhaps, lower physical stress but there are also risks. Virtual life is not real life and the representation of reality is not reality. Fourth, in any period of major social, economic and technological change, the balance of social costs and advantages shifts. The Information Society is no exception. Changes in the industrial structure are leading to job destruction, as well as new job creation. There are great challenges in terms of adjusting to the IS at the sectoral level, at the firm level, at the level of individual skills and occupations, and within both public and private service provision. Furthermore, there are similarly dramatic changes in the organisation and quality of work. Organisations have to be flexible to perform in the new paradigm of competition of quality, customisation and rapid innovation. Workers are increasingly required to be flexible in terms of the skills they have, the tasks they perform, and the new forms and structures of employment. New relationships between paid employment, work and activity are emerging. These raise questions about the place of work in people's lives, particularly for the large numbers of people faced with unemployment, under-employment, or unstable employment patterns.

The Information Society is a society in formation. The decisions we make now, and the opportunities we take now, to construct a strong social dimension for the future of Europe may well be with us for a long time. We can afford to miss out in the global stakes nor can we afford to weaken the solidarity of Europeans in a rush for a rapid move into the IS for some, but not for all. (HLEG, 1996, p. 52)

NOTES

1. Such as the needs for inter-operability technical standards, the appropriate R&D framework support policies, information infrastructure support policies, etc.
2. As summarised in the Bangemann Action Plan: the central role of the private sector in the development of the IS; the rapid liberalisation of the telecommunications infrastructure and services; and the limited role of the public sector in stimulating the development of applications and the creation of a stable and transparent competitive

regulatory framework. Issues such as intellectual property protection, privacy, security and broadcasting are gradually woven into the regulatory framework. Again, we will only address these issues here in so far as they can be related directly to the broader social and societal context.

3. One may e.g. remember the OECD McCracken report written in 1975, analysing the 1973 oil crisis primarily in terms of a Keynesian macroeconomic demand management crisis, or the EU Cecchini report predicting significant output and employment growth in Europe following the single market reforms in 1992.

4. The following text is an exact reproduction of pp. 5–12 of the HLEG Interim report 'Building the European information society for us all', published by the European Commission in January 1996.

5. The word 'shock' is probably not fully appropriate, as the changes to which we refer are neither sudden nor short-lived. They involve long-term and permanent decreases in prices for continuously improving ICT-related products.

6. Cordell developed the proposal for a 'bit tax' which could be applied to all interactive digital services (Cordell and Ide, 1994). It is based on a simple count of bits flowing over telecommunications lines. The argument in favour of such a new tax is based on the way globalisation has undermined traditional national tax bases. At the same time, the disincentive to the diffusion and use of new information and communication services can be assumed to be marginal, because these new services offer, generally speaking, a new bundle of product or service characteristics.

7. As von Mises put it: 'Lack of wages would be a better term than lack of employment, for what the unemployed person misses is not work but the remuneration of work. The point [is] not that the "unemployed" [cannot] find work, but that they [are] not willing to work at the wages they [can] get in the labour market for the particular work they [are] able and willing to perform' (as quoted in Gourvitch, 1940, p. 88, Footnote 14).

8. Both the OECD Jobs Study (1994) and McKinsey Global Institute (1994) can be said to have focused primarily on these market issues. The former emphasised the functioning of labour markets, the latter the functioning of product markets, particularly in services.

9. See Brynjolfsson and Hitt (2000) for an overview of the research on the interplay between organisational change and ICT adoption. Borghans and Ter Weel (2004) provide a very interesting theoretical and empirical analysis of how far one can go in explaining differences in the division of labour across firms as a result of computer technology adoption. They find that changes in the division of labour can result both from reduced production time and from improved communication possibilities.

BIBLIOGRAPHY

Aghion, P. and P. Howitt (1992), 'A model of growth through creative destruction', *Econometrica*, **60** (1), 323–51.

Berman, E. (2000), 'Does factor-biased technological change stifle international convergence? Evidence from manufacturing', NBER Working Paper 7964, November.

Borghans, L. and B. ter Weel (2004), 'The division of labour, worker organisation and technological change', Working paper Maastricht University.

Brynjolfsson, E. and L.M. Hitt (2000), 'Beyond computation: Information technology, organizational transformation and business practices', *Journal of Economic Perspectives*, **14**, 23–48.

Cairncross, F. (1998), *The Death of Distance: How the Communications Revolution Will Change Our Lives*, Cambridge, MA: Harvard Business School Press.

Cordell, A. and J. Ide (1994), *The New Wealth of Nations, Taxing Cyberspace*, Toronto: Between the Line Publishers.

David, P.A. (1991), *The Dynamo and the Computer: An Historical Perspective on the Modern Productivity Paradox*, Paris: OECD.

Freeman, C., J. Clark and L. Soete (1982), *Unemployment and Technical Innovation: A Study of Long Waves and Economic Development*, London: Pinter.

Freeman, C. and L. Soete (1985), *Information Technology and Employment: An Assessment*, Brussels: IBM.

Freeman, C. and L. Soete (1987), *Technical Change and Full Employment*, London: Pinter.

Freeman, C. and L. Soete (1994), *Work for All or Mass Unemployment; Computerised Technical Change in the 21st Century*, London: Pinter.

Gourvitch, A. (1940), *Survey of Economic Theory on Technological Change and Employment*, New York: Augusta M. Kelley.

Hansen, A.H. (1931), 'Institutional frictions and technological unemployment', *Quarterly Journal of Economics*, **45** (4), 684–97.

High Level Export Group (HLEG) (1996), 'Building the European information society for us all', Brussels: European Commission.

Kaldor, N. (1933), *Essays on Economic Stability and Growth*, London: Duckworth.

Katsoulacos, Y. (1984), 'Product innovation and employment', *European Economic Review*, **26**, 83–108.

McKinsey Global Institute (1994), *Employment Performance*, Boston: Mckinsey Global Institute.

Neisser, H. (1942), 'Permanent technological unemployment', *American Economic Review*, **32**, 50–71.

OECD (1994), *The OECD Jobs Study: Evidence and Explanations*, Paris: OECD.

OECD (1996), 'Technology, productivity and job creation', Paris: OECD.

Rifkin, J. (1995), *The End of Work*, New York: Putman's Sons.

US National Commission (1966), *National Commission on Technology, Automation and Economic Progress, Report and Appendices Vols. 1–6*, Washington, DC: US National Commission.

Weintraub, D. (1937), 'Unemployment and increasing productivity' in National Resources Committee, *Technological Trends and National Policy*, Washington, DC: National Resources Committee.

Womak, J.T., D. Jones and D. Roos (1990), *The Machine that Changed the World*, New York: Rawson Associates.

Young, A. (1928), 'Increasing returns and economic progress', *Economic Journal*, **38**, 527–42.

Index